READINGS ON
ENGLISH
AS A SECOND LANGUAGE

READINGS ON
ENGLISH
AS A
SECOND LANGUAGE:
for Teachers
and
Teacher-Trainees

EDITED BY

KENNETH CROFT

San Francisco State College

WINTHROP PUBLISHERS, INC.
Cambridge, Massachusetts

Cover by Daniel Thaxton

QE1128
A2
C1

ACKNOWLEDGEMENTS

"Initial Techniques in Teaching English as a Second Language," by Audrey L. Wright. Reprinted from *The ABC English as a Second Language Bulletin*, Vol. 1, No. 2, 1964. Used by permission of Litton International Publishing Company.

Miss Wright has been actively engaged in TEFL for many years as a teacher, teacher-trainer, and program administrator. She has served as a Fulbright Lecturer in Italy, Director of Courses at the Instituto Mexicano-Norteamericano in Mexico City, and Assistant Director of the Centro Colombo-Americano in Bogota, Colombia.

"Meanings, Habits, *and* Rules," by W. Freeman Twaddell. Reprinted from the October, 1948, issue of *Education* by permission of the publisher, The Bobbs-Merrill Company, Inc.

Dr. Twaddell is Professor of Linguistics and German at Brown University.

"Adding a Second Language," by Clifford H. Prator. Reprinted by permission of the author and the publisher from *TESOL Quarterly* 3 (1969): 95–104.

Dr. Prator is Professor of English and Vice-Chairman, Department of English, University of California, Los Angeles.

"Terminal Behavior in Language Teaching," by J. Donald Bowen. Reprinted by permission of the author and the publisher from *TESL Reporter* 1 (Winter, 1968): 1, 6, 7.

Dr. Bowen is Professor of English at the University of California, Los Angeles.

"Method in Language Teaching," by Edward M. Anthony and William E. Norris. Reprinted by permission of the authors and the Modern Language Association of America from *ERIC Focus Report* No. 8, 1969.

Dr. Anthony is Professor of Linguistics and Chairman, Department of General Linguistics, at the University of Pittsburgh.

Mr. Norris is Assistant Professor of Linguistics at the University of Pittsburgh.

"Rules, Patterns, and Creativity in Language Learning," by Wilga M. Rivers. Reprinted from *English Teaching Forum* 8 (1970): 7–10. This is a slightly modified version of "Grammar in Foreign Language Teaching" from *The Modern Language Journal* 52 (1968): 206–11. Used by permission of the author and the publisher.

Dr. Rivers is Professor of French at the University of Illinois.

"Learning Pronunciation," by Charles F. Hockett. Reprinted by permission of the author and publisher from *Modern Language Journal* 34 (1950): 261–69.

Dr. Hockett is Goodwin Smith Professor of Linguistics and Anthropology at Cornell University.

"Teaching a Pronunciation Problem," by Jeris E. Strain. Reprinted by permission of the author and the publisher from *Language Learning* 12 (1962): 231–40.

Dr. Strain is Senior Instructor, English, at the INTS Training Center (Page Communication Engineering, Inc.) in Tehran, Iran.

"Simple Classroom Techniques for Teaching Pronunciation," by Betty Wallace Robinett. From *On Teaching English to Speakers of Other Languages, Series I*, edited by Virginia French Allen. Copyright © 1965 by the National Council of Teachers of English. Reprinted by permission of the Publisher and Betty Wallace Robinett.

Dr. Robinett is Professor of Linguistics at the University of Minnesota.

"Listening Comprehension," by Wilga M. Rivers. Reprinted by permission of the author and the publisher from the *Modern Language Journal* 50 (1966): 196–202. This article is further developed with practical applications in Chapter 6 of Wilga M. Rivers, *Teaching Foreign Language Skills* (University of Chicago Press, 1968).

Dr. Rivers is Professor of French at the University of Illinois.

"Developing a Lesson Around a Dialogue," by George McCready. Reprinted from *The English Teaching Forum*, a publication of the Information Center Service of the United States Information Agency.

Mr. McCready is an English Teaching Specialist at USIS Belgrade, Yugoslavia.

"How to Teach English Grammar," by Lois McIntosh. Reprinted by permission of the author and the publisher from *Workpapers in English as a Second Language: Matter, Methods, and Materials* (Los Angeles: Department of English, University of California, 1967).

Dr. McIntosh is Associate Professor of English at the University of California, Los Angeles.

"Learning Syntactical Patterns," by Robert L. Politzer. From Robert L. Politzer, *Foreign Language Learning: A Linguistic Introduction*, © 1970. Reprinted by permission of Prentice-Hall, Inc., Englewood Cliffs, New Jersey.

Dr. Politzer is Professor of Education and Romance Linguistics at Stanford University.

"The Sequencing of Structural Pattern Drills," by Christina Bratt Paulston. Reprinted by permission of the author and the publisher from *TESOL Quarterly* 5 (1971): 2.

Dr. Paulston is Assistant Professor of Linguistics and Director of the English Language Institute, University of Pittsburgh.

"Learning to Read English as Part of the Oral Approach," by Charles C. Fries. Reprinted by permission of the English Language Education Council, Inc. from *ELEC Publications* 8 (June 1967): 6–11.

Dr. Fries founded the English Language Institute at the University of Michigan in 1941 and served as its director until 1956. He was Professor of

English Emeritus at the University of Michigan and Director Emeritus of the English Language Institute at the time of his death in 1967.

"Spelling and Sound in English," by Robert A. Hall, Jr. Reprinted by permission of The Center for Curriculum Development, Inc. from *Sound and Spelling in English* by Robert A. Hall, Jr. (Philadelphia: Chilton Books, 1966).
Dr. Hall is Professor of Linguistics at Cornell University.

"Advanced Reading: Goals, Techniques, Procedures," by William E. Norris. Reprinted by permission of the author and the publisher from *TESOL Quarterly* 4 (1970): 17–35.
Mr. Norris is Assistant Professor of Linguistics at the University of Pittsburgh.

"Breaking Down Your Writing Goals," by Gerald Dykstra. Reprinted by permission of the author from *English for American Indians,* Spring 1969, pp. 1–10.
Mr. Dykstra is Chief Curriculum Consultant at the Hawaii English Project and Professor of Speech-Communication at the University of Hawaii.

"Dictation in the Language Classroom," by Kenton K. Sutherland. Reprinted by permission of the author and the publisher from *TESOL Quarterly* 1 (March 1967): 24–29. Mr. Sutherland is Instructor of English at Cañada College

"Classroom Techniques for Controlling Composition," by William Slager. Reprinted by permission of the author and the publisher from *Selected Conference Papers of the Association of Teachers of English as a Second Language,* (1966), pp. 77–85. Dr. Slager is Professor of English at the University of Utah.

"Cultural Thought Patterns in Inter-Cultural Education," by Robert B. Kaplan. Reprinted by permission of the author and the publisher from *Language Learning* 16 (1966): 1–20.
Dr. Kaplan is Director of the English Communication Program for Foreign Students and Associate Professor of Linguistics at the University of Southern California.

"Linguistics and Language Teachers," by W. Freeman Twaddell. Reprinted by permission of W. Freeman Twaddell and the publisher from *On Teaching English to Speakers of Other Languages, Series II,* edited by Carol J. Kreidler. Copyright © 1966 by the National Council of Teachers of English.
Dr. Twaddell is Professor of Linguistics and German at Brown University.

"Patterns of Difficulty in Vocabulary," by Robert Lado. Reprinted by permission of the author and the publisher from *Language Learning* 6 (1955): 23–41.
Dr. Lado is Dean of the School of Languages and Linguistics, Georgetown University.

"The Psycholinguistic Concept of 'Difficulty' and the Teaching of Foreign Language Vocabulary," by Masanori Higa. Reprinted by permission of the author and the publisher from *Language Learning* 15 (1965): 167–79.
Dr. Higa is Associate Professor in the Department of English as a Second Language, University of Hawaii.

"Writing Proficiency and Achievement Tests," by Sidney Sako. Reprinted by permission of the author and the publisher from *TESOL Quarterly* 3 (1969): 237–49.

Mr. Sako is Chief, Test and Measurement Branch, English Language School, Defense Language Institute, Lackland Air Force Base.

"Constructing the Test," by David P. Harris. From *Testing English as a Second Language* by David P. Harris. Copyright © 1969 by McGraw-Hill, Inc. Used with permission of McGraw-Hill Book Company.
Dr. Harris is Director of the American Language Institute and Professor of Linguistics, Georgetown University.

"Language Testing—The Problem of Validation," by Bernard Spolsky. Reprinted by permission of the author and the publisher from *TESOL Quarterly* 2 (1968): 88–94.
Dr. Spolsky is Associate Professor of Linguistics and Elementary Education at the University of New Mexico.

"Gestures in the Language Classroom," by Robert L. Saitz. Reprinted by permission of the author and the publisher from *English Language Teaching* 21 (1966): 33–37.
Dr. Saitz is Associate Professor of English at Boston University.

"Try One of My Games," by Julia Dobson. Reprinted from *The English Teaching Forum* 8 (May–June 1970): 9–17, a publication of the Information Center Service of the United States Information Agency.
Ms. Dobson is an English Teaching Specialist, USIA Washington.

"Pictures for Practice," by Carol J. Kreidler. Reprinted by permission of Carol J. Kreidler and the publisher from *On Teaching English to Speakers of Other Languages, Series III*, edited by Betty Wallace Robinett. Copyright © 1967 by the National Council of Teachers of English.
Ms. Kreidler is Associate Director, English for Speakers of Other Languages Program, Center for Applied Linguistics.

"The Language Laboratory: Uses and Misuses," by Kenneth Croft. Reprinted by permission of the author and the publisher from *On Teaching English to Speakers of Other Languages, Series II*, edited by Carol J. Kreidler. Copyright © 1966 by the National Council of Teachers of English.
Dr. Croft is Professor of English and Anthropology at San Francisco State College.

"Development of a Manipulation–Communication Scale," by Clifford H. Prator. Reprinted by permission of the author and the publisher from *The 1964 Conference Papers of the Association of Teachers of English as a Second Language*, pp. 57–62.
Dr. Prator is Professor of English and Vice-Chairman, Department of English, University of California, Los Angeles.

"A Multiple-Register Approach to Teaching English," by J. Donald Bowen. Reprinted by permission from *Estudos Lingüísticos, Revista Brasileira de Lingüística Teórica e Aplicada* 1 (1966): 35–44, published by the Centro de Linguistica Aplicada do Instituto de Idiomas Yázagi, São Paulo, Brazil.

"Language and Categories: Some Notes for Foreign Language Teachers," by Kenneth Croft. Reprinted by permission of the publisher from *The English Record* 21 (April 1971) 1–12.
Dr. Croft is Professor of English and Anthropology at San Francisco State College.

PREFACE

The expression "teaching English as a second language" evokes various images among classroom teachers. Of course the expression implies promoting the learning of English in all its contexts, but the mental pictures that different teachers have of this learning activity are probably never the same. The ages of their students, the goals in the course, the students' motivation, the teacher's skills, the classroom conditions, the teaching materials—all these are factors in the learning that takes place. These and other factors determine the procedures that are followed in the classroom and, in turn, shape the image that each teacher has concerning teaching English as a second language.

One purpose of this book is to enlarge the teacher's perspective—to give the teacher a broader view of the field he works in. This collection of readings embodies much of the knowledge and many of the assumptions and beliefs we have about second-language teaching and learning. Its scope is broad and general, reflecting experience, observations, and opinions of practicing teachers and teacher-trainers, and it provides a representative sample of professional writing in the second-language field.

Teachers show varying degrees of competence, devotion, and conscientiousness. I have come to believe that the really *good* teacher is never completely satisfied that he is doing the best possible job with his students. He finds there is always more to learn—about the nature of language, about the structure of languages, about the presentation of language material, about the nature of language acquisition, about aids to learning, about student motivation, and the like. Through his classroom experience, his reading of professional literature, his discussions with colleagues and others, his participation in meetings and conferences, and his writing on professional subjects, he continually moves toward some sort of "perfection." This resembles, in part, Carl Rogers' concept of the *fully functioning person:* he is always in the process of becoming; he is never already there. "The process of the good life . . . involves stretching and growing, of becoming more and more of one's potential. . . . It means launching oneself into the stream of life. Yet the deeply exciting thing about human beings is that when the individual is inwardly free, he chooses as the good life this process of becoming."*

The second purpose of this book is to provide readings and bibliography for the teacher's professional growth. Some of the readings have been selected especially for new teachers and teacher-trainees, whereas others have been chosen with experienced teachers in mind. The readings are divided into nine sections, each with an introduction. The introduction is mainly a recapitulation of certain salient points contained in the reading selections of that section; but where they seemed appropriate, I have also added comments based on my own observations and experience.

Some of my colleagues have been very helpful to me in the preparation of this volume. For assistance in selecting the readings, I wish to express my appreciation to William E. Norris of the University of Pittsburgh, Kenton Sutherland of Cañada College, Milton Wohl of Fresno State College, and Sydney Sako of the English Language School, Lackland Air Force Base. I am also grateful to Thurston Womack of San Francisco State College for reading portions of the manuscript and giving me many useful suggestions and ideas.

* *On Becoming a Person* (Boston: Houghton Mifflin Company, 1961), p. 196.

CONTENTS

INTRODUCTION

There are three current expressions that describe the teaching of English to non-native speakers of the language: "teaching English as a foreign language" (TEFL), "teaching English as a second language" (TESL), and "teaching English to speakers of other languages" (TESOL). In American usage TEFL usually refers to teaching English overseas or to foreigners who are more or less temporary residents in the United States, such as foreign students, visitors, or diplomatic people. TESL, on the other hand, has to do with the teaching of English to non-native speakers who are more or less permanent residents in the United States, such as Mexican-Americans, American Indians, Puerto Ricans, or Chinese-Americans. (The TESL term also includes the teaching of English in the Philippines, India, and other countries where English is an official language.) TESOL, a broader expression, encompasses both the TEFL and the TESL groups; actually, as the term implies, it includes all teaching of English to non-native speakers everywhere.

The expression "English for the foreign born" still has some currency in urban adult-education programs, perhaps because a number of textbooks still carry the label *English for the Foreign Born;* but this expression, along with "English for new Americans," "English for non-native speakers," and the like, is rapidly giving way to "English for speakers of other languages" (ESOL), and "English as a second language" (ESL). Even the term "English as a foreign language" (EFL) seems to be on the decline. As a subtitle for textbooks, *For Students of English as a Second Language* now appears much more frequently than *For Students of English as a Foreign Language*. In the mid-60s the English Language Section of the National Association for Foreign Student Affairs decided to change its name to the Association of Teachers of *English as a Second Language* (my italics). Although the members of the association were mainly concerned with the teaching of English to foreign students on college and university campuses (EFL activities), "English as a second language" was chosen as part of its name rather than "English as a foreign language." This appears to be a contradiction in terms, but I think it simply indicates a trend toward ESL and TESL and away from EFL and TEFL.

THE TESOL ORGANIZATION

TESOL, /tíysŏl/ or /tésŏl/, is also an acronym for Teachers of English to Speakers of Other Languages—a professional association that officially came into being in 1966. Establishing TESOL (the organization) on a sound and continuing basis has perhaps been the most important recent development in the field.

The membership, numbering approximately 2,700, consists mainly of classroom teachers and program administrators. James E. Alatis, Associate Dean of the School of Languages and Linguistics at Georgetown University, has served as executive secretary for TESOL since its founding, and his office provides a clearinghouse for a large variety of matters concerning the profession. The officers and executive committee have worked vigorously, and with moderate success, on the national level, "to promote scholarship, to disseminate information, to strengthen at all levels instruction and research in the teaching of English to speakers of other languages," in accordance with the organization's constitution. But it will remain to the state and regional affiliates such as those now in operation in Arizona, California, the District of Columbia, Florida, Illinois, Puerto Rico, New Jersey, New Mexico, New York, and Texas, to provide direct assistance and guidance to the thousands of classroom teachers involved in one way or another with TESOL activities.

Through the national organization and its affiliates we can gain support in our efforts to equip the nation's non-English-speaking population with the language of the nation. These associations also need our support: collective action to influence legislation is one of the few devices we have to upgrade our profession and our programs. Federal and state funds are badly needed now and will be needed for years to come for teacher institutes, workshops, consultation services, more ESL teachers, teaching materials, and the like. We also need psycholinguistic and sociolinguistic research programs in such areas as attitudes, motivation, and learning styles to help improve the theoretical framework in which we work.

Prominent national leaders in the profession have served as presidents of TESOL: Harold B. Allen of the University of Minnesota (1966), Edward M. Anthony of the University of Pittsburgh (1967), Paul M. Bell of the Dade County (Florida) Board of Education (1968), David P. Harris of Georgetown University (1969), Mary Finocchiaro of Hunter College (1970), and Russell N. Campbell of the University of California at Los Angeles (1971). The organization has two regular publications: *TESOL Quarterly,* edited by Betty W. Robinett of the University of Minnesota, and *TESOL Newsletter,* edited by Richard L. Light of the State University of New York at Albany. These two serials, both ably produced, have provided the main avenues of publication for the profession since 1966.

The organizational (constitutional) convention was held in New York (1966), following two large-scale planning conventions in Tucson (1964) and San Diego (1965). Although the TESOL name has been used right along since 1964, the organization, officially constituted, is relatively new; its first annual convention was held in Miami (1967), the second in San Antonio (1968), the third in Chicago (1969), the fourth in San Francisco (1970), and the fifth in New Orleans (1971). Several well-known national organizations contributed varying amounts of time, effort, and money to help launch TESOL: the National Council of Teachers of English, the Modern Language Association, the Center for Applied Linguistics, the National Association for Foreign Student Affairs, and the Speech Association of America. There are still close ties between TESOL and these sponsoring organizations, as evidenced by the composition of their boards of directors, overlapping memberships, and joint undertakings in regard to TESOL activities. A similar tie has been developing between TESOL and the American Council on the Teaching of Foreign Languages (ACTFL): at each ACTFL annual convention TESOL has been arranging and sponsoring sessions devoted to ESOL, bilingual education, and SESOD (standard English for speakers of other dialects).

THE ASSOCIATION OF TEACHERS OF ENGLISH AS A SECOND LANGUAGE

The Association of Teachers of English as a Second Language (ATESL), a section of the National Association for Foreign Student Affairs (NAFSA), continues to function, but along somewhat different lines since the establishment of the TESOL organization. ATESL's annual *Selected Conference Papers* ceased publication with the 1967 issue. However, the *NAFSA Newsletter,* containing ATESL reports, has continued publication and may be replaced by a journal. ATESL (NAFSA) members, numbering between 300 and 400, are for the most part academic people associated with college and university programs devoted to English training for foreign students; a number of them are also involved in ESOL teacher training programs at colleges and universities.

For years ATESL operated as a kind of appendage to NAFSA, having relatively few interrelationships with the other sections and groups of the "parent" organization. But during the last few years, ATESL has become more integrated with the rest of NAFSA: joint projects and programs involving ATESL and the Admissions Section, ATESL and the Community Section, and the like have been undertaken. It has been found, generally, that ATESL and other NAFSA groups have more common interests, and their professional activities and concerns overlap in more areas than was previously believed.

Several proposals have been put forward to accommodate ATESL within TESOL or interlock the two organizations in some fashion, but as yet no concrete plan, satisfactory to all concerned, has emerged. The most promising suggestion is that ATESL form the nucleus of a college and university section within TESOL, at which time the latter would begin to reorganize itself along sectional lines. Another plausible idea is that TESOL and ATESL establish a joint membership arrangement whereby a member of ATESL would automatically be a member of TESOL as well.

The NAFSA Field Service has devised a framework to assist college and university personnel who work with foreign students; not only teachers of foreign students, but also admissions officers, foreign student advisers, and the like. A similar framework may prove desirable in the future for TESOL and its affiliates. The Field Service provides: (1) short-term travel grants that allow teachers and administrators from one campus to visit another campus and observe the methods of handling certain foreign-student activities and problems—also in some cases, travel grants permit college and university personnel to attend regional NAFSA conferences; (2) support for brief workshops, usually held on weekends in various parts of the country; (3) visits to campuses by NAFSA consultants to assist teachers and administrators in planning and carrying out specialized projects and programs. Around the country certain NAFSA members are designated as consultants, and when consultation at a given institution is requested, a consultant from the region goes to the campus and provides, insofar as possible, the needed assistance.

Inasmuch as ATESL is a section of a larger organization, it has a chairman rather than a president. The following have served as chairmen in recent years: William R. Slager of the University of Utah (1966–67), Bernard Spolsky of Indiana University (1967–68), Robert B. Kaplan of the University of Southern California (1968–69), Robert L. Saitz of Boston University (1969–70), Robert P. Fox of the University of Illinois (1970–71), and Gordon E. Ericksen of New York University (1971–72). Recent NAFSA annual conventions have been held in Houston (1967), San Francisco (1968), Boston (1969), Kansas City (1970), and Vancouver, B.C. (1971).

At the Houston convention a new suborganization came into being, the Commission on Intensive English Programs (CIEP), which later became an affiliate of ATESL. During its relatively brief existence, CIEP has worked toward nationwide uniformity in intensive English programs and has been developing guidelines for college and university personnel on the interpretation of scores on standard tests and what to expect in regard to English proficiency on the part of foreign students. An English proficiency-level chart has been prepared and made available in published form to college and university officials. Also, a set of guidelines covering staff and content for intensive programs has been published and distributed to persons and institutions expressing an interest in such programs. The seventeen or so members of CIEP, all administrators in intensive English programs, hope to establish a central office that will serve as an informational clearinghouse for all language institutes. Shigeo Imamura of Michigan State University was CIEP's first "president" (1966–68); Gordon E. Ericksen of New York University, the second (1968–69); Charles W. Gay of the University of Southern California, the third (1969–70), Allis Bens of San Francisco State College, the fourth (1970–71), and Austin Flint of Columbia University, the fifth (1971–72).

TEACHER TRAINING

TESL instruction and TEFL instruction are, of course, very much alike. The goals are often quite similar, and sometimes the same texts and methodology are found in both kinds of programs. As noted earlier, two main differences between TESL and TEFL have to do with where the programs are located and which groups they are supposed to serve. Assessment of domestic TESL programs is easier than assessment of international TEFL programs because there is considerable standardization throughout the United States in teacher training, school aims, procedures, and equipment. We know, for example, that the immediate objective of virtually all public school TESL programs is sufficient fluency in English to enable pupils to function like other children their own age. We also know a good deal about the kinds of teachers who staff such TESL programs, and this knowledge enables us to plan rather effective teacher-training courses and training materials for the teachers involved.

TEFL teacher training at the academic level dates from the early 1940s, when Charles C. Fries established the English Language Institute at the University of Michigan. By now there must be forty or fifty institutions of higher learning that have teacher-training courses in this field, but with the increased interest in providing English training to non-English-speaking elements of our own population, there has been a shift of emphasis at many institutions from TEFL to TESL. This shift is also reflected in the fact that most teacher trainees in TEFL and TESL remain at home to teach, rather than going abroad, upon completion of their training. At San Francisco State College, for example, almost all of the graduate students in the M.A. program in teaching English to non-native speakers find teaching jobs in the Bay Area after graduation.

INSTITUTES

The biggest boost to TESOL teacher training in recent years came with the 1964 amendment to the 1958 National Defense Education Act (NDEA). This amendment authorized NDEA institutes for advanced study in ESOL, similar to the ones already being supported by government funds for teachers of science and foreign languages. Two summer ESOL institutes were conducted in 1964, four in 1965, five in 1966, twelve in 1967, and sixteen in 1968. In addition, two institutes ran on a school-year basis from September 1968 to May 1969. Altogether, there were forty-one institutes authorized during the 1964–68 period.

These institute programs for teachers were administered by the U.S. Office of Education and were conducted by American colleges and universities. They typically included applied linguistics, methodology in second-language teaching, contrastive culture studies, and an opportunity to begin or continue the study of some modern foreign language. Most of them had practice-teaching somewhere in the program, and a few had instruction and practice in the preparation of teaching aids.

At the end of June 1968, new legislation replaced NDEA legislation— the Education Professions Development Act (EPDA), which expanded support for TESOL teacher training. EPDA provided for various forms of assistance, ranging from short-term institutes for teachers, supervisors, and teacher-trainers, to full-time fellowship programs for experienced teachers. The new act continued the Teacher Fellowship Program originally authorized in 1965 (the Higher Education Act) as well as the institute programs. All subjects usually taught in school became eligible for support, but the intention was to continue support for thirteen subject categories, including ESOL. The authority for the fellowship program was expanded, so that the projects could include graduate fellowships directed to any graduate degree, including the Ph.D.

EPDA also broadened the sponsorship of projects: state and local educational agencies, as well as colleges and universities, from 1968 on could design and submit proposals for projects to train or retrain teachers and other educational personnel. In the guidelines for project proposals under EPDA, three national priorities were set: (1) to train persons to work with the disadvantaged; (2) to train teachers and others in subjects that are in critically short supply; and (3) to cover areas of education where there are "particularly acute training needs." ESOL institutes have been clearly involved in the first two of these. Twenty-five ESOL and bilingual education institutes were conducted during the summer of 1969 and the 1969–70 academic year.

TEACHER QUALIFICATIONS

The preparation and qualifications of teachers has been one of the major concerns of the TESOL organization since its inception. The desired goal, of course, is excellence in teaching. But in order to achieve excellence, teachers should have certain personal qualities, attitudes, background, and training for their jobs. In May 1970, a conference was organized by James E. Alatis, Executive Secretary of TESOL, to develop statements concerning the preparation of teachers of English to speakers of other languages. This was a working conference with about thirty leaders in the TESOL field as participants.

The following eight broad guidelines were produced and adopted at the conference: *

1. The teacher of English as a second language should have personal qualities which contribute to his success as a classroom teacher, which will insure understanding and respect for the students and their cultural setting, and which will tend to make him a perceptive and involved member of his community.
2. The teacher of English as a second language should demonstrate proficiency in spoken and written English to a level commensurate with his role as a language model. His command of the language should combine the qualities of accuracy and fluency; his experience of it should include a wide acquaintance with writings in it.
3. The teacher of English as a second language should understand the nature of language, the fact of language varieties—social, regional, and functional—the structure and development of English language systems and their relations to the culture of English-speaking peoples.
4. The teacher of English as a second language should have had the experience of learning another language and a knowledge of its structure, and be provided with a conscious awareness of another cultural system related, if possible, to the population with which he is working.
5. The teacher of English as a second language should have a knowledge of the process of language acquisition as it concerns first and subsequent language learning and as it varies at different age levels.
6. The teacher of English as a second language should have an understanding of the principles of language pedagogy and the demonstrated ability to apply these principles as needed to various classroom situations and materials.
7. The teacher of English as a second language should have an understanding of the principles and knowledge of the techniques of second language assessment and interpretation of the results.

* "Statement of Qualifications and Guidelines for Preparation of Teachers of English to Speakers of Other Languages." (Foreword by Albert H. Marckwardt) *TESOL Newsletter* 4(1970):4–5.

8.   The teacher of English as a second language should have a sophisticated awareness and understanding of the factors that contribute to the life styles of various peoples, demonstrating both their uniqueness and interrelationships in a pluralistic society.

These statements provide a set of principles upon which programs of teacher preparation should be built. They also note the basic ingredients of a curriculum for teacher training and suggest requirements for teacher certification. Several TESOL affiliates are urging state departments of education (and state legislatures) to recognize English for speakers of other languages as a separate teaching field—separate, that is, from English for native speakers and also from foreign language teaching —and to adopt standards and procedures for the certification of teachers in this field.

PROFESSIONAL PUBLICATIONS

BIBLIOGRAPHICAL WORKS

During the last twelve years or so the Center for Applied Linguistics (CAL) in Washington, D.C., has provided services of inestimable value to the TESOL profession. Sirarpi Ohannessian, Director of the CAL English Program, and her staff have prepared numerous TESOL bibliographies and surveys, arranged and sponsored large conferences, and coordinated many developing TESOL projects and programs over the years. The Center has been and still is the largest and most efficient clearinghouse on TESOL and other professional language-teaching matters. It has an extensive library, an excellent staff, and an impressive publication record.

Among the many works CAL has published are three comprehensive, annotated bibliographies:

1.   Ohannessian, Sirarpi, ed. *Reference List of Materials for English as a Second Language, Part I: Texts, Readers, Dictionaries, Tests.* 1964.
2.   Ohannessian, Sirarpi, Carol J. Kreidler, and Beryl Dwight, eds. *Reference List of Materials for English as a Second Language, Part II: Background Materials; Methodology.* 1966.
3.   Pedtke, Dorothy A., Bernarda Erwin, and Anna Maria Malkoç, eds. *Reference List of Materials for English as a Second Language, Supplement: 1964–1968.* 1969.

Four other important bibliographical works, covering recent years, have been published in the U.S.:

4.   Allen, Virginia F. and Sidney Forman. *English as a Second Language —A Comprehensive Bibliography.* New York: Teachers College Press, 1967.

5. Croft, Kenneth. *TESOL, 1967–68: A Survey.* Washington, D.C.: Teachers of English to Speakers of Other Languages, 1970.
6. Malkoç, Anna Maria, comp. *A TESOL Bibliography: Abstracts of ERIC Publications and Research Reports, 1969–70.* Washington, D.C.: Teachers of English to Speakers of Other Languages, 1971.
7. Shen, Yao and Ruth Crymes. *Teaching English as a Second Language: A Classified Bibliography.* Honolulu: East–West Center Press, 1965.

Since 1966 CAL has operated the ERIC Clearinghouse for Linguistics, one of about eighteen clearinghouses monitored and funded by the U.S. Office of Education. ERIC (Educational Resources Information Center) is a nationwide service involving the collection, processing, and dissemination of information on significant literature in various educational fields. Documents are collected, evaluated, processed (indexed and abstracted), and made available to the public, for a fee, on microfiche or hard copy. ERIC also publishes lists of documents, newsletters, state-of-the-art papers, and the like. The ERIC Clearinghouse for Linguistics has four major components: (1) linguistics, (2) uncommonly taught languages, (3) teaching standard English to speakers of nonstandard dialects, and (4) teaching of English as a foreign or second language.

With the cooperation of ERIC, the CCM Information Corporation (a subsidiary of Crowell Collier and Macmillan, Inc.) began to publish the *Current Index to Journals in Education (CIJE)* in the spring of 1969. Issued monthly, with semiannual and annual cumulative volumes, *CIJE* covers articles in over 300 education and education-oriented journals. Actually, *CIJE* is a monthly companion piece to *Research in Education,* the U.S. Office of Education publication that announces the approximately 1,000 new and chiefly unpublished reports that are added to the ERIC document collection each month. The coverage of peripheral literature relating to educational fields is a unique feature and especially important to TESOL; a considerable amount of informational material about TESOL activities goes unnoticed because of its publication in scattered and out-of-the-way places.

Two British bibliographical tools are also of special value to ESOL teachers: *Language-Teaching Bibliography* (1968) and *Language-Teaching Abstracts* (Vol. 1, No. 1, January 1968). Both are edited jointly by the English-Teaching Information Centre of the British Council and the Centre for Information on Language Teaching, in London, and published by Cambridge University Press. TESOL publications figure prominently in these two items. The *Abstracts* is a quarterly, and it may be that the *Bibliography* will be serialized in some fashion or other, perhaps every few years, in the form of cumulative volumes of the *Abstracts.* This would be helpful.

TEACHERS' MANUALS AND COLLECTIONS OF READINGS

The number of training manuals and collections of readings for language teachers, particularly teacher-trainees, has grown considerably during the last few years. I am listing below the ones that have fairly wide use in ESOL teacher-training programs throughout the country. It should be noted that some of them were designed for general foreign-language teaching, and not specifically for TESOL.

1.   Allen, Harold B., ed. *Teaching English as a Second Language: A Book of Readings.* New York: McGraw-Hill Book Company, 1965.
2.   Allen, Virginia French, ed. *On Teaching English to Speakers of Other Languages, Series I.* Champaign, Illinois: National Council of Teachers of English, 1965.
3.   Brooks, Nelson. *Language and Language Learning: Theory and Practice.* 2d ed. New York: Harcourt Brace Jovanovich, 1964.
4.   Bumpass, Faye L. *Teaching Young Students English as a Foreign Language.* New York: American Book Company, 1963.
5.   Cornelius, Edwin T., Jr. *Language Teaching: A Guide for Teachers of Foreign Languages.* New York: Thomas Y. Crowell Company, 1953.
6.   ————. *Teaching English: A Practical Guide for Teachers of English as a Foreign Language.* Washington, D.C.: English Language Services, Inc., 1955.
7.   Dacanay, Fe R. *Techniques and Procedures in Second Language Teaching.* Edited by J. Donald Bowen. Quezon City, Philippines: Alemar-Phoenix Publishing House, Inc., 1963. Distributed in the U.S. by Oceana Publications, Inc., Dobbs Ferry, N.Y.
8.   English Language Services, Inc. *English Pronunciation: A Manual for Teachers.* New York: Collier-Macmillan International, 1968.
9.   Finocchiaro, Mary. *English as a Second Language: From Theory to Practice.* New York: Regents Publishing Company, 1964.
10.   ————. *Teaching English as a Second Language.* 2nd ed. New York: Harper and Row, 1969.
11.   Fries, Charles C. *Teaching and Learning English as a Foreign Language.* Ann Arbor: University of Michigan Press, 1945.
12.   Jakobovits, Leon A. *Foreign Language Learning: A Psycholinguistic Analysis of the Issues.* Rowley, Massachusetts: Newbury House Publishers, 1970.
13.   Kreidler, Carol J., ed. *On Teaching English to Speakers of Other Languages, Series II.* Champaign, Illinois: National Council of Teachers of English, 1966.
14.   Lado, Robert. *Language Teaching: A Scientific Approach.* New York: McGraw-Hill Book Company, 1964.
15.   ————. *Linguistics Across Cultures: Applied Linguistics for Language Teachers.* Ann Arbor: University of Michigan Press, 1957.
16.   Lee, W. R., ed. *E.L.T. Selections 1: Articles from the Journal*

English Language Teaching. London: Oxford University Press, 1967.

17. ———. *E.L.T. Selections 2: Articles from the Journal English Language Teaching.* London: Oxford University Press, 1967.

18. Lugton, Robert C., ed. *English as a Second Language: Current Issues.* Philadelphia: The Center for Curriculum Development, Inc., 1970.

19. Mackey, William Francis. *Language Teaching Analysis.* London: Longmans, 1965.

20. Moulton, William G. *A Linguistic Guide to Language Learning.* 2d ed. New York: The Modern Language Association, 1970.

21. Politzer, Robert L. *Foreign Language Learning: A Linguistic Introduction.* Englewood Cliffs, N.J.: Prentice-Hall, Inc., 1970.

22. Rivers, Wilga M. *The Psychologist and the Foreign Language Teacher.* Chicago: The University of Chicago Press, 1964.

23. ———. *Teaching Foreign-Language Skills.* Chicago: The University of Chicago Press, 1968.

24. *Selected Articles from Language Learning, Series I: English as a Foreign Language.* Ann Arbor: Research Club in Language Learning, 1953.

25. *Selected Articles from Language Learning, No. 2: Theory and Practice in English as a Foreign Language.* Ann Arbor: Research Club in Language Learning, 1963.

26. Stevick, Earl W. *Helping People Learn English: A Manual for Teachers of English as a Second Language.* Nashville, Tenn.: Abingdon Press, 1957.

27. ———. *A Workbook in Language Teaching: With Special Reference to English as a Foreign Language.* Nashville, Tenn.: Abingdon Press, 1963.

28. Valdman, Albert, ed. *Trends in Language Teaching.* New York: McGraw-Hill Book Company, 1966.

29. Wishon, George E. and T. J. O'Hare, eds. *Teaching English: A Collection of Readings.* New York: American Book Company, 1968.

SERIALS

Serial publications in the TESOL field—journals, newsletters, occasional papers, and "annuals"—have been increasing at a fast rate during recent years. Two old standbys—*Language Learning,* published by the Research Club in Language Learning at the University of Michigan, and *English Language Teaching,* published by the British Council in association with Oxford University Press—seem to be as vigorous as ever. Other serials, whose files do not date back so far, have continued publication over several years: *MST English Quarterly* (Manila), *English Teaching Forum* (Washington, D.C.), *ELEC Bulletin* (Kanda, Japan), *ELEC Publications* (Tokyo), *English Teaching Guidance* (Tel Aviv), *Englisch an Volkshochschulen* (Munich), *Journal of the Teachers of English in Ethiopia* (Addis Ababa), and *English Bulletin* (Hong Kong).

There are a number of newcomers to the field that are devoted wholly or for the most part to TESOL: *TEFL: Bulletin for Teachers of English as a Foreign Language* (Beirut), *English for Immigrants* (London), *Journal of the Nigerian English Studies Association* (Ile-Ife), *English Teaching* (Rio de Janeiro), *Journal of English Teaching* (Tokyo), *IATEFL Newsletter* (International Association of Teachers of English as a Foreign Language, London), *Englisch: Eine Zeitschrift für den Englischlehrer* (Berlin), *Workpapers in English as a Second Language* (Los Angeles), *TESL Reporter* (Laie, Hawaii), *English for American Indians* (Washington, D.C.), *SEAMEC Regional English Language Centre Newsletter* (Singapore), *English Language Journal* (Buenos Aires), *English Teachers' Journal* (Jogjakarta), and *English Teachers' Journal* (Jerusalem). *Occasional Papers* of the American Language Institute, New York University, changed its name in 1967 to *Journal of English as a Second Language;* the latter has now been replaced by serially-issued books published by the Center for Curriculum Development in Philadelphia.

This listing is by no means a complete one. I imagine that other serials devoted to the TESOL profession appear more-or-less regularly in different parts of the world, but they have not come to my attention. The list shows something of the international professional involvement in the teaching of English to non-native speakers of the language, and it gives an idea of the considerable number of ESOL teachers and students throughout the world.

Relatively few of the serials listed above are readily available to teachers in the United States. It is interesting to note, however, that in almost any part of the world you can find active programs in teaching English to speakers of other languages; you also find active teacher groups, many of them publishing a serial of some kind—a journal, newsletter, or the like. ESOL teachers in the United States receive the *TESOL Quarterly* and the *TESOL Newsletter* as members of the TESOL association. Also, state and local TESOL organizations generally publish newsletters and make them available to their memberships. Other serials published in the United States and Britain, of course, can ordinarily be obtained without difficulty.

ABOUT THIS BOOK

A program for ESOL teacher training typically includes descriptive linguistics, structure of English, pedagogical methods, and practice-teaching. Most programs are more elaborate than this, but virtually all of them cover the four areas noted. This volume of readings was designed for use in a pedagogical methods course, preferably with a pedagogical handbook. It presupposes prior or concomitant training in descriptive linguistics—structural linguistics in particular.

At this point in time structural grammar has much more practical value for classroom teachers than transformational-generative (TG) grammar. As Anthony and Norris point out, the predominant method in second-language teaching today is audiolingual—a method with theoretical underpinnings from structural linguistics and behaviorist psychology. They describe in some detail the development of the audiolingual method, its underlying assumptions, and its main characteristics. In connection with this methodology, it is important to note also that the currently accepted classroom procedures and textbooks are largely based on structural and behaviorist models.

Courses in English structure and in general and descriptive linguistics that are presently being taken by teacher-trainees often have TG, rather than structural grammar, as the major focus. As a consequence of the emphasis on TG, a good deal of the current thinking, talking, and writing about grammar is in TG terms: "deep and surface structure," "embedding," "terminal strings," "rewrite rules," and the like.

Many ESOL teachers and trainees are confused by the present situation in regard to grammar study and teaching. Obviously there is a discrepancy if their own study of grammar centers around TG and they subsequently employ the audiolingual method in their teaching.

Wilga Rivers outlines the TG point of view on the nature of language, based on statements by Chomsky, and she summarizes many of the arguments of the last few years about the value of TG in second-language teaching. She identifies two levels of foreign-language behavior in relation to the learner: "a level of *manipulation* of language elements . . . and a level of *expression* of personal meaning" — first and second levels, so to speak. In her opinion, TG insights and methods have a role to play at the second level, but not at the first.

Future research and experimentation will presumably show how TG may be applied to best advantage in second-language teaching. As of now we have very little teaching material with underlying TG models. But proponents of the TG approach among ESOL teachers seem to feel confident that this situation will change: with a more adequate theory of language behavior, better pedagogy will evolve.

The readings in this volume for the most part reflect attitudes and views that are appropriate to and consistent with the audiolingual method. They deal with habit formation through imitation and manipulation in accordance with audiolingual theory and practice. But the book is not devoted to oral language development exclusively. Reading and writing receive substantial treatment, too, and some attention is given to other communicative aspects of language. It may be noted, incidentally, that current practices in teaching reading and writing show less consistency than those in teaching speaking and listening. In our sequence of skills development—understanding, speaking, reading, and writing—we have more success with the first two than with the last two, particularly writing. Ongoing research and experimentation, however, point to improved techniques and materials for the teaching of reading and writing in the future.

Most of the readings in this book were prepared by ESOL teachers, some of whom are also linguists. A few of the readings have to do with the teaching of foreign languages to native speakers of English, but their implications for and applications to TESOL are obvious.

SELECTED READINGS

AARONS, ALFRED C., BARBARA Y. GORDON, and WILLIAM A. STEWART, eds. "Linguistic and Cultural Differences and American Education." *Florida FL Reporter* 7 (1969).

ALATIS, JAMES E., ed. *Report of the Twentieth Round Table Meeting on Linguistics and Language Studies* (Linguistics and the Teaching of Standard English to Speakers of Other Languages and Dialects). Washington, D.C.: Georgetown University Press, 1970. Georgetown University Monograph Series on Languages and Linguistics, vol. 22.

ALLEN, HAROLD B. "Challenge to the Profession." *TESOL Quarterly* 1 (1967): 3–9.

————. *TENES: A Survey of the Teaching of English to Non-Native Speakers in the United States.* Champaign, Ill.: National Council of Teachers of English, 1966.

————. "TESOL and the Journal." *TESOL Quarterly* 1(1967):3–6.

BROOKS, NELSON, *Language and Language Learning: Theory and Practice.* 2d ed. Chapter 1: "Theory of Language." New York: Harcourt Brace Jovanovich, 1964.

CHOMSKY, NOAM. "Linguistic Theory." In *Northeast Conference on the Teaching of Foreign Languages* edited by Robert C. Mead, Jr. Working Committee Reports, 1966.

DECAMP, DAVID. "The Current Discrepancy between Theoretical and Applied Linguistics." *TESOL Quarterly* 2(1968):3–11.

JACOBSON, RODOLFO, ed. "Studies in English to Speakers of Other Languages and Standard English to Speakers of a Non-Standard Dialect." *The English Record*, vol. 21, April 1971 (Special Anthology Issue and Monograph 14.)

LIGHT, RICHARD L. "English for Speakers of Other Languages: Programs Administered bv the U.S. Office of Education." *TESOL Quarterly* 1(1967):55–61.

————. "Teacher Training, Bilingual Education and ESOL: Some New Opportunities." *TESOL Quarterly* 2(1968):121–26.

MARCKWARDT, ALBERT H. "English as a Second Language and English as a Foreign Language." *Publications of the Modern Language Association* 78 (1963):25–28.

————. "Teaching English as a Foreign Language: A Survey of the Past Decade." *Linguistic Reporter,* Supplement Number 19, October 1967.

OHANNESSIAN, SIRARPI. "TESOL Today—A view from the Center." *TESOL Quarterly* 3(1969):133–44.

PERREN, G. E., ed. *Teachers of English as a Second Language: Their Training and Preparation.* Cambridge: Cambridge University Press, 1968.

ROBERTS, A. HOOD. "ERIC and Its Role in TESOL." *TESOL Quarterly* (1968): 198–200.

SCOTT, CHARLES T. *Preliminaries to English Teaching: Essays for the Teaching of English in Japan.* Chapter 1: "Language and Language Teaching"; Chapter 2: "Linguistic Science and the Teaching of English. Tokyo: The English Language Educational Council, Inc., 1966.

SPOLSKY, BERNARD. "TESOL." In *Britannica Review of Foreign Language Education,* vol. 2, edited by Dale L. Lange. Chicago: Encyclopedia Britannica, Inc., 1970.

"Statements of Qualification and Guidelines for Preparation of Teachers of English to Speakers of Other Languages." (Foreword by Albert H. Marckwardt) *TESOL Newsletter* 4(1970):4–5.

TWADDELL, W. FREEMAN. "A Focus Report: Linguistics and Foreign-Language Teaching." *Foreign Language Annals* 4(1970):194–99.

————. "Remarks Read at the 1966 Northeast Conference." *Studies in Linguistics* 17(1969–70):101–104.

WARDHAUGH, RONALD. "Linguistics, Psychology, and Pedagogy: Trinity or Unity?" *TESOL Quarterly* 2(1968):80–87.

————. *Teaching English to Speakers of Other Languages: The State of the Art.* Washington, D.C.: Center for Applied Linguistics/ERIC Clearinghouse for Linguistics, 1969.

SECTION ONE
TRENDS AND PRACTICES

In this section the authors review some of our general knowledge, assumptions, and beliefs about second-language teaching and learning. Wright provides us with a set of starting procedures, and Bowen describes the endpoint—the goals we strive to reach with our students. But the readings are concerned mostly with what goes on between the beginning and the end.

All the authors either explicitly or implicitly identify two levels of activity in second-language acquisition: *manipulation* and *communication*. Rivers' term for the second level is "expression of personal meaning." Twaddell speaks of the habitual aspects of language and the aspects of meaning and choice, roughly equivalent to manipulation and communication. The teacher's chief objective, of course, is to move his students from the first level to the second, and the language course must provide for training at both levels.

According to Rivers, "It would be a mistake . . . to believe that practice at the second level should be delayed until the student has learned all the common features of the manipulation type. . . . If he is eventually to understand the complex system with its infinite possibilities of expression, he must develop this understanding little by little. The student will learn to make higher-level selective decisions by being made aware at every step of the possibilities of application of operations he is learning at the manipulative level. No matter how simple the pattern he is practicing, he will become aware of its possibilities for communication when he attempts to use it for his own purposes and not just to complete an exercise or to perform well in a drill."

In Section Nine of this book, Prator outlines the development of a manipulation-communication scale: he sets up a classification of language-teaching techniques ranging from the most manipulative to the most communicative types. "In the beginning stages," he points out, "the teacher exerts such rigorous control as to reduce the possibility of error to a minimum; at least this is what happens in classes

taught by the methods that are most widely approved today. At
some later stage the time must inevitably come when these controls
disappear, when oral pattern practice is replaced by the discussion of
ideas, and dictation is superseded by free composition. The whole
process may be regarded as a prolonged and very gradual shift from
manipulation to communication which is accomplished through
progressive decontrol. We determine the speed of the transition by
allowing the student the possibility of making certain errors only
when we are reasonably sure that he will no longer be likely to make
them."

A NEW SET OF HABITS

The communicative aspects of language need no elaboration here;
communication goes on in our everyday lives as we talk, listen, read,
and write. It might be useful, however, to review some of the habitual
aspects of language, since forming new habits and overcoming old
ones lie at the very heart of the audiolingual method.

The noises we call *speaking* are actually sound waves that go
through the air from one person's mouth to another person's ear. If
the second person knows the language being spoken, and his hearing
and other faculties are functioning normally, we say that *understanding*
takes place. The movements of the tongue, lips, and vocal cords
in speaking one's native language are habitual; they were developed
in early childhood and reinforced throughout a person's lifetime.

Speech habits differ from language to language. There is a set of
habits for English, a set for French, and a set for Japanese. Some
habits found in one language are similar to habits in another language,
but they are never quite the same. Learning another language,
then, involves learning a new set of habits. The habits acquired in
learning a native language will not fit another language. It is necessary
for the student to begin by making conscious efforts to produce the
sounds of the new language as the native speaker produces them.
And because the sounds of the new language involve different and
unfamiliar motions of the lips, tongue, and other speech organs,
learning to make the right motions may require a good deal of time and
practice. However, with enough practice, the motions for the new
language eventually become as automatic as those for the native
language.

At the beginning stage of learning another language and often for a
long time after the learning has begun, the habitual aspects of the
new language are matters of conscious choice for the student. The
student's immediate goal is to gain automatic control of those aspects

of the language that are habitual for the native speaker. A great deal of conditioning or training may be required in order to free the student's attention and allow it to concentrate on the meaningful aspects of language. Twaddell's treatment of this topic is something of a classic.

CONTRASTIVE ANALYSIS

A language consists of a limited number of basic sound units, called *phonemes* in the terminology of structural linguistics, and the patterned arrangement of these units. "Patterned arrangement" refers to the way the phonemes are combined into meaningful utterances (or parts of utterances)—sentences, words, and the like—according to a limited number of patterns. In addition to learning new speech sounds, the student of a second language must learn how these sounds are organized into a system, called the *structure* or *grammar* of the language in the terminology of the structural linguist. The student must internalize this knowledge and make the use of it habitual.

For the purpose of description and study, language structure has traditionally been divided into three parts: phonology (sound structure), morphology (word structure), and syntax (sentence structure). This kind of division provides convenient labels for areas of concentrated study, but most language learning proceeds without a clear separation of one component from the other.

By comparing the structure (phonology, morphology, and syntax) of the student's native language with that of the language he is learning—the "target" language—it is possible to predict many of the difficulties that will be encountered. This kind of comparison is known as *contrastive analysis*. Twaddell (in Section Six) notes that "As between the habits of two languages, the non-reinforcements and downright conflicts are considerable. Comparison of two linguistic structures pinpoints the conflicts and reveals that they are often deeper than even an experienced foreign language teacher might have realized." A number of contrastive studies have been prepared and applied to the building of textbooks and courses of study. These studies help the teacher anticipate problems and enable him to construct or select appropriate drill materials for his students. Also, by means of overt explanation and classroom practice, the students can be made aware of the major points of conflict between the native and target languages; and they can take better advantage of the techniques used to help them acquire new language habits with a minimum of interference from their old ones. Hockett and Strain (in Section Two) treat the matter of interference with more detail.

METHODOLOGY

Anthony and Norris define *approach, method,* and *technique* and explain the interrelationships among them. They point out that method is procedural: "it is the sum and structure of the selection, gradation and characteristic pedagogy which is carried out on the basis of certain axioms which form the underlying assumptions." A special point of interest to language teachers is their answer to why methods change: "The reasons do not lie in the failure of any particular set of techniques, for often the same techniques appear in the next method to gain favor. The reasons are to be found in the shifts in linguistic, psychological and pedagogical concepts which in turn cause corresponding shifts in notions of what it means to acquire, teach, or learn a language."

Anthony and Norris outline the general characteristics of the grammar-translation method, the direct method, and the audiolingual method and describe the approach-level assumptions underlying each. Inasmuch as the audiolingual is the most favored method today they aptly dwell on it more than the other two. Teacher-trainees wisely concentrate their attention on this method and the various ramifications of it, for they will likely employ it in their subsequent teaching activities.

In Prator's paper "Adding a Second Language," he contrasts the learning of one's mother tongue (L1) with the learning of a second language (L2). The ten basic differences he describes have numerous implications for the teacher's planning, organizing, and conducting of activities to promote the learning of an L2. These areas of contrast should be carefully noted, in particular, by teachers of English to native speakers of the language who expect to become involved in TESOL. Prator does not agree with the often-expressed notion that language is speech only. For him, "It seems more realistic and helpful for teachers to regard English speech and writing as two closely related but distinct linguistic systems each of which should be given equal priority in education for urban living." This makes it easier to consider learning activities in school, where, in the study of an L1, students work largely at acquiring reading and writing skills, but in the study of an L2, students have to work at acquiring all four skills: understanding, speaking, reading, and writing.

Prator discusses the child's learning of his L1 at various stages of growth and development: the exploratory stage, the imitative stage, the analogical stage, and the stage of formal instruction. Most of his comparisons deal with activities at school. He notes that "L1 is merely *learned* whereas L2 must usually be *taught.*"

SELECTED READINGS

ALATIS, JAMES E., ed. *Report of the Nineteenth Round Table Meeting on Linguistics and Language Studies* (Contrastive Linguistics and Its Pedagogical Implications). Washington, D.C.: Georgetown University Press, 1968. Georgetown University Monograph Series on Languages and Linguistics, vol. 21.

BOSCO, FREDERICK J. and DI PIETRO, ROBERT J. "Instructional Strategies: Their Psychological and Linguistic Bases." *IRAL* 7 (1970):1–19.

BROOKS, NELSON. *Language and Language Learning: Theory and Practice.* 2d ed. Chapter 3: "Mother Tongue and Second Language"; Chapter 4: "Language Learning"; Chapter 5: "Language Teaching"; Chapter 10: "Methods and Materials." New York: Harcourt Brace Jovanovich, 1964.

FRIES, CHARLES C. *Teaching and Learning English as a Foreign Language.* Chapter 1: "On Learning a Foreign Language as an Adult." Ann Arbor: The University of Michigan Press, 1945.

HAMMER, JOHN H., ed. *A Bibliography of Contrastive Linguistics.* Washington, D.C.: Center for Applied Linguistics, 1965.

HEMPHILL, RODERICK J., ed. *Background Readings in Language Teaching.* Quezon City, Philippines: Phoenix Publishing House, 1962.

LADO, ROBERT. *Language Teaching: A Scientific Approach.* Part 1: "Language and Language Teaching." New York: McGraw-Hill, Inc., 1964.

———. *Linguistics across Cultures: Applied Linguistics for Language Teachers.* Ann Arbor: The University of Michigan Press, 1957.

MARCKWARDT, ALBERT H. "The Linguistic Background of the Oral Approach." *ELEC Bulletin* No. 8 (1963):7–14; No. 9 (1963):6–10.

MOULTON, WILLIAM G. *A Linguistic Guide to Language Learning.* 2d ed. Chapter 1: "Language and the Learner"; Chapter 2: "Some Misconceptions." New York: The Modern Language Association, 1970.

———. "Linguistics and Language Teaching in the United States, 1940–1960." In *Trends in European and American Linguistics, 1930–1960*, edited by Christine Mohrmann, Alf Sommerfelt, and Joshua Whatmough. Utrecht and Anthwerp: Spectrum Publishers, 1961.

POLITZER, ROBERT L. *Foreign Language Learning: A Linguistic Introduction.* Part I: "Language and Language Learning," pp. 3–18. Englewood Cliffs, N.J.: Prentice Hall, Inc., 1970.

RIVERS, WILGA M. *Teaching Foreign Language Skills.* Chapter 1: "Objectives and Methods"; Chapter 2: "The Audio-Lingual Method." Chicago: The University of Chicago Press, 1968.

SCOTT, CHARLES T. *Preliminaries to English Teaching: Essays for the Teaching of English in Japan.* Chapter 5: "The Oral Approach: Retrospect and Prospect." Tokyo: The English Language Educational Council, Inc., 1966.

TITONE, RENZO. *Teaching Foreign Languages: An Historical Sketch*. Washington, D.C.: Georgetown University Press, 1968.

WARDHAUGH, RONALD. "The Contrastive Analysis Hypothesis." *TESOL Quarterly* 4 (1970):123–130.

WELMERS, WILLIAM E. *Spoken English as a Foreign Language: Instructor's Manual*. Washington, D.C.: American Council of Learned Societies, 1953.

Workpapers in English as a Second Language. Los Angeles: Department of English, University of California, 1967–70. 4 vols.

INITIAL TECHNIQUES IN TEACHING ENGLISH AS A SECOND LANGUAGE

AUDREY L. WRIGHT

In recent years linguistic studies have radically altered language teaching. The traditional method of learning a new language by studying printed words and the rules governing their arrangement has been largely replaced by the audio-lingual approach. Language is now considered as a set of speech habits and the "rules of grammar" as a description of these habits. Thus, today, language is taught essentially as a tool of verbal communication.

This is not to say that reading and writing are neglected in favor of speaking and understanding. On the contrary, they are vital communication skills and receive due emphasis in modern foreign language teaching. However, since it is recognized that speech patterns are the basis of language, the teacher's primary task is to impart oral patterns to the student. From here, it is a relatively simple matter for the student to symbolize the orally-learned material in written form, and to comprehend the written form in the act of reading.

As a teacher of English as a foreign language, you have an important and challenging task to perform. The speech habits which you transmit to your students constitute a communication instrument of immense value in a world where English plays such an important role in the fields of international relations, science, commerce, and the humanities.

How can you perform your task most effectively? How can you best cultivate in your students the speech habits of the English language? Language habits, like any other habits, are acquired only slowly and through constant repetition; great patience and considerable skill are demanded of the teacher who would foster in his students the mastery of a foreign language.

It is simply not true that anyone who can speak English can teach it. Language teaching is both a science and an art; its methods must be based on a correct theoretical foundation and may be perfected only through a great deal of practice.

With all of these facts in mind, let us examine how you, the teacher, can best help your students to master a new set of communication habits, those of the English language.

SPEAK ENGLISH IN THE CLASSROOM

Students need to become accustomed as soon as possible to the unfamiliar sounds of the new language. Equally important, they need to develop an awareness of English as a living medium of communication, rather than as a "school" subject with which they are struggling.

At the beginning level, this can be accomplished by welcoming your students to class each day with simple greetings in English. If the room is too warm or too cool, ask John, in English, to open or to close the window. Employ gestures, sketches on the blackboard, demonstrations, objects, or pictures to make your meaning clear. *It is advisable not to speak to your students in their native language, nor to translate from English into the native language unless absolutely necessary.* Your aim is to enable your students to understand and to speak English automatically, without having to "stop and think" or to perform laborious mental translation before responding to, or in, English.

Use English in the classroom in preference to the students' language, but . . .

LET YOUR STUDENTS DO MOST OF THE TALKING

It's enjoyable talking about subjects which interest us, and, as English teachers, we may like to discuss the Anglo-Saxon origin of modern English words, or the symbolism of Shakespeare's plays. This type of discussion, however, has no place in a class intended to teach the English language. It is the student who needs speaking practice, not the teacher, and in order to learn the language, he must use it.

Many language teachers are inclined to talk too much; and certain students, in order to avoid the hard work of learning, are skilled at "keeping the teacher talking" by asking endless questions. Don't let your students involve you in lengthy explanations, arguments, or lectures. The best and most valid answer to the question "Why do you say it that way in English?" is frequently, "Because that is the custom of the English language." The sooner your students are made to realize that language habits derive from custom and usage, rather than from logic, the sooner they will stop asking "why" and get down to the serious business of mastering a new set of language customs.

As a general rule, we may say that the teacher should do no more than 25% of the talking in class, and that students should be permitted to do 75% of the talking. The good teacher is like the conductor of a symphony orchestra; not a performer, but the person who directs the performers. The teacher introduces a pattern; then, by means of carefully planned drills, leads the class in numerous rehearsals of the new material.

Often, the class responds as a group. Frequently, individual performers will be called upon to "solo." The teacher-conductor, by his signals, insures that the proper tempo is maintained, that there is a proper balance between ensemble and solo work, and that false notes do not go uncorrected.

Skillful student performance depends on careful teacher preparation, and the teacher's lesson plan is as essential to the foreign language class as sheet music is to the orchestra. A conductor cannot halt his musicians in the middle of a musical rendition to think how the next movement should be played without spoiling the performance; nor should a language teacher hesitate in the middle of a class hour while he debates what to do next.

CORRECT STUDENT ERRORS BY HAVING STUDENTS REPEAT THE RIGHT FORM

When a student makes an error, either in pronunciation or in structure, one shouldn't begin by explaining to the student what he has said that is wrong. Explanations are intellectualizations about language, and your aim is to enable your students to use English, not to intellectualize about it. Immediately produce the correct form and have the student repeat it after you several times. Adequate English language habits are developed by listening to and imitating correct models of English speech.

It is desirable not to let errors go uncorrected. On the other hand, too much correction of a student's mistakes may discourage him. Try to strike a happy balance, correcting and having the student correct through repetition his more serious errors, and letting the lesser errors pass if you feel that reference to them might dishearten your student.

To keep the number of student errors to a minimum, one should avoid using material that is too difficult or that has not been practiced. Incorrect responses, if repeated, will lead to the formation of incorrect language habits. Thus, "feeding" new material little by little and giving frequent review on material previously taught will help your students avoid making mistakes.

INTRODUCE ONE NEW STRUCTURE AT A TIME

Mastering a language is like building a house of bricks: one brick must be laid at a time, starting with the stones of the foundation and building upon them. Extreme care must be taken that the foundation is solid; if one or more of these basic bricks are loose, the whole construction is likely to be weak.

Introduce a new structure orally. Convey its meaning by the use of gestures, pictures, or paragraph context. Let your students hear the structure a number of times, then have them repeat it many more times. Write it on the blackboard for them, and have them write it. Be sure that they understand and are able to use the new structure correctly before you go on to new material.

INSIST ON PLENTY OF REPETITION

Language proficiency is a skill and like any skill may be developed only through a great deal of practice. We learn to type by typing, and to play the piano by practicing scales. We learn to speak a foreign language by repeating its basic patterns and vocabulary items over and over again until their production becomes automatic.

Repetition need not be boring, and what is an old story to the teacher may still be news to the student. Approach repetition drills with interest and enthusiasm, attitudes which are generally contagious. Maintain a lively pace, calling now on a single student, now on the class as a whole to repeat. Strive to obtain a good imitation not only of the words that constitute the structural pattern but of its pronunciation and intonation as well. Keep in mind that you are seeking to develop in your students automatic control of the patterns of English, a result which may be achieved only through constant repetition practice.

It is important that you train your students to *listen* attentively to your model utterance before they repeat it. If they attempt to speak the sentence along with the teacher, as students often do, they will neither be able to hear the correct model nor will the teacher be able to hear their errors; consequently, the value of the repetition exercise will have been lost.

GIVE PLENTY OF SUBSTITUTION DRILL

The value of the substitution drill is that it trains the student to use a great variety of words within a limited number of grammatical patterns, and hence be able to express in English a variety of concepts. For ex- ample. Suppose that you have just introduced and conducted repetition practice on the Present Continuous or "-ing" tense (I'm walking, etc.), and that you now wish to give further drill on its production, using a group of action words already familiar to the students: talk, write, erase, sit, stand, etc.

Say the basic pattern, "I'm walking," and have your students repeat it. Next, instruct them to substitute "talk." The students respond, "I'm talking." Then give the word "write," and let them compose the sentence, "I'm writing." And so on through the list of verbs.

You may then wish to have your students substitute personal pronouns, nouns, and names in subject position such as "I'm standing," "The man's standing," or "John's standing."

When students have become thoroughly familiar with the mechanics of the substitution drill, various sentence parts may be substituted within the same exercise: "He's writing," "John's writing," "John's speaking," etc. An even more advanced type of drill requires transformations (into question and negative forms, for example) as well as substitution. Complex forms of the substitution drill, however, must be used with discretion and only when students demonstrate readiness for them. The mental alertness demanded for their successful performance proves exhausting to many students if carried on over too long a period of time. Furthermore, if students must stop and think at length before producing a correct response, the whole purpose of the substitution drill—to *call forth automatic response in the foreign language*—has been lost.

An excellent feature of the substitution drill is that it may be readily adapted to any proficiency level, from complete beginner to very advanced; this is a more challenging and varied type of exercise than the simple repetition drill.

TRAIN YOUR STUDENTS TO ASK QUESTIONS IN ENGLISH

Much classroom time is spent in question and answer practice, with the teacher asking the questions and the students answering. Such drills provide good comprehension and oral production practice; however, they require the teacher to do 50% of the speaking, and they fail to give the student vitally needed experience in *asking* questions.

Suppose your student finds himself in an English-speaking country. If he is to learn to make his way around in the new environment, he will need to ask many questions of the local people: "Where is the nearest bus-stop?", "Can you cash this check for me?", "Do you have any apartments for rent?"

Give plenty of drill on question forms, and then have your students ask questions of each other. Control such exercises carefully, insisting that students keep their questions within the framework of a basic pattern. Or, you may wish to have the same question repeated by each student:

STUDENT A to STUDENT B: Where do you live?
        STUDENT B: I live at 9 West 11th Street.

STUDENT B to STUDENT C: Where do you live?
        STUDENT C: I live at 53 Maple Drive.

Most students enjoy asking questions in English. In so doing, they are actually using the foreign language as a communication tool to gain further insight into the environment.

PREPARE FOR YOUR CLASSES

Just as an architect plans each detail of a house before starting to build it, the teacher should plan his semester's work before the classes begin. Know approximately what structures and what vocabulary items you intend to teach. Divide the semester's work by the total number of teaching hours, and decide what you will teach in each period, not forgetting to allow ample time for review.

One should never go into a class without knowing what the objective is for that hour: to teach structure X and review structure Y by means of exercises A, B and C. Write out a lesson plan for each class hour and refer to it unobtrusively during the lesson.

After class, ask yourself whether you achieved the objectives you intended, and in what ways your plan might have been made more successful. Such frequent self-evaluation will insure that you continually develop your teaching skills.

Be flexible in amending your plan to suit the needs of your particular students; but remember, it is possible to make alterations in a plan, whereas it is not possible to build successfully without a plan.

TREAT YOUR TEXTBOOK AS A TOOL, NOT A TYRANT

A good textbook goes a long way towards easing the teacher's task. It sequences, illustrates by example, and provides drill exercises on new material. A textbook is not a teacher, however; it cannot speak, listen, correct, or encourage. Instruction must come from you, and not from a book, no matter how well organized or well written.

Novice teachers, overloaded teachers, and teachers who lack confidence in themselves sometimes fall into what might be called "the textbook trap." They greet their students with a "Good morning, class. Open your books to page 80." The entire class hour is then spent in reading and doing exercises from the textbook. Teacher and students become entirely dependent on the book, slaves to the written word, the printed instruction. The teacher does not teach, and the students do not achieve mastery of the patterns of English.

Use a textbook as a supplement to your teaching. Introduction of new material and preliminary oral drill should come from you, and textbooks should be closed while new structures and vocabulary are practiced. After a considerable amount of oral practice, have your students open their books and work with the material in its written form. Of course, textbook material previously studied will usually provide the basis for written homework.

Be creative in your use of a textbook, employing its materials in a variety of ways. Many textbook exercises lend themselves to a number of uses: performed with books open or closed, orally or in writing, by a single student or a group of students.

Above all, keep in mind that your textbook is simply a very useful tool to aid you in the achievement of your objectives. Don't use it as a crutch, or as a teacher substitute. The essence of language is two-way communication.

BE ENCOURAGING

Psychologists have confirmed that praise of good performance stimulates students to do better work than does punishment or criticism for bad performance.

One must keep in mind that learning a foreign language may be a difficult and often frustrating task for an adult. He is asked to discard his familiar mode of communication and to learn a new one. He must train the muscles of his tongue and lips to produce new sounds. New neurological patterns must form in his brain. Suddenly the familiar environment is full of strange objects for which he knows no name. He is reduced to the helplessness of childhood, and must learn to communicate all over again.

Many adults resent the feeling of helplessness, of "being a child" that is part of learning a foreign language. They are afraid to speak for fear of making errors or of appearing ridiculous. Help your students by praising their good performances and their progress. Ask the harder questions of your better students, save the easier questions for slower students. Compliments will make your students want to do their best, and when a real desire to learn exists, half of your job is already done.

HAVE FUN

Laughter is a great aid in releasing the tension and lightening the fatigue which build up during an hour of concentrated study. Let your English class be an enjoyable experience for you and your students. Use humorous stories, anecdotes and example sentences liberally in your teaching. Tell an occasional joke in English, simplifying structure and vocabulary as necessary. Your relaxed enjoyment of the teaching-learning function will surely evoke a corresponding enthusiasm on the part of your students, making the teacher-student collaboration a fruitful one.

In brief, the teacher of English as a foreign language should never lose sight of the fact that his task is to foster in his students the development of a new set of speech habits. He must demonstrate the new habits to his students one at a time in accord with a carefully planned sequence, and then insist on ample student repetition of the model in order that each new language habit may become an integrated element of his students' learned behavior.

Learning a new language is not an easy task; but with proper guidance and encouragement from the teacher, students will arrive at the agreeable discovery that English has become a habit—an enjoyable habit. This discovery is their key to a new and exciting world of communication.

MEANINGS, HABITS *AND* RULES

W. FREEMAN TWADDELL

We are analysts and teachers of that odd human practice known as language. Whether we are working with grammar or literature, we are working with and through language. It is our business whenever one human being affects another by disturbing the molecules of the air or defacing some surface with marks.

OUR RINGSIDE SEAT

This business of ours puts us at the ringside of an intricate and fascinating social activity. Language is one of the points of intersection in that network of habit and choice which is the pattern of our human doings. Nowhere, probably, do we human beings act with quite so intimate a fusing of habits and choices as when we talk and listen, write and read.

In a sense, we can say what we choose: we can talk about the weather, or Aunt Susie's operation, or the scandalous behavior of Mrs. Applethwacker, or little Oswald's last test, or—so it seems to us—we can talk about anything else. Within the limits of propriety and discretion and the patience of our listeners we have complete freedom of choice to talk about anything we please, and to say what we please about it. But if we're talking American English, we are absolutely certain to do that talking in certain sentence types, making certain kinds of noises and no others, using certain combinations of those noises and no others.

We may choose to call Mrs. Applethwacker a hussy; we cannot choose to call her a hwày-dan. If we were talking Mandarin Chinese, we could choose to call her a hwày-dàn, but we should neither be tempted nor be able to call her a hussy. Nor can we choose to tell the world that "Mrs. Applethwacker a hussy is." Nor can we choose to call Mrs. A. a "hoozie" or a "hassy." In sum, we can say what we please, but we have to talk in a particular way. There is an element of choice in language which we call meaning; that is an expression of the individual personality. But there is also an element of compulsion in language: that is the habitual aspect, which is predictable, which is below and above the control of the individual, it is a rule of the language.

A MATTER OF HABIT

In the practical affairs of social life, this habitual aspect of language is as much a matter of course as the air we breathe. The native speakers of a language talk and write in accordance with the rules of their language simply because that's the way they talk and write. They don't choose or invent a structure of pronunciation because they want to sound musical; they don't choose or invent a grammatical system because they want to talk logically; they don't choose or invent a repertory of words.

By the time we have learned to talk English, we don't have to think about using different pronunciations of *t* in "tin" and "still"; we do it right, every time, without thinking about it. We don't have to remember to set subject before verb in the statement sentence; that's the only sequence in statement sentences. We don't have to recall that the English word for "house" is "house" rather than *maison* or *casa* or *jyā* or *dom*.

We don't, for example, apply the rules describing adverbs between subject and verb: Certain general adverbs of time occur between subject and verb—"I usually take a bath on Saturday," "We never serve horseradish on ice cream," "He always blames somebody else"; but adverbs of place do not occur between subject and verb, and we don't say "I there had a good time," "We here will build a campfire," "He everywhere gets into trouble." This is a rather complicated rule of English grammar; speakers of English are largely unaware of it, but the English they speak is consistent in conforming to it.

When we talk or write a language which we command, and when we hear it or read it, we pay no attention to these habitual practices. They are habits; they are taken for granted; we have learned both to conform to them and to ignore them.

In our practical use of language, all our attention is focused on the factor of choice. We decide whether to say "yes" or "no"; we don't worry about a monophthong in one answer and a diphthong in the other. We decide to assert that Senator Jumbo is a windbag; we don't have to plan to use the third person singular verb "is" rather than "are." When we hear that our alma mater has defeated Slippery Rock Teachers' College in basketball, we don't reflect that subjects precede verbs and deduce from that analysis which team was victorious.

All these habitual aspects of English are below the level of attention. Whenever for some reason our attention is required by such matters—an unfamiliar pronunciation, an unaccustomed combination of grammatical elements—we are distracted and usually annoyed or contemptuous. Our concern normally is meaning, and meaning is a function of choice. What we pay attention to in listening and reading is the meaning, the speaker's or writer's choice of things to say.

A DIFFERENT PROCEDURE

How disturbingly different our procedure has to be in learning a new language! Here, everything attracts our attention, aspects of habit as well as aspects of meaningful choice. Precisely because we don't know the language, we are unable to take its habitual aspects for granted. We have to learn to ignore that which is habit in the new language, just as its native speakers have had to learn to ignore it; and some day we will be able to ignore it. But our skill in using our own language blinds us to the large element of habit in it; the only things we notice in our own language are the meanings, the acts of choice.

So, whatever we notice is a meaning for us. And in the new language we notice everything, the habitual aspects as well as the aspects of choice. We notice unfamiliar sounds, and unfamiliar sequences of sounds; so we conclude that the rate of speech is extremely rapid. After we have learned to identify some individual words, we notice that the order of words is different from the habitual order in English; so we are aware of it, and therefore react as though the word order of the new language were an expression of meaning, an act of choice of some kind. We find in the new language nouns with cases, where our habits are prepositions; we find tenses and moods of verbs, where we are in the habit of using auxiliaries.

NEW WORD HABITS

We find new word habits: the speakers of the language do not have separate word habits to correspond to a distinction between "swim" and "float"; but they have two different habits to correspond to our "know." Most perplexing of all, we find that the users of another language are addicted to idioms of a strange and alarming sort, whereas we are in the habit of just letting ourselves go and coming through with whatever we want to put across.

All of these features are habits for the native users of the language, and they are as unaware of their habits as we are of the phonetic and grammatical peculiarities of English which we practice with unconscious skill. But in a foreign language we notice them; and when we notice something in language we are conditioned to assume a meaning, an act of choice.

This is incorrect, of course. And we teachers of language have learned better. We know that a speaker of French doesn't use a certain verb because he has decided to select a third person plural imperfect; he uses the verb ending because that's what you use when you're saying that particular thing in French. But our students assume that the Frenchman uses it for the same reason that the student would use it in a translation exercise: because there's a rule that requires it. The student has to make an act of choice to decide what ending to use; so he assumes that the Frenchman has to go through the same soul-searching experience.

The learner, that is, is hypersensitive to the habitual aspects of a new language; he sees meanings and choices where for the native speaker there is no meaning or choice. For the naïve learner, the foreign language represents a much greater density of meanings than his own, for he notices both real choices and also the habitual features which do not involve choice. So far as the naïve learner is concerned, the speakers of all other languages perform prodigies of split-second choosings from among intricate arrays of grammatical forms, add them to items in the dictionary, and then put the products together according to various patterns of word order. The innocent freshman naturally regards this as a hard fate— and one that calls for an explanation.

RULES OF LANGUAGE

Alas, we have given him the explanation. We have told the freshman why the unhappy speaker of French or Spanish or German or Tibetan has to go to all this cruel and unusual trouble in order to talk: It is because of the rules of his language. We know what these rules are. We know that a "rule" of a language is the analytical statement of one of the habitual aspects of that language. We know that the habit is the reality and the rule is a mere summary of the habit. We know that the rule describes how people talk and not why they talk that way. But our students are not as sophisticated as we.

So far as they are concerned, they notice something. And when they notice something, they assume that the speaker or writer meant them to notice it. So they have to endow the grammatical habits of speakers of another language with some meaning. I dare say many students pity or despise the ancient Romans as people who had to be constantly on guard for or against the ablative absolute and the subjunctive; the French are people whose recollections of history are forever filtered through past definite and past indefinite; and the conversation of Germans is hampered by the necessity of deciding whether a clause is independent or subordinate, so as to know where to put the verb.

A LOGICAL CONSEQUENCE

It is quite natural for our students to have these absurd ideas. Not because the students are stupid; I have tried to show that these absurd ideas

are a logical consequence of a skill in speaking any language and igno-
rance of the processes of language. It would be pleasant, to be sure, if
our students had learned something of the body of knowledge we call
modern linguistics. But they are by and large as ignorant of modern
linguistics as the sixteenth century peasant was ignorant of the Coperni-
can theory. We have to take our student as we find him; and we find him
predisposed to think about language in terms of rules rather than habits.

This makes our job harder; there is no doubt of that. A good many
students simply find that the rules don't interest them, and the only
meaning they can see in a foreign language is the rather unprofitable
meaning of the disjunctive pronoun and the subjunctive verb. Without
that meaning they think they can live; and they do.

THE TEACHER'S PROBLEM

We know that they are mistaken in regarding these grammatical habits
as meanings; but we can't convince them. We know that the rules are
only temporary substitutes for habits, and the sooner a rule is forgotten
because it is absorbed and dissolved in a habit, the better. We want
the student to get to the point where he can forget the rule and take the
habit for granted, and give all his attention to the real meanings, to the
real choices. But this takes time and practice, more time and practice
probably than an Olympian curriculum committee has allotted us.

The sad result is that many of our students spend most of their language study time in this chrysalis stage, when they can't distinguish
between meanings and habits, when they are still noticing unfamiliar
habits and accounting for them as "rules," when they have not yet
learned to ignore the habitual aspects and focus on the real meanings.
It is those real meanings that we aim at; and, with the aid of Heaven and
a long spoon, some of our students do get to the desired stage. But many
of them don't; for *them* the study of a language is largely a study of rules
—and that means that these students are not able to pay attention to the
real things that are said and written in the language.

This is too bad, no doubt about it. We certainly prefer a student who
can read a book to one who can only conjugate verbs. But we know
that until he can take verb forms for granted he can't read the book and
concentrate on the real meanings in it. This, of course, is the reason we
spend so much time on the habitual aspects of a language: as a preliminary conditioning, to create the habit, so as to liberate the attention for
the meaningful aspects of speech and writing.

Must we then resign ourselves to working with many students who
will never emerge from this preliminary phase? Of course we must, just
as all teachers must. The teacher of mathematics knows that most of his
students will never read a mathematical treatise after the final examina-

tion. The teacher of chemistry knows that most of his charges will never perform any experiment more intricate than mixing a cocktail. The teacher of the social studies knows that most of his students will get their data from the radio, the newspaper, and gossip.

NOT WASTED

But the fact that these students do not reach the most productive, the most rewarding phase of their various studies does not mean that those studies are wasted. All those studies leave their residues in the little gray cells, and the world has more orderliness, more of the world is in the domain of the comprehensible, more of the actions of people are explicit and describable. Less of the world is irrationally magical, less of society is overlooked or attributed to individual caprice. The pupil product of even the preliminary phases is aware rather than stolid, rather more calculating and rather less excitable.

Just so, the preliminary phase of language study, the "mere rules" phase, has a value in itself. That value may not be as great as the experience of communion with Racine, or Cervantes, or Goethe, or Lucretius, but it is still a value.

It is, among other things, the value of seeing the difference between a single language and universal reality. The price we pay for our prodigious skill in speaking our native language is that we do many things unconsciously. Those aspects of our language which are habitual are beneath our attention; they are wholly a matter of course, and it is always dangerous for anything human to be wholly a matter of course. English grammar is our way of talking, and our naïve students cannot help believing that it is *the* natural way of talking. An acquaintance with some other way of talking is salutary—solely because it is another way of talking.

Our students of course take the difference between "one" and "more than one" quite seriously; all their grammatical habits are enforcing the distinction between singular and plural, hundreds of times every day—and they don't know it. But only a minority of the human beings now talking are so channeled by their grammars; for many people, many millions of people, the distinction between "older" and "younger" is dinned into them oftener than a distinction between "one" and "more than one." Our students partition the flow of time in a certain way, because our grammar does—and they don't know it. A different partition of time by a different grammar is salutary.

These particular details are relatively unimportant, probably, but it is not unimportant that all of our habits of talking are only one of many possible sets of habits.

The rules of grammar, as the student suspects, do have a meaning. But they are not mere un-American perversities. They are indexes of non-American habits. And if there is any one thing which Americans in the second half of the twentieth century will need to recognize, it is precisely that there are *non-American habits* which are *not anti-American choices*. If we must use the jargon of the school catalogue, grammatical rules are a segment of social anthropology. Grammatical rules are our summary of a community behavior of societies; they are not the expression of the wisdom of academies, nor are they built into the structure of the universe, nor even into human nature, if there is such a thing.

A FIRST INTRODUCTION

Grammatical rules are likely to be the student's first introduction to cultural relativity. They should be taught as such. To be sure, the other West European languages are not ideal for this purpose; Cantonese Chinese or Eskimo would be better. But we are not only social anthropologists, we are also humanists and historians (and participants in West European culture). So we must compromise between the values of cultural relativity and the—for us—absolute values of Hebraeo–Graeco–Roman–Mediterranean–Northwest European–British–American cultural traditions.

Those cultural traditions, in the widest sense, are our major goals. The students for whom we can make those traditions accessible are the students with whom we have succeeded, just as the teacher of physics has succeeded with a student who subscribes to and reads the *Journal of the American Physical Society*. But we also have succeeded with the student who becomes in some degree more aware of how language works. In however modest degree, if one of our students begins to be aware of the habitual aspects of language, and draws some of the obvious conclusions, we have been socially useful.

For we are, I repeat, at the ringside of an intricate and fascinating social activity. Language is one of the points of intersection in that network of habit and choice which is the pattern of our human doings. Nowhere, probably, do we human beings act with quite so intimate a fusing of habits and choices as when we talk and listen, write and read.

He is a better human being who knows the difference between habit and choice. We teachers of language can probably be a bit more explicit in pointing out to our students what is so obvious to us along these lines. The study of the human activity of language can be made a constant reminder that we act as we do because we are at one and the same time members of the human race, members of a community, and individuals.

OUR DESTINATION

The range of possible noises that *homo loquens* can produce is ultimately conditioned by the structure of the human vocal apparatus and hearing apparatus. Within these physiological limitations, the usage of a community imposes further restrictions: each language, each dialect has its phonemic structure, and only what is within that structure is possible for the speakers and listeners of the language or dialect. And, within the limits of structure imposed by the community, the individual speaker makes his choices. He who speaks and writes lives his social life along the network of his community's habits and his own choices among those habits. He sees his choices as free and he ignores the limitations. The beginning learner of a language sees that the choices are not free, and that is worth seeing. The advanced learner of a language comes to ignore the limitations and move about among them comfortably, so that the real choices become the only choices he sees. And that is a skill of great value.

Meaning is our destination; the way to it, through rules, is a journey with its own rewards.

ADDING A SECOND LANGUAGE*

CLIFFORD H. PRATOR

This paper attempts to sum up, in non-technical terms, the essential differences between the acquisition of a first and a second language. It represents a conviction that a large number of the key concepts of TESOL can be drawn out of this type of comparison.

1. ACQUIRING THE MOTHER TONGUE

A very significant difference between the acquisition of one's mother tongue (L1) and adding a second language (L2) is that the former is merely *learned* whereas the latter must usually be *taught*. Though the difference is not absolute, it still has enormous consequences.

There is a great deal of interest today in finding out exactly how a child does learn his L1, and a large amount of research is being carried out in an attempt to discover just how and when the various components of language mastery are developed. Though few incontrovertible facts are as yet available for the guidance of the language teacher, the various stages in which the learning process takes place are coming to be understood with increasing clarity.

THE EXPLORATORY AND IMITATIVE STAGES

The first phase is often labeled *the exploratory stage.* Just as the newborn child instinctively exercises his limbs in order to develop them, he also exercises his lungs, mouth, tongue, and lips to produce sounds. His early cries of anger, pain, fear, or hunger are soon supplemented by increasing amounts of babbling activity, apparently aimed at exploring the range of his own vocal possibilities. He often makes a wide variety of sounds which he can never have heard before and which he would find it very difficult to emit later as an adult: velar spirants, voiceless nasals, retroflex sibilants, or simultaneous labio-velar stops plus vowels.

---

* This was the opening paper presented to the Pre-Convention Study Groups at the TESOL Convention, March 1969. (Footnotes for this paper have been supplied by the editor with the author's permission.)

The second phase of language learning has been called the *imitative stage*. There are signs that the infant is beginning to pay more attention to the speech sounds made by other people, and he may even become temporarily less vocal himself as he concentrates on listening to others. The sounds he produces become progressively more similar to those made by his elders, and he abandons many of his earlier sounds altogether. His parents find that, by giving him the benefit of every doubt, they can identify some of his sounds as the vowels and consonants of the mother tongue.

At first there are very few of these recognizable sounds, and each production of one of them may vary widely from other productions of what the infant and eventually his listeners come to think of as the same sound. Little by little, successive productions of the same sound grow more standardized and the distinction between sounds is therefore clearer. What has happened so far can be explained in terms of B. F. Skinner's theory that a habit is formed by a shaping process involving successive approximations to a behavioral model.[1] Perhaps the infant is motivated at this stage by his urge to imitate and by the approval of his elders.

In his earliest efforts to speak, the child typically favors one vowel and one consonant, seeming to prefer to produce them with the consonant first and the vowel following it; his first syllable is often recognized by his delighted parents as /ma/, /da/, or /ga/. The child may then split his general, all-purpose consonant into a stop and a continuant, learning to distinguish between a sound something like /na/ and another a little like /da/. The general vowel may then split into a high vowel and a low vowel. The stop may split into a pair, one of whose members is voiced, the other voiceless. Somewhat as a primitive organism develops through the splitting of cells, the child's phonological system becomes more complicated as he learns to make use of the various features—such as voicing, aspiration, and nasalization—that are used in his mother tongue in various combinations to distinguish between sounds and between words.

He now has what can be thought of as a stock of words to which he can attach meanings. This is when he begins to produce one-word sentences and finds that they can effect more specific desirable results than can be effected by mere noise-making. "/ap/" may result in his being picked up and cuddled. He can obtain the box he wants to play with by articulating "/ba/." A good, clear "/dada/" will attract the attention of the male parent. More and more he relies on speech to fulfill his basic physical and emotional needs. His linguistic successes are immediately reinforced by tangible rewards.

---

[1] B. F. Skinner, *Verbal Behavior* (New York: Appleton-Century-Crofts, Inc., 1957), pp. 29–33.

THE ANALOGICAL STAGE

Sometime during the child's second year he usually begins to enter the third phase of learning his mother tongue, the *analogical stage*. He has developed a small vocabulary of content words that symbolize people, things, actions, qualities, places, directions, etc. He now draws on his innate language ability to try to relate these ideas one to another.

Still without any awareness that he is learning a language, he explores the various possibilities of patterning among words. When does one make a certain group of words end with a certain sound as his elders do? What is the effect of making one word precede or follow another? Or of pronouncing one word on a higher pitch than another? What is the meaning of those obscure little words that people seem to insert between important words? In other terms, he becomes aware of the existence and potential significance of inflectional and derivational endings, word order, stress, intonation, and function words as opposed to content words.

In experimenting with patterns he produces word forms that he has never heard before and, eventually, completely new sentences that no one has ever before uttered. His listeners detect only a few of these— those that violate the accepted norms of the local adult speech community. Many children independently invent such forms as *feets, childs, brung, catched,* and *more better*. I shall never forget some of the analogical creations of my own children. Upon being somewhat violently admonished to behave, one of them answered in an aggrieved voice: "But Dad, I *am* being have." Another replied to a warning about diving into shallow water with a memorable: "Yeah, I know. Many a people have cracken their head on the bottom of the pool."

Seldom is the child corrected for such "mistakes." He gradually learns to avoid them because his listeners do not understand him, laugh at him, or simply never use those patterns themselves. In Skinnerian terms, the stimulus responses no longer occur because they are not positively reinforced.

Though sentences of this aberrant type, in which each departure from accepted norms can be justified by an impeccable analogy with acceptable patterns, do not persist long in the child's speech, the irrefutable fact that all normal children do produce such sentences may have great significance for the language teacher. It seems clear that a child does *not* learn to speak his mother tongue by imitation alone. Nor can such creations as "many a people have cracken their head" be satisfactorily explained as the result of a mechanical process of habit formation. The most convincing explanation of the child's ability to create new sentences appears to be that put forward by the current school of transformational grammarians: he acquires his competence by internalizing the rules that the grammar of his L1 prescribes for the generation of sentences. And he normally does this without ever knowingly formulating the rules himself or hearing them formulated.

THE STAGE OF FORMAL INSTRUCTION

When the child enters school, he begins the fourth and final phase of acquiring his mother tongue, the *stage of formal instruction*. Up to now he has merely been *learning* the language; it would be grossly inaccurate in most cases to say that he has been *taught* it. Now, for the first time, someone undertakes to teach it to him; but what remains to be taught? Charles C. Fries used to go so far as to say that nothing essential remains to be taught and that the child has already mastered his language before he goes to school.

Today we tend to regard such statements as considerable exaggerations, but there is certainly a large amount of truth in them. Fries was equating "language" with "speech." What he was really saying was that a pre-school child has already mastered the essentials of speaking his mother tongue: its phonological and grammatical systems. All that remains to be done in school is to enlarge his vocabulary and to teach him to read and write, to make him literate.

Many of us would not agree with his conviction that the spoken language *is* the language and that writing is merely an imperfect symbolization of speech. It seems more realistic and helpful for teachers to regard English speech and writing as two closely related but distinct linguistic systems each of which should be given equal priority in education for modern urban living.

Moreover, research such as that of Milfred Templin, Frederick Davis, and Jean Berko has shown that the average six-year-old is still far from having mastered many basic essentials of the spoken form of his L1.[2] Phonemicization—the process described earlier in this paper whereby the child singles out certain sounds as the only distinctive sounds in his language—is far from complete at the age of six. Many children have still not learned to produce some of the rarer sounds in the mother tongue's phonological inventory. Many have not yet internalized some of the most basic rules of the grammar, such as that which in English governs the alternation among the three forms of the plural endings: $/-s/$, $/-z/$, and $/-\partial z/$.

[2] Mildred C. Templin, *Certain Language Skills in Children: Their Development and Interrelationships* (Minneapolis: University of Minnesota Press, 1957), see especially pp. 142–52. See also Frederick B. Davis, *Philippine Language-Teaching Experiments* (Quezon City, Philippines: Alemar-Phoenix, 1967, Philippine Center for Language Study, Monograph Series, Number 5); and Jean Berko, "The Child's Learning of English Morphology." *Word* 14(1958):150–77.

Be that as it may, most pupils get very little intentional help from their teachers in their efforts to increase their command of the spoken language after they have entered school. In some well developed school systems an organized attempt is made to augment the child's vocabulary through activities designed to lead him to form new concepts. But over most of the world teachers concentrate almost all their efforts during the first year or two of schooling on teaching their pupils to read and write. Henceforth, most vocabulary development takes place as a by-product of reading.

2. TEACHING A SECOND LANGUAGE

From time to time theoreticians have championed a so-called "natural method" of second-language teaching. The basic tenet of the method is that children should, in so far as possible, be allowed to learn L2 in exactly the same way they learned their L1. This implies that there is no need for the teacher to concern himself with drills, or correctness, or organizing his subject matter. All he needs to do is to create situations in which the child will feel a sufficiently strong need to use the L2. He can then content himself with encouraging the child to persevere through a prolonged period of trial-and-error activity, and the language will eventually be learned. The method would seem to be about as sensible as trying to train a telegraph operator by giving him exciting news to transmit and then leaving him to work out the Morse Code for himself without benefit of systematic instruction.

There is actually no way whereby the circumstances under which a child learned his mother tongue can ever be reduplicated for the learning of a second language. The rest of this paper will be devoted to a consideration of the basic differences between acquiring an L1 and adding an L2. These differences will be classified under ten headings:

1. Time available
2. Responsibility of the teacher
3. Structured content
4. Formalized activities
5. Motivation
6. Experience of life
7. Sequencing of skills
8. Analogy and generalization
9. Danger of anomie
10. Linguistic interference

TIME AVAILABLE

One of the most self-evident differences is the much more limited amount of *time available* for acquiring the second language. The child normally has at his disposal almost all the waking hours of whatever number of years he needs to master his mother tongue. During that time he can experiment with new sounds, try out novel structural patterns at his leisure. He constantly hears authentic models of the type of speech he needs to learn and can usually afford to listen or not as he pleases. If he doesn't understand a word the first time he hears it and it is really something he needs to know, he can be sure that he will have many further opportunities to grasp its meaning.

But, unless his circumstances are quite exceptional, he must learn his second language largely at school, within the brief hours set aside in the schedule for teaching it. The total amount of time available varies considerably from school system to school system. If he wishes to be a polyglot, the Filipino child is lucky. He will begin to study English at least one period per day in the first grade, and from the third grade on he may receive all of his instruction in English. He will probably hear it spoken and sometimes may even have an opportunity to speak it outside of class. On the other hand, the cards are stacked against the average American who wants to learn French. He will be fortunate if his school offers two full years of instruction in the language and if his teacher allows him actually to try to speak French for a few hours of that time. He may never, alas, have an opportunity to use his L2 for any practical purpose in school or out. Even the Filipino, however, has to learn his second language in a small fraction of the time he had at his disposal for learning his first.

RESPONSIBILITY OF THE TEACHER

The shorter the time available for instruction, the greater the *responsibility of the teacher* to see to it that full advantage is taken of every precious minute. The necessity for careful planning and timing is still further increased by the fact that, whereas the L1 teacher is responsible for only a tiny portion of his pupils' language experience, the L2 teacher is responsible for almost all of it. In the second-language classroom there is both much more to be taught and much less time in which to teach it. The teacher of the mother tongue can afford to devote a great deal of attention at an early stage to the mechanics of writing and at a later stage to the niceties of usage, but his second-language counterpart must first deal with much more basic elements of language. One of the chief concerns of the former is to build up his pupils' vocabulary; the latter can allow himself to introduce only a small, carefully selected stock of the most useful new words.

Because of the pressure of time, the L2 teacher can afford to use only the most economical and effective instructional techniques. There may be differences of opinion as to what these are, but I think almost no one would argue, with regard to the most elementary stages of teaching a second language, that it is either economical or efficient to allow pupils to flounder through long periods of trial-and-error activity. Such activity inevitably leads to the formation of incorrect speech habits, which then have to be unlearned. And few processes can be more time consuming than unlearning well established habits.

One of the principal responsibilities, then, of the L2 teacher is to see to it that his pupils use correct language as often as possible. This does not mean that he must constantly correct them for the slightest error. That is seldom either feasible or desirable. Too many corrections by the teacher can render activities meaningless and reduce sensitive children to stubborn silence. What it does mean is that the teacher finds as many ways as he can to prevent the occurrence of errors. In other words, he begins by supplying the best possible model for imitation; he controls the language to be used. Then, little by little, when he is convinced that his pupils have mastered the material at hand, he relaxes his control to the extent that the absence of errors permits relaxation. The whole process, repeated each time new language material is to be taught, can be thought of as a gradual progression from the manipulation of language to communication through language.[3]

STRUCTURED CONTENT

Another consequence of the pressure of time is that the linguistic *content* of an L2 course, and even the content of each class of such a course, needs to be carefully *structured*. In an elementary L1 class, where attention is focused on developing the skills of reading and writing, there is room for a very large amount of spontaneity and improvisation. Structural controls are not essential in the reading selections, provided that the sentences are not too long and complicated. But the L2 teacher must be aware at all times of just what elements of the language he is teaching. There is a clearly determined inventory of sounds and combinations of sounds that his pupils must master. He cannot

[3] See Clifford H. Prator, "Development of a Manipulation-Communication Scale." In *The 1964 Conference Papers of the Association of Teachers of English as a Second Language,* edited by Robert P. Fox (New York: The National Association for Foreign Student Affairs, 1965), pp. 57–62. Reprinted in this volume (pp. 402–408).

afford to omit or slight any of them, and he should observe an ordered sequence in introducing them.

Completeness and sequencing are perhaps even more important in his major task, which is that of making certain that his pupils have an adequate opportunity to master the basic structures and sentence patterns that the grammar of the language permits. The pupils must then be given a chance to internalize the various formulas whereby the basic patterns are expanded, shortened, transformed, and embedded in other patterns to generate more complex sentences. All this requires practice and more practice. If a basic structure is overlooked somewhere early in the sequence, there can be no assurance that it will sooner or later reappear as a matter of chance sufficiently often to be learned. This is not to say that there is no room at all in the second-language class for spontaneity and improvisation. Without improvisation there is probably no true communication. It does seem to mean, however, that even spontaneity must be timed and rationed.

FORMALIZED ACTIVITIES

The rate at which a child acquires a second language probably depends above all else on the amount of time he spends in actually using the language. Whereas the L1 teacher can encourage pupils to speak one at a time and even allow them the option of remaining silent if they feel so inclined, the L2 teacher is forced to rely much more heavily on *formalized activities* in which participation is obligatory. He must have at his command an extensive repertory of drill techniques. These should range from purely manipulative drills in which all the child has to do is to imitate a model, through predominantly manipulative drills that require the child to supply certain linguistic elements within a framework provided by the model, through predominantly communicative activities over whose linguistic content the teacher still retains some slight degree of control, to purely communicative activities such as free conversation and the writing of original compositions.[4] Many L2 teachers feel that choral drills, in which groups of pupils or all the members of the class participate simultaneously, are an essential part of the repertory because they effectively multiply the amount of time each child spends in actually using the language.

Since formalized activities tend to be boring if they are continued for too long, the L2 teacher must learn to move from one activity to another in a rhythm that provides sufficient drill for mastery but that also moves fast enough to give the pupils a sense of achievement. As Earl Stevick has pointed out, this probably involves skill in recognizing technemes;

[4] *Ibid.*

Stevick defines a techneme as a classroom technique that pupils will react to as being different from a previously used technique.[5]

MOTIVATION

Most of the remaining basic differences between acquiring an L1 and adding an L2 arise not so much from the fact that a more limited amount of time is available for the L2 but that the child usually begins to learn his second language at a more mature stage in his general development. Perhaps the most far-reaching in its effects of these differences is the difference in *motivation*. Recent research has been rather inconclusive as to the importance of some of our cherished methodological dogmas, such as our preference for presenting grammar inductively rather than deductively and our earlier insistence that structural patterns be drilled to the point of over-learning. On the other hand, all the pertinent research that I am aware of, particularly that of Wallace Lambert and his colleagues at McGill University in Montreal, has clearly demonstrated the central importance of motivation.[6]

The child learns a great deal of his mother tongue without awareness that he is learning. His most basic drives—hunger, fear, the need for affection—urge him to communicate. His very existence depends on his ability to make his needs known in some way to those upon whom he is utterly dependent. It is hard to imagine how stronger motivation could exist. As he grows older his degree of independence of course increases, and he is certainly aware in school that he is being taught how to read and write. Even so, his motivation usually remains fairly high: it is not hard to comprehend the value of becoming literate, and many children really do discover that reading is fun.

But how inferior is the natural motivation for learning a second language! Instead of being a tool for the satisfaction of immediate needs, it may seem more like a questionable superfluity. It may be associated with unsympathetic foreigners or an objectionable social group rather than with the learner's family, peers, and favorite people.

Obviously, the L2 teacher must bend every effort toward supplying at least a portion of the natural motivation that is lacking. He must try to show that native speakers of the language are an interesting and even an

[5] Earl W. Stevick, "Technemes and the Rhythm of Class Activity," *Language Learning* 9(1959):45–51.
[6] See, in particular, W. E. Lambert, "Psychological Aspects of Motivation in Language Learning," *Bulletin of the Illinois Foreign Language Teachers Association* (May 1969), pp. 91–106; also W. E. Lambert, R. C. Gardner, R. Olson, and K. Tunstall, "A Study of the Roles of Attitudes and Motivation in Second Language Learning." In *Readings in the Sociology of Language* (The Hague: Mouton Publishers, 1968), edited by J. A. Fishman, pp. 474–91.

admirable lot who have said and written many things that can enrich anybody's life. He may be able to convince his pupils that mastery of the language will open doors to professional advancement that would otherwise remain closed. Above all he will need to make sure that his pupils often experience that simplest and most solid of the satisfactions that accompany the successful learning of an L2, the pleasure of being able actually to communicate thought in a language other than one's own. He certainly cannot allow them to conclude, basing their judgment on what goes on in the classroom, that most of what is said in the second language is empty verbiage unrelated to reality. Even manipulative drill can be made meaningful.

EXPERIENCE OF LIFE

A second consequence of increased maturity is a wider *experience of life*. The L2 teacher has less need than does the L1 teacher to provide his pupils with new, non-linguistic experiences. A child normally brings to learning his second language a larger stock of more sophisticated concepts than he brought to acquiring his first. This is one reason why readers in English, for example, that have been written for American children are not usually suitable for, say, Filipino children. Such texts tend to be too difficult linguistically and too simple conceptually. Unless this difference is kept in mind, L2 drills prepared for adolescents and adults may turn out because of the simple-minded language in which they are written to be an insult to the intelligence of the learners.

SEQUENCING OF SKILLS

Almost inevitably the native speaker of a widely written language learns the skills involved in mastering his mother tongue in a certain fixed order: first hearing, then speaking, then reading, then writing. Is this *sequencing of skills* equally inevitable in the teaching of a second language? There is a great deal of evidence that it is certainly not inevitable and, indeed, that it may sometimes not even be desirable. Every year thousands of graduate students in American universities learn to read French or German, because they must do so to fulfill advanced degree requirements, without ever having spoken either language. It may be argued that they do not really read but merely decipher with the aid of a dictionary. I am not sure that this is anything more than a verbal quibble. It cannot be denied that they do manage to get meaning from the printed page. And if that is all they need to do with their French or German, then it hardly seems justifiable to criticize the method on the grounds that that is not the way in which children learn their mother tongue.

Perhaps it is wise to maintain, except in cases of special need like that of the graduate students cited above, that the pupils in an L2 class should generally speak only what they have first heard and understood well, should read only what they have spoken, and should attempt to write only what they have read. This seems to be a particularly wise policy in a school system like that of Kenya or the United States, in which English is almost universally the medium of instruction at all levels. In the lower grades of such schools teachers—and parents—tend to measure achievement in terms of reading alone, and the pressures to begin reading early may therefore become nearly irresistible. If, however, the children are required to read large amounts of material with which they have not earlier familiarized themselves in oral form, they have no other recourse than to parrot, to mouth words without understanding their meaning. In time parroting may become a fixed habit, a besetting sin that imperils the mental development of the child. Anyone who has worked in the schools of Kenya or who has studied the problems of Spanish-speaking children in American schools will recognize the reality of the danger.

There is a great and, it seems to me, insufficiently recognized difference between sequencing skills in terms of the linguistic material contained in one lesson or unit of lessons, as described at the beginning of the preceding paragraph, and sequencing them in terms of the total skills. Some methodologists, basing their judgment on the analogy with first-language learning, have gone so far as to say that the L2 teacher should not ask his pupils to begin to speak until they have learned to hear the differences between all the sounds that the language distinguishes, that pupils should not be allowed to read before they have mastered all the essentials of the spoken language, etc. Such a doctrine seems to ignore the well-established fact that, as children mature, they tend rapidly to become more visually-minded. That is to say, they find it increasingly difficult to learn and remember a word without having seen it in writing. There is evidence that prolonged postponement, over a period of months or even years, of all contact with the written form of the language in an L2 class may be definitely counter-productive. Therein may lie another basic difference between acquiring an L1 and adding an L2.

ANALOGY AND GENERALIZATION

As his maturity increases, a child also becomes more capable of learning through *analogy and generalization*. We have noted that in his linguistic development he begins to make good use of these processes as early as his second year. It seems reasonable to assume that they can be even more useful in teaching him his second language than they were to him in learning his mother tongue. We are not yet sure whether it is better actually to formulate the rules that govern the generation of sentences in the L2 or merely to lead the child to internalize them without overt formulation. There are also differences of opinion as to whether the formulation should be done by the pupils or by the teacher. But rules can obviously provide a short-cut to learning. This belief is in harmony with the modern view of language as rule-governed behavior rather than as the result of mechanical process of habit formation. Provided that the rules are phrased in the simplest and most non-technical language possible and that learning them is never confused with being governed by them, it is difficult to see how formulating them could be other than helpful.

DANGER OF ANOMIE

By acquiring his L1 a child relates himself more closely to his own speech community and culture. When he learns an L2, he is in *danger of anomie,* or alienation from his own culture. How can the danger be avoided or at least minimized, especially in a situation in which the L2 is begun early and eventually becomes the medium of instruction? This is one of the most significant problems of second-language teaching. Unless it can be solved, English may in time lose much of the favor it now enjoys in many of the world's newly independent countries. The spokesmen for ethnic minority groups within the United States are becoming increasingly insistent that it be solved in American schools. The search for a solution is made more difficult by the teachers' conviction, already alluded to in this paper, that a language cannot be well taught apart from the culture of which it is an expression and that adequate motivation for learning an L2 is impossible unless the pupils are favorably disposed toward those who speak the language natively. Part of the solution may lie in dividing instruction into two phases, in Africanizing or Hispanizing the subject matter dealt with during the first phase, and in postponing any attempt to explain British or traditional American culture until the second phase. Until a more complete solution is worked out, second-language teaching will continue to be characterized and bedeviled by the need for serving two apparently contradictory sets of goals.

LINGUISTIC INTERFERENCE

I have saved until last the difference that is perhaps of most interest to linguists, the difference that arises from the *linguistic interference* which affects every element of teaching a second language. Whereas the child acquires his L1 without prejudice or predisposition toward certain forms of language, when he comes to add his L2 he must do so against the ingrained and often misleading influence of his mother tongue. I have saved this point until last and include it here only for the sake of completeness. Its importance is so obvious and it has so frequently been discussed at length that it hardly seems necessary to consider it further in this paper.

TERMINAL BEHAVIOR
IN LANGUAGE TEACHING

J. DONALD BOWEN

In modern education one often hears of the concept "terminal behavior." This is a term supplied from the field of psychology, a term which reflects the belief that the measure of any successful educational activity is the degree to which the student's behavior is modified. To what extent does he do or can he do things he did not or could not before the lessons were presented.

The term fits comfortably in second-language teaching, where we wish to influence behavior of students by enabling them to communicate effectively in a medium other than their native language. The extent to which they can do this can be measured and evaluated as a reflection of the effectiveness of the teaching (plus whatever aptitude and motivation the student brings to the classroom).

Knowing what terminal behavior we seek should be useful in the design of our teaching. We should select and arrange activities that lead directly to the acquisition of the required behavior. The trouble is we do not know explicitly what sequence of activities does lead to the skill of communicating effectively in a new language.

We observe that all normal human infants in a socially typical environment do learn their mother tongue, but we also know that this experience cannot be recreated for a teenager or an adult. Natural language learning seems to be possible only with the optimum combination of age and circumstance.

INTERMEDIATE BEHAVIOR

The desired terminal behavior in a second language is communication within a relevant range of experience, ideally the same range the student commands in his first language. But obviously for a non-infant this is a highly developed and complex pattern of behavior involving physiological and neurological coordinations that can be controlled only with extensive practice. It is an activity never yet successfully described in all its specific detail, nor yet imitated by any machine.

We know as teachers that we can't ask beginning students to practice by simply imitating what we desire as their terminal behavior. They are not capable of doing so. Rather we substitute various types of intermediate behavior which we hope will lead to the desired terminal behavior. We cannot, in other words, ask them to communicate in a language they have just begun to study, so we employ various repetition exercises, substitution drills, etc., postponing communication for the more advanced levels of training.

This is necessary; we have no choice. But teachers must assume two important responsibilities: (1) to understand how intermediate-type activities can be meaningfully related (in pedagogical terms) to terminal behavior and (2) to move steadily toward communication in the selection and design of activities in the classroom.

Teachers will usually accept this view, especially on an intellectual plane, as a reasonable picture of what they must accomplish. But how is it implemented in the classroom? How do we move from manipulation to communication? How do we get students to a point where they can operate in the realm of the desired terminal behavior?

Manipulative activities are characterized by predictability—the teacher knows all the answers and his corrections are based on his knowledge. But communicative activities presume that the listener does not know all the answers—only the limitations within which the answers must fall. Choices are left to the speaker—otherwise there is no point to the communication, and it would never normally occur.

ACTIVITIES THAT ARE NOT PREDICTABLE

The application to language teaching, then, seems to be the use of activities (questions, answers, rejoinders, reactions, etc.) which are not predictable. The skill with which a teacher can direct such activities is a measure of his professional efficiency and, incidentally, the teacher's best guarantee that his job will not soon be taken over by a machine.

Every teacher should ask himself whether he is using all the communication activities his students are capable of participating in. He should be able to analyze each classroom activity (usually each drill or exercise) to know whether it involves communication and to what extent. He should utilize communication-type activities as early as possible and increase the percentage of their use as his students increase their capability.

A consideration of terminal behavior is the touchstone to identify the elements of communication that are available in the classroom. For each activity a teacher should ask two questions: (1) Does the response to this stimulus represent a skill the student will need when he is on his own? and (2) Does this activity stretch the student's capacity by requiring that he express a thought of his own, one that the teacher cannot fully predict? Then, of course, the teacher must know if he is offering enough of these activities that require independent student action, enough so that the student can operate effectively when eventually he is left to his own resources.

In short, manipulation activities such as repetition, substitution, and transformation are useful, even necessary, to the beginner. But he must go beyond these if he is to achieve a useful control of his second language in situations that demand real and authentic communication. And it is the teacher's responsibility to see that he does.

METHOD
IN LANGUAGE TEACHING

EDWARD M. ANTHONY and WILLIAM E. NORRIS

WHAT METHOD IS

Participants in discussions of the methodology of language teaching frequently lack the common ground upon which to build fruitful debate. At one extreme is a philosophical and psycholinguistic dialogue, largely on the axiomatic level—a level which may provide an approach to methodology, but which cannot in itself be labeled method. On the other hand, anecdotal presentations of pedagogical tricks, however well classified and no matter how diverting and perceptive, are not really methodological. Classroom techniques may reflect a particular method, or may implement a method—they may even provide data to evaluate a method, but they are not, in and of themselves, method.

Method is, then, neither the intricate set of assumptions, explicit or implicit, about language and language acquisition that characterizes a particular approach to language teaching, nor is it the list of drills, exercises, diagrams and explanations that makes up the technique of the talented classroom teacher. Method lies somewhere between the labyrinthine algebra of the grammarian and the psychologist and the actions of an overworked teacher industriously following her lesson plans.

It is possible to initiate discussions of method in the philosophical labyrinth or in the classroom; to begin with approach or with technique. For example, let us begin with the classroom teacher. A skilled teacher may develop over the years certain techniques that "work"—that bring about a desired language learning event—that guide the behavior of the student in the direction the teacher wants. If these classroom strategies show structurally unifying characteristics and tend to form a coherent procedure, they may come to be regarded as components of a method. This route to method has been traveled time and again, as is evident from those many methods which are named after one of their successful practitioners or after a characteristic technique. But though a particular method may historically derive from a set of techniques, a method may, by definition, be found only where pragmatically acceptable techniques are supported by theoretical assumptions.

A DEFINITION OF METHOD

As one of the authors of this article has written elsewhere: "Method is an overall plan for the orderly presentation of language material, no part of which contradicts, and all of which is based upon, the selected *approach*. An *approach* is axiomatic, a *method* is procedural."[1] In a perfect world an assembly of savants might decide for all time just what language really is, and how we acquire a first language, or learn a second. These precious truths would then be passed on to an omniscient language-pedagogy engineer who would transform them into an all-purpose, fool-proof method for language teaching. The set of procedures, in the form of a syllabus, textbook, program, curriculum, or whatever, would be passed on to the teacher, who then could choose the weapons to accomplish the high purpose of language teaching. But, in our less than perfect world, instead of a smooth one-way route from approach through method to technique, we find a busy intersection where each of these three aspects of the total language learning process is continually modifying the others.

Language teaching methods come and go, ebb and flow. Some achieve wide popularity, then decline. Why the swing from oral learning to rule learning, back to oral learning, and yet again to rules? If a method is successful, why doesn't it remain in wide favor? The reasons do not lie in the failure of any particular set of techniques, for often the same techniques reappear in the next method to gain favor. The reasons are rather to be found in the shifts in linguistic, psychological and pedagogical concepts which in turn cause corresponding shifts in notions of what it means to acquire, teach, or learn a language. For example, language learning tended to mean quick and accurate translations of readings in the 1930's, but by the 50's it meant facile ability in aural comprehension and oral production.

METHODS GAIN AND LOSE FAVOR

As our beliefs about the nature of language change, our faith in a method is affected, since we all value consistency. When language is seen as a closed system of contrasting patterns of phonology and syntax, a method which aims to teach aural-oral mastery of a finite set of sentence patterns enjoys theoretical support. But if we accept the view that language is a small set of basic relationships capable of infinite variation through expansion and transformation, we will feel constrained to adjust our methods to fit these new "facts" of linguistic theory.

[1] Edward M. Anthony, "Approach, Method and Technique," *English Language Teaching* 17 (January, 1963):63–67.

Again, as the psycholinguists' view of language acquisition processes changes, so must classroom teaching techniques. If language is a set of habits, then mim-mem and stimulus-response practice to shape new habits dominates the lessons. Some recent psycholinguistic theory, however, holds that children are born with an innate set of linguistic universals which they use to acquire their first language. Stimulus-response explanations are alien to this theory and consequently, as applications of the theory are extended to second language teaching, the value of learning through habit formation and the most common practice procedures of the audiolingual approach are brought into question.[2] Methods, then, are shaped by many different theories, and the popularity of a method may depend on the popularity of any of these theories.

Nevertheless, all language teaching worthy of the name must follow some sort of method. That method must include, as does all teaching, the selection of materials to be taught, the gradation of those materials, their presentation, and pedagogical implementation to induce learning.[3] Method, we repeat, is by definition procedural; it is the sum and structure of the selection, gradation, and characteristic pedagogy which is carried out on the basis of certain axioms which form the underlying approach.

TWO EARLIER METHODS IN PROTOTYPE

Man can study his principal means of communication in three different ways. One of these is traditionally considered "training," while the other two are usually considered "education."

First, an individual may study a foreign language so that he can participate in the cultural affairs of the society which uses that language. Whether the society is living or long dead is irrelevant to this particular reason for study. The Peace Corps candidate who studies Hausa in order to teach Africans malaria prevention and the scholar who studies Hittite in order to read history in cuneiform inscriptions are brothers under the skin. Each wishes to use the language he studies as a means to a basically non-linguistic end. Each needs to control the language sufficiently well to operate in some corner of the culture. He must be trained in some skill-building way designed to help him accomplish his specific goals. Indeed, we often speak of the "four skills" of aural understanding, oral production, reading ability, and writing ability. The Peace Corps candi-

[2] Leon A. Jakobovits, "Implications of Recent Psycholinguistic Developments for the Teaching of a Second Language," *Language Learning* 18 (June, 1968):89–109. David McNeill, "Developmental Psycholinguistics," in *The Genesis of Language: A Psycholinguistic Approach*, Frank Smith and George A. Miller, eds. (Cambridge, Mass., 1966), pp. 67–73.
[3] William F. Mackey, *Language Teaching Analysis* (London, 1965), pp. 156–157.

date may have an interest only in the first two; the scholar, with access only to written records, has interest only in the third and, perhaps, the fourth.

Second, and usually considered "educational," is the study of artistic language. Certain gifted individuals respond to their environments with greater sensitivity than do we ordinary mortals, and some of these individuals (whom we often call poets), are able to communicate their sensitivity to the rest of us through language. Their language is considered worthy of educational academic study, both by those who speak the poets' native languages and by those who do not, in an effort to arrive at a wider understanding of the meaning of life.

Third, some students of language are interested in gaining insights into how language works—its peculiarities, its geographical, temporal, or social spread, and how it is acquired, either as a native or as a foreign language. This is generally considered educational study as well.

We will, within our present discussion, call these three ways of investigating language the study of *language,* the study of *literature,* and the study of *linguistics* respectively. It is useful to keep them separate in speaking of language teaching—especially in discussing earlier methods— because the proponents of these methods did not always separate them on the approach level, and did not always take advantage of the findings of one kind of language study to benefit another kind of language study. This is evident in the two central methods described in this section. While they are referred to as "earlier" methods, they are still, in some instances, followed today.

THE GRAMMAR-TRANSLATION METHOD

The first of these methods is often called the *grammar-translation* method. By *grammar* here is usually meant the series of rules or generalizations that is intended to describe the target language. A successful "grammar" performance by the student usually means his ability to recite the list of German prepositions which take the dative, or to give the forms of the Latin verb "to be" in the particular arbitrary order *sum, es, est . . . ,* or to name the conjugation to which the Spanish verb *cantar* belongs. In a more sophisticated use, it may mean that the student is successful if he can puzzle out a fill-in-the-blanks exercise, oral or written, on the model "el perro _____ un animal." That is, he must extract from his *soy, eres, es* conjugation the form that is labeled third person singular present and fit it into the blank. His performance is then judged by the speed and accuracy with which he can do these tasks.

The question that is always raised about the grammar portion of this method is "Is this the study of language or the study of linguistics?" If it is the former, it should, according to our earlier statement, enable the student to operate in some or most of the aspects of the society in which the language is used to conduct its cultural business. But it is doubtful if the Germans spend much of their time discussing the prepositions used with the dative case, or if Spanish speakers ask each other to fill in the blanks in sentences. To the extent that they do so, the study is valuable and relevant. Some teachers would see that this kind of study of grammar provides only the basis for studying the language rather than the language itself. To this extent, it is a sort of study of low-grade linguistics—that is, it gives some insights into how the language under study works, even though these insights are often phrased in terms more appropriate to the native language grammar than to the target language grammar.

But what of the other end of the grammar-translation method? How does *translation* fit in? When students of the grammar-translation method are not reciting rules or filling in blanks, they are frequently rendering foreign language passages into English or putting English passages into the foreign language. Again, one must ask, what is this the study of? Is it language? If it enables the student to operate in the society which uses the language, such translation must become an instantaneous skill, as indeed it may for some students after long years of agonizing practice. Is it the study of literature? Marginally perhaps, if one begins with a literary work to translate. Is translation the study of linguistics? Again, the answer must be that the linguistic insights gained are elementary and are on the truistic level for most linguists: perhaps that decent word-for-word translation is impossible; that different languages use different structures to express different things differently.

All this is not to say that it is impossible to learn a language through the grammar-translation method. The above-average student can gain a good deal from the method, can collect a vast amount of information that some day, somewhere, given the right circumstances, just might "nucleate"[4] into a useful command of the language. The odds, however, are not attractive. A good deal of the difficulty with the grammar-translation method seems to arise from the confusion of linguistic, literary, and language aims—possibly out of a misguided effort to include respectable "educational" material in a "training"-centered academic exercise.

THE DIRECT METHOD

The *direct method*, the second of the two central methods, is much more focused and makes no pretension toward literary or linguistic aims, nor does it take into account literary or linguistic findings. Direct method

[4] Kenneth L. Pike, "Nucleation," *The Modern Language Journal* 44 (November, 1960): 291–295.

teachers attempt to use only the target language on all levels, ask for no statements about grammar, proceed through conversation, reading, and writing in the target language, and give no attention to translation. It is, in its purest form, the direct antithesis of the grammar-translation method. The direct method is clearly aimed at giving students sufficient control of a language to operate in the society which employs that language. The direct method teaches without the emphasis on choice of materials that characterizes the method described in the following section. The valuable increase in relevance and efficiency that arises from the linguistic description and comparison of the target and native languages is lacking in the direct method. Nevertheless, it clearly shows an advance over the grammar-translation method when the goal is language control.

Although we have commented here upon two widely-used and well-established methods as if they occurred only in pure form, a cursory examination of texts and syllabuses will show many that illustrate a mixed language-teaching methodology. It is perhaps unnecessary to mention that such mixed methods often reflect a curious inconsistency at the approach level.

THE DOMINANT METHOD TODAY: AUDIOLINGUAL

"What teaching method do you use?" Ask this question of almost any foreign language teacher in our schools today, and the reply will be "the audiolingual method," "oral approach," "aural-oral method," "linguistic method," or one of the other terms used to indicate certain procedures which share the same approach level assumptions.[5] An examination of current journal articles, a look at the introductions to new textbooks (and even revisions of old ones) will confirm this—the currently accepted method is audiolingual. Nearly all of us use it, or claim to use it.

What then is this method? Certainly the question should not be hard to answer considering the number of articles, books, lectures, conferences,

[5] For us the use of a term like *audiolingual* alternatively with *approach, method,* or *technique* never implies that these combinations are synonymous. *Audiolingual approach* embraces an intricate series of postulates and assumptions about language and learning, a number of possible methods, and innumerable techniques. *Audiolingual method* is used to describe a set of cumulative curricular procedures toward a stated language goal, again involving a large number of varying techniques. An *audiolingual technique* may be merely a classroom procedure during which the teacher and student talk and listen, and might easily be used in, for example, grammar-translation methodology:

TEACHER: Alvin, list the German prepositions which govern the dative.
ALVIN: *aus, ausser, bei, mit, nach, seit, von,* and *zu.*
TEACHER: Very good. You may to the head of the class go.

This use of the technique would, of course, be completely at odds with the aural-oral approach as usually understood.

and courses on the subject in recent years. But these discussions are often overly concerned with techniques. Perhaps it would be worthwhile to reconsider the basic assumptions of the audiolingual method before we take a look at the techniques most commonly employed to implement it.

LINGUISTIC AND PSYCHOLOGICAL CONSIDERATIONS

This modern method has its theoretical base in an understanding of the nature of human language and the psychology of second language learning quite different from that underlying grammar-translation or even the direct method. Twentieth-century linguistic science has been the main source of the new ideas and knowledge from which language teachers have developed this method. Charles C. Fries set forth the implications of linguistics for language teaching most forcefully and effectively in his now classic 1945 monograph *Teaching and Learning English as a Foreign Language*. He there insists that the initial tasks in learning a new language are "first, the mastery of the sound system . . . second, the mastery of the features of arrangement that constitute the structure of the language." Thus Fries applies to language teaching two basic premises of structural linguistics concerning the nature of language: language is primarily oral, and language is a system of contrasting structural patterns. To this is added a third premise: language is a communicative activity of human societies, and therefore "accuracy," not mere "correctness," must be the standard for mastery from the beginning, "an accuracy based upon a realistic description of the actual language as used by native speakers in carrying on their affairs."[6]

These linguistic premises are reflected in the audiolingual method by the following requirements, at least for the first stages of language learning:

1) The student must learn to use orally with normal speed the foreign language response that is required by any of the situations that he has studied.

2) The major structural patterns of the linguistic system, presented in meaningful contexts, are the language materials to be learned.[7]

The psychological assumptions about the nature of human language acquisition and behavior which have influenced the method have been drawn from behaviorist theory. Its influence is clearly seen in Bloomfield's description of language behavior in stimulus-response terms, and

---

[6] Charles C. Fries, *Teaching and Learning English as a Foreign Language* (Ann Arbor, Mich., 1945), p. 3.
[7] Fries, "On the Oral Approach," *ELEC Publications* 4,2 (Tokyo, 1960).

his view that language consists of a great many complex activities united into a single far-reaching complex of habits.[8] Psychologists themselves, although long interested in child language development, until recently took little direct interest in problems of second language learning; however, they assented to the linguist's and language teacher's assumption that "language is a system of extremely well-learned habitual responses."[9] A more direct application of psychological theory has come from the concepts of operant behavior and instrumental learning formulated by B. F. Skinner who first pointed out that verbal behavior exemplifies operant behavior, thereby describing the mechanism for establishing new language habits. Moreover, in learning a second language it is assumed that the already established first language habits tend to interfere with the process of acquiring the set of second language habits wherever the native language and foreign language systems are in conflict.

These psychological conclusions are reflected in the method in the following ways:

1) Memorization and practice drills are used extensively to establish the new language skills as habits.

2) Materials take into account contrasts between the native language and the foreign language systems.

Over the past twenty-five years, these few assumptions by linguists and psychologists about language and language behavior have been the source from which modern teaching methods have developed, methods which have brought far-reaching changes in classroom procedures (emphasizing oral language habit formation) and teaching materials (employing sound linguistic description and contrastive analysis to select and order the language features to be taught).

"MIM-MEM" AND "PATT-PRAC"

The terms "mimicry-memorization" and "pattern practice," which are frequently used in describing the new methodology, each reflect the influence of both linguistic and psychological concepts. "Mimicry" recognizes the linguists' assertions that language is primarily oral and that native speaker models are ultimately the only completely acceptable models for imitation. "Pattern" represents the system of the language, each pattern a part of the system of systems of which the language is constructed. The language "item" to be learned is not an individual sound, word, or sentence, but that sound in contrast to other sounds of

[8] Leonard Bloomfield, *Language* (New York, 1933), pp. 22–37.
[9] John B. Carroll, *The Study of Language* (Cambridge, Mass., 1953), pp. 99, 191.

a phonological system; that word as the member of a lexical cluster; that sentence pattern in relation to other sentence patterns. The influence of behaviorist psychology is shown by the second term in each pair— "memorization" and "practice" are the chief mechanisms for establishing habit. "The command of language is a matter of practice . . . language learning is overlearning, anything less is of no use," says Bloomfield,[10] echoing three hundred years later the words of Comenius, "Every language must be learned by practice rather than rules. . . ."

"Mim-mem" and "patt-prac" are two important and complementary classroom tools of an audiolingual method. One or the other may dominate in a given lesson or even a whole set of lessons, but fundamentally they can be viewed as steps in a procedure by which the student is first presented with the new foreign language item and gains familiarity with and conscious control over it (through mim-mem), and then progressively gains language mastery as recognition and production of the item are made unconscious habit (through pattern-practice). The precise steps in this procedure are recognition, imitation, and repetition, followed by variation and selection.[11] To these steps we may add another which is commonly used with older students: explication. Usually coming between repetition and variation, explication typically consists of linguistic comments about the pattern or item, often elicited from the students as an inductive generalization from examples. The approach principle here seems to be that mature students, at least, are helped in language learning by some sort of systematic organization, overtly presented.

SUMMARY

Our purpose here has been to present a concept of method in terms of its relationship to the other components of language teaching. We have, hopefully, demonstrated that method, while it exists apart from basic theoretical assumptions on the one hand and day-to-day teacher-pupil interaction on the other, is nevertheless dependent upon them. We can make assumptions without feeling obliged to invent procedures to implement them; we can use classroom techniques without relating them to a particular method. But method must be based on axioms, and it must be implemented through techniques selected to lead the student to the desired language behavior, as defined by those axioms.

We believe that keeping these interrelationships in mind will clarify discussions of a particular method.

[10] Leonard Bloomfield, *Outline Guide for the Practical Study of Foreign Languages* (Baltimore, 1942), p. 12.
[11] Freeman W. Twaddell, "Preface to the First-Year Seminar Script, 1958" *ELEC Publications* 3,2 (Tokyo, 1959).

REFERENCES FOR FURTHER READING

Fries, Charles C., *Teaching and Learning English as a Foreign Language.* (Ann Arbor, Mich.: University of Michigan Press, 1945).

Mackey, William F., *Language Teaching Analysis.* (London: Longmans, Green, 1965).

Moulton, William G., *A Linguistic Guide to Language Learning.* (New York: Modern Language Association, 1966).

Valdman, Albert, ed., *Trends in Language Teaching.* (New York: McGraw-Hill Book Co., 1966).

RULES, PATTERNS, AND CREATIVITY IN LANGUAGE LEARNING

WILGA M. RIVERS

In 1966, Chomsky shocked many participants at the Northeast Conference by casting doubt on the validity of the direct and uncritical application of linguistic theory to teaching practice. "I am, frankly," he said, "rather skeptical about the significance, for the teaching of languages, of such insights and understanding as have been attained in linguistics and psychology."[1] He went on to say: "It is possible—even likely—that principles of psychology and linguistics, and research in these disciplines, may supply insights useful to the language teacher. But this must be demonstrated and cannot be presumed. It is the language teacher himself who must validate or refute any specific proposal."

With an obvious, though unstated, reference to methods of foreign-language teaching of recent years which it has been believed were consistent with what was known of the nature of language and of the learning process, Chomsky declared: "Linguists have had their share in perpetuating the myth that linguistic behavior is 'habitual' and that a fixed stock of 'patterns' is acquired through practice and used as the basis for 'analogy.'" To Chomsky, "Language is not a 'habit structure.' Ordinary linguistic behavior characteristically involves innovation, formation of new sentences and new patterns in accordance with rules of great abstractness and intricacy." For this reason, he speaks continually of the " 'creative' aspect of language use."

Linguistic science has made teachers very conscious of the fact that grammar is the core of language. Without an internalized set of rules, or syntax, they are told, no one can understand or use a language: Language is "rule-governed behavior."[2] In the past, many teachers have uncritically adopted habit-formation techniques because language, it appeared, was

---

[1] Noam Chomsky, "Linguistic Theory," in Robert G. Mead, Jr. (editor), *Language Teaching: Broader Contexts,* Northeast Conference Reports, 1966, p. 43. Other quotations in this and the next paragraph are from pages 44 and 45 of the same source.
[2] Sol Saporta uses this term in "Applied Linguistics and Generative Grammar" in Albert Valdman (editor), *Trends in Language Teaching,* New York: McGraw-Hill, 1966, p. 86.

"a set of habits."[3] Now many are ready to seize upon a new slogan and begin to inculcate rules in the hope of establishing "rule-governed behavior," even though they have only a vague concept of what this phrase can mean as it has been used by linguists or psychologists.[4] In this way they hope to take their students beyond the arid fields of mechanical repetition, where pure habit-formation techniques seem so often to have left them, into the greener pastures of creative production of foreign-language utterances.

Before adopting any such approach, we need to clarify our ideas about the essence of language use (which in Chomsky's terms is a question of performance based on competence) and then select methods appropriate to the type of learning involved in its effective acquisition. It is at this point that there is most confusion.

LINGUISTIC vs. PEDAGOGIC GRAMMAR

First, it is important to distinguish, as Chomsky has done in *Topics in the Theory of Generative Grammar*, between a linguistic and a pedagogic grammar. A linguistic grammar, as Chomsky sees it, aims to discover and exhibit the mechanisms that make it possible for "a speaker to understand an arbitrary sentence on a given occasion," whereas a pedagogic grammar attempts to provide the student with the ability to understand and produce such sentences.[5]

This leaves the question wide open for the foreign-language teacher. A linguistic grammar is an account of competence (the knowledge of the language system that a native speaker has acquired) expressed in terms of an abstract model that does not necessarily represent, and may not even attempt to parallel, the psychological processes of language use. It can give the informed teacher insights into language structure and clarify for him various aspects of his subject matter, but methods of linguistic description do not *per se* provide any guidance as to how a student may be taught to communicate in a foreign language. This is the preoccupation of the writer of a pedagogic grammar who, in the light of what the linguistic grammar has established about the subject matter, decides what are psychologically (and therefore pedagogically) the most appropriate ways of arranging and presenting the material to the students.

---

[3] William G. Moulton, "Linguistics and Language Teaching in the United States 1940–1960," in C. Mohrmann, A. Sommerfelt, and J. Whatmough (editors), *Trends in European and American Linguistics,* Utrecht: Spectrum, 1961, p. 87.

[4] George A. Miller, "Some Preliminaries to Psycholinguistics," *American Psychologist,* 20 (1965), pp. 15–20. Reprinted in L. A. Jakobovits and M. S. Miron (editors), *Readings in the Psychology of Language,* Englewood Cliffs, New Jersey: Prentice-Hall, 1967, pp. 172–79; see especially p. 175.

[5] Noam Chomsky, *Topics in the Theory of Generative Grammar,* The Hague: Mouton, 1966, p. 10.

The form a particular pedagogic grammar will assume will depend on such factors as the objectives of the language course, the age and intellectual capacity of the students, the length and intensity of the study, and the degree of contrast between the foreign and native languages.

How, then, can the foreign-language teacher establish "rule-governed behavior" that will enable his students to produce novel utterances at will? In conformity with Chomsky's position, we need to make it possible for the foreign-language learner to internalize a system of rules that can generate an infinite number of grammatical sentences that will be comprehensible and acceptable when uttered with the semantic and phonological components appropriate to specific communication situations.[6] With the word *internalize* we are at the heart of the problem: *"Rule-governed behavior" in the sense in which it is used by linguists or psychologists does not mean behavior that results from the conscious application of rules.*

According to Chomsky, "A person is not generally aware of the rules that govern sentence-interpretation in the language that he knows; nor, in fact, is there any reason to suppose that the rules can be brought to consciousness." Neither can we "expect him to be fully aware even of the empirical consequences of these internalized rules"[7]—that is, of the way in which abstract rules acquire semantic interpretations. The behavior is "rule-governed" in the sense that it conforms to the internalized system of rules. These rules are not the pedagogic "grammar rules" (often of doubtful linguistic validity) of the traditional deductive, expository type of language teaching, according to which students docilely constructed language sequences. They are rules, as Chomsky puts it, of "great abstractness and intricacy" inherent in the structure of a language, which through the operation of various processes find expression in the overt forms that people produce.

Generate, in the mathematical sense in which Chomsky uses the term, does not then refer to some unexpected production of language sequences that reflects originality of thought on the part of the speaker, but to a mechanical process: The outworking of the internalized rules will automatically result in what are recognizably grammatical utterances. When Chomsky talks, therefore, about the " 'creative' aspect of language use," he is not referring to free play with language elements where students "create language," grammatical or ungrammatical, to suit their purposes, as in some direct-method situations (foreign-language camps and clubs or foreign-language houses, for instance), or as people do in moments of need in a foreign country. He is referring to the fact that once the system of rules of the language has become an integral part of the student's store of knowledge he will be able to produce, to suit his purposes, an

6 Ibid., p. 16.
7 Ibid., p. 10.

infinite variety of language sequences, whether he has previously heard such sequences or not, and these sequences will be grammatically acceptable, and therefore comprehensible, to the person to whom he is speaking. The mere supplying of rules and the training of the students in using these for the construction of language sequences is not in itself sufficient to ensure the "internalizing" of the system of rules so that it operates in the production of sentences without the students being conscious of its role. Unless foreign-language teachers are aware of the technical meaning of the terms Chomsky was using in his speech on language teaching, they may be left with erroneous impressions of his viewpoint.

CREATIVE USE OF LANGUAGE

Exercising the language teacher's prerogative that Chomsky has so clearly assigned us, we may well question his statement that it is a myth that linguistic behavior is "habitual" and that a fixed stock of patterns is acquired through practice and used as the basis for "analogy."[8] "Repetition of fixed phrases," he says, "is a rarity," and "it is only under exceptional and quite uninteresting circumstances that one can seriously consider how 'situational context' determines what is said."[9] Despite these assertions, Chomsky himself would be the first to admit that a theory of language performance has yet to be developed. With his continual emphasis on creative and innovative use of language, Chomsky is likely to lead us astray in the teaching of foreign languages by fixing our attention on a distant rather than an immediate goal. It is certainly true that our final aim is to produce students who can communicate about anything and everything in the foreign language, creating at will novel utterances that conform to the grammatical system of the language. But, as in every other area of teaching, we must map out our program step by step.

Creative and innovative use of language still takes place within a restricted framework, a finite set of formal arrangements to which the speaker's utterances must conform if he is to be comprehended and thus to communicate effectively. The speaker cannot "create" the grammar of the language as he innovates: He is making "infinite use of finite means."[10] His innovative ability will exist only to the degree that underlying competence exists—that the set of rules has been internalized. Foreign-language students must acquire the grammar of the foreign language so that it functions for them as does the grammar of their native language.

[8] Noam Chomsky, "Linguistic Theory," p. 44.
[9] Ibid., p. 46.
[10] Noam Chomsky, quoting Humboldt, in *Aspects of the Theory of Syntax,* Cambridge: Massachusetts Institute of Technology Press, 1965, p. 8.

Basically, the question of how to inculcate the grammar of a language will depend on the type of activity we believe communication in a foreign language to be: Is it a skill or an intellectual exercise? If foreign-language learning is the acquiring of a skill or a group of interrelated skills, then our students need long and intensive practice until they are able to associate without hesitation or reflection the many linguistic elements that are interrelated in a linear sequence. This approach has been basic to mimicry-memorization and pattern-practice procedures. If foreign-language use is an intellectual exercise, then training is necessary to ensure that students can make correct choices of rules and modifications of rules in order to construct utterances that express their intentions. This has been the traditional grammar-learning approach.

TWO LEVELS OF LANGUAGE BEHAVIOR

If we can identify two levels of foreign-language behavior for which our students must be trained, then it is clear that one type of teaching will not be sufficient for the task. These two levels may be designated: (1) the level of *manipulation* of language elements that occur in fixed relationships in clearly defined closed systems (that is, relationships that will vary within very narrow limits), and (2) a level of *expression* of personal meaning at which possible variations are infinite, depending on such factors as the type of message to be conveyed, the situation in which the utterance takes place, the relationship between speaker and hearer or hearers, and the degree of intensity with which the message is conveyed. A place must be found for both habit formation and the understanding of a complex system with its infinite possibilities of expression. The problem is to define the role of each of these types of learning in the teaching of the foreign language.[11]

It is essential to recognize first that certain elements of language remain in fixed relationships in small, closed systems, so that once the system is invoked in a particular way a succession of interrelated formal features appears. Fluent speakers are able to make these interrelated adjustments irrespective of the particular message they wish to produce. The elements that interact in restricted systems may be practiced separately in order to forge strong habitual associations from which the speaker never deviates (this applies to such elements as inflection of person and number, agreements of gender, fixed forms for interrogation or negation, formal features of tenses). These elements do not require intellectual analysis: They exist, and they must be used in a certain way

11 This subject is discussed in relation to all four fundamental language skills in Wilga M. Rivers, *Teaching Foreign-Language Skills,* Chicago: University of Chicago Press, 1968.

in certain environments and in no other way.[12] For these features, drill is a very effective technique. They may be inductively learned by the student, without more than an occasional word of explanation by the teacher when there is hesitation or bewilderment. In fact, lengthy explanation can be a hindrance rather than a help because it is *how* these systems operate that matters, not *why*. In structured classroom practice, the use of these formal features may be extended, by the process of analogy, to other utterances with different combinations of lexical items.

On the other hand, other elements of language, mainly at the level of syntax, involve decisions more intimately connected with the contextual meaning. A decision at this higher level has implications for structure beyond the word or the phrase, often beyond the sentence. A slight variation in the decision will often mean the construction of quite a different message.

Elements of this second type usually involve several features in interaction and, therefore, a more complicated initial choice, which entails further choices of a more limited character. In order to express exactly what one wishes to say, one must view it in relation to the potential of the structural system of the language as a whole. This is the higher-level decision that sets in motion operations at lower levels that are interdependent. The decision to make a particular type of statement about something that has taken place recently involves a choice of register, a choice of degree of intensity, the use of lexical items in certain syntactical relationships that will involve the production of certain morphological elements, certain phonemic distinctions, and certain stress and intonation patterns. The interrelationships within the language system that are involved in these higher-level decisions may need to be clarified in deductive fashion by teacher or textbook. Practice at this level must be practice with understanding, where the student is conscious of the implications and ramifications of changes he is making. This he will best do if the practice involves making decisions in real communication situations devised in the classroom, rather than in continual drills and exercises. In such interchange the feedback from the other participants brings a realization of the effect of the decision the speaker has made.

There must be in the classroom, then, a constant interplay of learning by analogy and by analysis, of inductive and deductive processes—according to the nature of the operation the student is learning. It is evident that he cannot put higher-level choices into operation with ease if he has not developed facility in the production of the interdependent lower-level elements, and so learning by induction, drill, and analogy will be the commonest features of the early stages. Genuine freedom in language

[12] It is interesting to note that many of these features, particularly the morphological ones, are excluded by Chomsky from his system of rewrite rules and included in the lexicon as parts of complex symbols. See *Aspects*, pp. 82–88.

use, however, will develop only as the student gains control of the system as a whole, beyond the mastery of patterns in isolation.

PRACTICAL APPLICATION

It becomes clear that the second level of language use, which we have just considered, is of a more advanced type than the first level, requiring as it does sufficient knowledge of the total possibilities of the language to be able to make higher-level choices, as well as skill in the manipulation of numerous lower-level elements in accordance with the higher-level decision. Too often in the past, foreign-language teaching has concentrated on an understanding of the language system as a whole without providing for the amount of sheer practice that the lower-level elements demand. This has led to hesitancy in language use. On the other hand, some modern methods, in which only the problems of the early stages seem to have been considered to any serious extent, have worked out techniques for developing the lower-level manipulative skill while leaving the student unpracticed in the making of decisions at the higher level. The language course must provide for training at both levels.

It would be a mistake, however, to believe that practice at the second level should be delayed until the student has learned all the common features of the manipulative type—that is, that the student should first learn to manipulate elements in fixed relationships and not begin until a year or two later to learn the selection process of the higher level. If he is eventually to understand a complex system with its infinite possibilities of expression, he must develop this understanding little by little. The student will learn to make higher-level selective decisions by being made aware at every step of the possibilities of application of operations he is learning at the manipulative level. No matter how simple the pattern he is practicing, he will become aware of its possibilities for communication when he attempts to use it for his own purposes and not just to complete an exercise or to perform well in a drill.

As the pattern becomes a medium of communication, it takes its place in the communication system that the student is gradually beginning to control; by using it in relationship with what he has already learned, he sees this isolated operation as part of a whole, with a definite function within the language. As he acquires more knowledge of the language, he may need some explanation of how the various elements he has become accustomed to using interact within sentences and discourse. Such explanations will be brief and to the point. Since their sole purpose is to prevent mislearning through mistaken assumptions about relationships, they will be fruitful only if followed immediately by thorough practice in the expression of these relationships. Intensive practice is essential and must be continued until it is evident that the student has internalized the underlying rule so effectively that it governs his production without conscious and deliberate application of the rule on his part.

At a further stage, which will be sooner or later according to the age and maturity of the class, the student will need to see the parts and the interacting sections he has learned in relation to the whole functioning system of the language. (Having learned, for instance, different ways of expressing past action, he will need to see how the past fits into the general expression of temporal relationships in this particular language.) In most cases, he will have had most practice in those areas where the danger of native-language interference is the greatest (that is, where the native and foreign languages are most divergent in their usage). At this advanced stage, the student will need to grasp, to understand, without referring to an external and therefore irrelevant criterion, how apparent similarities and differences interact within the complete system of the language he is learning.

But let me emphasize again that the student cannot realize this understanding of the whole before he has experienced, through practice and use, the functioning of the parts. If he attempts to possess the whole too soon, he will achieve only rote learning of grammar rules and the ability to describe rather than to use the grammatical system. On the other hand, where the teacher can present the system as a whole to students who already have a practical knowledge of the functioning of the parts, he can freely use authentic language material to demonstrate what he wishes to convey. And by showing how the grammar works for real purposes the teacher can convey far more to the students than he can by making numerous abstract explanations supported by isolated, out-of-context examples.

Textbooks and courses of study—and teachers—must make ample provision at appropriate stages for both types of learning discussed here. Neglect of the repetitious practice needed to acquire such things as interrelated inflectional systems will force students to make decisions for each element as they proceed, and their use of the language will remain hesitant. On the other hand, it is only by going beyond the repetitious practice stage that students can learn to make the higher-level choices that will bring the lower-level adjustments they have learned into operation at the appropriate time.

There has been much experimentation in recent years with techniques for the lower-level manipulative operations. We need now to give more thought to effective ways of inducing language behavior at the second level. This, I believe, is the direction in which we should be moving.

SECTION TWO

SPEAKING AND UNDERSTANDING

In second-language study, particularly at the beginning stages, we devote a great deal of attention to pronunciation and selective listening. *Pronunciation* is the production of speech sounds for communication. But for communication to take place, these sounds must be comprehended by another person. Control of the speech mechanism for the purpose of communicating in one's own native language is completely automatic. The effort put forth in speaking is largely in the area of *what* one is going to say rather than *how* one is going to say it. In the area of what to say, the speaker has an almost infinite number of choices— up to the limit of the particular culture in which he functions. How he is going to say something, on the other hand, is restricted to the conventional speech habits that he acquired as a child and that he shares with other members of his social group or community. In addition, he shares the same framework of expectations, built up by long practice and familiarity. Rivers points out that "The acoustic patterning of a language has not only acceptable sound sequences but anticipated degrees of loudness, levels of pitch and lengths of pause. With experience the child learns to recognize groupings of these features as clues to meaning. Some sequences recur with great frequency and in certain contexts alternatives are inconceivable."

In this section the authors discuss problems of pronunciation and comprehension in second-language learning, they give us some background concerning the nature of these problems, and they offer suggestions for approaching them. Hockett, Strain, and Robinett deal largely with the articulatory aspects of communication, whereas Rivers deals with the acoustic aspects. Hockett provides us with a well-organized summary of basic information on learning pronunciation. Strain reviews the rationale and methodology for teaching pronunciation at the English Language Institute (University of Michigan), and he sets up a model lesson plan for teaching a specific pronunciation problem. Robinett lists and describes the use of various classroom devices that can be of help to students in overcoming pronunciation problems. Rivers, concerned with the reception of speech messages, approaches comprehension learning on two levels: the recognition level and the selection level. She suggests materials and procedures for improving listening comprehension at both levels and techniques for leading students from the first level to the second.

GOOD PRONUNCIATION

Hockett mentions that *good* pronunciation "is one which will *not* draw the attention of a native speaker of that language away from *what* we are saying to the *way* in which we are saying it." If a native speaker of Spanish or Russian comments on how "well" you speak his language, this may or may not be considered a compliment. It may mean that he has noticed some kind of non-native flavor in your use of his language. If he had not noticed something "foreign" in your speech, he would have made no comment at all about it. Pronunciation is *acceptable*, of course, if it serves the purpose for which it was learned, but it may fall short of *good* pronunciation, which is so like that of a native speaker that it does not call any special attention to itself. Probably the best pronunciation, from the standpoint of the second-language learner, is that of an educated native speaker of a dialect that for cultural, political, and other reasons enjoys high prestige.

"No two speakers of a language have absolutely identical habits of pronunciation," Hockett notes, "and in some cases there is a great deal of variation from person to person or from region to region. Where this is the case, as, for instance, with Chinese, the native speakers themselves are accustomed to hearing a relatively wide variety of pronunciations, without necessarily having their attention drawn to pronunciation itself instead of to content. Consequently, a good pronunciation of such a language need not be an *exact* counterpart of any one native speaker's pronunciation; if we establish habits well within the range of variation found among native speakers themselves, our pronunciation will count . . . as good."

A similar situation obtains with regard to English in the United States, especially in urban areas. Every language, unless it is spoken by an extremely small group, has a number of dialects. Which dialect should the student learn? A good practical rule suggests that he should become accustomed to hearing most, if not all, of the major dialects, but, obviously, when it comes to speaking he will have to concentrate on one.

TRANSCRIPTION

Many languages have writing systems: sets of graphic symbols used to represent the sounds of language. All conventional writing systems seem to be inconsistent and incomplete in that there is no perfect match between the phonemes and the symbols that represent them, and all the phonemes are not represented. The way the English writing system "fits" the English sound system, for example, leaves much to be desired. Linguists often use a *transcription* for representing the speech sounds of a language—an invented writing system with one symbol for each phoneme and no more. Some language teachers also use a transcription for a more accurate guide to the sound system they are teaching.

Two transcription systems are widely used in the United States today: (1) the Trager-Smith transcription, named for the linguists who developed it, George L. Trager and Henry Lee Smith, Jr., and (2) the one sometimes called the IPA-Kenyon-Pike transcription. The latter has the alphabet of the International Phonetic Association (IPA) as a basis, but has been adapted to American English by John S. Kenyon, Kenneth L. Pike, and others. (See Hall's paper in Section Four.) ESOL teachers should become familiar with at least one of these transcriptions. (The main difference between them is the method of recording certain English vowels, not much else.) Even if a teacher does not use a transcription in his teaching activities, he will still find it useful in talking with other teachers about particular speech sounds, in sequencing pronunciation material for his students, and in reading professional publications. Without some familiarity with a transcription and its articulatory basis, for example, a teacher would not be able to read the paper by Robinett (in this section) with complete understanding.

SELECTED READINGS

Bowen, J. Donald. "A Pedagogical Transcription of English." *Language Learning* 10(1960):103–14.

Brooks, Nelson. *Language and Language Learning: Theory and Practice.* 2d ed. Chapter 2: "Language and Talk." New York: Harcourt Brace Jovanovich, 1964.

Dacanay, Fe R. *Techniques and Procedures in Second Language Teaching.* Edited by J. Donald Bowen. Chapter III: "Pronunciation Lessons." Dobbs Ferry, N.Y.: Oceana Publications, Inc., 1965.

English Language Services, Inc. *English Pronunciations: A Manual for Teachers.* New York: Collier-Macmillan International, 1968.

Fries, Charles C. *Teaching and Learning English as a Foreign Language.* Chapter 2: "The Sounds: Understanding and Producing the Stream of Speech." Ann Arbor: The University of Michigan Press, 1945.

HALL, ROBERT A., JR. *Sound and Spelling in English*. Chapter 1: "The Relation of Spelling to Sound"; Chapter 2: "The Phonemes of English." Philadelphia: Chilton Books, 1961.

KENYON, JOHN S., and KNOTT, THOMAS A. *A Pronouncing Dictionary of American English*. 4th ed. Springfield, Mass.: G. & C. Merriam, 1953.

LADO, ROBERT. *Language Teaching: A Scientific Approach*. Chapter 7: "Phonemes across Language"; Chapter 8: "Intonation and Rhythm"; Chapter 9: "The Consonant and Vowel Network." New York: McGraw-Hill Book Company, 1964.

————. *Linguistics across Cultures: Applied Linguistics for Language Teachers*. Chapter 2: "How to Compare Two Sound Systems." Ann Arbor: The University of Michigan Press, 1957.

MOULTON, WILLIAM G. *A Linguistic Guide to Language Learning*. 2d ed. Chapter 3: "How Language Works"; Chapter 4: "Sounds." New York: The Modern Language Association, 1970.

NIDA, EUGENE A. "Selective Listening." *Language Learning* 4(1952–53):92–101.

NILSEN, DON L. F., and NILSEN, ALLEEN PACE. *Pronunciation Contrasts in English*. New York: Simon and Schuster, 1971.

OWEN, GEORGE H. *Effective Pronunciation*. Experimental Edition. Detroit: Department of Adult Education and Summer Schools, Detroit Public Schools, 1957.

POLITZER, ROBERT L. *Foreign Language Learning: A Linguistic Introduction*. Chapter 4: "The Sounds of English"; Chapter 7: "Pronunciation Problems." Englewood Cliffs, N.J.: Prentice-Hall, Inc., 1970.

RIVERS, WILGA M. *Teaching Foreign-Language Skills*. Chapter 5: "Teaching Sounds"; Chapter 6: "Listening Comprehension"; Chapter 7: "The Speaking Skill: Learning the Fundamentals"; Chapter 8: "The Speaking Skill: Spontaneous Expression." Chicago: The University of Chicago Press, 1968.

SCOTT, CHARLES T. *Preliminaries to English Teaching: Essays for the Teaching of English in Japan*. Chapter 3: "A Contrastive Sketch of English and Japanese Phonology." Tokyo: The English Language Educational Council, Inc., 1966.

SHEN, YAO. *English Phonetics*. Ann Arbor: The University of Michigan, 1962. (Especially for Teachers of English as a Foreign Language.)

SITTLER, RICHARD C. "Teaching Aural Comprehension." *English Teaching Forum* 4(1966):3–9.

TRAGER, GEORGE L., and SMITH, HENRY LEE, JR. *Outline of English Structure*. Norman, Okla.: Battenburg Press, 1951. (*Studies in Linguistics*, Occasional Papers, 3).

WARDHAUGH, RONALD. "An Evaluative Comparison of Present Methods for Teaching Phonology." *TESOL Quarterly* 4(1970):63–72.

LEARNING PRONUNCIATION[1]

CHARLES F. HOCKETT

An essential part of learning a new language is to acquire a good pronunciation. Tied up intimately with this is the task of learning to *hear*
the new language correctly. Success in all other phases of foreign language learning depends, at least in part, on success in these two phases.

WHAT IS PRONUNCIATION?

When anyone speaks, in any language, he moves his lips, jaws, tongue,
and certain other parts of the mouth, nose, throat, and diaphragm, in
certain ways. These motions produce sound waves, which travel through
the air to the ears of someone else; if that second person happens to
know the same language, there follows (usually) the type of behavior
which we call *understanding*.

The motions of lips, jaws, tongue, and so forth for any one language
are *habitual*. In the native speaker of the language, the habits involved
were acquired largely in early childhood, and have been reinforced since
then by incessant practice. The habits involved in pronunciation are
entirely automatic and unconscious; when we open our mouths and say
something, we do not worry about where we should put our tongue from
moment to moment—all such mechanical matters are taken care of by
our long-standing habits, and our attention is concentrated rather on *what*
we are going to say—"yes" or "no," "it's raining" or "the sun is shining,"
"I like him very much" or "he's a stinker."

The habits of pronunciation for different languages, however, are not
the same. Different motions of the "organs of speech" are involved in

[1] This paper is a reworking, with specific emphasis on Chinese taken out, of introductory material in the writer's *Progressive Exercises in Chinese Pronunciation,* to be
published in the *Mirror Series* of the Institute of Far Eastern Languages of Yale
University. When available, the book will serve as an example of the practical
working-out of the theory presented here—though only, be it emphasized, a first
approximation, which in course of time will need thorough-going revision.

Some of the points made here about pronunciation apply also to grammatical habits,
at least at the lower levels, but we concentrate our attention on the former. See W.
Freeman Twaddell, "Meaning, Habits, and Rules," *Education,* October, 1948; reprinted in *Language Learning* 2:4–11 (January–March, 1949).

different languages, and even where the same or almost the same motions occur, they are apt to occur in different sequences relative to each other. Thus *k* and *n* differ little in English and German, but in German one may begin an utterance with *kn-*, an arrangement unknown initially in English. So it is that when we start to learn a new language, matters of pronunciation cannot be left to automatic habit. We simply do not *have* the necessary habits. We have to start by consciously guiding our tongue and lips, practicing until those organs are making the right motions. Then we must continue the practice until those motions for the new language are as habitual, as unconscious, as effortless as are the more or less different motions for our own language. And as we try to do this, the main interfering factor is the set of habits we already have for our own native language.

WHAT IS A GOOD PRONUNCIATION?

It is not enough for us to attain some vague approximation to the pronunciation of the new language, even if we would fairly often be understood if we spoke the new language that way. We must attain a *good* pronunciation.

A good pronunciation cannot be defined—as some have suggested—in terms of its pleasing quality to the ears of a native speaker of the new language. The Spanish coloring we hear in the English of many a Latin American can be quite pleasing, and yet it is undesirable. The vary fact that we are pleased by it means that when we listen to such a person, our attention is being drawn away from *what* is being said to the *way* in which it is said. A good pronunciation of a foreign language is one which will *not* draw the attention of a native speaker of that language away from *what* we are saying to the *way* in which we are saying it.

No two speakers of a language have absolutely identical habits of pronunciation, and in some cases there is a great deal of variation from person to person or from region to region. Where this is the case, as, for instance, with Chinese, the native speakers themselves are accustomed to hearing a relatively wide variety of pronunciations, without necessarily having their attention drawn to pronunciation itself instead of to content. Consequently, a good pronunciation of such a language need not be an *exact* counterpart of any one native speaker's pronunciation; if we establish habits well within the range of variation found among the native speakers themselves, our pronunciation will count, by the above criterion, as good. This, however, is the most we can usually hope to do even if we try slavishly and exactly to imitate the pronunciation of some one individual. For the most part, until one has learned a great deal of a foreign language, the thing to do is to follow a single model as accurately as possible.

WHY IS A GOOD PRONUNCIATION IMPORTANT?

This question has more than one answer, depending on our aim in learning the foreign language and the use we expect to make of it.

For the student who is learning a language because he expects to be in face-to-face contact with its speakers, and to carry on business with them, the importance of a good pronunciation is obvious, following automatically from the definition of "good pronunciation" we have given above.

Many students, however, have primarily a "reading" aim, as it is often called; they have no expectation of ever residing or touring in the country where the language is spoken, but do want to be able to read the literature, newspapers, scientific material, or other documents, of that country, as efficiently and understandingly as possible. It might seem that for the student with this aim, time and energy expended in learning to pronounce well would be largely wasted.

This is true to some extent, but not nearly as true as has sometimes been thought. Let us ask ourselves: why is it that we find it so easy to read our own language? It is easy because all we have to do, in reading our own language, is to interpret the strings of symbols we see before us into a string of thoroughly familiar speech sounds; the latter are in turn interpreted immediately and effortlessly into "understanding," just as are the strings of speech sounds we hear when something is said to us in our own language.[2] This latter process—interpreting heard speech sounds into "understanding"—was acquired very early in life, as outlined above. When we learn to read, always at a somewhat later age and sometimes very much later, we do not have to begin all over again; written material is not something completely unrelated to our spoken language, not some completely different system of symbols, but a symbol system which bears a direct and immediate relation to the language we already speak. In learning to read, we learn to associate written symbols with speech sounds, rather than directly with meanings; it is the speech sounds which carry the meanings.

Now if we approach a foreign language in its written form, with no advance knowledge and control of its spoken form, and try to train ourselves to interpret the strings of graphic shapes directly into meanings, we are trying something which is completely alien to the structure and

[2] Reading, when one has learned how, is like hearing under ideal acoustic conditions, for there is none of that static from extraneous sources (see later in the paper) which may impair oral communication. Thus when we misunderstand a word, say, over the telephone, and ask that it be spelled, we are taking a longer but surer way round; if we hear the letter-names correctly, we can then assemble the graphic shape and transform it, inside our heads, into the speech-sounds *we* would make for the word in question. Such resorts to writing are often misunderstood as evidence pointing to some kind of priority of writing over speech.

capacities of the human nervous system. What happens, when such an attempt is made, is that the learner actually makes up his own set of speech-sounds to go with the alien graphic shapes, perhaps not even realizing that he is doing so; these private speech-sounds, easier for him because they can be virtually identical with those he already uses for his own language, are *not* the speech sounds actually associated, in the nervous systems of literate speakers of the new language, with the graphic symbols the learner is trying to learn, and as a consequence the learner is forever precluded from real efficiency in handling material in the new language. The only efficient way, in the long run, to put oneself in the position to read with maximum understanding, intellectual and emotional, material written in some foreign language, is to get at least an elementary control of the spoken form of that language first. And this is equally true whether or not the learner has any expectation of face-to-face oral interchange with native speakers.

An exception to the above statements is the technical specialist, say the chemist, whose only aim is to be able to follow the technical literature in his own field. Scientific material is the most translatable material of all; if emotional overtones are lost in the translation, it does not really matter. The chemist can be permitted, with perfect safety, to make up his own set of speech sounds for the new language, providing he learns the vocabulary and the grammatical structure as it is for native speakers, for the content of the foreign material which concerns him will not be obscured by his failure to match the pronunciation habits of the native speakers. At the other extreme from this is the case of the would-be student of literature. One obviously cannot learn to appreciate the nuances of French or German poetry and drama, based on features of rhythm and sound, unless, in reading, one can make the proper speech sounds without conscious effort. Literary material must be received by the student in the acoustic shape in which it was originally cast, or some literary values will be lost. This is also true, though to a lesser extent, in such documentary material as that for history or philosophy, which does not share the rather special status of chemical, mathematical, or other technical scientific writing.

There is one other factor making for the importance of a good pronunciation, especially for the learner who expects face-to-face dealings, but to some extent for others. This is the fact, not easy to recognize and yet undeniably so, that one cannot even *hear* a new language correctly until one has learned to pronounce it reasonably well oneself. As we hear someone say something in our own native language, we ignore a good deal of the gross acoustic output that reaches our ears, since experience has taught us that it is irrelevant. For, when anyone talks, he produces a certain amount of irrelevant noise or "static" in addition to the relevant message-carrying sounds. If A is talking over the telephone to B, and C is in the room with *A*, then *B* and *C* receive the same *message*, but the static is quite different for the two. If *A* is slightly drunk, or has a cold, or is salivating more freely than usual, the moisture conditions in his speech organs change the acoustic qualities of his speech sounds; normally we compensate for such conditions and understand anyway. The first of these examples is mainly of *external* static, and the second of *internal* (produced within the speaking organs) but *abnormal* static; what is not so easily realized, because we are so accustomed to ignoring it, is the presence of a considerable amount of *internal* static even under *normal* conditions.

But the line of demarcation between relevant sound and static is not the same in one language as it is in another. When we first hear, say, Chinese, our ears are trained only to hear English; we are apt to interpret some of the Chinese static as relevant, and to ignore some of the relevant sound as static. As we practice pronouncing and speaking the foreign language ourselves, the necessary filtering and sorting apparatus is built into the parts of the nervous system which handle incoming stimuli from the ear, and slowly but surely we begin to hear the relevant and ignore the irrelevant. In extreme cases, this can perhaps be accomplished without simultaneous training in *producing* the speech sounds of the new language; but the natural and most efficient way is to develop at one and the same time ability to pronounce correctly and to hear correctly.

WHY IS THE PRONUNCIATION OF A FOREIGN LANGUAGE DIFFICULT?

This question has already largely been answered in the course of our discussion, but here we can gather together the factors involved and itemize them specifically.

The first source of difficulty is the habits we already have for pronouncing our own language. In the case of a speech sound in the new language which is produced by a motion almost, but not quite, like one which is part of the repertory for our native language, the tendency is simply to substitute the familiar articulation, instead of training ourselves in the new one. This occasionally makes for total lack of intelligibility; more often, the native speaker of the language can still understand us, but has to work too hard to do so. In the case of a speech sound totally unlike anything in our own language, it may at first be almost impossible for us to twist our tongue and lips into the proper contortions to produce it. In the face of either of these experiences the thing to remember is that, barring cleft palates, hare-lips, and other physiological defects *any human in the world* has the requisite physical apparatus (musculature and bony parts) for the production of any speech sound of any language. Claims to the contrary are old wives' tales. It is the nervous system that makes the trouble; and here, enough learning is bound, in time, to be successful.

A parallel source of difficulty is the habits of hearing which we already have. A speaker of the foreign language may actually be saying X, but if we have not yet learned to say X, we may persist in hearing what he says as Y, something more familiar to us; consequently, when we think we are imitating him we are actually producing something like Y; he hears the difference and is not satisfied. This can be helped by an explicit demonstration of the difference between X and Y. Once the difference has been heard, then X may be fairly easy, or it may still involve difficulties arising from the first factor. Here, also, it must be remembered that any physiologically normal human being has all the necessary apparatus; Chinese has distinctive *tones* (contours of pitch), and even a person who thinks he is tone-deaf can learn them correctly, for there are tone-deaf Chinese who cannot carry a tune but who yet speak like everyone else.

HOW CAN ONE GO ABOUT ACQUIRING A GOOD PRONUNCIATION?

A good pronunciation of a language is a matter of *motor skills*, coupled with ear training. We can build a useful analogy between the task of learning to pronounce a foreign language and the task of learning to play a musical instrument, although the analogy will not be exact in all details. The fine muscular motions involved in, say, playing the violin, are also motor skills, and one has to have ear training along with motor-skill drill in order to judge the results of one's efforts at the latter. The beginner at the violin is first shown how to hold the instrument, where to put his hands, how to hold the bow, and so on. Then he is given very simple things to play, perhaps just long tones on open strings. Then he is given things which involve the left-hand fingers with the hand in just one position on one string, say five different notes. Then with that hand in the single position but crossing from one string to another, he learns to switch the bow from one string to another—first to an adjacent string, then skipping one or two. Then the left hand is trained in another position, and another, and eventually in moving from one position to another.

In other words, the practice is progressive, beginning with those motions or positions of muscles which are either most *universally* necessary, or are *easiest*, and going on to more difficult matters. At any stage, all that has gone before is supposed to have been practiced so much that it has become easy, so that the only difficulties faced at a given stage are the few new items presented for mastery.

The material used in such drill is often enough not really "music" at all—it has, that is to say, no musical interest. Rather it is exercise material, incorporating motions which have to be mastered for the performance of "real" music; but in fact a good deal of such practice is necessary before anything of any real musical interest can possibly be attempted. For the young learner, exercise material is sometimes "sugar-coated" by such titles as "Basket of Roses," or "The Brownies' Picnic" or by a simple accompaniment for the teacher to play; but although this may (or may not) change the child's attitude towards practice, it does not transform the material from motor-skill exercise into real music.

An interesting aspect of this, valuable for our analogy, is that even the virtuoso, the Heifitz or the Elman, who does indeed perform extremely difficult pieces full of musical interest—even such a virtuoso still finds it advisable to spend some part of his practice time at the same old motor-skill drill material. Apparently the point of virtuosity is never reached after which motor-skills can be allowed to take care of themselves; if they are left alone, they will begin to deteriorate.

Now what is our analogy? The beginner at a new language has a set of motor skills to acquire: the articulatory motions requisite for the new language. Just as the would-be violinist is already, we shall say, fairly competent at the piano, so the would-be learner of a new language already has a set of thoroughly ingrained habits for his own language. These may partly help, but will also partly interfere with, the habits to be acquired for the new language.

For the task he faces, the would-be learner needs sets of motor-skill drill materials comparable to the fingering and bowing exercises of the incipient violinist. These materials need to be organized as much as possible in the same way, starting with what is either universally necessary or easy, or both, and going ahead progressively. He needs to go through these materials slowly, and thoroughly enough that at each stage all that has gone before will indeed be easy, and only the new material to be mastered will represent any difficulty. And, finally, it is quite probable that even when he, too, has reached the "virtuoso" stage, some continuing review drill is desirable.

The differences between the two situations are revealing too. The incipient violinist already has a fair idea of what violin music is supposed to sound like, for he has participated at least to some extent in the musical culture of his civilization. Therefore he can be relied on, after the crudest initial stages, to do a great deal of practice on his own. He himself can judge whether or not the sounds he produces are satisfactory as to pitch, tone quality, length, and loudness. But, as has already been pointed out, the beginner at a new language does *not* know in advance what the language sounds like, and so the bulk of his practice, for a very long time, must be carried on in the presence of a native speaker who can check on his production.

A second difference is that the violinist's ultimate aim is the playing of *pieces*—set sequences of notes organized by someone else and put down for him in a notation which he has learned. This is not the ultimate aim of the language learner, who must, in the end, make up his pieces as he goes along—must *improvise*, to continue the analogy, rather than simply recite set sequences. If anything, this requires that his motor-skill habits be mastered even more thoroughly. For if a violinist encounters a particularly difficult passage in a piece that he is learning, he can spend a great deal of time practicing it before ultimately performing the piece in public. The language learner must eventually have so little worry about his pronunciation that he can devote his entire attention to the improvising itself, to choosing what he is going to say, planning it (as we all do) a second or so in advance as he goes along.

There is a less ultimate stage of the language learner's activity which more closely matches the violinist's ultimate stage. In the course of his work, the learner will be confronted by monologues or dialogues prepared by someone else which he is to memorize and to perform from memory (like the violinist's rehearsal of a piece for performance), or which he is to read off naturally and effectively at sight (like the violinist's sight-reading). Up to and including this stage, the analogy holds well; beyond it, the differences only emphasize the importance, for the language learner, of thorough mastery of pronunciation.

PRACTICAL CONCLUSIONS

The foregoing sections present an analysis of pronunciation and of the problem of learning to pronounce (and hear) a new language. From the discussion, we can draw certain conclusions about the types of implementing materials needed and the types of classroom procedure which will effectively put the theory into action.

1. Materials for the teaching of the pronunciation of language A to speakers of language B have to be prepared on the basis of a thoroughgoing analysis of the pronunciation habits of both languages. In order to know which features of pronunciation of language A are easy, which are hard, this analysis, though necessary, is not enough: we need empirical evidence based on actual classroom experience.

2. In theory it would be fine if we could *first* learn everything about the pronunciation of a new language—master all the habits—and *then* go on actually to learn to talk it. In practice, the first step would become so dull that all motivation would be annulled. As a practical alternative, we can begin the learning of a foreign language with graded pronunciation practice, turning from it to the acquisition of vocabulary and sentence-patterns as soon as the point of boredom comes into sight; then a certain proportion of learning time can be set aside, each week or each hour, for continued pronunciation practice; this proportion can slowly decrease.

Until all points of pronunciation have been drilled on at least once, some of the words and sentences which are learned will be pronounced imperfectly. But they can be taken up again, and the rough edges smoothed down; and in the meantime the variety of activities maintains motivation.

3. Students may have a tendency to feel that pronunciation practice (or any other special activity concentrating on some one phase of the whole language learning task) has no necessary relation to the rest of their work; specifically, they may feel that having worked at pronunciation during special time set aside for that, they can forget about pronunciation the rest of the time. Ultimately, of course, the aim of the kind of instruction here discussed is that they should be able to do just that. But that ultimate aim is a long way off; in the meantime, they must constantly be reminded, during all their learning activities, that pronunciation is important, and must not be allowed to slip from whatever level of accuracy they have attained during the special practice.

4. In our society the written word is emphasized at every turn. Students consequently are apt to work more efficiently—even at learning pronunciation—if they have something to *look at* as they work, instead of working entirely through imitation. Unfortunately, most traditional writing systems are not sufficiently regular to be used for this purpose without confusing the issue; some, such as those of Chinese and Japanese, are totally useless for the purpose. Materials for the students to follow as they practice pronunciation therefore need a *transcription*—an invented writing system which represents with absolute regularity the speech sounds they are to learn to make and recognize.

The mastery of such a transcription, however, forms no part of their learning aim. It is a *scaffolding*, put up to help in the complex task of erecting the structure they must erect: the control of the language. As a scaffolding it must be respected; but as only a scaffolding, it will eventually be torn down (or be allowed to "wither away").

Students must be warned time and again that nothing they *look* at can possibly tell them what anything *sounds* like. This is just as true of a transcription as of any traditional writing system. The transcription becomes useful only as they learn, by direct imitation and practice, what the sounds of the new language are, and build up an association between those sounds and the symbols used in the transcription. When this has been accomplished, then the transcription is useful for many classroom purposes: testing pronunciation ability other than in immediate echoing, testing hearing ability without immediate repetition aloud, training in "sight-reading." In time, the traditional orthography can assume these functions, insofar as they still need to be performed, but most traditional orthographies are themselves systems which have to be learned systematically before they can perform any function at all, and one useful function of a well worked-out transcription is in teaching the traditional orthography.

The above discussion does not in itself tell us which languages need a special transcription and which do not. Chinese and Japanese do. Finnish orthography can itself serve efficiently in the role of a transcription. For cases intermediate between these extremes, more empirical evidence is needed; German, for example, can undoubtedly be taught well either with or without a transcription, though obviously with slight differences in technique.

5. Finally—and important: regardless of the amount of motivation a learner brings to his task, he will work more efficiently if he is able to understand clearly the reasons for the procedures and materials that he encounters. The importance of pronunciation, the reasons for the techniques used to give him a good pronunciation, the reasons for a transcription and the proper way to use a transcription, the reasons why the pronunciation of a new language is difficult, and all the other points touched on in this discussion, need to be brought home to the beginning student as forcefully as possible. Explanations and discussion take time, true enough, but the gain in long-term efficiency is well worth the slight initial delay.

TEACHING
A PRONUNCIATION PROBLEM

JERIS E. STRAIN

1. There are without doubt a vast number of ways to teach a given pronunciation problem. The general approach and methodology outlined here are certainly not new; as a matter of fact, they have been employed to teach English as a Foreign Language at the English Language Institute for over two decades. At the same time, however, knowledge of this point of view has been confined to a relatively small group as attested by the lack of literature available to the interested reader. Our main purpose here is to fill in a small portion of this gap.

2. Our task is to teach the sound system of a foreign language. To do so we attempt to bring as much linguistic knowledge as possible to bear on the "what" of our task and complement it with the best "how" ideas that are known to us.

In defining our task, we take certain propositions for granted, propositions based on conclusions reached in the scientific study of language; namely:

(a) that the sound system of a language is made up of a certain rather small set of elements which function significantly as carriers of the message (usually called phonemes).

(b) that the sound systems of two languages are never the same.

(c) that pronunciation problems can be predicted at least in part by comparing the native-language sound system with that of the target language.

(d) that skill in pronunciation consists of a set of automatic habits involving the hearing organs and the speech organs, plus the ability not only to recognize significant sounds in a stream of speech but also to react to them in an acceptable manner.

(e) that a prerequisite to developing the ability to produce significant sounds is development of the ability to recognize the significant sounds.

(f) that learning to speak a language should precede learning to read and write it.

Pedagogy, on the other hand, provides us with the procedure to be outlined below, based on these important principles:

(a) that spoken language habits can be most effectively developed by drilling.

(b) that the conscious drilling of a learning point during an exercise should gradually become unconscious drilling by shifting the learner's attention to a point that is related but irrelevant to the learning point, such that the point being learned comes to be produced automatically.

(c) that learning the few but essential points of the target sound system and developing the necessary automatic habits can best take place with a restricted number of vocabulary items.

(d) that to be effective, learning must take place with regard for meaning in a contextual setting, not in isolation.

(e) that classroom procedure should consist of a minimum of explanation and a maximum of practice.

3. Application of these "what" and "how" principles leads us to two problems: (1) the nature of the phonological problem that we intend to teach and (2) the method to be followed in teaching it. Suppose we take as an example the problem of teaching the English high-front vowels to a speaker of Persian.

3.1. Phonetic studies provide the following information about the English and Persian sound systems:

(a) Both English and Persian have a higher high-front tense unrounded vowel which might be designated /i/; the English vowel, however, is usually followed by a high-front glide, giving the contrast of English [iy] and Persian [i].

(b) English also has a lower high-front lax backed unrounded vowel which may be designated /ɪ/; Persian has no counterpart.

(c) The following examples illustrate the problem:

	PERSIAN		ENGLISH	
	[i]		[iy]	[ɪ]
	/ʔíl/	'tribe'	eel	ill
	/ʔín/	'this'	——	in
	/píč/	'screw'	peach	pitch
	/bíd/	'willow'	bead	bid
	/sí/	'thirty'	see	——
	/kí/	'who'	key	——

For teaching purposes the above information may be summarized from the point of view of (a) recognition problems and (b) production problems.

(a) The Persian speaking student will have difficulty
   (1) in distinguishing between English [iy] and [ɪ] and
   (2) in hearing and recognizing [ɪ].

(b) The Persian speaking student must learn (1) to produce the high-front glide found in English [iy] and
   (2) to lower and back his tongue to produce [ɪ].

3.2.   One procedural method that might be followed in teaching this pronunciation problem is as follows:

GOAL	TECHNIQUE
1. Attention pointer	1. Teacher calls student's attention to the learning point.
2. Focus attention on the problem-area	2. Student just *listens* to teacher's pronunciation of items containing the target sounds.
3. Sharpen recognition	3. Student tries to *recognize* each sound in different consonantal environments.
4. Generalize	4. Teacher points out and emphasizes the *significant features* that must be mastered.
5. Produce new sounds	5. a. Student *mimics* teacher's production of one-syllable items. b. Teacher pronounces items containing one of the sounds; student *produces* the opposite sound. c. Student *mimics* teacher's pronunciation of two-syllable items. d. Student *mimics* teacher's pronunciation of longer utterances.
6. Check perception	6. Teacher presents *minimal sentences;* students try to recognize the new sounds.
7. Drill	7. a. Teacher presents *substitution drills;* students are cued to supply items containing one of the new sounds. b. Teacher presents *pattern practices,* the frames containing frequently missed items; student again gives a cued response.
8. Reinforce and stabilize sounds taught	8. Student practices in laboratory, at home, or both.

Notice that the first seven steps can be broken down in the following fashion: Step 1 *introduces* the lesson; Steps 2, 3, 6 deal with *recognition;*

Step 4 deals with brief, concise statements based on *linguistic insights;* Steps 5, 7 deal with *production.* In teaching, a minimum of time should be spent on Steps 1–4 and a maximum of time on Steps 5–7; Step 8 would probably take place outside of the classroom. At each step, accuracy should be continually emphasized and demanded.

4. An actual lesson plan might be as follows. (Only the teacher's role will be illustrated.)

4.1. *Step 1. Attention Pointer.* Using pictures, actions, or some other device, the teacher calls the students' attention to a minimal contrast between the new sounds—for example, "sheep" and "ship"—and designates each with an appropriate symbol on the blackboard—for example [iy] and [ɪ]. Henceforth, the symbols may be referred to by the teacher as a cue and point of reference.

4.2. *Step 2. Focus Attention.*

    a) Listen to words containing this sound. (Teacher points to [iy] on the blackboard; students listen and *do not* repeat.)

sheep	sheep
leave	leave
he's	he's

    b) Listen to words containing this sound (Teacher points to [ɪ]);

ship	ship
live	live
his	his

    c) Now listen to the contrast (Teacher points to the appropriate symbols):

sheep	–	ship	sheep	–	ship
leave	–	live	leave	–	live
he's	–	his	he's	–	his

    d) Can you hear the difference? (The students will probably say "yes," which leads into Step 3.)

Notes: 1. Words containing problem consonants that have not yet been taught should not appear here or anywhere in the lesson; for example, /θ/, /ð/, /r/, /w/.

2. The focus is at this point on the two target sounds as such, without reference to the meanings of the words.

3. The choice of items may be limited to minimal pairs; nonsense words might be used, but if minimal pairs are available, they should be used.

4.3   *Step 3.   Sharpen Recognition.*   (The students have replied that they can distinguish between [iy] and [ı].)

   a) Then identify the vowel sound in these words:

   b) Let's call [iy] No. 1, and [ı], No. 2. (Teacher writes the numbers above the symbols.) If the vowel sound is [iy] say "one"; if it is [ı] say "two."

   c)

he's	(1)	ship	(2)	ship	(2)
sheep	(1)	leave	(1)	he's	(1)
his	(2)	live	(2)	his	(2)

   d)

is	(2)	seem	(1)	key	(1)
it	(2)	seen	(1)	did	(2)
if	(2)	sin	(2)	miss	(2)
in	(2)	he's	(1)	she	(1)

   Notes: 1.   Items used should provide a wide variety of consonant environments.

   2.   Minimal pairs need not be used; words that are frequently mispronounced should be included.

   3.   The focus is still on the target sounds.

   4.   The exercise should begin with choral response for three or four items and then switch to individual responses.

4.4   *Step 4.   Generalize.*

   a) Fine! Now tell me how [iy] and [ı] are different.

   b) Say "he's" and "his" to yourself. The front part of the tongue isn't the same, is it?

   c) When we say [iy] the tongue is high and close to the top of the mouth; when we say [ı] the tongue is low and toward the middle of the mouth. (Reference to a cross-section of the mouth is quite useful.)

   d) In addition, English [iy] is usually long and followed by a gliding movement of the tongue.

   e) Pronounce [iy] after me: [iy-iy-iy . . .]

   f) Pronounce [ı] after me: [ı-ı-ı . . .]

   Notes: 1.   This step should be brief and to the point; long explanations are unnecessary and a waste of time.

   2.   The significant feature or features to be mastered should be emphasized.

4.5.   *Step 5.   Develop Flexibility.*

   a) Now let's practice.

b) Pronounce these contrasts after me:

sheep	–	ship		ship	–	sheep
he's	–	his		his	–	he's
leave	–	live		live	–	leave
seen	–	sin		sin	–	seen
deed	–	did		did	–	deed

c) Pronounce these words after me:

beat	it	me	fill
bit	is	him	in
live	tea	see	did
leave	he	itch	she

d) Pronounce a word with the opposite sound: If I say "beet," you say "bit."

live	he's	seat	leave
sheep	Tim	deed	eat
beat	did	feel	seen
it	sin	ship	bit

e) Pronounce these phrases after me:

[iy-iy]	[ɪ-ɪ]	Contrast
she eats	it did	his feet
he sees	it is	he did
she sees	his lip	it's tea
he eats	his ship	it's me

f) Pronounce these sentences after me:

[iy-iy . . .]	1. He's eating meat.
[ɪ-ɪ-ɪ . . .]	2. It's his fish.
(contrast)	3. Give me his key.
(contrast)	4. Give me his tea.
(contrast)	5. Did she see it?

Notes: 1. Using primarily the target sounds creates several restrictions in making up exercises; nevertheless, utterances of this type can be very effective in developing speech-organ flexibility.

2. A problem is the need of vocabulary items; even though the focus is on production of the sounds as such, useful and meaningful items should be the rule.

3. Each exercise may begin with choral response but should soon switch to individual responses.

4.6. Step 6. Check Perception.

a) Tell me if these sentences sound the same or different: (Observe the intonation peaks—stressed words.)

1.	He bít me. He béat me.	(Different)
2.	Tim béat me. Tim béat me.	(Same)
3.	Did he líve? Did he léave?	(Different)

4.	Fíll it. Fíll it.	(Same)
5.	Please féel it. Please féel it.	(Same)

b) Which of these sentences are the same?

1.	He bít me. He bít me. He béat me.	(1–2)
2.	Féel it. Fíll it. Féel it.	(1–3)
3.	Did he líve? Did he líve? Did he líve?	(1–2–3)
4.	Tím beat me. Tím beat me. Tím bit me.	(1–2)
5.	Pléase fill it. Pléase feel it. Pléase feel it.	(2–3)

Notes: 1. Notice that the loud stress has been put on the key words at first and then moved; perception may thus be checked in both stressed and unstressed positions.

2. There should be not more than one difference in each set of utterances, and that difference should pertain to the target sounds.

4.7.   *Step 7.   Drill.*

a) Complete this sentence: (Teacher may use pictures or charts to cue the responses.)

b) It's his _____.

ship	lip	chin	meat
sheep	tea	knee	milk
key	cheek	fish	

c) Give me his _____.

key	meat	sheep
dish	fish	milk
tea	ship	

d) Did she _____ it?

eat	
fill	leave
see	feel
fix	kiss

Notes: 1. The major aim in each of these exercises is correct pronunciation of the sentence frame first and of the cued items second.

2. Meaning is essential at this point, both on a structural and lexical level; charts, pictures, gestures, and actions are a few techniques that could be used to provide cues to the meaning.

3. Exercises of this type could be used to expand the student's vocabulary while mastery of structural patterns is being reinforced; that is, "Tim is _____-ing." could form the basis for another exercise, providing the /ŋ/ problem has been taught. "Please" could be used on the production level, providing the initial consonant cluster has been taught. The question structure "Is it (his) _____?" could be used for still another exercise.

4. Very frequent and often-mispronounced items containing the target sounds should be worked into the structural frames and drilled until they are automatically pronounced correctly.

4.8. *Step 8. Reinforcement.*

a) Since this step may take place in a language laboratory or out of class, a brief review of the target sounds should be provided first. One procedure would be to quickly go over Steps 2 (presentation), 5 (mimicry production), and 6 (recognition check) again.

b) If a tape recorder is available, oral exercises on tape can be correlated with pictures in a workbook. The pictures should be accompanied by regular spelling as well as the special alphabet used for teaching. For example:

Picture 1.	Tape voice:	"It's his ———."
	Student:	"Sheep. It's his sheep."
[šiyp] sheep	Tape voice:	"Sheep. It's his sheep."
	Student:	(Repeats.)
Picture 2.	Tape voice:	"Picture 2."
	Student:	"Ship. It's his ship."
[šip] ship	Tape voice:	"Ship. It's his ship."
	Student:	(Repeats.)

c) A major point in stabilizing the target sounds is to correlate them with their usual orthographic representation; therefore, a statement in the workbook summing up the various spellings is in order. For example: "Note that in pictures 1,3, . . . Vowel No. 1 [iy] is spelled: ee, ey, ea, etc., and that in pictures 2,3, . . . Vowel No. 2 [ɪ] is always spelled i.

d) Pattern practices of the type in Step 7, but using words in regular spelling as cues, might be used at this point:

1. sheep	Tape voice:	"1. Is it his ———?"
	Student:	"Sheep. Is it his sheep?"
	Tape voice:	"Sheep. Is it his sheep?"
	Student:	(Repeats.)
2. key	Tape voice:	"Two."
	Student:	"Key. Is it his key?"
	Tape voice:	"Key. Is it his key?"
	Student:	(Repeats.)

e) Paper and pencil exercises to check production might be as follows:

1. Students circle the correct answer.

i) I believe he'll ————.	leave	live	(leave)
ii) Is the ———— going to tip?	sheep	ship	(ship)

2. Students circle the correct answer.

   i) A _____ is a boat.   sheep   ship   (ship)
   ii) This is _____ ship.   he's   his   (his)
   iii) A _____ is an animal. sheep   ship   (sheep)

f) A short paragraph or conversation using the target sounds as much as possible (to be memorized) completes the lesson plan.

A. Did she see it?

B. No, she didn't see it.

A. Is it his sheep?

B. Yes, it is his sheep.

5. In drafting this lesson plan, we have assumed that about twenty minutes could be devoted to teaching the one problem-area and that other class periods would be devoted to learning points of structure and vocabulary. There is, of course, an inescapable degree of overlap between pronunciation, structure, and vocabulary.

Depending on the level of the students and the competence of the instructor, the lesson plan outlined above could be either expanded or reduced. It may be that the plan given is more elaborate and detailed than necessary; but this was our intention. Regardless of how such a plan is adapted or changed, it is important not to deviate too much from the "what" and "how" principles underlying the approach and to make each step in the process relate clearly to the basic goals toward which the methodology is directed.

SIMPLE CLASSROOM TECHNIQUES FOR TEACHING PRONUNCIATION

BETTY WALLACE ROBINETT

In teaching pronunciation it is seldom sufficient for the student simply to imitate the teacher: the majority of students need more direct help. One helpful device is the simple face diagram in which the various "organs of speech" are shown:

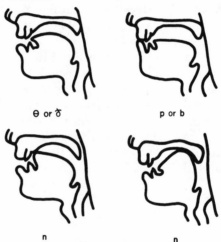

Θ or ð   p or b

n   ŋ

FIGURE 1.   Sample Face Diagram

FACE DIAGRAMS

English sounds which can be shown clearly by the use of such diagrams are /θ, ð/ with the tongue between the teeth; /p,b,m/ with the lips completely closed; /t,d/ with the tongue on the tooth ridge; the contrast between /n/ with the tongue on the tooth ridge and /ŋ/ with the tongue against the velum; and the contrast between the "clear" l of *leave* and the "dark" l of *veal*. Even other articulatory movements such as the thrusting outward of the lips in the pronunciation of /š/ in *shoe* or the jaw movement in the /w/ of *wall* can be shown on these so-called "static" diagrams. Movable face diagrams have been devised by ingenious teachers to show the difference in tongue position between sounds which are frequently confused, such as the /n/ and /ŋ/ sounds.

The points of articulation for the various vowel sounds are less easily taught than those for the consonant sounds because in producing vowel sounds the tongue moves freely without contact within the mouth cavity. If, however, we superimpose a chart of the vowel sounds on a static or face diagram, the student will have a clearer understanding of the relationship between the tongue position and the resulting sound. Here contrast produces effective results. If we are teaching the contrast in *leave* and *live*, for example, we can show through the use of the face diagram that the vowel sound of *leave* is produced with the front of the tongue in a higher and more forward position than the vowel sound of *live*—the important point being not the exact position of the tongue but a difference in height of the tongue.

Flexibility exercises are very desirable to help the student become adept at changes in position of the tongue. General exercises for attaining this flexibility of articulation can be made with the sounds /iy/, /a/, and /uw/. These sounds can be repeated several times in sequence to enable the student to become aware of the movement of his tongue. Then, when he attempts to pronounce such sounds as /iy/ and /i/, in which the tongue movement is less discernible, he will be better able to notice this movement.

Some students have greater difficulty than others in controlling tongue movement. These students often have a greater problem in producing the vowel sound in *live*. It helps these students to use the so-called "bracketing" exercise.[1] That is, the two sounds nearest to the "difficult" one are pronounced in contrast several times: /iy-ey, iy-ey, iy-ey/. Then the

FIGURE 2.   Vowel Grid Superimposed on a Face Diagram

[1] Kenneth L. Pike, *Phonemics* (Ann Arbor: University of Michigan Press, 1947), p. 16.

tongue is moved to a position approximately midway between these two sounds: /iy-i-ey/.

After the approximate positions of the various vowel sounds have been pointed out by the use of the vowel chart superimposed on the face diagram, the chart itself can be used alone each time a new sound is introduced without the necessity of including a careful drawing of the face. When the students see the chart, they will associate the various vowels with the actual tongue position in the mouth.

MINIMAL PAIRS

Pictures of objects typifying the common contrasts such as *pen* and *pan* or *sheep* and *ship* are especially helpful as visual aids with younger students. With students of any age, the use of minimally different words, "minimal pairs," has been found very effective in teaching the recognition and production of pronunciation elements. Such words can be arranged in lists on the blackboard, and a variety of exercises can be developed with these lists as a basis.

Using such a contrastive set of words as *sin-thin, sick-thick, sink-think,* the following types of exercises could be used:

a)   The teacher pronounces the words in each list and the students repeat them in unison.

b)   Individual students are asked to pronounce all the words in one list. If the student encounters difficulty in producing an acceptable production of the sound, the teacher can then give an articulatory description of the sound, using diagrams or charts, bracketing or flexibility exercises in order to help the student attain a more accurate pronunciation.

c)   The teacher pronounces pairs of words in contrast, e.g., *sin-thin,* and the students repeat in unison. The falling intonation is used on both words so that the only difference in sound will be that of the sound under practice.

d)   The teacher pronounces a word from either list and individual students tell which list it is from.

e)   Individual students are asked to pronounce pairs of words in contrast.

f)   Individual students are asked to pronounce a word from either list and the teacher tells which list it is from.

g)   Individual students are asked to pronounce a word from either list and *another student* tells which list it is from. This student, in turn, pronounces a word and another student tells which list it is from.[2]

---

[2] B. J. Wallace, *The Pronunciation of American English for Teachers of English as a Second Language* (rev. ed.; Ann Arbor: George Wahr Publishing Company, 1957).

As variations on these exercises, the students can be asked to write on a piece of paper the number of the list in which the word appears or the phonemic symbol of the sound under practice.

This same type of minimally contrastive utterance can be extended to include an entire sentence. Again it is essential that the same intonation be used on both sentences. For example, the /ə/ and /a/ contrast could be practiced in the following minimally different sentences:

The *cut* was long. | The *cot* was long.

MORE ON VOWELS

The techniques described above are usually built into the materials. Now I would like to go on to some specific techniques which are not usually found in published texts.[3]

First, let us consider the vowel sounds.

In teaching the /æ/ sound, emphasis should be placed on the spread position of the lips. This can be achieved by the simple admonition to smile when pronouncing this sound.

The /ə/ sound can be described as that which one makes when he is suddenly hit in the stomach, but it must be made without rounding the lips. This sound can then be contrasted with the /a/ sound by having the students watch the jaw position. The first sound is made with the jaw almost closed and the second with the jaw quite low.

The upward movement of the jaw in the pronunciation of the /ey/ and /ow/ sounds, emphasizing the diphthongal quality of these sounds, should be called to the attention of the students.

The contrasts between the /iy/ and the /i/ sounds and between the /uw/ and /u/ sounds can be made clearer by the mention of muscular tension. A kinesthetic correlation between clenching the fists when pronouncing the tense sounds and opening and relaxing the hand when pronouncing the lax sounds has been found helpful.

MORE ON CONSONANTS

In teaching specific consonant sounds one humorous device which I have used—if I am teaching a group with whom I am using a phonemic alphabet—is to make the /θ/ symbol serve as a memory clue. I enlarge the symbol to represent an open mouth with the crossbar on the symbol acting as the tongue protruding between the teeth.

In teaching the English /r/ sound, presentation of the sound in a certain sequence is important. Here a knowledge of phonetics will help

[3] Betty Wallace Robinett, *A Workbook in Phonetics and Phonemics of American English.* Unpublished manuscript.

the teacher select the more effective sequence even though this presentation is not built into the materials. The student should first pronounce /a/ and then raise the tip of the tongue slightly being sure that he does not touch the roof of the mouth. If he can do this satisfactorily, he should then be able to practice many words in which the sound appears in postvocalic position: *car, far, near, door, clear, wear.*

The next step is to be able to produce /r/ before a vowel sound in the word *road* or *read.* Ask the student to pronounce /a/ plus /r/ again, lengthening the /r/ and following it with /ow/ (thus rounding the lips): /a rrrr ow/. Repeat this exercise several times to be sure that the student is not touching the roof of the mouth with his tongue. Then omit the vowel sound before the /r/: /row/.

Lip rounding is an essential part of the pronunciation of the /r/ before vowels and must be emphasized and practiced. Words in which the /r/ appears before rounded vowels should be practiced first. After this, the student is ready to try such words as *read, write, ran, run* in which the vowel sounds themselves are not rounded but the /r/ must be.

The "match trick" is a device which can be used to enable a student to observe whether or not he is producing an aspirated /p/, /t/, or /k/ sound. The student holds a lighted match in front of his mouth and attempts to blow it out as he pronounces a word like *pie.* A piece of paper, not too thick, can be substituted for the lighted match where fire laws prohibit such experimentation—or where nonsmokers do not have matches readily at hand.

The difference between the /s/ and /z/ sounds can be illustrated by comparing them to various hissing and buzzing sounds. The sound which a snake makes, the steam coming from a teakettle, air coming from a tire, illustrate the /s/ sound. The /z/ sound can be made in imitation of a mosquito, an airplane motor, or a power saw.

The pencil trick is helpful in distinguishing between the /n/ and /ŋ/ sounds. The student places a pencil crossways in his mouth and pronounces the words *thin* and *thing.* If he pronounces the /n/ sound accurately, his tongue will touch the pencil for both the /θ/ and the /n/. If he pronounces the /ŋ/ sound accurately, his tongue will touch the pencil for the /θ/ sound but not for the /ŋ/.

CONSONANT CLUSTERS

Once the individual consonant sounds have been mastered, the problem remains of learning to pronounce these consonants in combinations or clusters. The student may have learned to pronounce the word *wash* with an accurate production of the final consonant sound, but when he needs to use the form *washed,* he encounters a cluster of consonants which may be impossible for him to produce at first trial. We can first ask the student to say *wash two cups* in which the difficult consonant sequence occurs between two words. Then we can change the phrase to *washed a cup* in which the sounds are more closely combined, at the same time pointing out how they can be separated by the following vowel sound: *wash-ta-cup*. This is sometimes referred to as phonetic syllabication. Once the student has learned such phrases as *washed it, looked at it, changed it,* it will be easier for him to produce these sequences before other consonants as in *cashed them, looked for them, changed them.*

Another type of sequential exercise involving consonant clusters is the use of series of words such as *were, word,* and *world.* Beginning with a single final consonant, the student must add one or more consonants to pronounce the other words.

Minimally distinctive sentences containing consonant clusters are also useful. Practice on such pairs of sentences as *they talk about it, they talked about it* or *they learn about it, they learned about it* can be used both for recognition and for production.

STRESS, RHYTHM, AND INTONATION

Now for some ways of teaching word stress. When students need practice in stressing the right syllable of a word, such familiar words as *table, pronounce, alphabet, important, understand* can be set up as models. Other words are then pronounced, and the student is asked to list them under the proper model.

Many students have difficulty in changing sentence stress when the situation demands it. Using the sentence, *The woman received many letters yesterday,* varied word stress can be elicited through the use of questions. The teacher asks, "What did the woman receive yesterday?" The student answers first, "Letters," and then pronounces the entire sentence with stress only on the word *letters.* Questions with *who* or *when* can be used in the same manner.

The reverse pyramid type of exercise is effective for the teaching of sentence rhythm. English speakers tend to produce stresses at somewhat regularly spaced intervals, thereby necessitating relatively equal amounts of time between the stressed syllables. By starting with a short sentence containing perhaps just two stresses, the sentence can be built up in a reverse pyramid to a relatively long sentence still containing only two stresses but repeated with just about the same amount of time.

The boy's in the house.
The boy's in the old house.
The little boy's in the old house.
The little boy's not in the old house.

It must always be remembered that this is an unnatural type of sequence (we would normally give contrastive stress to the two sentences: the boy's in the house, the boy's in the *old* house, and before the practice period ends, each of the sentences should be put into a natural context. This type of exercise is what Clifford Prator would term manipulative—as so many pronunciation drills necessarily are, in the earlier stages of language learning—but the sentences from a manipulative drill can then be placed in communicative contexts once the purely articulatory difficulties have been overcome.

For practicing intonation, the most successful technique seems to be imitation or mimicry. The use of gestures also seems to give the student a feeling for change in pitch. Showing the direction of the pitch change by raising or lowering the hand seems to help students. I have even had students who used the kinesthetic approach here, lifting a shoulder or raising an eyebrow in imitation of the pitch level.

The falling intonation is sometimes difficult to obtain from students under certain circumstances where the situation demands it. It has been found helpful to begin with the final word in the utterance and to move backward. For example, in the sentence, *Do you want coffee or tea?* the student can first be asked to say *tea* using the falling intonation as if it were an isolated word; then he is asked to say *or tea, coffee or tea, want coffee or tea,* and so on, until the entire sentence has been completed by this backward buildup sort of exercise.

Obviously many of the things that I have been discussing are exaggerated, unnatural kinds of activities which are drills of the type we must use in any skill building process. What has to be remembered is that pronunciation is only one part of this system we call language and must be integrated with the structure and lexicon at every point along the way, in order to produce a speaker who can really be said to have mastered the language.

LISTENING COMPREHENSION

WILGA M. RIVERS

Teaching language as communication has become an accepted aim of the foreign-language teacher throughout the world. To most this has come to mean that we must teach our students to speak the language with some fluency and authentic idiom. What has been less emphasized, however, is that communication is a process involving at least two people. Speaking does not of itself constitute communication unless what is said is comprehended by another person. The greatest difficulty for a traveller in a foreign country is not primarily that he cannot make himself understood; this he can frequently do by gesture, by writing or by pointing to something written in a bilingual book of phrases. His first difficulty, and one that leads to considerable emotional tension and embarrassment, is that he cannot understand what is being said to him and around him. Even if the native speaker enunciates his words slowly and distinctly, elements of stress, intonation and word-grouping, often exaggerated in an earnest attempt at clarity, add to the confusion of the inexperienced foreigner. As a result there is no communication and the traveller's speaking skills cannot be exercised to great advantage. His enjoyment of and participation in community life and thought are further curtailed by his inability to comprehend announcements, broadcasts, lectures, plays and films.

Teaching the comprehension of spoken speech is therefore of primary importance if the communication aim is to be achieved. A long-neglected area, listening comprehension has its peculiar problems which arise from the fleeting, immaterial nature of spoken utterances.

THEORETICAL CONCEPTS BASIC TO LISTENING COMPREHENSION

Much attention has been paid in recent years to problems of discrimination of sounds, stress and pitch, but these are only a few of the elements involved in understanding what is being said to us.

Of great value to foreign-language teachers interested in teaching listening comprehension is the extensive research which has been carried out in recent years by communications engineers concerned with the maximum efficiency of telephonic and telegraphic equipment. Research engineers have given considerable thought and study to the nature of the message to be communicated, the particular qualities of the channel by which it passes from emitter to receiver, and the state in which it is received and interpreted by the listener. The foreign-language teacher who understands his theoretical formulations and terminology can extract many seminal lines of thought from their observations.

INFORMATION IN COMMUNICATION

The language emitted by the communicator, which contains the message, has phonic patterning distinctive for each language. This conventional patterning limits the possible sequences of sounds for that particular language and determines their frequency of occurrence. As the child learns his native language he comes to expect certain patterns of sound and not others. He is therefore disconcerted by the sound sequences of a foreign language until he has had sufficient experience with them to build up a frame of expectations. This process requires long practice and familiarity. The phonic patterning of a language has not only acceptable sound sequences but anticipated degrees of loudness, levels of pitch and lengths of pause. With experience the child learns to recognize groupings of these features as clues to meaning. Some sequences recur with great frequency and in certain contexts alternatives are inconceivable. Such items are considered to contain little "information," in the technical sense of the term. "Information" in this sense does not refer to meaning but to the range of possible alternative words which could occur in a certain position in speech. As Weaver has put it, "the word information in communication theory relates not so much to what you *do* say, as to what you *could* say. That is, information is a measure of one's freedom of choice when one selects a message." [1] The concept of information in terms of probabilities is mathematical, but the basic idea is useful for extrapolation to comprehension situations. If in the context any other word would be most unlikely, the word is said to give little information. If the range of possibilities is great, then the use of one particular word conveys a great deal of information. If I hold a book in my hand and state: "This is a book," the word conveys little information. Possibilities have been reduced by visual and situational clues which help to delimit the alternatives. On the other hand, if I say of someone who is not present: "He is reading," the word "reading" conveys much information because of the great number of words which could easily have occurred in that context. In the native language, we have learned to

---

[1] Claude E. Shannon and Warren Weaver, *The Mathematical Theory of Communication,* Urbana: University of Illinois, 1959, p. 100.

recognize a number of factors which reduce the possibility of occurrence of any particular word: elements such as syntactic relationships, sequences of words and combinations of sounds of high frequency, clichés, conversational tags and formulae. The effects of these factors in reducing the amount of information conveyed in any one utterance is of great importance because the human organism has a limited capacity for reception of information. When someone is conveying to us a message which is not entirely expected or obvious, we often say: "Wait a minute! Not so fast!" or "Say that again!" These expressions make it clear that we can absorb only a certain amount of information at one time.

REDUNDANCY

In order to reduce to manageable proportions the amount of information in any one sound sequence each language has developed a certain amount of redundancy. It has been estimated, for instance, that the English language is fifty percent redundant.[2] Were this redundancy eliminated, the human organism could not absorb information at the rate at which it would be emitted in normal speech. Redundancy in languages is to be found in elements of sound and morphological and syntactical formations which reinforce each other in the conveying of meaning. A French sentence may begin with "est-ce que," which signals a question for which the response will normally be "Yes" or "No." At the same time the voice will continue to rise in pitch until the end of the sentence, this being also an indication that a question of this type is being asked. The listener who was not attending to the first words of the sentence will be guided by the rising intonation. Both of these features are conveying the same element of meaning and one of them is therefore redundant.

It is redundancy in language which helps us to piece together the information we hear. Even in communication in our native language we do not hear everything that is said to us clearly, nor do we pay full attention to every element of each utterance. In a language we are learning as foreigners our difficulties are compounded by so many items which we do not recognize or with which we are as yet unfamiliar. Artificially constructed messages, such as those frequently used in foreign-language classes, often unwittingly reduce the amount of redundancy supplied by a speaker in a normal situation. In this way the perception of the foreign-language message is made more difficult even for a person familiar with the language clues.

Over and above the clues provided by sound sequences, we convey further elements of meaning by body movements, facial expressions, slight changes in breathing, length of pauses and degrees of emphasis. These elements, usually classed as kinesics and paralanguage, vary from

[2] *Ibid.,* p. 104.

language community to language community, and even within language communities at various levels of intercourse. No comprehension of oral communication is complete without taking these aspects into consideration as further delimitation of the message.

The problems of the message itself, then, may be studied in terms of the amount of information it conveys and the rate at which this information is encoded.

IRRELEVANT SOUND OR "NOISE"

Further problems arise, however, in the transmission of the message from communicator to receiver. If the message is transmitted with an accompaniment of irrelevant sound or "noise," some of the message may not be received by the listener. In a foreign-language situation, unfamiliar elements of the message may be perceived in much the same way as noise, so that some parts of it will be lost in the process of transmission to the receiver. The listener is then faced with several problems: the identification of patterns and their combinations in the somewhat mutilated message which he has received, the reconstruction of the defective sections according to probabilities of occurrence, and the organization of these patterns in a meaningful way. This organization will depend on his previous experience with words, syntactical groupings, situational context and the cultural elements reflected in the foreign-language usage. His degree of familiarity with these elements will determine what he selects from the stream of sound which is providing information at a rate at which it is beyond his capacity to assimilate it totally.

Probabilities of occurrence of certain sequences of sounds are built up through experience with a language. These probabilities determine what we hear; in other words, we hear what we expect to hear. A non-conventional, and therefore improbable, sequence of sounds will at first be interpreted as a familiar, or probable, sequence and in this way acquire intelligibility. Psychologists have found that if a non-conventional sequence of sounds is presented to a listener just below the threshold of audibility it will be organized by the listener into a conventional sequence; in other words, a series of meaningless syllables with sentence intonation will be interpreted as an intelligible sentence. In the learning stages of a foreign language many sequences of sounds have low probability of occurrence for the inexperienced learner, and will therefore be misinterpreted, while others which he has never before encountered provide an accompaniment of "noise." His ability to distinguish sequences which are slightly familiar from the unfamiliar will also be affected by the emotional stress and anxiety which not infrequently accompany aural comprehension experiences in a foreign language.

STAGES IN COMPREHENSION

The student learning a foreign language passes through several stages in the comprehension of spoken speech. On first contact, the foreign-language utterances strike his ears as a stream of undifferentiated noises. As he listens, he gradually perceives some order in the noise: a regularity in the rise and fall of the voice and in the breath groups. As he learns some of the arbitrary associations of the particular language (i.e., vocabulary, verb groups, simple expressions) he begins to distinguish the acoustic and syntactic patterning: the recurring elements which give form to segments of speech. Comprehension, however, requires selection of what is crucial for the particular situation in which the utterance is heard. The student then passes through a stage when he recognizes familiar elements in the mass of speech but is unable to recognize the interrelationships within the whole stream of sound; he does not therefore fully comprehend the message. It is only with much practice that he can pass beyond this stage in which he feels rather like a man walking in a fog which clears in patches and floats back to obscure other points. As the student hears much foreign-language speech, he eventually acquires facility in recognizing the crucial elements which determine the message. We shall discuss later the teacher's role in helping him to reach this level of achievement. At this more advanced stage, he may recognize the essentials of the message, but not be able to remember what he has recognized. This is because he is unable to concentrate his attention on the crucial elements of the message long enough to rehearse them subvocally before moving on with the continuing voice. All his attention is taken up with recognition. In comprehension of native speech he anticipates certain sequences of low information content, which in his previous experiences with the language had occurred in similar contexts, and his full attention is given to the high information items. While the foreign language is still rather unfamiliar territory there are few low information items which may be anticipated and so occupy little of his attention. Furthermore, anticipation based on experience with the native language (as with homonyms and structures which appear to parallel those of his own language) may be extremely misleading. Because of the high rate of information contained in sound sequences with which he is not very familiar, he has not sufficient capacity left for retention.

TEACHING LISTENING COMPREHENSION

Before the teacher can devise a sequence of activities which will train students in listening comprehension, he must understand the nature of the skill he is setting out to develop.

Listening to a foreign language may be analyzed as involving two levels of activity, both of which must be taught. The first, the recognition level, involves the identification of words and phrases in their structural interrelationships, of time sequences, logical and modifying terms, and of phrases which are redundant interpolations adding nothing to the development of the line of thought. The second is the level of selection, where the listener is drawing out from the communication those elements which seem to him to contain the gist of the message. This process requires him to concentrate his attention on certain sound groupings while others are aurally perceived without being retained. This parallels the process in visual perception where we see the object which attracts our attention but do not absorb surrounding details, which, from the physical point of view, are equally within the range of our view. For the student to be able to listen with ease to the foreign language in normal situations, he needs thorough training at the recognition level and much practice in selecting specific details from the stream of sound.

RECOGNITION AND SELECTION LEVELS

Training at the recognition level must begin from the first lesson. This does not mean the presentation of much ungraded and ill-designed aural material in the hope that something will happen. There was a period when teachers were urged to surround their students from the very beginning with a veritable mist of foreign-language speech, thus recreating in the classroom, so it was believed, the situation in which students would find themselves if suddenly transported to the country where the language is spoken. It is true that, when plunged completely into the foreign-language atmosphere, people do learn to interpret the sounds they are hearing, but to varying degrees of accuracy. One fact which is conveniently overlooked is that many migrants in a new land are unable, after many years of residence, to interpret more than the simple interchanges of daily life. Some do go beyond the comprehension of banalities but certainly not without effort on their part. When we take into consideration the number of hours during which the average migrant listens to the new language before he understands it to any degree of effectiveness we appear justified in assuming that he is not learning aural comprehension in the most economical and efficient way. In the considerably fewer hours at the disposal of the teacher in the classroom, methods must be adopted which will lead more directly to the objective, developing the greatest degree of skill that is possible in the time available.

For a method to be economical as well as efficient it must take into account all the skill elements which should be developed. As we have seen, in a listening situation the student must be so familiar with the components of a stream of speech that he can react quickly to some of them and pass rapidly over others which are redundant or irrelevant to his immediate purpose. He must be able to recognize without effort sound patterns (sound discriminations affecting meaning, intonation patterns, significant levels of pitch, word groupings), grammatical sequences and tenses, modifiers and function words, clichés, expletives or hesitation expressions which can be ignored as irrelevant to the message, levels of discourse (colloquial or formal), emotional overtones (excited, disappointed, peremptory, cautious, angry utterances), as well as regional, social or dialectal variations. As these aspects of speech become familiar to the student his expectation of their occurrence in certain contexts rises and their information content is, as a consequence, lessened. As the human organism is able to absorb only a certain amount of information at one time, this familiarity, by decreasing the information content, increases the number of items with which the student can cope in one utterance. Systematically prepared listening comprehension materials will provide training, in a steady progression, for all the areas listed, not leaving essential learning to chance. If suitable materials are not available, the teacher will choose, adapt and re-fashion those which are obtainable, or prepare his own, with these basic requirements in mind.

DIALOGUE-LEARNING

The first step in training in listening comprehension is well provided for in dialogue-learning. The student is continually hearing the material he is learning repeated by the model, by other students and by himself. In this way, he forms an acoustic image of these short utterances so that he is able to recognize them without analysis. The danger in this situation is that such recognition may remain only at the acoustic level, the student not being more than dimly aware of the meaning of what he is saying. To ensure that the phrases he is learning will be useful also at the selective level, frequent opportunity must be provided for their application to communication situations within the class group, where actual degree of comprehension can be clearly demonstrated by an appropriate response, either physical or oral. This response, if oral, should as a general rule be in the foreign language. If the student is habitually asked to demonstrate his comprehension by translation into his native language a further danger develops. He will acquire the habit of analysing the elements of every utterance for comparison with what seem to be the most nearly appropriate categories of his native language and he will not learn to perceive short utterances and segments of longer utterances as meaningful in themselves. He will also not develop facility in listening to and registering an ongoing stream of sound for retention. With each utterance he will be busy decomposing the first segment he has heard in order to retain a native-language version of it, when his attention should have been fully engaged in forming an acoustic image of the second segment and in selecting from it the elements relating it to the first.

In the early stages, the teacher should concentrate on teaching the immediate apprehension of a segment of sound, not on long-term retention of it: that is, on recognition, not on total or delayed recall. The student, for instance, may not be able to recall a sequence of utterances in a dialogue but may yet be able to respond promptly and appropriately to any one item in the dialogue. He will not be capable of total recall until the material has been overlearned, and he has built up a strong frame of expectations in the language. It is debatable whether time should be wasted on bringing a long series of dialogue sentences to this pitch of overlearning, as the value of the dialogue lies in the usefulness of the individual utterances not in any intrinsic value in the devised sequence.

The potentialities of a dialogue for improving listening comprehension have not been fully exploited until the student is hearing recombinations of the material in the current and earlier dialogues, particularly in the context of actual situations, as in dramatizations acted out by groups of students or in actual conversational interchanges among students. The sense of reality can also be created by filmed situations where these recombinations are appropriate. In classes where dialogues are not being used, the language material of the current lesson and those preceding it should be similarly exploited in recombinations in a situational context.

Recombinations of listening comprehension material can, with a little ingenuity, be included in games requiring a physical or oral response. Often these can take the form of guessing games. Games imaginatively devised give the students comprehension practice in a situation where interest is heightened by the competitive element and their attention is distracted from the skill being practiced. If comprehension is thus demonstrated in a real situation where it is an instrument rather than an objective the teacher will have tangible evidence that the students have passed beyond the recognition stage to that of selection. A few minutes of listening comprehension games at regular intervals, usually at the end of class lessons, will enable the teacher to re-introduce systematically material which is not currently being actively practiced. In this way, retention of material from earlier lessons will be constantly reinforced by active recapitulation without tedium.

AUTHENTIC MATERIAL

All material used for listening comprehension, even in the earliest lessons, should be authentic, that is, it should consist of utterances with a high probability of occurrence. Teaching students to comprehend artificial language combinations which would rarely be heard from a native speaker is a waste of time and energy, and can only confuse the student when he is later confronted with natural speech.

Authentic material will frequently involve details of customs, behavior and attitudes typical of the foreign culture. Unless the teacher prepares his class for such cultural elements, they may pass completely unnoticed by the student or appear to him to be ridiculous or peculiar. Yet it is the understanding of these cultural differences which is one of the most valuable experiences in foreign-language learning. If all comprehension material consists of foreign-language words and phrases applied to native-language behavior, the students will begin to feel that it is a burdensome way of expressing themselves when the native language seems so much more adequate. The concept that foreign-language words and phrases are exact counterparts of certain native-language words and phrases will be fostered and the opportunity of opening the eyes of students to other attitudes and values will be lost. The understanding of cultural differences will often be hastened by the presentation of some visual representation of the situation, by picture, film or film-strip, which highlights the cultural implications.

The visual stimulus can, however, be more of a hindrance than a help if it is introduced without due attention to context. A picture which is ambiguous in concept may concentrate the attention on a misleading feature and arouse false associations which it is hard for the teacher to identify and correct at a later stage. The student may also acquire incorrect notions about the foreign culture if certain elements in the visual accompaniment have not been fully explained. The teacher must study carefully the visual aids he is to use in order to ensure that they are reinforcing what he is trying to teach and not merely distracting attention from the oral language. Reliance on a visual representation at all times may certainly mean that the student comprehends less well when he is left to depend on his ear alone. In some cases it may be impossible in the school situation to determine whether the student has actually comprehended the aural message or deduced it from the visual stimulus. It is important, therefore, to ensure that the student has abundant practice in listening without the support of visual clues other than the situational clues of normal conversation.

PRESENTATION

Certain procedural features of the presentation of listening comprehension exercises have been the subject of experimental study. Physical aspects of the classroom or laboratory presentation, such as speed of utterance, length of segments, length of pauses, and the acoustics of the classroom should be carefully studied by the teacher because of their decisive effect on the value of the exercise.

All utterances for listening comprehension should be delivered at normal speed from the earliest lessons. Normal speed does not mean rapid native speech, but a speed of delivery which would not appear to a native speaker to be unduly labored—a speed which retains normal word groupings, elisions, liaisons, consonant assimilations, natural rhythm and intonation. Utterances which are delivered at an unnaturally slow pace are inevitably distorted and the acoustic images stored by the student will not be immediately useful when he hears a natural form of speech. It may be argued that, in a foreign-language situation, the native speaker will, on request, speak very slowly, but in so doing he exaggerates what to the listener are already confusing liaisons, elisions and phonemic distinctions of his language or tries to incorporate into it, in an unsystematic fashion, what he believes to be the distinctive characteristics of the language of his interlocutor. This labored delivery, running contrary to the expectations of the foreigner, is often as difficult for him to interpret as undistorted speech at normal speed. Even in the very early stages familiar material can be understood when spoken at normal speed. It is obvious that difficulties will arise when unfamiliar material is included, thus increasing rapidly the amount of information to be assimilated. At more advanced stages, when unfamiliar words and phrases are intentionally included in comprehension exercises, they should be embedded in so much easily recognized material of low information content that the student is able to concentrate on comparing the new elements with the surrounding context and deducing their meaning in this way. These new elements are also more easily assimilated at this stage because their characteristic acoustic and structural patterning is recognized by the trained ear of the student.

The length of the segments emitted in each breath group and the length of the pauses between the segments are of more importance than the actual speed of delivery within the segments. The amount of information in a segment increases rapidly with the length of the segment, a greater number of words allowing for a greater number of alternatives. The longer the segment the greater is the strain on the auditory memory. During the pause between segments, the organism rehearses what it has heard, thus strengthening the memory trace. Research has shown that the auditory memory span for foreign-language material is considerably less than for native-language material, probably on a ratio of nine words to fifteen.[3] With segments of from eight to ten words (less in the early stages) the mind can recirculate the material during the pause, relating it to what preceded and anticipating to some extent what will follow.

[3] Robert Lado: "Memory Span as a Factor in Second Language Learning," *International Review of Applied Linguistics*, III/2 (1965), p. 127.

Such pauses are supplied in natural speech by hesitations, a certain amount of hemming and hawing, some re-stating, and by certain conventional expressions contributing nothing to the meaning of the utterance but having a high frequency of occurrence which reflects their usefulness in extending the pauses in a normal utterance. As artificially prepared material usually omits these common features of natural utterances it tends to deliver information at a much higher rate than normal speech. A slight lengthening of the pauses will supply the extra time which the organism requires to absorb the information presented to it, without adding a time element not available in normal conversation.

For the same reason, listening comprehension exercises should contain a certain amount of repetitious material. This may take the form, for example, of explanations or descriptions in slightly different versions. Such repetition is another characteristic of normal speech. In conversation and other forms of extempore speech there is redundancy of content as well as linguistic redundancy. It is because redundancy of content has been eliminated that following a close-knit discourse or the reading of a well-written paper, even in the native language, requires a concentrated effort on the part of the listener. This fact is often overlooked with the result that listening comprehension materials in the foreign language contain features which make them even more difficult to follow than similar material in the very familiar native language.

Teachers should be aware of certain emotional problems which may arise in connection with listening comprehension exercises. Any trepidation on the part of beginning students not accustomed to paying close attention to aural messages can be overcome by the early introduction of much practice in listening to a limited amount of linguistic material. Considerable difficulty is experienced by students trained to study the language through written texts when they are suddenly confronted with listening comprehension material of a similar standard of difficulty to that which they are accustomed to studying at their leisure in graphic form. The emotional tension associated with this experience is frequently compounded by the near approach of some examination for which this type of activity is preparing the students.

LISTENING ACTIVITIES

Materials for listening comprehension at an elementary level will consist mostly of the give-and-take of simple conversational situations, short sketches or short stories containing a considerable amount of conversation, and brief reports from fellow-students. The material will be a recombination of words and phrases which the student recognizes with ease. A listener cannot concentrate his attention on every constituent of an utterance with the same intensity. The familiar expressions form a matrix from which he selects certain elements which are interrelated from segment to segment and which outline the developing pattern of the ideas which he is pursuing. If the student is confused by an effort to comprehend every element as he hears it, thus concentrating his attention fully on every constituent, he will not perceive these interrelationships and what he has not perceived he will not retain. It is in listening comprehension particularly that the teacher can easily underestimate the difficulties of the student. To the teacher the comprehension of elementary material is immediate and effortless. He must try to see the processes involved from the student's point of view and provide plenty of practice in hearing well-rehearsed material while requiring the extraction from it of different lines of thought. It is only at an advanced stage when so many more features of the language are familiar, that the teacher may begin to allow the student the opportunity of working with uncontrolled material where he must deduce meanings from context in a very rapid mental process of association. This process is possible only when the effort involved in retention has been considerably reduced by almost automatic recognition of language patterns. At this stage the teacher may seize the opportunity from time to time to enliven the lesson by recounting in the foreign language some amusing incident which has occurred during the day, or by providing some anecdotal background to a subject under discussion. When the teacher uses the foreign language as he would use the native language, the students begin to look upon it as a normal instrument for communication.

When the student has acquired confidence in listening to ungraded material much practice may be given in individual situations: in a language laboratory, in listening booths established in the library, in a listening room equipped with a tape-recorder or a record-player. At this stage direct listening practice can be divorced from a conversational situation. Material for listening may be drawn from literature being studied and may provide a basis for oral reports in class. Practice in listening may be given by taped lectures on informational subjects, sustained scenes from plays, or readings from poetry and prose. Students may attempt to follow radio broadcasts or the sound track of a commercial film or documentary. They may relax with a program of popular songs. Training should be given, too, in listening to group conversations and discussions. In the excitement of the discussion speech will be slightly slurred, but this will be compensated for by the hesitations, interruptions, and repetitions characteristic of natural speech. Conversations and discussions of this type may be taped and used over and over again. Simulated telephone conversations are also worthwhile, for they give practice in listening to slightly distorted speech with no visual clues available to counteract the effect of the distortion.

Groups of schools in the same supervision area should cooperate in the production of material for listening comprehension, freely exchanging tapes which they have had the opportunity to make. One school may be able to tape an interview or conversation with a native speaker who has visited them. This material should be immediately circulated to other schools in the district. In areas where contact with native speakers is rare no opportunity should be lost of building up through cooperative action a supply of semi-informal material in the foreign language. In this way students will have the opportunity to hear a variety of voices of differing quality, and accents representative of several regions and educational backgrounds.

Above all, it must be clearly borne in mind by teacher and student alike that listening comprehension is not a skill which can be mastered once and for all and then ignored while other skills are developed. There must be regular practice with increasingly difficult material. This practice must, however, be regularly spaced over the language-learning period and not massed urgently in great blocks at some moment preceding an examination. Listening comprehension increases with growing familiarity with the vocabulary and structures of the language and can provide one of the most enjoyable activities associated with the language program and one which the student continues to enjoy after he has left the classroom.

SECTION THREE

GRAMMAR

In learning our first language we get virtually no instruction, but we get plenty of correction. Through trial, error, and correction, we eventually learn to use our language in a more or less acceptable fashion. The language system becomes a matter of automatic habit: we focus our attention of *what* we want to say, and not on *how* we have to say it. As has been noted previously, this is also a desired goal in second-language learning. For our purposes here, the systematic use of the resources of the language, which are habitual for the native speaker, constitutes the *grammar* of the language.

McIntosh points out that "Today we consider . . . there are two ways to 'know' grammar. The most important is to have a recognition of the functioning of the language we know how to speak. The structures required to signal various meanings . . . must be used in relation to each other. The second is the ability to talk analytically about the language in the terms of descriptive linguistics." She suggests that the first way of knowing grammar should precede the second.

A structural linguist may observe the speech habits of the native speakers of a language for a time and make statements based on his observations. In the end he may produce a structural sketch or *descriptive grammar*, recording facts about the language in terms of its actual use by its speakers. He describes the overall system and the various subsystems that operate within it. Descriptive grammar, then, provides a guide to real, observed usage.

We have emphasized the fact that speech habits differ from language to language: each language has its own set of phonemes and its own devices for organizing these into meaningful stretches of speech. We can notice also that languages differ in the way they categorize and report experience. The description of one language will not serve as a model for describing another language (although the same descriptive techniques are applicable to both). The many points of dissimilarity make such a procedure impracticable, in spite of the fact that there may also be many points of similarity, particularly among related languages. *Prescriptive grammar*, which most of us studied in school, illustrates some of the difficulty. With concepts and models from the study of Latin and Greek applied to English, we easily become confused about what the structure of our own language is like. The best guide to the language is a description in terms of the language's own configurations. A descriptive grammar is by design a configurational grammar, whereas a prescriptive grammar is not.

As ESOL teachers we often have to make statements about the structure of English. These statements should relate to actual usage of the language, and not to some fancied notion of "correctness" that conflicts with acceptable usage. "Acceptable," in this case, refers to your own usage and the usage of native speakers you habitually associate with. For example, to insist that students say *It is I*, rather than *It's me*, is absurd. We should take seriously the old slogan of World War II days: "A language is what the native speakers say, not what someone thinks they ought to say." Not long ago I heard an ESOL teacher-trainer giving some good advice to one of her trainees: "Listen to yourself," she said. "You're a speaker of English."

MIM-MEM AND PATT-PRAC

This section provides a tiny sample of the voluminous literature on structural drills and exercises for second-language learning. Paulston's bibliography gives an idea of how extensive this literature is and how much work has gone into the development of techniques for teaching "grammar." *Mimicry-memorization* (mim-mem) *and pattern practice* (patt-prac), as described by Anthony and Norris in Section One, are two important and complementary tools of the audiolingual method. Anthony and Norris note that "One or the other may dominate in a given lesson or even a whole set of lessons, but fundamentally they can be viewed as steps in a procedure by which the student is first presented with the new foreign language item and gains familiarity with and conscious control over it (through mim-mem), and then progressively gains language mastery as recognition and production of the item are made unconscious habit (through pattern practice). The precise steps in this procedure are recognition, imitation, and repetition, followed by variation and selection."

McCready demonstrates this procedure nicely: he begins with a dialogue containing a new grammar problem that the students learn through mim-mem; then he proceeds to manipulation drill using model sentences from the dialogue as "frames" for manipulation. "In one sense," he points out, "the dialogue-oriented lesson provides simulated conversation activity from the very beginning . . ." Later in the drill, dialogue material enters into "a series of activities that gradually make the transition from simulated conversation (the practice of predetermined utterances) toward real communication."

MORPHOLOGY AND SYNTAX

In simple terms *morphology* has to do with word structure, and *syntax* has to do with the structure of grammatical units larger than words— phrases, clauses, and sentences. *Grammar,* in the terminology of structural linguistics, includes both morphology and syntax. Two important grammatical devices in English are word forms and word order; students have to learn what goes with what and in what order. But it should be remembered that the patterns of form and arrangement are limited. Learning activities must be centered around these patterns until they have been internalized.

McCready describes mim-mem, followed by patt-prac, as a route for accomplishing habit formation in the use of grammatical elements. McIntosh, Politzer, and Paulston continue the discussion of pattern practice devices (also called "structural pattern drills") and their function in helping students gain automatic control over the grammatical system (and subsystems) of the language. They provide sample drills and suggest ways of exploiting them to best advantage. (For a discussion of laboratory drills, see Croft's paper in Section Eight.)

Politzer stresses the importance of structural signals in language learning. He notes that "Your ability to comprehend the spoken or written form of *any* language (including your own) depends largely on the quick 'deciphering' of the signals that carry the structural meaning." Ordinarily, he points out, "(1) a knowledge of structure, (2) knowledge of 'vocabulary' (i.e., knowledge of the words carrying lexical meaning), and (3) knowledge of the general context or situation in which language is used will combine or interact to convey the meaning of what is being expressed. Sometimes knowledge in one or two of these areas can be used to make up for lack of knowledge in the others." This notion is best illustrated perhaps in the introduction of new vocabulary items: "Once you have acquired a knowledge of structure and a limited vocabulary, you can use this knowledge to help you understand new words and to comprehend sentences that are—partially at least—made up of unknown words."

Paulston reviews the literature of the last two decades or so on structural pattern drills and sets up a classification of such drills. She contends "that there are three classes of drills: mechanical, meaningful, and communicative and that we may distinguish the three . . . if we analyze the drills in terms of (1) expected terminal behavior, (2) degree of response control, (3) the type of learning process involved, and (4) of criteria for selection of utterance response." A classification is needed, she continues, "for grading and sequencing drills in order to obtain a systematic and more efficient progression . . . from mechanical learning to the internalizing of competence."

The term "transformational drill" used by Politzer and Paulston appears to have a vague reference to the transformational-generative approach to language description. But as Croft points out in Section Eight, surface transformations as exercises have been around a long time, familiar to language teachers in such instructions as "change the statements to questions" or "change the sentences to passive."

SELECTED READINGS

Bowen, J. Donald. "Applications of Grammatical Analysis to Language Teaching." In *On Teaching English to Speakers of Other Languages, Series I.* Edited by Virginia French Allen. Champaign, Ill.: National Council of Teachers of English, 1965, pp. 57–64.

Brooks, Nelson. *Language and Language Learning: Theory and Practice.* 2d ed. Chapter 11: "Pattern Practice." New York: Harcourt Brace Jovanovich, 1964.

Campbell, Russell N. "An Evaluation and Comparison of Present Methods for Teaching Grammar to Speakers of Other Languages." *TESOL Quarterly* 4(1970):37–48.

Dacanay, Fe R. *Techniques and Procedures in Second Language Teaching.* Edited by J. Donald Bowen. Chapter 1: "Presenting English Structure"; Chapter 2: "Pattern Practice or Structural Drills." Dobbs Ferry, N. Y.: Oceana Publications, Inc., 1963.

Fries, Charles C. *Teaching and Learning English as a Foreign Language.* Chapter 3: "The Structure: Making Automatic the Use of the Devices of Arrangement and Form." Ann Arbor: The University of Michigan Press, 1945.

Hok, Ruth. "Oral Exercises: Their Type and Form," *Modern Language Journal* 48(1964):222–26.

King, Harold V. "Oral Grammar Drills." *English Language Teaching* 14 (1959):13–18.

Lado, Robert. *Language Teaching: A Scientific Approach.* Chapter 10: "From Sentences to Patterns"; Chapter 11: "Pattern Practice." New York: McGraw-Hill, Inc., 1964.

———. *Linguistics across Cultures: Applied Linguistics for Language Teachers.* Chapter 3: "How to Compare Two Grammatical Structures." Ann Arbor: The University of Michigan Press, 1957.

Moulton, William G. *A Linguistic Guide to Language Learning.* 2d ed.

Chapter 5: "Sentences." New York: The Modern Language Association, 1970.

————. "What is Structural Drill?" In *Structural Drill and the Language Laboratory*. Edited by Francis W. Gravit and Albert Valdman. The Hague: Mouton and Co., 1963.

POLITZER, ROBERT L. *Foreign Language Learning: A Linguistic Introduction*. Chapter 5: "The Forms of Language: English Morphology"; Chapter 6: "Syntactical Patterns: Some Examples of English Syntax"; Chapter 8: "The Problems of Morphology." Englewood Cliffs, N.J.: Prentice-Hall, Inc., 1970.

PRATOR, CLIFFORD H. "Guidelines for Planning Classes and Teaching Materials." *Workpapers in English as a Second Language: Matter, Methods, and Materials*. Los Angeles: Department of English, University of California, 1967, pp. 27–31.

RIVERS, WILGA M. *Teaching Foreign-Language Skills*. Chapter 3: "The Place of Grammar"; Chapter 4: "Construction of Grammatical Drills and Exercises." Chicago: The University of Chicago Press, 1968.

STRAIN, JERIS E. "Drilling and Methodology." *Language Learning* 18(1968): 177–82.

DEVELOPING A LESSON
AROUND A DIALOGUE

GEORGE MC CREADY

The short dialogue is frequently used as one of the steps leading from imitative repetition toward free conversation. However, it is often possible and desirable to develop an entire lesson around a good dialogue. If the textbook you are using offers dialogue material, you may wish to use the considerations presented here as a guide in judging the suitability of the material or its role in the lesson plan. If your textbook does not contain dialogue material, you may find the suggestions on how to construct a dialogue useful.

A dialogue is any oral interchange between two or more people. It may be a question and its answer:

> Do you have any ink?
> Yes, I have some.

It may take the form of a statement with a statement response:

> It's a lovely day today.
> Yesterday was warmer, though.

It may limit itself to one new grammar problem embedded in known vocabulary, or to new vocabulary in known grammar structures, or it may (as in many tourist phrase books) treat entire utterances as semantic units without consideration to grammar or vocabulary grading.

THE TEACHING DIALOGUE

For the purposes of this article, the good teaching dialogue is defined as one which:

1) Contains from three to ten exchanges. It is long enough to develop a believable conversation, and short enough for the average student to memorize.

2) Limits any one utterance to a length the student is capable of pro-

ducing with fair success after hearing it twice. This may be as few as five syllables per utterance for beginning students.

3) Adequately illustrates new grammar or vocabulary of the lesson but strictly controls the number of new items presented.

4) Represents a natural interchange which could take place between native speakers of English.

5) Takes into consideration, in content and style, the age and interests of the students.

THE ROLE OF THE DIALOGUE IN THE LESSON

1) *Dialogue Material in Imitative-Repetition Drills.* If the dialogue is well constructed, most of the sentences can serve as the pattern sentences for imitative-repetition drill. Instead of being unrelated sentences illustrating a point of grammar, the dialogue sentences are related to each other in a meaningful interchange. This gives point and adds interest to the imitative-repetition drill. In the illustrative dialogue given below, the dialogue utterances which serve as pattern sentences for the imitative-repetition (or substitution) drills are printed in bold type. The dialogue here is designed to introduce the grammatically distributed words *some* and *any*.

A: Excuse me, (name of B). **I need some envelopes.**

B: Sorry. **I don't have any. Maybe** (name of C) **has some.**

A: Thanks. I'll ask him (her).

As the students listen to the utterances of the dialogue and then repeat them, they are hearing and using the new forms in the context of a natural conversation. They are also beginning the task of memorizing the dialogue. Experience has shown that successful memorizing—and by that I mean mastery of the utterances to a point approximating the speed and style of native oral delivery—requires a strong "head start" through controlled practice in the classroom. Of course you must make sure that the students understand the meaning of the dialogue utterances. The fact that the pattern sentences appear in a dialogue rather than in semantically unrelated sentences makes it easier for the students to grasp the word and sentence meaning.

2) *Dialogue Material in Structure-Demonstration Drills.* After the students have had an opportunity to imitate the dialogue sentences several times and have begun to grasp the meaning of the new forms, you can have them make substitutions in the dialogue sentences in order to achieve the purposes of the structure-demonstration drill.

Step 1. Manipulate the sentences independently of the dialogue:

> I need some **envelopes.**
>> **paper clips**
>> **stamps**
>> **ink**
>> **paper**
>> **paste**
>
> I **want** some envelopes.
>> **need**
>> **have**
>
> I don't have any **envelopes.**
>> **paper clips**
>> etc.
>
> I don't **have** any.
>> **need**
>> **want**

Step 2. Using the same substitution technique, drill the sentences within the framework of the dialogue:

A: Excuse me, (name of B). I need some **envelopes.**
> **paper clips**
> etc.

B: Sorry, (name of A). I don't have any.

As this drill proceeds, the essential structure of the dialogue is being increasingly mastered by the students as the application of the grammar point is being extended and clarified through sentence variation.

3) *Dialogue Material in Substitution Drills.* Up to this point, the dialogue has been varied to demonstrate the function of the new grammar point. With the grammar function now clear, the substitution-drill technique is continued to strengthen the student's oral mastery of the item. At this stage, any element of the base sentence can serve as the "slot" for substitution, whereas in the structure-demonstration phase only elements grammatically related to the item under study were used as slots for substitution. You might, for example, now substitute as follows:

> Maybe **Gordon** has some envelopes.
>> **Jane**
>> etc.

Again, the sentences may first be extracted from the dialogue for independent substitution drill and then practiced within the framework of the dialogue. In the early stages of the substitution drill you yourself give the items for substitution; later, you may encourage the students to supply their own substitutions—keeping, of course, within well-known vocabulary—perhaps choosing from a list of words on the blackboard.

4) *Dialogue Material in Simulated-Conversation Drills.* In one sense, the dialogue-oriented lesson provides simulated conversation activity from the very beginning—since even the imitative repetition drills are within the framework of a conversation. This is one of the decided advantages of this type of lesson organization. But now you will want to use the dialogue in a series of activities that gradually make the transition from simulated conversation (the practice of predetermined utterances) toward real communication. Examples of three possible steps in this transition are given below.

Step 1. Present a chain-dialogue drill, with the students selecting substitution words at random from a list of words well known to them written on the board:

A: Excuse me, (name of B). I need some (word from list).

B: Sorry, (A). I don't have any. Maybe (C) has some.

A: Thanks. I'll ask him (her).

A (turning to C): Excuse me, (C). I need some (same word).

C: Sorry, (A). I don't . . . etc.

After two times through the dialogue, Student A surrenders his role to another student and the drill continues.

Step 2. Present a chain-dialogue drill with optional sentence selection. Here the students select one of a set of sentences written on the board to provide development of the *dialogue situation* rather than to practice particular sentence forms. All sentence choices should contain familiar words in known grammar structures. For example:

A: 1) Say, (B). Do you have any _____?
    2) Excuse me, (B). I need some _____.
    3) Excuse me, (B). Can you lend me some _____?
    4) (B), can I borrow some _____ from you?

B: 1) Sorry, (A). I don't have any. Maybe (C) has some.
    2) No, I don't, (A). But I think (C) has some.
    3) Sorry, (A). But I can't spare any right now.
    4) Sure, I have some. How many (much) do you want (need)?

A: 1) Thanks. I'll ask him (her).
   2) Thanks, anyway.
   3) Appropriate answer to B's fourth choice.

Notice that *A*'s choice of opening sentence can limit *B*'s appropriate response. On the other hand, *B* can choose between a negative or a positive response, thus forcing *A* to make a suitable selection for the final remark.

The option sentences may be written on the blackboard as a guide during the first part of the drill, but they should be erased or covered as the students become familiar with them. As a further move toward "real conversation," *B* might answer negatively or affirmatively according to the truth of the matter as it applies to him. The important element in Step 2 of the drill is the practice in selecting the appropriate response as the dialogue situation develops.

Step 3. Conduct "cued" conversation, with optional selection within the "grammar set." In previous illustrations of the drill, everything has been varied except the words *some* and *any* and the classes of nouns that can be used with them. That, in fact, is the secret of the rapidly conducted substitution drill: By focusing the attention of the student on the slot into which substitution is to be made (which is never the new grammar feature) and the words to be substituted, it leads the student to repeat the new grammar feature over and over to the point of unconscious mastery. Assuming that the students have already learned the use of such phrases as *a book, the book,* and the corresponding pronouns that substitute for them, the dialogue can now be used to review and practice the "grammar set"

a—the—some / any
one—it—some / any

Only the framework of the basic dialogue situation is retained in these drills. The items requested by *A* may be such things as "my watch," "the book," "any ink," "a match," and the form of the request and *B*'s response may vary as in Step 2. For example:

A: Excuse me, (B). Do you have (1) **my watch?**
                                 (2) **the new book**
                                 (3) **the new books**
                                 (4) **a dictionary**
                                 (5) **a match**
                                 (6) **any matches**
                                 (7) **any ink**

B: Sorry, (A). I don't have (1) **it.**
                                           (2) **it**
                                           (3) **them**
                                           (4) **one**
                                           (5) **one, any**
                                           (6) **any**
                                           (7) **any**

Then go on and complete the dialogue.

There are several ways to "cue" the conversational exchange of the students. Some are purely mechanical:

1)   You give each student a "cue card." One card might have the following cues:

a)   You need a dictionary.

b)   You have the object(s) that (A) wants.

2)   You say, "You need a dictionary" and indicate the student who will act as A. A directs his request to a student you indicate or to one of his own choice, who reacts to the stimulus.

Sometimes you can give the cue in a more realistic way: You say, "(A), can you get a dictionary for me?"

A: I'll try. Excuse me, (B). Do you have a dictionary?

B: Answers according to the truth of the matter as applied to him.

THE DIALOGUE, THE TEXT, AND THE LESSON PLAN

It would not be wise to attempt to develop the dialogue treatment described under the main heading "The Role of the Dialogue in the Lesson" in one period or to dedicate any one period solely to oral dialogue work. (Developing a lesson around a dialogue means that the dialogue is the focal point of the work for the period, not that it is the only matter dealt with during the period.) The following is a suggested plan for coordinating dialogue development with the lesson materials in the class text. It is assumed in this example that the text lesson contains a reading passage, grammar explanation, exercises of various types, and a vocabulary list.

The plan would require two, or possibly more, class periods for its execution.

Step 1.   Present the dialogue as in number 1 under "The Role of the Dialogue in the Lesson," which is "Dialogue Material in Imitative-Repetition Drills."

Step 2. Use the dialogue material as in number 2 of the same main section above, which is "Dialogue Material in Structure-Demonstration Drills."

Step 3. Read and discuss the grammar explanation section of the lesson in the text.

Step 4. Use the dialogue according to the following subsection number 3 above, which is "Dialogue Material in Substitution Drills."

Step 5. Do appropriate exercises from the textbook.

Step 6. Do a final imitative-repetition drill on the basic dialogue. Be sure that the students have copied the dialogue correctly from the board and have marked it with pronunciation reminders. Assign the dialogue to be practiced aloud and memorized for home work.

END OF THE FIRST CLASS PERIOD

Step 7. Check to see if the students have memorized the dialogue.

Step 8. Do the reading passage in the text and appropriate exercises.

Step 9. Return to the dialogue material as indicated in subsection number 4, above, which is "Dialogue Material in Simulated-Conversation Drills."

The nature of the text material and of the new language item treated in the lesson will naturally affect the sequence and emphasis that you give certain activities in your lesson plans. The plan outlined above is meant only to indicate the points at which the usual text offering can best be co-ordinated with dialogue development in the dialogue-oriented teaching plan.

CONSTRUCTING A DIALOGUE

1) *When the class textbook contains no dialogue material,* you should:

a) Isolate the new items presented in the lesson.
b) Build a dialogue with the following consideration in mind:

i) The characteristics of a good teaching dialogue as presented under "The Teaching Dialogue," above.

ii) The theme of the text lesson, if any. Usually the text lesson will contain a reading passage. When at all possible, the theme of the dialogue should be related to the theme of the reading passage.

iii) The need for item substitution. The utterances in the dialogue should be designed to allow the substitution of items necessary for structure demonstration and drill. The list of substitution items should include as many words from the text vocabulary list for the lesson as is feasible.

iv) The need for variation and extension. If the use of the dialogue is to go beyond simple memorizing and the repetition of set utterances, you must plan for the gradual introduction of believable *utterance variations*. The students must learn to recognize, react to, and use different levels of formality in their conversation drills; they must learn to handle unexpected responses to their requests or questions. It is also desirable to plan for *extension* of the dialogue to more than two participants. Notice that the dialogue used as an example in this article may involve more than two speakers:

A: Excuse me, (B). I need some envelopes.

B: Sorry, (A). I don't have any.

c (interrupting): Maybe (D) has some.

A (to c): Thanks. I'll ask him.

The second type of extension to plan for is that required by the technique of chain drill. Notice that in the exchange immediately above, A can continue his search for envelopes quite naturally by turning to D and developing the same dialogue theme with him.

v) The desirability of contrasting and combining new items with review items, either in the basic dialogue or in later developments of the dialogue.

2) *When the text offers an unsuitable dialogue,* you should attempt to improve it, to adapt it, rather than abandon it. Where the dialogue uses stilted or otherwise unnatural utterances, often the change of a few words or phrases will bring it to life. Where the text dialogue is too long, you might select that part of it which best illustrates the new grammar point for intensive drill as described in this article.

There is always a strong temptation to add sentences to a dialogue to "set the scene" or to illustrate all possible uses of the new language item; the result is often a dialogue too long to be manageable. It is important to set the scene for language interchange in a dialogue, but you can often do this more efficiently by a short narrative introduction which can then be taken for granted and excluded from the oral drills. It is equally unnecessary—and undesirable—to illustrate all possible uses of the new grammar item in the body of the basic dialogue. The most generally useful ones should be there, but others can be introduced and treated according to their merits in the later variations of the dialogue or in separate exercises.

SUMMARY

The dialogue-oriented lesson allows presentation of a new language item in a normal oral framework related to a situation. Thus, while permitting strictest teacher control at the beginning to reduce the students' opportunity for error and to focus attention on the new material, the dialogue format encourages oral practice in a meaningful context.

Later substitutions within the dialogue utterances, and variation of the utterances themselves within the dialogue situation, serve to demonstrate the functional range of the new item. In this manner, a wide range of possible utterances—all employing the new item—are practiced in relation to a given situation.

Finally, the dialogue format for oral practice encourages the use of the gestures, facial expressions, and vocal modifiers which are also very much a part of communication. Naturalness does not lie in the utterance alone; it depends in equal, or even greater, degree upon the way the utterance is delivered. Where each sentence drilled is a related part of a larger communication problem, the students can be more easily persuaded to practice the accompanying gestures and expressions. Just as the dialogue format permits the students more practice with these gestural elements of communication, they in turn contribute to understanding and mastery of the language content of the dialogue.

HOW TO TEACH ENGLISH GRAMMAR

LOIS MCINTOSH

1. THE QUESTION OF GRAMMAR RULES

All of us have, at one time or another, memorized statements about English. We have been able to tell what *nouns* are, what *verbs* do, and what *pronouns* consist of. As teachers we expect our students to follow in our paths.

When we are learning to speak of a language, at some stage in our learning, we need to be aware of the facts *about* language. We need to know what kinds of sentences there are, what parts of speech there are and what they do, what arrangements of word order are possible and significant. WHEN do we need this information? HOW can we benefit from knowing it?

We should never talk ABOUT language until we know how to speak the language. This means that beginners, whether they are six or sixty, in kindergarten or adult night school, should not talk about language until they have had some experience with it.

For example, a class in elementary school somewhere abroad, in its second year of language study, might have a lesson like this:

TEACHER	STUDENTS
Listen: I was in Grade Two last year.	
I'm in Grade Three now.	
How many of you were in Grade Two	
last year?	(Show of hands)
Say, after me: I was in Grade Two last year.	I was in Grade Two. . . .

As the lesson continues, with choral repetition, row by row and individual repetition, the children are using sentences about themselves, in terms of past time and present time. Now the teacher, in preparing to give that class, no doubt said to herself that she would "review past tense forms of *be*." But she didn't tell the class that. Instead, she led them into a conversation that ensured plenty of practice in selecting the right verb form to go with the time expressions of *now* and *last year*. The class learned grammar. As they talked they gained control of those forms of the present and past of *BE*. But they weren't talking about "present tense" and "past tense." They were speaking about language, and showing by their speech that they had mastered that particular phase of the grammar.

In the early years of school, and in later years, if the students are beginners, they learn grammar by mastering the basic sentences of the language. This is exactly what they did when they learned their first language, long before they came to school. They learned it by using it. Only in school did they come in contact with "rules of grammar," and they learned to talk about the language they already knew how to speak.

It is even more important for us to remember that in learning a second language, discussion of its structure does not ensure mastery of its sentences. After the beginning stages, learners may find it helpful to know something *about* the language they are speaking. But this must be done only after they are able to use it so well that they can stop and consider what it is they are communicating with. But here too, and with more advanced learners, we should come to our conclusions about language from a consideration of what we have been saying.

For example, an intermediate student might be asked to "define" past tense in English. He might then say, "Past tense expresses past action or state of being. We add *-ed* to verbs to make them past."

He probably found some such statement in a book, memorized it until he had it letter perfect. Then in class, in another situation, he said, "I *walk* there *yesterday*." No relation between rule and use has been established, and much time has been wasted. Another student began by hearing his teacher read a short paragraph about a rabbit.

TEACHER (with pictures of a rabbit): Listen to the story of the rabbit (Reading to the class):

Yesterday a rabbit looked out of his hole under a tree. He hopped along the path. He stopped and lifted his nose in the air. What did he smell? Was it a carrot? His nose wiggled and his tail did too. Where were those carrots? He looked and looked and looked. He wanted those carrots, but he didn't find any.

TEACHER: Now tell the story of the rabbit with me.

Yesterday a rabbit looked out of his hole under a tree.

CLASS: (repeating the story sentence by sentence)

TEACHER: Did the rabbit look out of his hole?

CLASS: Yes, he did.

TEACHER: Did he hop along the path?

CLASS: Yes, he did.

The questions and answers continue, the class responding *Yes, he did; No, he didn't*. (If the *did* is introduced for the first time, of course the teacher models it. But this is Grade 6—they have had these forms before.)

TEACHER: When did the story happen?

CLASS: Yesterday.

TEACHER: What did the rabbit do yesterday?

STUDENT 1: He looked out of his hole.

STUDENT 2: He hopped along the path.

    (and so on through the story)

Generalization:

When we tell what happened yesterday what do we add to the verbs?

Listen:	he looks	—he looked	/t/
	he wiggles	—he wiggled	/d/
	he lifts	—he lifted	/əd/

Can you find other verbs in the story? How are they pronounced?

With /t/ /d/ or /əd/?

How do we spell these sounds (-ed)
How do we ask a question about past time? (We use *did*)
How do we make a sentence negative? (We use *didn't*)

Compare these generalizations with those of the first student. You will notice how much more territory is covered in the second set: The sounds of past tense, the spelling, the question sentence, the negative sentence . . . all essential to a complete picture of past tense. (If this tense is a brand new concept, introduced for the first time, you might use the same context, but you would proceed a step at a time. First the statement, . . . then practice with statements; then questions and their related answers, and more practice, contrasting this form with the statement form; and then negatives, introduced, practiced, and contrasted.)

2. IMPLEMENTING THE GRAMMAR LESSON

Following the *generalization,* there are more exercises to reinforce and make the new material automatic. The past tense of regular verbs has fewer difficulties than present tense. Only one form—*did*—as against the two *do/does,* demanding correlation with singular and plural forms, only one ending, although the three phonetically determined endings must be learned. And these endings (walked—kt; moved—vd; waited—əd) cause real difficulty for speakers of languages in which final consonants do not cluster, or in which final consonants are always voiceless.

At this stage, to ensure aural recognition of the new structure, a substitution of items and choral repetition may prove helpful.

TEACHER: The rabbit looked and looked and looked.
    (Repeat)

Then he	hopped and hopped and hopped.
Then he	wiggled and wiggled and wiggled.
And he	lifted his nose and waited a while.
He	wanted those carrots but he didn't find any.

The substitution drill has many variations. (See Section 3 of this paper) *Conversion drills* make heavier demands on students. The learner needs to understand and react to English time signals. He can learn to do this through conversion drills.

1. *Statement to question*

The rabbit looked for carrots: did he look for carrots?

2. *Affirmative statement to negative statement*

The rabbit looked for carrots. He didn't look for rice. (If possible, the resulting conversions should be more than a mechanical switch over—it should make sense. In order to get the negative statement, you could ask "Did he look for rice?").

3. *From one time to another*

The rabbit looked for carrots.	—He looks for carrots every day.
Did he look for carrots?	—Does he look for carrots?
Did he look for carrots?	—Is he looking for carrots?
He isn't looking.	—He didn't look.

Correlation drills reinforce the use of substitute verbs.

The rabbit likes carrots, and *we do too.*
He didn't find any, and we *didn't either.*

Tag questions:

He doesn't like them, . . . (does he)
He likes them, . . . (doesn't he)

Continue with statements in all the tenses they have studied, with varying subjects:

He liked them, didn't he?
They liked them, didn't they . . . and so on.

The same lesson can be used for further study. Returning to the original paragraph, we can take up spelling problems connected with suffixing *-ed* (*study, hop, hope* not in the story are sources of some misspelling. Examples of each kind could be the subject of a spelling lesson at this time). Then a new attack can be made on *was/were.* Again, as in the two present tenses, the problem of singular/plural agreement must be recognized and drills provided. A generalization can be made from the text:

> Was it a carrot? It was a carrot.
> Where were the carrots?

Then: *I was, he was, she was, it was . . . we were, you were, they were* are compared.

Then follow exercises to make the choice of subject and verb automatic:

(a) Simple substitution:

TEACHER		CLASS
Repeat after me:	It was there.	It was there.
	He	He was there.
(continuing)	They; we; she; you; I	

(b) TEACHER: It was a carrot.   They were carrots.

Change the sentence according to the last word. Example:

> cat: It was a cat.
> cats: They were cats.

(continue with singular and plural items).

3. THE ASSIGNMENT

The assignment, following extensive class use of past tense forms in meaningful situations, should be considered an additional opportunity to reinforce the matter being taught. Depending on the maturity of the class—for past tense can be taught at all levels and all stages—the assignment can be used to exercise the student's productive ability. For the beginner, make the assignment very specific. Give him a group of related verbs and ask him to tell a little story with them. Or, ask him to write a series of sentences, like the model that you give him: The boy *skipped* (jump, shout, play, hurry, stop). For the intermediate student, in higher levels, give a more general assignment, but don't hesitate to help with examples and models and suggested vocabulary if he needs it. Assignments aren't tests, they are further ways to use the language.

4. BUT WHAT ABOUT FORMAL GRAMMAR?

The rabbit story and its exercises are all very well for younger learners you will say at this point. But when does the student learn *formal grammar?* Whether he is talking about rabbits in Grade 6, or philosophers in a university class, he is learning formal grammar when he learns to control the past tense forms and to correlate these forms with such time expressions as *yesterday, once upon a time,* and all the others.

The rabbit as subject matter was suitable for the younger learner, while the procedures of the lesson can apply to any level and any stage. The story and the verbs at university level may not concern rabbits—they may concern explorers and philosophers. But the noises /t/, /d/, and /əd/ at the end of the verbs still mean *yesterday; did* followed by subject and verb still asks a past time question; and subject followed by *didn't + verb* still makes a past time negative statement. When the speaker uses these devices without resorting to his first language, when he produces statements and questions correlating the time and the forms, he is using formal grammar. If he can make a generalization about all this, he is talking about the formal grammar that we hope he already controls. But the recognition and use of the grammar should precede the talking about it.

The pattern approach to language learning replaces the item by item consideration of the grammar. We may pause to recognize *noun* as concept, after we have been introduced to it through use. We may pause and change some forms from singular to plural. But the nouns must operate in a total structure, in a sentence, in relation to other elements in the sentence. The underlying pattern of the formation of plural must be tied to agreements like these:

> It is a . . . . they are . . . -s; There's a . . . There are . . . -s.
>   (and: was/were; have/has; do/does)
> A thing is . . . . Things are . . . . Boys play ball. A boy enjoys games.

It isn't enough to say that a noun forms its plural by adding -s. We must consider how that -s sounds—/s/, /z/, /əz/—as we considered the past tense endings, /t/, /d/, /əd/. We must consider the whole problem of number—how some nouns select only singular verbs: *news is;* others only plural: *people are.*

Today we consider that there are two ways to "know" grammar. The most important is to have a recognition of the functioning of the language we know how to speak. The structures required to signal various meanings . . . the suffixes on verbs, the suffixes on nouns, must be used in relation to each other. The second is the ability to talk analytically about the language in the terms of descriptive linguistics. This second way of knowing grammar must be deferred until the first has been acquired. The best way to learn formal grammar is to speak English well and meaningfully. If you can use English sentences effectively, you control the formal grammar of the language. When you need to stop and talk about the language, you can do so more effectively if you draw on your actual conversation and make generalizations from it. In brief, control and accurate production of the language mean knowing the formal grammar. Unfortunately, examinations do take place, and the terminology of these does not always match the linguistic descriptions of the language. But if the examination expects the student to underline nouns and verbs in a sentence, surely he can do that, if he has undergone the processes described here. If the examination calls for "choosing the correct form," he should be able to do that, if he knows the grammar by speaking the language accurately. If he is asked to re-write a sentence to make it correct, he should be able to do it. If, however, examinations call for parsing or defining in older terms, we will simply have to change the examinations.

5. THE GRAMMAR LESSON FOLLOWS CERTAIN STAGES

The first [stage] consists of presenting the problem to be taught. There are several ways in which this can be done.

1. The Analytical Presentation. The grammar book with a rule followed by a sentence or two of illustration, and followed by some exercises to write is familiar to us all. Some text books in the newer tradition of language learning retain some of the features of that approach. Such text books are not suitable for young learners. They can be used by adults who wish to be aware of the bony structure of the language they are trying to master. The present day language text that offers an analytical approach usually does so by selecting one or two "key" sentences that illustrate the problem to be mastered. These are put in a frame showing the different divisions of the sentence. The sentences are repeated. Then a generalization follows, and exercises of various kinds follow the generalization to ensure mastery of the sentence in question.

The procedure is still that of language learning—hearing, repeating, and mastering. It is well suited for the kind of mature student in a hurry to review the structure of the language. But it has the serious drawback of providing sentences that are not easily transferred to normal everyday conversation. Although the drills have the classes talking about small experiences (I wash my face every day), there is rarely sufficient challenge in the material of the lesson to stimulate the language learner to thorough and enthusiastic control.

2. The Contextual Presentation. Other textbook writers believe that the language experience should precede analysis, and that the language should be related to the realities of the student's life. The dialogue or two-part conversation is the basis of many context presentations. It has many advantages. When two people talk to each other, they use language in several of its basic forms. They ask questions and answer briefly. They do not harangue one another, but rather exchange pertinent information. Dialogues can not only present a grammar point, they can reveal social attitudes and facts about the background of the users of this language. Dialogues are good, too, for pronunciation control.

A disadvantage of this form is that it is not always possible to control the language completely if the dialogue is to sound natural. While this is not serious in intermediate or advanced learning situations, it is a difficulty in materials for beginners. The beginner should not have to be burdened with language matters he will use once and not soon again, nor should he be bewildered by variant forms of the same structure. (Far too many texts give both forms of the negative in the same lesson [*he isn't* and *he is not*] making no distinction between them). Unnecessary confusion has resulted from that kind of thing. A third disadvantage is that a dialogue is somewhat like the lines in a play. Each depends on a set response. For if as student A in a dialogue with student B, you ask a question, student B will respond with the right memorized response. If, outside the classroom, you ask Neighbor B the same question, you may get a wrong answer and the dialogue will grind to a stop. There is no cut and dried response to any question.

But these difficulties to one side, the dialogue is an excellent way to acquire a lively section of the language and master it. Exercises stemming from the dialogue give it some adaptability to new situations. Contextual presentations vary according to the preference of the writer of the materials. The story about the rabbit happens to be the kind of context I like to use to present a grammar problem. The questions that follow check comprehension, and give the students a chance to use the language before they talk about it. This approach works for adults as well as for children, and the introductory material may be a short paragraph, an anecdote from a publication, or a longer context. The longer context— perhaps an article in the newspaper, or in a textbook accessible to all the students—will not be entirely controlled. However a single sentence from the context can be pulled out and imitated as well as analyzed.

The purpose of all these presentations is to provide an experience in the use of the language first. Realization of the way in which the language operates follows its use. It is far more important to speak the language and communicate with it, than to talk about it. All of us reading that familiar sentence will nod, but how many of us in our classes follow that precept? How many of us have a guilty feeling that if we don't tie up the grammar with a neat rule, they'll never never learn it? To overcome that deep-seated attitude, which we all share, remember how you learned your first language. You did not sit in the corner memorizing rules. You went out in the sun and played with your friends and learned from them and taught them, as you summoned up those noises you needed to get on with the game of the moment. Analysis of the language, talking about it is all right after we are able to speak it well enough to have some curiosity about its behavior.

The first step in the lesson on past tense was, you will remember, hearing a story or a conversation or a key sentence spoken by the teacher. The next step was imitating the teacher. The third step for some kinds of material is repetition of them until they are mastered. This is especially true of material introduced in a dialogue. I am talking here about the kind of lesson represented by the rabbit story in this article.

The class listens to the teacher, repeats after the teacher. The class hears questions and repeats them. The class answers each question using the sentences from the story. When they are able to use these sentences without help from the text or from the teacher, they are ready for the generalization about them. Remember that the generalization isn't necessary for young learners, and for older learners it should be postponed until the class is sure of the introductory sentences. The story of the rabbit was followed by some statements about the pronunciation of past tense endings, the past tense question and negative signals (*did, didn't*). There was no mention of action or state of being, but the focus of attention was on the shape and function of this entity recognized as a verb.

After the generalization, we come to a stage that is sometimes labelled "pattern practice." This practice consists of drills to provide sufficient repetition of the structure to be learned to ensure control of it. The possible devices for providing this practice are described here. Let me say very emphatically that merely repeating one word or one sentence over and over again is not one of them. The word *drill* may recall long hours at the piano or on the parade ground to some of us. Drill in language learning situations should not consist of doing the same thing over and over. Variety is possible and desirable, as the activities described here will show.

Let us consider some of the aids to mastery of the grammar of English.

1. Hearing Activity

   A. Listening to the structure to be mastered either analytically or contextually (i.e., hearing the story of the rabbit).

   B. Hearing minimal pairs of sentences revealing a grammatical fact: Example 1: the meaning of the sound on the end of verbs in terms of time:

TEACHER	CLASS
The boy walks fast.	every day
The boy walked fast.	yesterday

(More advanced classes should respond: *he does; does he?* or *he did; did he?*)

Example 2: the meaning of the sounds /s/, /z/, and /əz/ when they occur on the verb, compared to their meaning when they occur on the noun:

TEACHER	CLASS
The boy studies. How many?	one
The boys study. How many?	two

(More advanced classes should respond: *he does,* or *they do; does he?* or *do they?*)

Comment: A certain amount of practice on hearing and responding to the *sounds* that mean singular/plural or time shifts is useful to speakers of many different language backgrounds. Many Oriental languages, for example, use a particle preceding the noun to express plural, or a particle following the verb that never changes its form to express time or aspect. With the language habits implied by these devices, the learner must be led to *hear* what is going on in English. If his language has no final consonant clusters, he must learn to hear those significant noises that tell time and number in English.

2. Producing the Language: Preliminary Activity

A. Basic activity: Imitation of the teacher and repetition after him of the introductory material. He models all new material and expects the class to imitate it. Guessing the answer does not belong in language learning. *Nothing should be assigned in advance to be studied for the first time.* Homework should be based on what was first presented and practiced in class.

B. Response to questions that force the particular grammar structure. The questions following the story of the rabbit tested comprehension of the material that the class had listened to and repeated. They afforded an opportunity for the learner to make statements using the structure to be mastered. This sequence of questions has been suggested to elicit a gradually increasing amount of language:

(1) Questions that can be answered *yes* or *no.* Answers of this type demand correlation with the subject and verb of the question. *Does X do something? Yes, he does,* or no, *he doesn't.*

(2) "or" questions offering a choice of answers: Does X do this or that? He does that. This question forces a complete statement in answer, and it gives clues in the question as to what the answer will consist of.

(3) *What, where, when, who, how* information questions (sometimes called *thought provoking*) will bring out fully structured answers if the material under discussion has been thoroughly understood.

Comment: At first glance, the questions following a text may seem very obvious and easy. Remember that the questions have been carefully constructed to give practice in producing certain language relationships and to lead the student into using controlled language at a time when he must master that particular segment of the language.

3. Producing the language: Pattern Practice drills and devices

A. *Substitution*

(1) Any drill involving replacing or changing the form of a part of the sentence, without re-arranging the word order of the sentence may be considered a substitution drill.

(2) Substitution drills are of three kinds: simple, replacement, and conditioned form changes.

a. Simple substitution:

The teacher sets a model sentence which the class repeats. The teacher suggests a replacement for one item in the sentence. The class repeats the model sentence, replacing one item as suggested.

Example: Model sentence: He ate his lunch yesterday.
    Substitution:

breakfast	He ate his breakfast yesterday.
dinner	He ate his dinner yesterday.

In this exercise, all the student has to do is to put a different item in the same place in the sentence. This exercise would be useful for teaching him to associate the names of meals with the verb "ate." The class is also practicing, unconsciously, the correlation of time "yesterday" and the past form "ate."

b. Replacement substitution:

Example: Model sentence: He ate his lunch yesterday.
    Substitution:

she	*She* ate *her* lunch yesterday.
dinner	She ate her *dinner* yesterday.
they	*They* ate *their* dinner yesterday.

This exercise demands a replacement in more than one part of the sentence. When the subject changes from "he" to "she" or to "they," the possessive pronoun must also change. When "dinner" replaces "lunch," attention shifts to that part of the sentence, while the student keeps all the other elements in place.

Other possibilities of this exercise:

(i) Time substitutes:

	They ate their dinner yesterday.
now	They're eating their dinner now.
every day	They eat their dinner every day.

(ii) Number:

(a). Single word changes:

(singular to plural)	a cat . . . cats
	a man . . . men
(plural to singular)	men . . . a man
	mice . . . a mouse
(zero to -s)	I walk . . . he walks
	I run . . . he runs
	I watch . . . he watches
(general to specific)	a book . . . the book on the table

(b). Subject-verb agreement:

(forms of be)	They're eating now.
he	He's eating now
I	I'm eating now.

(and so on; include was/were)

(do/does in question)	Do they eat here every day?
we	Do we eat here every day?
he	Does he eat here every day?
she	Does she eat here every day?
people	Do people eat here every day?

(c). Number agreement in the complement:

	They are friends.
he	He's a friend.
	I see this book.
books	I see these books.
pencil	I see this pencil.
pencils	I see these pencils.
this	I see this pencil.
book	I see this book.
books	I see these books.
those	I see those books.
that	I see that book.
pencil	I see that pencil.
pencils	I see those pencils.

(d). Replacement of several parts of the sentence:

	He gave the boys some food.
them	He gave them some food.
sent	He sent them some food.
to them	He sent some food to them.
to us	He sent some food to us.
passed	He passed some food to us.
us	He passed us some food.

This drill makes heavy demands on the alertness of the student, and helps him to order sentences according to their relationships. It is a drill for adults, to be used sparingly, as it can easily become mechanical and meaningless language manipulation. Young children should *not* be asked to do this kind of drilling. And adults should not be expected to stop there. They need to go on to communication.

B. *Transformation drills*

(1) Any drill involving change in the word order of a sentence is considered a transformation drill.

(2) Transformation drills vary in length and complexity.

　　a. Single constructions causing change

| (me . . . to me) | He gave me a book. |
| to me | He gave a book to me. |

(always; never)	I'm always late.
never	I'm never late.
work	I never work late.
he	He never works late.
is	He's never late.

　　b. Total sentence changes

statement to question:	He goes there: Does he go there?
question to statement:	Did he see them?: Yes, he saw them.
question to command:	Did you tell him?: Tell him.
included question:	What did he do? Do you know?
	Do you know what he did?

　　c. Time substitution in three basic kinds of sentences: statement, question, negative statement.

We go to school every day.
Do you eat lunch at home?
Yes, we don't have lunch at school.

There are two ways to proceed:

(1—one sentence at a time)

now	We're going to school now.
yesterday	We went to school yesterday.
tomorrow	We're going to go to school tomorrow.
since June	We've gone to school since last June.

now	Are you eating lunch at home now?
yesterday	Did you eat lunch at home yesterday?
tomorrow	Are you going to eat lunch at home tomorrow?
since June	Have you eaten lunch at home since June?

now	We aren't having lunch at school.
yesterday	We didn't have lunch at school yesterday.
tomorrow	We aren't going to have lunch at school tomorrow.
since June	We haven't had lunch at school since June.

(2—the three sentences together)

now	We're going to school now.
	Are you eating lunch at home now?
	Yes. We aren't eating at school.

(and so on through the time signals)

The advantage of this drill is that it includes the auxiliaries needed for questions and negatives, and gives a more complete review of tense changes than a series of statements would do.

(3—total sentence changes)

. . .

. . .

This child is happier than that one.
These children are happier than those.

Comment: Strictly speaking, exercise three is substitution rather than transformation. However, the whole sentence undergoes a change in this. The title of the exercise isn't important. What is important is that a total sentence has many small relationships that must change when the problem of singular-plural is introduced. The ability to handle this kind of transformation will ensure control of many of the more troublesome problems of number.

C. *Completion drills*

(1) Any drill requiring conditioned production of a part of a sentence in order to make it complete.
(2) The addition of elements tied to the rest of the sentence by requirements of number, time, word order make up these drills:

a. Simple addition

	I want to go.
you	I want *you* to go.

	Do you want to tell me?
what	*What* do you want to tell me?
why	*Why* do you want to tell me?

b. Lexical choice

(because, although)   I went to the dance. . . . I had a fever.

I had a new dress.

c. Verb-subject correlations

> John smiles, and I . . . (do, too)
> John smiles, and Mary . . . (does, too)
> John swims, but Mary . . . (doesn't)
> John doesn't dive, and Mary . . . (doesn't either)

Comment: This exercise has infinite possibilities. By changing the tenses and the subject the drill can continue through the verb and pronoun systems. The (too–either) contrast is a particular problem, as is the use of substitute verbs (do, does, did).

> He's a student . . . (isn't he?)
> This is yours . . . (isn't it?)
> They used to live here . . . (didn't they?)
> She doesn't have to do that . . . (does she?)

Comment: The "tag question" has a number of teaching points:

(i) The verb of the tag must be the same tense and number as the verb in the statement.

> he is . . . isn't he?
> he goes . . . doesn't he?

(ii) The subject of the tag must always be a personal pronoun.

> *That's* a new dress, isn't *it.*

(iii) In the most common pattern, if the statement is affirmative, the tag is negative; if the statement is negative, the tag is affirmative.

(iv) The response is tied to the statement . . . not to the tag. (Particularly confusing for speakers of several Oriental languages)

> He's here, isn't he. . . .   Yes, he is.
> He didn't go, did he. . . .   No, he didn't.

(v) If the tag ends in a rising contour, it is probably a genuine question implying uncertainty on the part of the questioner.

> If it ends in a rising-falling intonation contour, the speaker probably expects agreement and is just politely including the listener in his comments.

D. *Conditioned Response*

(1) Any drill calling for answers that are controlled by the possibilities of the question can be considered a conditioned response drill.

(2) They range from relatively restricted to relatively free.

a. Answers to questions based on context:

"yes"/"no"   Did the rabbit go out? Yes, he did.
              Did he smell a carrot or eat one?
"or"   He smelled it.
"where"   Where did he go? Along the path.

b. Cued responses:

Tell us what the rabbit did first.   He sniffed the air.
Ask Fely what the rabbit did.   What did the rabbit do, Fely?
                                      He sniffed the air.

c. Controlled "conversation" to elicit various structures:

(i) Modal auxiliaries:

What *can* a cat do that a dog *can't* do?   It *can* climb a tree.
Which would you rather do: eat or
sleep?   I'd *rather* sleep.
Should men be polite to women?
Should women be polite to men?

(ii) The -s form of the present:

I know a man who does some things well.
    He sings.
    He plays golf.
But he doesn't do everything well:
    He sings, but he doesn't dance well.
    He plays golf, but he doesn't play tennis.

continue with:

He drives a car, but . . .
He raises pigeons, but . . .
What else does he do?
What are the things he doesn't do?

(This exercise illustrates the principle of gradual release of control of the material until the student is producing his own sentences modeled on the earlier ones.)

(3) [They] encourage freer production.

Ask Mr. X what he did yesterday.
What did you do, Mr. X?
Tell Miss Y what you saw.

define sentences.

He teaches . . . what is he?
    He's a teacher.
He's a teacher . . . what does he do?
    He teaches.

What is a shoe store?
    A shoe store is one that sells shoes.
A store that sells shoes is a . . . shoe store.

(speak slowly)
I like girls who . . . speak slowly.
I like a girl who . . . speaks slowly.

These drills were suggested by Harold King in *English Language Teaching*, Vol. XIV, No. 1, p. 17. He calls them substitution-concordance drills.

The *letter* was there, but nobody noticed *it*.
I was there, but nobody noticed *me*.

or

They're *doing* the same thing they *did* yesterday.
They're *buying* the same thing, they *bought*.

and

Why doesn't Mr. White play something for us?
He forgot to bring his music with *him*.

Why don't the children play something for us?
They forgot to bring their music with *them*.

CONCLUSION

The drills described on these pages are merely *devices* to help provide oral/aural practice necessary for acquiring grammatical mastery. They serve to replace the activities of former days in which we recited rules and wrote out a series of unrelated sentences.

Who can benefit from these exercises? Are they all equally good for the language learner of any age at all levels of language learning? No, they are not.

The young child, pre-school or in the early elementary grades does not benefit from the language manipulation demanded by many of these drills. This young learner needs to hear the story or take part in the dialogue suited to his age and interests. He needs to imitate the sentences, play the roles suggested, and apply the sentences to new situations provided by the teacher.

The older learner in the upper grades of elementary school or in junior high school can use some, but not all, of these devices. He too needs the story or dialogue. In addition, he can respond to questions about introductory material and consider generalizations about the grammar under study. Substitution, conversion, completion exercises from explicitly stated models should be possible, and gradually "de-controlled" conversation a desirable possibility.

High school, college, and adult learners generally can do all the foregoing and can include "controlled conversation" activities which allow more freedom of choice. Written assignments following each lesson can further reinforce the oral practice. Composition topics can and should force the use of structures under consideration. Guided composition, suggested vocabulary, sentence clues can also be furnished as aids to the less fluent adult learner.

Our aims and procedures are focused on *oral* mastery, on acquiring the ability to use the sentences of the new language without having to stop and translate from the first language. We begin to ensure this control by controlling the speech of the learner. We model for him, and he repeats after us. Then step by step, we release our control of him and push him further into using language, accurately, fluently, without conscious effort, in order to communicate with others, an end which is the ultimate purpose of all language teaching worth doing.

LEARNING SYNTACTICAL PATTERNS

ROBERT L. POLITZER

In our discussion of learning vocabulary we did not include consideration of the function words. . . . These words are part of the syntactical pattern and function only partly in conveying *word meaning.* Their main function is to convey *grammatical meaning,* in other words to show how the units of the sentence are related or to which word classes the words belong. What in English is represented by function words is in many languages represented by grammatical endings. English itself has at least one grammatical ending that can be equated with a function word, namely the *s* of the possessive function of the noun: My father's garden = the garden of my father.

One good way of demonstrating the operation of function words and the grammatical meanings they convey is to apply grammatical structure to nonsense syllables. . . . These nonsense syllables . . . become "words" simply because we treat them as such from the grammatical point of view. A favorite example among linguists for the demonstration of grammatical function in isolation is Lewis Carrol's poem "Jabberwocky" in *Through the Looking Glass:*

(A)   (B) (C)
'Twas *brillig* and the *slithy toves*
(D)   (E)   (F)
Did *gyre* and *gimble* in the *wabe;*
(G)   (H)
All *mimsy* were the *borogoves,*
(I) (J) (K)
And the *mome raths outgrabe.*

The italicized words of the poem are "non-sense" words. They are held together by function words and grammatical patterning. The nonsense words tell a story—a story told by grammatical meaning alone without the help of lexical meaning. If we look at the nonsense words, one after the other, we see that the spot of (A) could be filled by either a noun or an adjective (*'Twas summer, 'Twas peaceful,* etc.). However (C) is unam-

133

biguously a noun because of the preceding *the* and the *did* that follows. (B), because of its position before the noun and its ending (*y*), is clearly marked as an adjective. (D) and (E) are felt as verbs because of the preceding *did*. (F), preceded by the unambiguous noun marker *the*, must be a noun. In the third line the plural function verb *were* and the plural marker *s* at the end of (H) indicate that this word, preceded by *the*, must be a plural noun and subject of the sentence; (G), not marked as a plural and ending in a derivational morpheme used for adjectives, is immediately classified as such. In the last line you probably interpreted (J) as a plural noun, subject of the sentence. Because of the English rule of position of adjectives, this would immediately make (I) an adjective and (K) a verb [probably an irregular verb in the past—the rest of the "story" is in the past, cf. *were* (line 3), *was* (line 1), and *outgrabe* sounds like the past of a verb *outgribe; give/gave, outgribe/outgrabe*— why not?]. Note, however, that the last line could be interpreted differently: e.g., if (I) is a noun, then (J) could also be a noun, but the object of the verb (K). This possibility is somewhat farfetched, but in a poem it is conceivable to have that kind of word order: *The mome raths outgrabe—the ruler peace proclaimed* (instead of the *ruler proclaimed peace*). Of course if our English vocabulary only included either the word *mome* or *raths*, the ambiguity would be resolved.

Poems like Carroll's "Jabberwocky" underline the tremendous importance of being able to recognize structural signals and grammatical patterns. Your ability to comprehend the spoken or written form of *any* language (including your own) depends largely on the quick "deciphering" of the signals that carry the structural meaning. In your native language you have the ability to comprehend these signals instantly in their spoken form. When it comes to reading, you should have the ability to understand the written counterparts of those structural signals almost as rapidly as if they had come to you through speech. A person who does not will probably be a slow reader and have difficulty assimilating materials rapidly.

We have shown in the analysis of "Jabberwocky" how the recognition of the structural signal goes a long way in helping us to make sense out of what would otherwise be just a complete garble of nonsense syllables. This same process is characteristic of the comprehension of real language just as it is of the "comprehension" of nonsense words. Once you have acquired a knowledge of structure and a limited vocabulary, you can use this knowledge to help you to understand new words and to comprehend sentences that are—partially at least—made up of unknown words. As a matter of fact, this process of starting with a limited vocabulary and a knowledge of grammatical structure and using these initial assets for increasing your ability in the language is precisely the same process that you have used (and should use) in your native language. You increase your English vocabulary and your sensitivity to English structure and usage by a great deal of reading. Note also that in this process you will usually not go to the dictionary to look up the meaning of words. This looking up—while necessary and advisable in some cases—could be overdone and slow up your reading to the point where it would most certainly become unenjoyable. In fact you learn most words simply by meeting and becoming acquainted with them. Most of the time you don't remember how you learned new words and you are not even conscious of learning them. You absorb their meaning because of two important helps at your disposal: (1) a general knowledge of the context, the situation in which the words are used, and (2) the knowledge of the grammatical structure in which the words are used. This grammatical structure not only supplies part of the meaning, it also helps to define the words grammatically.

Even if your goal in foreign language learning is to acquire a reading knowledge, it is thus very important that you learn to understand the structural signals quickly and easily. In most situations (1) a knowledge of structure, (2) knowledge of "vocabulary" (i.e., knowledge of the words carrying lexical meaning), and (3) knowledge of the general context or situation in which language is used will combine and interact to convey the meaning of what is being expressed. Sometimes knowledge in one or two of these areas can be used to make up for lack of knowledge in the others. Thus people who know the technical vocabulary of their field of specialization (e.g., mathematics, chemistry, economics) in a foreign language are sometimes able to read technical materials in the foreign language even if their knowledge of the grammar is very poor. In a sense they are doing the exact reverse of what you as a native speaker of English could do with "Jabberwocky": they know the meaning of the words that have lexical significance and use the lexical meaning to supply the grammatical meaning (which for them, since they do not know the grammar, is made up of nonsense words and syllables like *the, will, -s, -y, may*, etc., and perhaps a strange and therefore meaningless word order). The writer of this book has heard of at least one case where knowledge of the general context or situation was used to make up for all the factors that normally interact to supply meaning. The experiment that the Russian scientist Pavlov performed with his dog is very well known and is described in most elementary textbooks of psychology. A graduate student, who had little or no knowledge of French was asked to give an English summary of a French text for his reading examination in French. In the French text he recognized the name Pavlov, and the word *chien* (dog). He passed the examination. Yet the instances in which you can rely on context, situation, and knowledge of vocabulary to make up for the lack of an understanding of structure will normally be few and limited. Situations are unpredictable and the vocabulary of a language is vast. Only structure and grammar are limited and finite. In other words, in most instances in which you want to understand the foreign language you will not be able to get along without the help that comes from structure and grammar, and—just as in your native language —you will most likely have to use it to fill the *lacunae* that exist in your knowledge of the vocabulary items. (Did you grasp the meaning of the italicized word from the context?)

When it comes to speaking the language, the necessity for the control of structure is obvious. We have already stressed the idea that probably the best way of speaking a foreign language is to remember sentences in the language and to convert them into what you want to say. In order to go through this conversion process, you must have some idea of the structure of grammar of the foreign language. This does not mean that you must necessarily be able to analyze a sentence and identify parts of speech, but it does mean that you must know what part of a sentence that you have learned is basic to the structure and what is a replaceable vocabulary item.

Assume for a moment that you are teaching English to a foreign student who, because of interference coming from his native language, says sentences like: *I have Charles recently seen, I have him the book given,* etc. Wouldn't it be a good idea to have him *say* and *remember* many sentences like *I have seen Charles recently, I have given him the book,* and at the same time get across the idea that he can use these sentences as models to form many others of the same grammatical construction? For the purpose of giving this kind of practice and creating the realization of "model" and "pattern," we use the so-called substitution exercises that are found in many grammars. The pupil is given a sentence, e.g., *I have not given him the money,* and the teacher shows, first by example, how this sentence can be changed by varying the words carrying lexical meaning without changing the grammatical construction:

I have not given him the money.	The teacher then says:
you and models the answer	*You have not given him the money.*
sent "	*You have not sent him the money.*
her "	*You have not sent her the money.*
letter "	*You have not sent her the letter.*

Once the pupil has observed and repeated after the teacher, he will provide the answer himself if he gets the substitution word as a cue. For example, let us assume that you are learning English as a foreign language. Your base sentence is *We did not understand this idea.*

The teacher says *you;* you respond: *You did not understand this idea.*
"   "   *study;*   "   "   *You did not study this idea.*
"   "   *problem;*   "   "   *You did not study this problem.*

and so on.

This procedure would not only give you practice in saying these sentences, but more importantly, the next time you had to say *We did not understand this book,* or *We did not find the book,* you would probably remember the sentence that you had practiced and convert it into the sentence that you wanted to say, by the very substitution procedure that was part of your practice session. It is for this reason that it is very important that you do not go through the substitution procedure mechanically, but try to associate each sentence with a situation in which it could possibly be used. If you don't do this, the sentences will probably not suggest themselves again as possible responses or as models for possible responses.

Let us assume once more that we are teaching English to a foreign student who can very accurately say sentences like: *I speak English and I understand you very well.* But when it comes to the negative, he says *I not speak English, I not understand you.* We can at least interpret his difficulty as due to the fact that he does not know how to make positive sentences negative, most likely because his native language does it differently. So we want to give this student practice in the correct way to make positive sentences negative. Not only will this kind of practice force him to say a lot of correct negative sentences, but it will also show him how to make up negative sentences if and when he must do so on his own. So we have our student practice an exercise that consists of transforming sentences like *I speak English* to *I don't speak English.* After this procedure has been modeled by the teacher, the positive sentences serve merely as cues. Putting yourself now into the student's situation, what will be your response if the teacher says:

I follow your advice. You will say: *I don't follow your advice.*
I write poetry.   "   "   "   *I don't write poetry.*
I love Joan.   "   "   "   *I don't love Joan.*

and so on.

The procedure and goal of foreign language learning is then simply the following: *to have at your disposal an ever-growing stock of model sentences associated with specific situations that you can transform into what you want to say by a limited number of substitution and transformation procedures that you learn to perform at ever-increasing speed.*

Just what are the substitution and transformation procedures involved? Of course they will vary according to the foreign language involved, but we can give a general classification from the point of view of English—a classification that will be applicable to most of the languages you are likely to study. This means that the categories that we mention will be usable, although the operations involved will take various and different forms.

The ways of creating new sentences out of old ones involve first of all a series of operations which we might classify as:

A. REPLACEMENT PROCEDURES

When you use a replacement operation, you do not change the basic structure of the model sentence, but simply replace one element by another identical element. The most important replacement procedures are:

(1) *Noun replacement:* Simply substitute one noun for another:

> The *child* came late. ⟶ The *boy* came late.
> I saw the *man.* ⟶ I saw the *dog.*

(2) *Pronoun replacement:* Replace a noun by a pronoun or a pronoun by another pronoun:

> I saw *the man.* ⟶ I saw *him.*
> *We* saw the man. ⟶ *They* saw the man.

In English, at least, the pronoun merely takes the place of the noun in practically all cases without further change of structure. (The notable exception occurs with certain two-part verbs that require a change in word order, e.g., *I called up MY FRIEND,* but *I called HIM up.*) Thus this category is for English merely a subdivision of the preceding category, and truly a mere replacement operation. In many foreign languages this may not be the case. The pronoun may, for instance, take a different position in the sentence than the one occupied by the noun. In that case it would be technically more correct to speak of a pronoun *transformation* than of a pronoun *replacement.*

(3) *Verb replacement:* Replace one verb by another:

> Charles *sees* the boy. ⟶ Charles *knows* the boy.
> Robert will *follow* orders. ⟶ Robert will *understand* orders.

(4) *Adjective replacement:* Replace one adjective by another:

> My *good* friend knows the answer. ⟶ My *old* friend knows the answer.
> Charles is *lazy.* ⟶ Charles is *intelligent.*

(5) *Adverb replacement:* Replacement of one adverb by another:

Robert works *continuously*. ⎯⎯⎯⎯→ Robert works *slowly*.
Charles arrived *late this morning*. ⎯→ Charles arrived *early last night*.

Slightly more complicated are the operations that we might call:

B. BASIC EXPANSION OPERATIONS

In these operations you do change the structure of the original sentence somewhat by adding to or expanding one of its original elements. The most important basic expansion operations are:

(6) *Verb expansion:* By this operation we understand simply what the name says, making the verb bigger. For English this would involve . . . (a) replacing the simple form of the verb by have (had) + past participle; (b) putting an auxiliary verb (function word) before the verb; or (c) replacing the verb by the progressive tense (be + -ing form):

Robert *works* all the time. ⎯→ Robert *has worked* all the time.
Robert *works* all the time. ⎯→ Robert *should work* all the time.
Robert *works* all the time. ⎯→ Robert *is working* all the time.
Robert ought to *work*. ⎯⎯⎯⎯→ Robert ought to *have worked*.

(7) *Adverbial expansion:* This involves adding to the verb part of the sentence by adding an adverb or adding to an already existing adverb:

Charles *sings*. ⎯⎯⎯⎯⎯→ Charles sings *beautifully*.
Charles sings *every day*. ⎯→ Charles sings *beautifully every day*.

(8) *Noun expansion:* This operation involves adding to the noun by various means; the most common are by using (additional) modifying adjectives or by prepositional expressions (preposition type function word + noun):

My *friend* is here. ⎯⎯⎯⎯→ My *good friend* is here.
I know that *old man*. ⎯⎯⎯→ I know that *good, wise old man*.
The *boy* is here. ⎯⎯⎯⎯→ The *boy with the papers* is here.

Note that in English the possessive of the noun can of course be used just like a prepositional expression for expanding another noun:

This pen doesn't write. ⎯⎯→ My *aunt's pen* doesn't write.
The *leg* is broken. ⎯⎯⎯→ The *dog's leg* is broken.
The *leg* is broken. ⎯⎯⎯→ The *leg of the chair* is broken.

Another way in which nouns can be expanded in English is by the use of another noun as modifier:

The *bottle* is on the *table*. ⎯→ The *milk bottle* is on the *coffee* table.

The next group of important changes are the ones that we might call:

C. SIMPLE TRANSFORMATIONS

These changes involve not just a replacement or expansion of the existing grammatical structure, but a change in the structure itself. The most important of these simple transformations are:

(9)   *Change in verb form:* This means replacing the verb form by another. We consider this operation, because of its importance in speaking the language, as a special operation of the transformation type. Notice, however, that from the point of view of English (and many other languages) the change involved is a morphological one rather than a change in the structure of the sentence.

> I *speak* to Charles. ⟶ I *spoke* to Charles.
> We *know* the answer. ⟶ We *knew* the answer.

Note also that within our classification and for the purpose of discussing English grammar we have classified changes like *I speak English* ⟶ *I can speak English* ⟶ *I have spoken English* ⟶ *I am going to speak English* as verb expansion rather than change in verb form.

(10)   *The negative transformation:* This involves making a positive statement negative:

> Charles *understands* me. ⟶ Charles *doesn't* understand me.
> Charles *can* write. ⟶ Charles *cannot* write.

(11)   *The interrogative transformation:* Making a statement into a question:

> Charles understands me. ⟶ *Does* Charles understand me?
> Charles can write. ⟶ *Can* Charles write?

Note that very often in actual practice the interrogative transformation is accompanied by the use of a question word or other function word replacing a noun (or pronoun) in the sentence:

> Charles understands me. ⟶ *Why* does Charles understand me?
> ⟶ *Whom* does Charles understand?
> ⟶ *Who* understands me?

(12)   *The passive transformation:* In English this is accompanied by replacing the verb by the corresponding form of *be* plus the past participle of the main verb, and putting the object in subject position:

> 1   2   3   3   2   1
> The man *beats* the boy. ⟶ The boy *is beaten* by the man.
> The detective *followed* the man. ⟶ The man *was followed* by the detective.

The most complicated of the sentence creation procedures are the ones that we shall call:

D. SUBORDINATE CLAUSE OPERATIONS

These might also be called the "replacement-transformation" procedures, since what is involved in using the subordinate clause is a transformation as well as a replacement. First of all, we can think of a
subordinate clause as a main clause that has been transformed or changed
into a subordinate one, and secondly, the clause is used either to replace
a noun, or to take the place of an adverb or a noun modifier. At least
we can assume that it fits into the place that might have been occupied
by one of these. To give an example, we take the sentence *He has told
the truth* and transform it into a subordinate clause→*that he has told the
truth.* Then we take this clause and fit it, so to speak, into the sentence
I know this fact by replacing the noun (and its modifier) *this fact* by that
clause. Result: *I know that he has told the truth.* The above is an example of a *noun clause.* Other examples would be:

(13)   *Noun clause expansion:*

(a)   This is true ⟶ *that this is true*
       [*the truth*] is obvious ⟶ *That this is true* is obvious.
(b)   We understand his objection ⟶ *that we understand his objection*

       I doubt [our understanding] ⟶ I doubt *that we understand his
                                                         objection.*

(14)   *Adverbial clause expansion:* In this procedure a sentence is transformed into an adverbial clause and then fitted into the place of an adverbial modifier.

The moon was shining ⟶ *while the moon was shining.*
Charles worked [late] ⟶ Charles worked *while the moon was shining.*
We answered without thinking ⟶ *because we answered without think-
                                                ing.*
Robert was upset [by our answer] ⟶ Robert was upset *because we
                                                answered without thinking.*

(15)   *Relative (adjectival) clause expansion:* Here the subordinate clause
is fitted into the place that could have been occupied by a noun modifier:

Charles is my good old friend ⟶ *who is my good old friend*
[Good old] Charles didn't come ⟶ Charles, *who is my good old friend,*
                                                didn't come.
Jack's work is not very accurate ⟶ *whose work is not very accurate*
[lazy] Jack didn't win any prize ⟶ Jack, *whose work is not very ac-
                                                curate,* didn't win any prize.

To review the procedure that we have just described, let us take some
simple sentences and perform on them the "sentence creation" operations
that we have outlined. Let us perform the simple replacement operations

(in succession) on the sentence *The boys understand this difficult problem quite well.*

1. The *students* understand this difficult problem quite well.
2. *We*   understand this difficult problem quite well.
3. We   *grasp*   this difficult problem quite well.
4. We   grasp   this *complicated* problem quite well.
5. We   grasp   this complicated problem *very easily.*

Now let us try the simple expansion operations (in succession) on the sentence *We understand the question.*

6. We *may understand* the question.
7. We may understand the question *very easily.*
8. We may understand *our teacher's* question very easily.

We can try the transformation operations in succession on the sentence *He understands the answer.*

9. He *understood* the answer.
10. He *didn't* understand the answer.
11. (Why) didn't he understand the answer?
12. (Why) wasn't the answer understood by him?

Finally let us take the sentence *He knows English grammar* and try to transform it into a subordinate clause to be fitted into various positions in the sentence: *Charles understands everything clearly.* In other words, let us transform the subordinate clause in such a way that it can be used (1) in place of the subject noun, (2) in place of the object noun, (3) as an adverbial modifier, (4) as an adjectival modifier:

13. (a) Whoever knows English grammar understands everything clearly.
    (b) Charles understands clearly that he knows English grammar.

14. Charles understands everything clearly because he knows English grammar.

15. Charles, who knows English grammar, understands everything clearly.

Another way of reviewing the basic operations is to think of them as the operations that you yourself are using—though unconsciously—all the time, even in your native language, in order to express yourself. The only real difference is that in the foreign language these operations—this conversion of known "raw material" into sentences for self-expression—

must, initially at least, be a conscious process. But let us see how it works in the native language.

Someone says *Charles speaks French very well.* And you answer *Yes, but I don't speak it at all.* You can think of this answer as derived from the original statement by the basic operations we have just discussed:

Charles speaks French very well.

(2) *I* speak it very well.
(10) I *don't* speak it very well.
(5) I don't speak it *at all.*

Or another example: *The United States is a powerful country.* Your reaction may be: *I hope that it will always be a powerful and peaceful country.* The steps involved in arriving at your statement would be:

The United States is a powerful country.

(2) *It* is a powerful country.
(6) It *will be* a powerful country.
(7) It will *always* be a powerful country.
(8) It will always be a powerful *and peaceful* country.
(13) I hope *that it will always be a powerful and peaceful country* (i.e., converting the statement into a subordinate clause and fitting it into the sentence "I hope . . .").

We have already stated that in your native language the replacement and transformation operations are rapid, automatic, unconscious. You might think of the way in which you control your native language as a series of such operations performed instantaneously and simultaneously by that wonderful "electronic computer" that operates in the speech areas of your brain. Learning a foreign language means, in the last analysis, teaching this computer the rules that operate in the foreign language, and training it to perform the foreign language operations. The more rapidly, the more easily the computer performs, the more you approach fluency in the foreign language. Once the computer has learned to operate in the foreign language with the same instantaneous, unconscious rapidity that characterizes its function in your native language, then you can truly say that you are speaking the foreign language "like a native."

LEARNING EXERCISES

1. Just to show how much meaning can be supplied from context, and to what extent we can rely on guessing the meaning of words, we have taken at random a text and left out some of the lexical items. See whether you can understand the text anyway, and whether you can

supply the missing items or words that approximate their meaning. (The words omitted from the original text are supplied as answers to the exercise.)

"Of Gottfried von Strassburg we only know that he was ___(1)___ a native of the ___(2)___ for which he is named, that he was not of ___(3)___ family, but well educated and apparently in good ___(4)___ and that he must have died still ___(5)___ young, before 1210. One of the old manuscripts has a ___(6)___, which represents him as a ___(7)___ man with long, curling ___(8)___, but its ___(9)___ cannot be relied upon. He was perhaps a ___(10)___ friend of Hartmann von Aue. It is not known whether he ever ___(11)___ Wolfram von Eschenbach. Gottfried also ___(12)___ the subject of his one ___(13)___, "Tristan," from English and French ___(14)___. It had even been ___(15)___ before him by a German poet, Eilhart von Oberg.

Answer: 1. probably 2. city 3. noble 4. circumstances 5. comparatively 6. portrait 7. young 8. locks 9. authenticity 10. personal 11. met 12. drew 13. epic 14. sources 15. used

2. Apply all of the replacement operations (1–5) in succession to each of the following sentences:

(a) My friend will gladly follow your good advice.
(b) Charles has never understood your complicated explanations.

Sample Answer:

(a) My friend will gladly follow your good advice.

    1. My *son* will gladly follow your good advice.
    2.   *He*   will gladly follow your good advice.
    3.   He   will gladly *seek* your good advice.
    4.   He   will gladly seek your *fine* advice.
    5.   He   will *always* seek your fine advice.

(b) Charles has never understood your complicated explanations.

    1. Charles has never understood your complicated *actions*.
    2.   *He*   has never understood your complicated actions.
    3.   He   has never   *liked*   your complicated actions.
    4.   He   has never liked   your   *strange*   actions.
    5.   He   has *always* liked   your   strange   actions.

3. Apply the expansion operations (6–8) in succession to each of the following sentences:

(a) I know the answer.
(b) The boy may succeed.
(c) We know this man.

Sample Answer:

(a) I know the answer.

    6. I *may* know the answer.
    7. I may *never* know the answer.
    8. I may never know the *whole* answer.

(b) The boy may succeed.

    6. The boy may *have succeeded.*
    7. The boy may have succeeded *brilliantly.*
    8. *My friend's* boy may have succeeded brilliantly.

(c) We know this man.

    6. We *have known* this man.
    7. We have known this man *very well.*
    8. We have known this *fine old* man very well.

4. Apply—again in succession—the transformation operations (9–12) to each of the following sentences:

(a) The farmer kills the duckling.
(b) John understands Mary.
(c) The man cheats the girl.

Answer:

(a) The farmer kills the duckling.

    9. The farmer *killed* the duckling.
    10. The farmer *didn't kill* the duckling.
    11. *Didn't* the farmer *kill the duckling?*
    12. *Wasn't the duckling killed by the farmer?*

(b) John understands Mary.

    9. John *understood* Mary.
    10. John *didn't understand* Mary.
    11. *Didn't* John *understand* Mary?
    12. *Wasn't Mary understood by John?*

(c) The man cheats the girl.

    9. The man *cheated* the girl.
    10. The man *didn't cheat* the girl.
    11. *Didn't* the man *cheat* the girl?
    12. *Wasn't the girl cheated by the man?*

5. Transform each of the following sentences into subordinate clauses and use them in the replacement-transformation procedures (13–15):

(a) This is true.

(b) His son is sick.
(c) He is a conceited fool.

Sample Answer:

(a) This is true.

    13. *I know that* this is true.
    14. *He left because* this is true.
    15. *An answer* that is true *must be accepted.*

(b) His son is sick.

    13. *I realize that* his son is sick.
    14. *He is staying here although* his son is sick.
    15. *Charles, whose* son is sick, *won't come to the meeting.*

(c) He is a conceited fool.

    13. That he is a conceited fool *should be obvious to anybody.*
    14. *She loves him although* he is a conceited fool.
    15. *Charles,* who is a conceited fool, *manages to be quite successful.*

6. The following are a series of "statements" and "reaction statements." See whether you can connect them through the replacement, expansion, and transformation operations:

(a) His father was born in Russia.—(No), I am sure that Charles' father was born in Poland.
(b) Robert speaks French.—He can't even speak English.
(c) I want to go to England.—Some day I may want to go to England too.
(d) Do you want to leave?—No, I'll always want to stay.

Answer:

(a) His father was born in Russia.

    1. His father was born in *Poland.*
    8. *Charles'* father was born in Poland.
    15. *I am sure that* Charles' father was born in Poland.

(b) Robert speaks French.

    1. Robert speaks *English.*
    2. *He* speaks English.
    6. He *can speak* English.
    10. He *cannot* speak English.
    7. He cannot *even* speak English.

(c) I want to go to England.

6. I *may* want to go to England.

7. *Someday* I may want to go to England *too*.

(d) Do you want to leave?

10. (in "reverse"). You want to leave.

2. *I* want to leave.

3. I want to *stay*.

6. I *will* want to stay.

7. I will *always* want to stay.

.   .   .

THE SEQUENCING
OF STRUCTURAL PATTERN DRILLS

CHRISTINA BRATT PAULSTON

INTRODUCTION

There is at present in the field of language learning and teaching a re-examination of many of its basic tenets and assumptions. This paper is an attempt to reexamine the role and function of structural pattern drills in language learning. The first part of the paper seeks to examine the relevant literature pertaining to drills in order to (1) bring together some of the major references for comparison of agreements and disagreements and (2) to consider the implications for language teaching. The second part of the paper proposes a theoretical classification of structural pattern drills, incorporating the implications found relevant, in order to provide a systematic and more efficient working model for the classroom.

PART I
THEORIES OF LANGUAGE LEARNING AND DRILLS

A cursory glance at the literature during the last two decades reveals a consistent concern about drills, their function, construction, and role in language teaching. This concern naturally reflects the assumptions about language learning held by the advocates of the present major approach to teaching foreign languages, the audio-lingual method. Language learning is seen as basically a mechanical system of habit formation, strengthened by reinforcement of the correct response; language is verbal, primarily oral, behavior and as such learned only by inducing the students to "behave."[1] It is not by accident that most of the proponents of this method are, or are trained by, descriptive structural linguists, since, as Croft points out, pattern practice and substitution drills—the very backbone of the original Fries' oral method—developed from techniques

---

[1] A summary of Wilga River's "Table of Content" in *The Psychologist and the Language Teacher* (Chicago: University of Chicago Press, 1964), pp. vii–viii, which examines the major assumptions of the audio-lingual method.

of linguistic field methods.[2] It is interesting to speculate that part of the theoretical foundations of the audio-lingual method was based on a fortuitous, albeit very felicitous, fit between the then major linguistic method of analysis and psychological learning theory.

Scientists tend, as Kaplan has pointed out, to research what they have the instruments to investigate and linguists are no exception. Surely there is a relationship between kinds of linguistic analyses and kinds of drills, in that drills attempt to teach what linguistic analysis reveals of language structure and typically, different linguistic analyses explore different characteristics of language structure. So Moulton as early as 1963 pointed out the relationship between tagmemics and substitution drills, between immediate constituent grammar and expansion drills and between transformation-generative theory and transformation drills.[3] I think this is important to consider in light of the present challenge of the basic tenets of the audio-lingual method. "Linguists have had their share in perpetuating the myth that linguistic behavior is 'habitual' and that a fixed stock of 'patterns' is acquired through practice and used as the basis for analogy. These views could be maintained only as long as grammatical description was sufficiently vague and imprecise."[4]

Chomsky's admonition that "it is the language teacher himself who must validate and refute any specific proposal"[5] would lead, of course, to an empirical rather than a theoretical approach and would open a Pandora's box of problems. It is entirely true that language teaching as a field shows a dearth of controlled experimentation, and as Eugene Briere has pointed out, the primary value of *Language Teaching: A Scientific Approach*[6] lies in specifying all the assumptions in the field that need verification. However, the predictive power of theory would be lost if the language teacher has to validate every new proposal and the result would be an endless ad-hoc list of techniques. What the linguist and the language teacher jointly need to do is to reexamine the theory of language learning and to make changes in the theory according to new data.

[2] Kenneth Croft, "TESL Materials Development," *NAFSA Studies and Papers, English Language Series, No. 11*, ed. K. Croft, p. 45.
[3] William Moulton, "What is Structural Drill?" *Structural Drill and the Language Laboratory*, ed. F. W. Gravit and A. Valdman (The Hague: Mouton, 1963), pp. 11–15.
[4] Noam Chomsky, "Linguistic Theory," *Northeast Conference on the Teaching of Foreign Languages*, ed. Robert G. Mead. Reports of the Working Committees, 1966, p. 44. See also Chomsky's review of Skinner's *Verbal Behavior in Language*, 35 (1959): 26–58; Eric Lenneberg, "The Capacity for Language Acquisition" *The Structure of Language*, ed. J. Fodor and J. Katz (Englewood Cliffs, N.J.: Prentice-Hall, 1964); and Leon A. Jacobovits, "Implications of Recent Psycholinguistic Developments for the Teaching of a Second Language," *Language Learning*, XVIII: 1 and 2 (June, 1968), 89–109.
[5] Chomsky, 45.
[6] Eugene Briere, Review of *Language Teaching: A Scientific Approach*, by Robert Lado, *IJAL*, 31 (1965): 170–78.

AREAS OF CONCORD AND DISAGREEMENT ABOUT DRILLS

There has been relatively little disagreement on the purpose of structural pattern drills when one looks at the literature of the past twenty years. Drills "are undertaken solely for the sake of practice, in order that performance may become habitual and automatic," and "make no pretense of being communication."[7] "The function of drill is to provide sufficient repetition in meaningful context to establish correct habitual responses."[8] "The fact that language operates largely on the basis of habit should be obvious to everyone . . . what is needed is practice that will gradually force the students' attention away from the linguistic problem while forcing them to use language examples that contain the problem. This will engage the habit mechanism and more quickly establish the new habits."[9] Linguists from Fries[10] to Haugen[11] to Moulton[12] have echoed the belief that language learning is habit formation. Obviously we need now to look very closely at how this is reflected in structural pattern drills.

There seems to be disagreement on the degree of meaning necessary in drills and I shall return to this question. There is also disagreement as to the focus of the drill. Lado maintains the view that the student's attention should be forced away from the teaching point and defines pattern practice as "rapid oral drill on problem patterns with attention on something other than the problem itself."[13] Rivers on the basis of a good deal of psychological research[14] states, "If the drill is to be effective, the student must be aware of the crucial element in the operations he is performing."[15] This is certainly an area that needs systematic study with experimental verification of the above assumptions.

There is a great deal of varying practice, if not disagreement, in

[7] Nelson Brooks, *Language and Language Learning* (New York: Harcourt Brace Jovanovich, 1964), p. 146.

[8] J. Donald Bowen, "Appendix: Pedagogy," in R. P. Stockwell, J. D. Bowen, and J. W. Martin, *The Grammatical Structures of English and Spanish* (Chicago: University of Chicago Press, 1965), p. 295.

[9] Robert Lado, *Language Teaching: A Scientific Approach* (New York: McGraw-Hill, 1964), p. 105.

[10] Charles C. Fries, *Teaching and Learning English as a Foreign Language* (Ann Arbor: University of Michigan Press, 1945), pp. 8–9.

[11] Einar Haugen, "New Paths in American Language Teaching," ELEC Publications, III (March, 1959), 23.

[12] Moulton, 5.

[13] Lado, 105. See also, Jeris E. Strain, "Drilling and Methodology," *Language Learning*, XVIII:3 and 4 (December, 1968), 177–82.

[14] Rivers. Chapter XI.

[15] Wilga M. Rivers, *Teaching Foreign Language Skills* (Chicago: University of Chicago Press, 1968), p. 82.

terminology. Most attempts at classification of drills are purely descriptive (Brooks,[16] Dacanay,[17] Finocchiaro,[18] Hok,[19] etc.). An exception in Stanislaw P. Kaczmarski's "Language Drills and Exercises: A Tentative Classification," which classifies drills according to various types of stimulus-response sequences in terms of spoken, written, and non-linguistic media.[20] Drills thus are exclusively classified according to the medium of the communicative activity with no attention to learning process or degree of information (although he says "one of the principal tasks of the methodics of language teaching is to work out the most efficient . . . process of habit and skill formation in the learners."[21] V. J. Cook in an article called "Some Types of Oral Structure Drills," attempts to define structure drills in terms of the number of operations the learner has to perform in a drill.[22] "This approach treats the output as a master sentence into which successive items are inserted according to information selected from the input, rather than as a process of changing the whole input into an output."[23] She concludes that "one point which does emerge from this framework is the extremely limited number of operations that the learner has to perform in a structure drill. . . . It does appear that what is happening in a drill is much more limited than had been previously thought."[24] This conclusion is not really astounding because, for unstated reasons, Cook defines a structure drill as a mechanical drill only (see later discussion) and her discussion therefore only deals with mechanical drills.

There is within the last five, six years a definite increase in the demand for some form of meaning and communication in the drills. Wilga Rivers throughout her *Teaching Foreign-Language Skills*[25] emphasises the need for meaningful learning and communicative classroom activities. Clifford

[16] Brooks, 156.
[17] Fe R. Dacanay, *Techniques and Procedures in Second Language Teaching* (Dobbs Ferry, New York: Oceana Publications, 1963), pp. 107–51.
[18] Mary Finocchiaro, *English as a Second Language: From Theory to Practice* (New York: Regents, 1964), pp. 60–65.
[19] Ruth Hok, "Oral Exercises: Their Type and Form," *Modern Language Journal*, 48:4 (1964), 222–26. See also, T. Grant Brown, "In Defense of Pattern Practice," *Language Learning*, XIX:3 and 4 (December, 1969) 191–203; and James W. Ney, "Oral Drills—Methodology," *NAFSA Studies and Papers, English Language Series*, ed. David Wigglesworth, 1967, pp. 57–63.
[20] Stanislaw P. Kaczmarski, "Language Drills and Exercises: A Tentative Classification," *IRAL*, III:3 (August, 1965), 195–204.
[21] Kaczmarski, 195.
[22] V. J. Cook, "Some Types of Oral Structure Drills," *Language Learning*, XVIII:3 and 4 (December, 1968), 155–64.
[23] Cook, 157.
[24] Cook, 164.
[25] Rivers, *Teaching Foreign Language Skills*.

Prator[26] has a very useful paper where he outlines Bowen's,[27] Stevick's[28] and his own viewpoints on this and their variances, but basically they all agree that there are two poles in language learning, i.e. from manipulation to communication and that in efficient language teaching there needs to be some form of communication built into the drills. For once, there is experimental evidence to support this assumption. Oller and Obrecht report on an experiment carried out in a Rochester, New York high school with the conclusion that "the effectiveness of a given pattern is significantly increased by relating the language of that drill to communicative activity in the teaching/learning process." They conclude that from the very first stages of foreign language study meaningful communicative activity should be a, if not the, central point of pattern drills.[29]

To sum up, there are fairly adequate procedural descriptions of types of drills available although we need to consider the implications[30] of recent linguistic theory on new types of drills (not within the scope of this paper.)[31] There is growing concern with the necessity to teach not only parroting of the teacher but also some form of communication within the classroom. We do not have as yet a generally accepted theoretical framework for classifying structural pattern drills, which deals with these problems.

[26] Clifford Prator, "Guidelines for Planning Classes and Teaching Materials," *Workpapers in English as a Second Language: Matter, Methods, Materials,* Department of English, University of California, Los Angeles, April, 1967, pp. 27–31.
[27] Bowen, 292–309.
[28] Earl W. Stevick, "UHF and Microwaves in Transmitting Language Skills," *Language Learning: The Individual and the Process,* ed. E. W. Najam, *IJAL,* 32:1 (January, 1966), 84–94.
[29] John W. Oller and Dean H. Obrecht, "Pattern Drill and Communicative Activity: A Psycholinguistic Experiment," *IRAL,* VI:2 (May, 1968) 165–174.
[30] Rivers in *The Psychologist and the Foreign Language Teacher,* Chapter V, pp. 31–42, was one of the first FL teaching specialist in a major work to question the Skinnerian concept of conditioning. See also Leon J. Jacobovits, *Foreign Language Learning: A Psycholinguistic Analysis of the Issues* (Rowley, Mass.: Newbury House Publishers, 1970).
[31] See e.g. Mark Lester, ed. *Readings in Applied Transformational Grammar* (New York: Holt, Rinehart and Winston, 1970); Robin Lakoff, "Transformational Grammar and Language Teaching, *Language Learning,* XIX:1 and 2 (June, 1969) 117–40. William E. Rutherford, "From Linguistics to Pedagogy: Some Tentative Applications," *Preparing the EFL Teacher: A Projection for the '70's* ed. R. C. Lugton (Philadelphia: Center for Curriculum Development, Inc., 1970), 29–44; Sol Saporta, "Applied Linguistics and Generative Grammar," *Trends in Language Teaching,* ed. Albert Valdman (New York: McGraw-Hill, 1966). This language teacher would like to express her validation of most TG proposals for classroom teaching as quite impractical. Hauptman is quite right when he says, "We must be aware of the fact that in many areas, transformational grammar is not ready to be applied except in the most cursory way. We can look to it for insights, but it is a mistake to expect firm answers." (Philip C. Hauptman, Review of *Readings in Applied Transformational Grammar,* ed. Mark Lester, *Language Learning,* XX:2 (December, 1970), 284–89.

PART II

A CLASSIFICATION OF STRUCTURAL PATTERN DRILLS

I have recently attempted in an article called "Structural Pattern Drills:
A Classification"[32] to suggest such a conceptual framework; that is, a
classification, which recognizes that language learning is partly but not
only habit formation, which proposes to put meaning and communication
into classroom activities, and to do so in a consistent and orderly procedure. This paper is an attempt to further expand and clarify this proposi-
tion for classifying drills. We need such a classification for grading and
sequencing drills in order to obtain a systematic and more efficient
progression in the classroom from mechanical learning to the internalizing of competence. I believe with John Carroll, Wilga Rivers and others
in our field that "there is no reason to believe that the two positions
(language teaching as formation of language habits versus the establishment of rule governed behavior) are mutually exclusive."[33] Rivers points
out in a fascinating footnote that many of the language features which
are most efficiently taught by drills (person and number inflections,
gender agreements, formal features of tense, etc.) "are excluded by
Chomsky from his system of rewrite rules and are included in the lexicon
as parts of complex symbols."[34]

If, as the evidence seems to suggest, language involves more than one
level and there are at least two types of learning,[35] then this should be
reflected in the nature and types of drills. Both Stevick[36] and Titone[37]
conceive of language learning as a three stage process, but as Prator[38]
points out, there is no way of accurately assigning a drill to a specific
stage. My contention is that there are three classes of drills: mechanical,
meaningful, and communicative and that we may distinguish these three
classes from each other if we analyze the drills in terms of (1) expected

[32] Christina Bratt Paulston, "Structural Pattern Drills: A Classification," *Foreign Language Annals,* IV:2 (December, 1970), 187–93.
[33] Rivers, *Teaching Foreign-Language Skills,* 78.   See also John B. Carroll "Current
Issues in Psycholinguistics and Second Language Teaching," paper read at the
TESOL convention, New Orleans, March 3–7, 1971.
[34] Rivers, *Teaching Foreign-Language Skills,* 79.
[35] Rivers, *The Psychologist and the Language Teacher,* 47, 50.
[36] Stevick, 85. Stevick actually talks of a two-phase cycle from the M-phase of mimicry, manipulation and meaning to the C-phase of communication. This process is
analyzable along the three dimensions of "habituation," "vividness," and "responsibility."
[37] Renzo Titone, "A Psycholinguistic Model of Grammar Learning and Foreign
Language Teaching," *English as a Second Language: Current Issues,* ed. R. Lugton
(Philadelphia: Center for Curriculum Development, 1970), pp. 41–62, and especially
58–59. He refers to grammar learning as a three stage process: (1) Association of elementary linguistic units, (2) Induction and integration, and (3) Deduction.
[38] Prator, 31.

terminal behavior (2) degree of response control, (3) the type of learning process involved, and (4) of criteria for selection of utterance response.

TESTING DRILLS AND TEACHING DRILLS

But before I proceed to a discussion of the criteria for classifying drills, we need to consider an important aspect of drills, which cuts across this classification. Many have recognized a basic division in kinds of drills. Etmekjian[39] refers to them as teaching drills and testing drills, Rivers as the teaching phase and the testing phase, and Fries spoke of patterns produced "on the level on conscious choice."[40] What is involved is the difference between drills that serve primarily to help the student memorize a pattern with virtually no possibility for mistake and the drills which test or reinforce the learning of that pattern. (For a detailed discussion of reducing a grammatical pattern to "minimal items" see Gunter's "Proportional Drill as a Technique for Teaching Grammar.")[41] The concord of person and verb in the Romance languages serves as a good example for a teaching drill:

Model:	andar (tú)	R:	andas
	cantar (tú)		cantas
Continue the drill:			
Cue:	trabajar (tú)	R:	
	pasar (tú)		
	hablar (tú)		

This is a memorizing drill, where even the reader who does not know (or understand) Spanish can complete the drill correctly. But as soon as we change the cues to include all persons, that is, to change the cues so as to require an answer of more than minimal items, we require that the student know all the verb endings for the *ar*-verbs, present tense, and by his response we know whether he does or not. The response depends on the conscious choice of the student:

Model:	andar (tú)	R:	andas
	cantar (Vd.)	R:	canta
Continue the drill:			
Cue:	trabajar (él)	R:	

---

[39] James Etmekjian, *Pattern Drills in Language Teaching* (New York: New York University Press, 1966), pp. 33–36.

[40] Fries, 9.

[41] Richard Gunter, "Proportional Drill as a Technique for Teaching Grammar," *Language Learning*, X;3 and 4 (1960), 123–34. See also Andrew Macleish, "Composing Pattern Practice Drills," *On Teaching English to Speakers of Other Languages*, ed. B. W. Robinett, Series III, 1966, 141–48, and "Questions and Directed Discourse," *TESOL Quarterly*, 2:4 (December, 1968), 262–67.

Only the student who has previously memorized these patterns can complete the drill successfully.

I have constructed a tentative design to clarify the overall division of drills. (See Figure 1.)

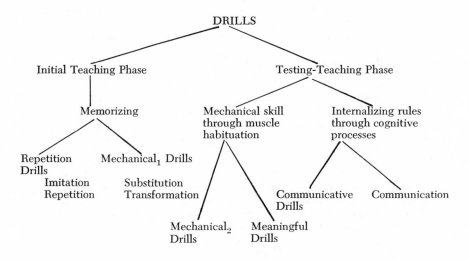

FIGURE 1

Drills are basically divided into teaching (memorizing, habituation) drills and testing (feedback, quizzing) drills.[42] There are two types of drills to help the student memorize: repetition drills and mechanical drills$_1$ which basically tend to be substitution drills but transformation drills are also possible. The testing drills in turn can be divided according to purpose: acquiring mechanical skill through muscle habituation on the one hand and on the other internalizing of rules through cognitive processes. The mechanical skill drills subdivide into mechanical$_2$ and meaningful drills while the internalizing of competence drills subdivide into communicative drills and actual communication. It can thus be seen that it is possible for mechanical drills to be either testing or teaching drills, depending on their breakdown into minimal items. I mention this before discussion of the three classes—mechanical, meaningful, and communicative—of drills because this duality of mechanical drills troubled me for a long time and contributed to some confusion in my other article.

The chart in Figure 2 may make the following discussion somewhat clearer.

[42] I find the terminology of teaching and testing drills infelicitous, in that the testing drills are also designed to teach language and "testing" easily becomes confused with the technical sense of that word. I am at a loss though to find a more apt terminology.

	MECHANICAL DRILLS	MEANINGFUL DRILLS	COMMUNICATIVE DRILLS
Expected terminal behavior	Automatic use of manipulative patterns— formation of habits	Automatic use of manipulative patterns— formation of habits still working on habit formation	Normal speech for communication— free transfer of patterns to appropriate situations
Degree of Control	Complete	Less control but there is a "right answer" expected	No control of lexical items—some control of patterns. Answer cannot be anticipated
Learning process involved	Learning through instrumental conditioning by immediate rein- forcement of correct response ANALOGY	Learning through instrumental conditioning by immediate rein- forcement of correct response ANALOGY trial-and-error ANALYSIS	Problem solving ANALYSIS
Criteria for select- ing response	Teacher	Teacher, situation, readings (knowledge common to the class)	Student himself (new information about real world)

FIGURE 2

MECHANICAL DRILLS

A mechanical drill is defined as a drill where there is complete control of the response, where there is only one correct way of responding. Be- cause of the *complete* control, the student need not even understand the drill although he responds correctly, as in the first Spanish drill. One might possibly consider repetition drills as the most extreme example of this class of drill. Substitution drills lend themselves particularly well to this. Here is another mechanical drill that all readers can complete be- cause it has been broken down to minimal items. It is a memorizing drill on the subject-adjective word order in Thai:

Example: Poom: nakrian Poom
$+$ ... 3 ... $+$

suun: nakrian suun
$+$ ... 3 ... $+$

ʔuan: nakrian ʔuan
2 ... 3 ... 2

Continue the drill:

1.   naaw
$+$

2.   roon
3

3.   dii

4.   suay[43]
2

The following drill is also a mechanical drill but unless you have studied (and memorized) the various classifiers you will not be able to complete it. It is a mechanical testing drill and (apart from the choice of numeral) there is only one correct answer:

6:   V 22 Complete the sentence with a numeral and a classifier.

Example: Kaw suu roon Taaw
$+$ ... 3 ... 3

Kaw suu roon Taaw soon Kuu
$+$ ... 3 ... 3 ... $+$ ... 2

Continue the drill:

1.   Kaw suu Paanun
$+$ ... 3 ... 2 ... 2

2.   Poo Puuk nekTay
2 ... $ꞌ$ ... 3

3.   maeae say soyKoo
2 ... $ꞌ$ ... 2

4.   noon sak sua
3 ... 3 ... 2

8.   nakrian say suanaaw
3 ... $ꞌ$ ... 2 ... $+$

9.   Kruu suu roonTaaw
3 ... 3

10.   Pii sak kaankeen
2 ... 3

11.   dek Puuyin say waeaen[44]
$ꞌ$ ... 2 ... $+$ ... $ꞌ$ ... $+$

The difference between a mechanical memorizing drill and a mechanical testing drill lies in the ability of the student to respond which again depends on how well he has memorized certain patterns, but understanding what he is saying is not a necessary requisite. It is perfectly possible to supply a verb with a correct ending in, e.g., Spanish, without necessarily knowing what the verb means: given Cue: *gratar (nosotros) any docile student will respond with *gratamos and he no more than I will know the meaning of that nonsense word. I remember perfectly well drilling classifiers in Thai without knowing the lexical meaning of the words; I just divided the world in terms of fruits, containers and people, but what kind of people or fruits I did not need to know. The ability to drill mechanical drills without necessarily understanding them is an important criterion in distinguishing them from meaningful drills.

[43] Edward M. Anthony, et al., *Foundations of Thai—Book 1, Part 1* (University of Pittsburgh, 1967), p. 31.
[44] Anthony, 115.

Transformation drills may be mechanical:

John kicked the door.
The door was kicked by John.

All the student need memorize is the structural change and he can complete such a drill without understanding exactly what he is saying. Response drills, which so frequently are being masqueraded forth as communication, can be some of the easiest mechanical drills for the student:

Which would you prefer, tea or coffee?
wine or beer?
nectar or ambrosia?

I know very well that the student is going to answer *ambrosia* without the foggiest notion of what it is.

The expected terminal behavior of such drills is the automatic use of manipulative patterns and is commensurate with the assumption that language learning is habit formation. It involves the classical Skinnerian method of learning through instrumental conditioning by immediate reinforcement of the right response. Learning takes place through analogy and allows transfer of identical patterns. This is clearly the mechanical level of learning, and this class of drills provides practice in mechanical associations such as adjective-noun agreement, verb-endings, question-forms and the like. This is a very necessary step in language learning, and as long as the student is learning, he won't mind the mechanical nature of the drill. The teacher needs to remember that the student can drill without understanding and to make sure that in fact he does understand. Because of the response-control, it is eminently suited for choral drills.

The student knows how to select his utterance response on the basis of the teacher's cue, be it oral or pictorial, but the teacher is the sole criterion for supplying the correct response. This becomes an important distinction between meaningful and communicative drills.

MEANINGFUL DRILLS

Much of the criticism of the audio-lingual method is based on the mechanical drill or rather the overuse to which it has been put. There are a number of psychological studies which demonstrate that there is a limit to the efficiency of mechanical drills in the language learning.[45] While not denying the need for mechanical drills, we may note that on the mechanical level alone the student certainly cannot yet express his

[45] William E. Rutherford, *Modern English: A Textbook for Foreign Students* (New York: Harcourt, Brace and World, 1968), p. 234.

own ideas fluently. He next needs to work through a set of meaningful drills:

1. Teacher: for five years   Student: How long did he (study)?
2. Teacher: during March   Student: When did he (register)?
3. Teacher: until four o'clock   Student:

In a meaningful drill there is still control of the response although it may be correctly expressed in more than one way and as such is less suitable for choral drilling. There is a right answer and the student is supplied with the information necessary for responding, either by the teacher, the classroom situation or the assigned reading, but in all cases the teacher always knows what the student ought to answer. Everyone is always aware that these drills are only language exercises and that any answer will do as well as another as long as it is grammatically correct and conforms to the information supplied. The student cannot complete these drills without fully understanding structurally and semantically what he is saying. I have attempted very hard to exclude lexical meaning from structural in the definition of meaningful drills, but I doubt that it is either possible or desirable. With the new license for mentalism I shall include both. The result is that some pattern drills come very close to being vocabulary drills. Compare the above "Which would you rather have, tea or coffee?" with "Which would you rather be, rich and healthy or sick and poor?" In other words, some meaningful drills may have the check for feedback that the student really understands the pattern built into the lexical components.

Comprehension type question and answers based on assigned readings fall in this class of drills:

TEACHER: What time did John come to school?
STUDENT: John came to school at 9 o'clock.

as well as much "situational" teaching as in this drill on post-nominal modification using prepositional phrases, where the students were instructed to describe each other.

TEACHER: Which boy is in your class?
STUDENT: The thin boy with long sideburns.
            The handsome boy with black hair.
                                              Etc.

It will be noticed that in the question-answer drill above, the long answers were given. The expected terminal behavior is the same as for mechanical drills. We still want an automatic use of language manipulation; we are still working on habit formation. Although for the language teacher, who is fluent in the target language, it may be difficult to appreciate the enormous difference in difficulty in these two classes of drills.

This is not to deny that a response like "The man was bitten by the dog," albeit in a mechanical drill, is much more difficult for the learner than a single lexeme substitution drill. Language learning is also the ability to control increasing amount of language in mechanical manipulation, and we need to consider the difficulty level within the "amount range" as well.

But the method is different. Mechanical drills by their nature can be drilled without grammatical analysis with the students left to "analogize" the pattern on their own. This is not possible with meaningful drills. Unless the student understands what he is doing, i.e. recognizes the characteristic features involved in the language manipulation, he cannot complete the drill. Politzer reports on an interesting experiment in "The Role and Place of the Explanation in the Pattern Drill" and points out that an early introduction of the explanation seems to be a more effective treatment than its postponement or omission and that it is preferable to show the application and relevance of the new material in some sort of context before explaining it.[46] The place for the explanation then is following the mechanical drills; those students who grasped the analogy will be rewarded with positive reinforcement and those who did not will be helped to understand the specific characteristics of that language structure.[47] The learning process varies depending on the structural pattern drilled, and while there may still be instrumental conditioning involved, there is very often a trial-and-error process involved in finding the correct response.

COMMUNICATIVE DRILLS

At this point, however, there is still no real communication taking place. Students have a tendency to learn what they are taught rather than what we think we are teaching. If we want fluency in expressing their own opinions, then we have to teach that. The expected terminal behavior in communicative drills is normal speech for communication or, if one prefers, the free transfer of learned language patterns to appropriate situations.

The degree of control in a communicative drill is a moot point. I originally stated that there is no control of the response, that the student has free choice to say whatever he wants. However, this turns out not to be true. All classroom teachers, using this system of sequencing drills, have reported back saying that there is indeed control, not of lexical items

---

[46] Robert L. Politzer, "The Role and Place of the Explanation in the Pattern Drill," *IRAL*, VI:4 (November, 1968): 315–331.
[47] Richard Barrutia, "Some Pedagogical Dangers in Recent Linguistic Trends," *IRAL*, IV:3 (1966), 157–164.

as we had at first thought but of structural patterns. The difficulty lies just in retaining this control so that the students indeed practice what they have learned; they themselves lose track of the fact that they are drilling and become engrossed in exchanging information. But it is a drill rather than free communication because we are still within the realm of the cue-response pattern. Communication "requires interpersonal responsiveness, rather than the mere production of language which is truthful, honest, accurate, stylistically pleasing, etc.—those characteristics which look at language as language rather than as behavior, which is the social purpose of language. Our end product is surely getting things done, easing social tensions, goading ourselves into doing this or that, and persuading others to do things. Communication arises when language is used as such interpersonal behavior, which goes beyond meaningful and truthful manipulation of language symbols."[48] To recapitulate, the differences between a meaningful drill and a communicative drill lie in the expected terminal behavior (automatic use of language manipulation versus free transfer of learned language patterns to appropriate situations) and in response control. But the main difference between a meaningful drill and a communicative drill is that in the latter the speaker adds *new* information about the real world. All of us have seen a meaningful drill turn communicative when the students suddenly took the question or cue personally and told us something about himself that we did not know from the classroom situation: "I have three sisters" is communicative, but "My shirt is red" is merely meaningful; that information is supplied by the situation, and I can see it as well as the student.

Language teachers have always used communicative drills in the classroom (where else is one asked such personal questions as "Did you brush your teeth this morning?"), but my point is that there should be an orderly progression from mechanical drilling through meaningful to communicative drills, that the teacher should know one from the other, and that one should not rely on chance that the students will turn a drill into communicative activity.

Communicative drills are the most difficult to arrange within the classroom. They can, of course, never be drilled chorally. Still, if we want fluency in expressing personal opinion, we have to teach that. One way of working with communicative drills is to structure the classroom activity so that it simulates the outside world of the students and to work within this situation. Need I point out that running through a memorized dialogue with accompanying gestures and action is not communicative drill nor necessarily language learning; non-language teachers refer to such activity as acting. Another, simpler way of working with communicative drills is simply to instruct students to answer truthfully.

[48] Dr. Francis C. Johnson, Professor of English, University of Papua and New Guinea. In personal communication, 31 July, 1970. He states his objection better than I could paraphrase it; as always I am grateful for his comments.

Example:

1. What is your responsibility?
   My responsibility is   to (learn English).
                                               (learning English).

2. What's your hobby?   to (make models).
   My hobby is   (making models).

3. What's your favorite pastime?

4. What are your lab instructions?

5. What will your occupation be?

6. What are your interests?

7. What is your advice to (Ahmed)?[49]

Gone is the instrumental conditioning; there is no facilitating of the correct response. What we have is John Carroll's " 'problem-solving' situation in which the student must find . . . appropriate verbal responses for solving the problem, 'learning' by a trial-and-error process, to communicate rather than merely to utter the speech patterns in the lesson plan."[50] We are clearly working within a level of language that involves thought and opinion and teaching it in a way that necessitates an understanding of the essential elements of what is being learned. It is a very different experience from mechanical drilling. It is indeed practice in performance by practice in generating new utterances in order to internalize the rules of grammar so that competence will not be defective. I am not saying that language teaching should be concerned solely with communicative type drills, but I am suggesting that any amount of mechanical drills will not lead to competence in a language, i.e., fluency to express one's own opinions in appropriate situations.

To summarize, in language teaching we ought to classify the drills we use into three classes: mechanical, meaningful, and communicative in order to reach free communication. We then need to proceed systematically, not leaving out any one step. Mechanical drills are especially necessary in beginning courses and in learning languages markedly different from the native tongue, such as Thai is for me. I do not believe that this is the only way of teaching languages because it patently is not. Rather, given what we know about languages and learning today, this classification of drills will provide for more efficient language learning.

[49] Rutherford. 175. The teaching point here is using the compliment to $V_t + O$ (as in to *learn English*) in free variation with V+ing+O (as in *learning English*). The teacher asks the questions and the students answer.
[50] John B. Carroll, *The Study of Language* (Cambridge, Mass.: Harvard University Press, 1953), p. 188.

SECTION FOUR
READING

The authors in this section review some of the fundamental notions of language in relation to graphic systems that are employed to represent speech sounds. They deal with English orthography, in particular. Fries compares the English writing system with other kinds of graphic systems —syllabic and logographic—and points to various problems that students, especially oriental students, have in acquiring a "productive reading" ability in English. Hall proceeds to show that "Even though our English spelling system may seem capricious, it is by no means wholly so; there is a basic pattern to the way in which it symbolizes language." And, of course, only by utilizing the "basic pattern" can efficient reading be brought about. Norris outlines goals, techniques, and classroom procedures for developing reading skills, along with other "language" skills, in the ESL program.

From time to time I have gone to meetings that, according to the announced topic, were to be concerned with "How to teach reading in ESL programs." In almost all instances, however, the real subject has turned out to be "How I use reading materials in my classes." Nobody, it seemed, had any contributions to make to a general theory of teaching reading. I did discover one (not particularly educational) thing at these meetings—that some teachers habitually use reading materials as a starting point for various kinds of oral work in the classroom: structural pattern drill, pronunciation drill, and the like.

Teachers who use reading materials as a guide to oral aspects of the language are obviously confused about the nature of language and graphic systems. This confusion, I think, stems largely from our traditional education concerning "language" and our visual-oriented society. Since we spend so much time in our school years learning to read efficiently, spell correctly, and write effectively—activities carrying the designation "language arts"—we come to believe that the "real" language is graphic. Our school tradition has tended to reinforce this notion. As ESOL teachers we must make a clear distinction between speech on the one hand and graphic symbols on the other. Letters are used to represent speech sounds, but letters themselves are not speech. In reading we go from letters to speech (vocally or subvocally) and then to meaning. We do not get meaning directly from the printed page.

At the early stages of English instruction, reading has been regarded mostly as incidental to or reinforcement to oral performance. According to Norris, "by and large there has been little attention to the systematic teaching of reading in beginning and intermediate ESL classes, especially the sort of preparation that might be expected to facilitate the student's acquisition of reading fluency at the advanced level of instruction." Fries emphatically points out that "the signals that perform the communicating function of a language are, first of all, patterns of vocal sounds. These patterns . . . are primary. For reading, man has invented various types of graphic representations . . . [that are] secondary. In connection with reading activities at the lower levels of instruction, he notes that "To provide support for the basic oral patterns, reading exercises must contain only the structure, the vocabulary, and the intonation contour that have already been taught and practiced. The reading selections for this purpose should never be the starting point out of which the oral practices arise. They must be the final focus point of a lesson in which all that has been learned is put to use in reading."

GRAPHEMICS

Hall uses the term *grapheme* as a basic unit of visual shape in language symbolization, and he charts the graphemic representations of English phonemes. It would be inaccurate, I think, to say that graphemes are simply the visual counterparts of phonemes, although this general idea is clearly evident. We can, however, draw a parallel in regard to English orthography and speech: graphemes are to visual shapes as phonemes are to speech sounds.

In an alphabetic writing system, such as the one for English, the ideal is one symbol consistently applied to represent each phoneme. Fries, Hall, and Norris all note that our English orthography falls short of this ideal. But "In general," according to Hall, "English orthography does afford to each phoneme of the language at least one regular, clear and consistent alphabetic representation." Also he makes two important points about irregularities in our orthography: (1) "very few words are wholly capricious in their spelling: most irregular spellings are irregular only in the representation of one or two of the phonemes contained in the word (usually, though not always, the vowels)," and (2) "our irregular spellings are by no means wholly random; they fall, to a large extent into certain sub-sets which are consistent within themselves." He notes in conclusion that "When we have set up both the 'regular' spellings of English phonemes, and the sub-systems of 'regular irregularities,' there is left a hard core of really irregularly spelled words. (The surprising thing, however, is how few these are in comparison to the great mass of regular and semi-regular spellings.)"

Fries, Hall, and Norris all note that some phonemes are not symbolized in our orthography and that some graphemes are superfluous. Fries notes that "If one is to read the graphic representations with comprehension, he must learn to supply those portions of the language signals that are not represented in any of the graphic signs. Satisfactory reading shows itself in oral reading, in what has been called reading 'with expression.' Reading English 'with expression' consists of supplying the tone sequences, the stresses, and the pauses that English uses to signal a whole range of cumulative meanings." Hall mentions the very widespread situation in which a grapheme is written, but nothing is pronounced: "Many letters are written in this way, especially 'mute *e*' at the ends of words . . . a number of consonant letters at the beginning of words and in the middle of words. . . ."

ADVANCED-LEVEL READING

Norris assumes that advanced-level students have had some training in reading at the beginning and intermediate levels of English instruction, either in support of oral performance or as a "by-product" of their oral language study. "In any event," he says, "since our students are literate, it is not the 'process' of reading as such that they must learn, but rather skills for reading a foreign language, English." His paper concentrates "on matters of immediate and practical classroom application by focusing on three primary aspects of the teaching task: (1) definition of advanced-level reading goals [in particular, to get information from the printed page efficiently, rapidly, and with full understanding], (2) varied techniques and exercises for achieving improvement in five reading skill areas, and (3) suggested classroom procedures for conducting the reading lesson." He draws his material from a wide variety of sources and does a very competent job of presenting it "in a context broad enough so as not to obscure its relevance and applicability in the majority of teaching situations."

In the terminology of structural linguistics, *language* refers only to *speech:* language consists of vocal symbols and nothing else. This, of course, excludes graphic symbols. According to an old cliché, "Language is the noises we make with our faces, and not the marks we make with our fists." Fries' and Hall's papers seem to reflect this notion more than Norris'. For example, Norris speaks of the "spoken" language and the "written" language and mentions that "written English differs considerably from spoken English in many features of structure and style." Prator's comment on this distinction (Section One) deserves careful consideration, I think: "It seems more realistic and helpful to teachers to regard English speech and writing as two closely related but distinct linguistic systems. . . ." Hockett (in Section Two) and Politzer (in Section Three) discuss the problems of students whose only purpose in foreign language study is to gain a reading knowledge of the language.

SELECTED READINGS

ASTON, KATHARINE. "Another -Eme in Language Teaching: The Grapheme." In *On Teaching English to Speakers of Other Languages, Series I,* edited by Virginia French Allen. Champaign, Ill.: National Council of Teachers of English, 1965.

BROOKS, NELSON. *Language and Language Learning: Theory and Practice.* 2d ed. Chapter 12: "Reading and Writing." New York: Harcourt Brace Jovanovich, 1964.

BUMPASS, FAYE L. "Learning to Read in a Foreign Language." *The ABC English as a Second Language Bulletin.* Vol. 1, No. 4, 1965.

DACANAY, FE R. *Techniques and Procedures in Second Language Teaching.* Chapter 4: "Reading English." Edited by J. Donald Bowen. Dobbs Ferry, N.Y.: Oceana Publications, Inc., 1963.

DALE, EDGAR. "Teachers and Reading." *English Teaching Forum* 1(1963): 11–14.

FRIES, CHARLES C. "To Read English as a Second Language." In *On Teaching English to Speakers of Other Languages, Series III.* Edited by Betty Wallace Robinett. Champaign, Ill.: National Council of Teachers of English, 1967.

———. *Linguistics and Reading.* New York: Holt, Rinehart and Winston, 1963.

FRANCIS, W. NELSON. *The Structure of American English.* Chapter 8: "Writing It Down: Graphics." New York: The Ronald Press Company, 1958.

KING, HAROLD V. "Linguistic Aspects of the Reading Program." *Language Learning* 9(1959):19–23.

KREIDLER, CHARLES W. "Reading as Skill, Structure, and Communication." In *On Teaching English to Speakers of Other Languages, Series II.* Edited by Carol J. Kreidler. Champaign, Ill.: National Council of Teachers of English, 1966, pp. 97–103.

LADO, ROBERT. *Language Teaching: A Scientific Approach.* Chapter 13: "Reading." New York: McGraw-Hill, Inc., 1964.

MACLEISH, ANDREW. "Adapting and Composing Reading Texts." *TESOL Quarterly* 2(1968):43–50.

PLAISTER, TED. "Reading Instruction for College Level Foreign Students." *TESOL Quarterly* 2:164–68.

RIVERS, WILGA M. *Teaching Foreign-Language Skills.* Chapter 9: "The Reading Skill." Chicago: The University of Chicago Press, 1968.

SCOTT, CHARLES T. "The Linguistic Basis for the Development of Reading Skill." *Modern Language Journal* 50(1966):535–44.

THONIS, ELEANOR WALL. *Teaching Reading to Non-English Speakers.* New York: Collier Macmillan International, 1970.

WEST, MICHAEL. *Learning to Read a Foreign Language and Other Essays on Language Teaching.* London, Longmans, Green, 1955.

LEARNING TO READ ENGLISH
AS PART
OF THE ORAL APPROACH

CHARLES C. FRIES

To emphasize the needs and problems of learning to read English does not in any way conflict with our primary insistence upon the oral approach. As we have practiced it the "oral approach" does not confine or limit the classroom practices of the teacher; it provides the measure for the degree of achievement to be attained by the pupil. During the first stage of learning a foreign language the basic materials must be so completely and thoroughly learned that they can be produced orally by the pupils when stimulated solely by the meaning situations in which they are required. Both writing and reading can be made to contribute to the thoroughness and precision of that learning for oral production.

We thus have included reading in courses of study that aimed at the greatest possible efficiency in learning a foreign language, both for the purpose of supporting and supplementing the basic oral practices, and also for the purpose of teaching the pupil how to read the language he is studying.

Let me then briefly center attention upon one or two of the special tasks that the speaker of another language must struggle with if he would read English. We have tried to bring to bear upon the problems of reading English some of the knowledge and understanding concerning the nature and functioning of English that has been achieved during the last century. We are concerned here with the reading of Late Modern English, that is, English of the 19th and 20th centuries.

I.

In order to read Modern English, the pupil must master the *writing system of Modern English.* All the basic writing systems of the languages of the world have as their purpose the representation of a language as that language is used orally to carry on the affairs of a society. They aim to provide a graphic code through which one who has learned both the code of the language signals and the code of the writing system can interpret the written materials in terms of the language they represent. To read any writing efficiently, one must develop high speed discrimination and recognition responses to the graphic signs as representations of significant language parts.

Writing systems applied to languages can be put into three groups, roughly, according to the nature of the language-part or language-unit which constitutes the chief basis of the graphic representation.

a. In word writing, the (logographic) signs represent words as wholes. The oldest hieroglyphics of Egypt are word writing, as are the Chinese characters, the Kanji of Japanese.

For example, some of our own English writing is logographic—our numerals and other mathematical signs:

$$3 \quad \times \quad 3 \quad = \quad 9$$
three times three equals nine.
(is)
$$5 \quad - \quad 2 \quad = \quad 3$$
five minus two equals three
(less)   (is)
$$2 \quad + \quad 5 \quad = \quad 7$$
two plus five equals seven
(and)   (are)
$$10 \quad \div \quad 2 \quad = \quad ?$$
ten divided by two equals what

The letters of the alphabet also sometimes represent words that have the same pronunciation as the names of the letters.

I   C   U   R   A   J
I see you are a jay.

b. In syllable writing, the signs represent whole syllables. The signs of syllable writing do, of course, represent whole words when applied to one syllable words. See the use of I C U R A J above. The syllable signs do not separate the consonants of a syllable from the vowels that go with the consonants to make the syllable. The two sets of *kana* (katakana and hiragana) that the Japanese use are syllabaries, as was also the Hittite and Sumarian cuneiform writing.

We can and do at times use the letters with their English names as "syllable" writing. The letters MT can represent the two syllable word *empty*. The letters KT read by their English names represent the two syllable word *Katy*. Calling the National Council of Teachers of English the NCTE is using our letters as a syllabary. On the other hand, pronouncing the sequence of letters NATO as the two syllable word /neigh-to/ (for the North Atlantic Treaty Organization) is treating the letters as an alphabet and not as a syllabary.

c. In alphabet writing, the signs represent *not* the syllable as a unit but rather the separate consonants and vowels which make up the syllable.

For example, the name of the letter B constitutes a syllable, made up of a consonant plus a vowel. In our alphabet writing we spell that syllable *be*. We spell the names of the following letters in similar fashion. C, *se*; D, *de*; G, *ge*; P, *pe*; T, *te*; V, *ve*; Z, *ze*. We spell the names of the following letters with the vowel before the consonant. F, *ef*; L, *el*; M, *em*; N, *en*; R, *ar*; S, *es*; X, *ex* or *ecks*.

All of these three kinds of writing systems seek to represent a language as that language is used to carry on the affairs of a society. Both the syllable systems and the alphabet systems are tied to the *sound-system of the language*. Each of these two writing systems can represent a language sound-system. But the syllabary system of writing and the alphabetic system of writing are tied to different units of the sound-system of a language. For a language that has morphemes with many consonant clusters, both initial and final, and more than five vowel phonemes, alphabetic writing seems more convenient than syllabic writing. English writing from the time of its earliest records has used an alphabetic system. It used the western Greek alphabet modified to fit the language of the Romans, Latin, and probably adapted for Old English by the practices of scribes from Ireland. The basic question for us, is, "What *language parts or units* does *Modern English spelling represent?*"

Historical evidence shows that a fundamental change in the basic principles of English spelling came about during the hundred years from 1450 to 1550. In general, for the languages that have used a Greek-Roman alphabet for their writing, each letter has had a basically regular correspondence with one of the phonemes of the language. Such a regularity characterized the spelling of Old English and that of Middle English. But by the end of the hundred years from 1450 to 1550 that basic regularity for a large section of the English vocabulary had been displaced by a different system. For example, Modern English spelling to represent the so-called "long vowels" is quite out of line with that of the older periods of English. It is also quite out of line with the spelling of the familiar European languages that also use an adaptation of the Roman alphabet.

Judged by the conventional ideal of spelling, that is, a one for one correspondence between each individual "sound" and a distinctive letter to represent it, the spelling of Modern English ever since 1550 has been vigorously condemned. John Hart's manuscript "The Opening of the Unreasonable Writing of Our English" (1551) led the way.

"For even so I have opened the vices and faultes of our writing which cause it to be tedious and long in learning: and learned hard, and evil to read. . . . And then have I sought the meanes (herin writen) by the which we may use a certaine, good and easi writing, onli following our pronunciation; and keping the letters in their auncient Simple and Singular powers."

John Hart's vigorous condemnation of the English spelling of 1550 furnished only the beginning of such condemnations. Many others from that time to the present have echoed the criticisms of Hart and more than fifty prominent writers have published fully developed schemes to reform Modern English spelling. They have all sought to produce a spelling for Modern English in which there would be no "silent" letters[1]; in which there would be no "etymological" spellings (with "letters silent to the ear but eloquent to the eye")[2]; in which there would be none of the hundreds of words pronounced alike but differing in meaning and in spelling[3]; in short, a Modern English spelling in which it would be possible to match individual "distinctive sounds" and individual letters, and state simple rules for these correspondences.[4]

English spelling developed a basically different system of representation for Modern English. The old system based on a correspondence of items and a distribution of items was displaced by a system based on correspondences of word-patterns with spelling-patterns. The changes in the basic system of representation did destroy many of the regular correspondences of individual phoneme and individual letter, but they did serve to establish a much larger range of regularity, when measured by riming morphemes as represented by patterns of spelling.

Measured by *this* different systematic base of significant phoneme sequences as word-patterns represented by letter sequences as spelling-patterns, there appears a tremendous degree of regularity in Modern English spelling that does not appear otherwise;—a regularity that can be structured systematically in small steps to lead the non-native speaker much more efficiently into a satisfactory control of the Modern English spelling system for both reading and writing.[5]

II.

Although his speed recognition responses to the spelling-patterns of Late Modern English do constitute a basic essential of reading English, these responses must become so automatic that they sink below the

[1] *stage, know, whole, sight, chief, breath, gnarled.*
[2] *reign, feign, deign, impugn, doubt, debt, island.*
[3] *rite-right-wright; pare-pair-pear; lode-lowed-load; mete-meet-meat.*
[4] The major computer studies that now exist have not furnished the evidence for any such rules. See also the study by Theodore Clymer, "The Utility of Phonic Generalizations in the Primary Grades." *The Reading Teacher.* 16:252–58. (Jan. 1963)
[5] With this approach there are only two major sets of spelling-patterns and eighteen minor sets. There are very few "irregulars" left over and these are all partly patterned. The "irregular" word *answer*, for example, except for the *w* fits into the first major set of patterns; *people*, except for the *o*, fits with *steeple*, one of the matrixes of the second major set of patterns.

It is only the spelling-patterns approach that will make sense out of the hundreds of words that are "alike in sound but different in meaning and in spelling." See Richard Hodges, *A Special Help to Orthographie*, 1643, for a list of more than seven hundred such words in use in the first half of the seventeenth century.

threshold of attention before the reader can do the kind of productive reading that is required in our reading-centered society. I shall discuss briefly only what I call "reading for the cumulative meanings." As I said at the beginning we have included reading both for the purpose of supporting and supplementing the basic oral practices, and also for the purpose of teaching the pupil how to read productively the language he is studying.

To provide support for the basic oral practices, the reading exercises must contain only the structures, the vocabulary, and the intonation contour, that have already been taught and practiced. The reading selections for this purpose should never be the starting point out of which the oral practices arise. They must be the final focus point of a lesson in which all that has been learned is put to use in the reading. The pupil should not attempt to read such selections until after the oral practices of the materials have been completed, and the dialogues in which they are contained, thoroughly learned. When they are read the reading must be oral reading and real reading, not just saying the words.

As you well know, the signals that perform the communicating function of a language are, first of all, patterns of vocal sounds. These patterns of vocal sounds are primary. For reading, man has invented various types of graphic representations of these vocal sounds. These patterns of graphic representations . . . are secondary. These secondary representations used for reading contain less of the language signals than do the primary representations—i.e. the patterns of vocal sounds themselves. In the graphic representations there are left out markings for such language signals as intonation (sequences of tones of various pitch), differences of stress, and pauses to mark grouping.

Our punctuation system is quite limited when measured by the range of these vocal signals. If one is to read the graphic representations with comprehension, he must learn to supply those portions of the language signals that are not represented in any of the graphic signs. Satisfactory reading is not simply a matter of speed and fluency. It shows itself in oral reading, in what has been called reading "with expression." This reading "with expression" is not simply avoiding a monotone in producing the sound-patterns that make up the separate words. Reading English "with expression" consists of supplying the tone sequences, the stresses, and the pauses that English uses to signal a whole range of cumulative meanings. It is these cumulative meanings that are the function of the intonation sequences and the distribution of so-called "sentence" stresses and pauses for grouping.

These cumulative meanings attach to sequences of sentences in a discourse.[6] It may be a discourse of only two sentences, as, for example, a simple greeting:

Good | morning   How | are | you

Fine | thank you   How are / you

(Note the change of the intonation pattern on the repetition of the words *How are you*.)

It is these special oral signals of the cumulative meanings of sequences of sentences in a discourse that must be supplied by the reader if he is to do the "productive reading" of complete comprehension.

In most of our efforts to develop ability to read English as a foreign language we have not given enough practice to the reading of materials that are being learned orally, and in which all the signals have been thoroughly grasped and marked. This first step in learning to read requires attention throughout most of the materials of the first stage of learning the foreign language.

The next step is the oral reading of new materials that have been carefully marked by the student for such a reading exercise. The third step is the oral reading of new material "at sight." And only, as the final step, would there be the silent reading of new materials and the demonstration by comment, of complete comprehension.

Learning to read well a foreign language, after the age of ten or twelve, presents a quite different set of problems from those of learning to read the first (or native) language. These problems deserve much more consideration than we have yet given them.

SPELLING AND SOUND IN ENGLISH*

ROBERT A. HALL, JR.

With graphemes,[1] as with phonemes, we must distinguish several different classes. Not only vowel and consonant letters, but also punctuation marks, form part of our graphemic system. We must also differentiate between simple and compound graphemes.

Our traditional grammatical doctrine tells us that the vowel letters are "*a, e, i, o, u,* and sometimes *w* and *y.*" As for the letter *y*, its use to represent a vowel phoneme is fairly frequent, as in *myth* /míθ/ or *myrtle* /mɔ́rtəl/; but *w* occurs as a vowel letter only in a few Welsh words such as *cwm* /kúwm/ (a "cirque," or kind of recess in a mountain) or the feminine name *Gwladys* /gúwladis/ (a variant of Gladys), and we might just as well forget about this use of the letter *w*. This leaves us with only one letter, *y*, which really has the function of both a vowel and a consonant grapheme. The other nineteen consonant letters need no special comment. The Arabic numerals from 0 to 9 also count as separate simple graphemes, but form a separate non-alphabetic subsystem of their own, whereas the Roman numerals are simply alphabetic graphemes (I, X, V, etc.) used in a special non-alphabetic way.

The difference between small and capital letters, roman and other fonts of type (italic, bold-face, etc.) is not significant in the representation of phonemes. However, it on occasion has other types of linguistic mean-

---

* Editorial adjustments have been made in this material with the publisher's permission.

[1] Hall defines *grapheme* as "a significant unit of visual shape. We use the expression visual shape so as to cover not only writing, but also all other kinds of shape perceived by the eye, e.g. carving, letters and other forms spelled out by bands on football fields, by floral designs, etc. The grapheme, as a unit, is to visual shape what the phoneme is to speech-sound. Thus, in English spelling, our basic graphemic units are the twenty-six letters of the Roman alphabet; but in other systems of writing, certain differences which we regard as non-significant have graphemic significance, and some which we consider significant have none. For instance, if one of us writes the small letter *i* without a dot over it, this, in English spelling, is just a childish mistake; but in modern Turkish orthography, *i* stands for one phoneme and *ı* for another, and the two letters are distinct graphemes in Turkish and must not be confused. Like phonemes, graphemes also can be either simple or compound: instances of the latter are English *th* or *ng*, which are combinations of two single graphemes but which in themselves function as one. (Traditional terminology recognizes this fact by using such expressions as *digraph* for combinations of two letters, etc.)" *Sound and Spelling in English.* Philadelphia: Chilton Books, 1961. p. 5.

ing, as when we capitalize the first letter of a spelling to indicate that the word represented is a proper noun or adjective, or when we use italic type to show that a word has extra loud stress. Note also that in English graphemics accent marks are normally not used except in reproduction of a foreign spelling (e.g. *fiancé* or *rôle*); even in such words, naive spellers often (perhaps usually) omit the accent marks, and write, say *coupé* as *coupe*, occasionally with resultant effects on the pronunciation of the word (e.g. /kúwp/ instead of /kuwpéy/).

The compound graphemes of English include a great many sequences of vowel letters, graphic diphthongs such as *ae, ai, au, ea, ei, eo* (as in *people* /píypǝl/), *eu, ie, oa, oi, ou, ue,* in addition to double vowel letters like *ee* or *oo*. There are also certain combinations of consonant letters which function as single units and hence must be considered as compound graphemes: e.g. *ch, gh, ph, rh, sh, th; ng;* and again all the double consonant letters such as *bb, dd,* etc. These combinations function as compound graphemes even when some of them (such as *gh*) are almost "silent," or others (like *ph, rh*) have the same linguistic meaning as do certain simple graphemes (e.g. *ph* and *f* both = /f/; rh and r both = /r/).

This is the proper place to take care of certain automatic losses or substitutions of graphemes, such as those which take place when suffixes are added to words—for instance, the loss of final "mute *e*" before *-ed, -ing* (*hate, hated, hating*). In a similar way, certain graphemes are automatically replaced in certain positions: for example, *-ay* at the end of a word is always replaced by *-ai-* when it comes to stand before further graphemes (e.g. *gay* + *-ly* becomes *gaily*). Stating such alterations at the outset as over-riding rules has the advantage of saving space in later explanations and of making over-all patterns clearer than they would otherwise be.

We shall have to take punctuation marks into account as graphemes when considering the way in which suprasegmental phonemes are notated in English writing. The punctuation marks include, of course, the comma, period, colon, and semi-colon; the exclamation and interrogation marks; the hyphen and various types of dashes; and the quotation marks (single and double) and parentheses and square brackets. There are still further types of marks which function in essentially the same way as do punctuation marks, but only in special kinds of discourse such as chemistry or mathematics, and hence we need not go into them here.

GRAPHEME AND PHONEME

Since the function of graphemes, in an alphabetic writing system, is to represent phonemes, we must now examine the way in which our English orthography performs this function. Our first approach will be through a listing of the phonemes in a modified Trager-Smith transcription[2] (The IPA-Kenyon-Pike transcription,[3] whatever its scientific merits or demerits, is not easy to write on a typewriter or to set up in print), together with the graphemes used to represent them, and examples of each.

In addition to these correspondences, we must also mention the very widespread situation in which no phoneme is pronounced, but a grapheme is written, the case of the so-called "silent letters." Many letters are written in this way, especially "mute *e*" at the end of words (*judge, sense*), and a number of consonant letters at the beginning of words (*knee, gnat, psychology, pshaw*) and in the middle of words (*debt, paradigm* /pǽrədim/, *drachm* /drǽm/, etc.). Perhaps some of the phoneme-to-grapheme correspondences listed in Table I could also be interpreted as containing "silent" letters, e.g. *foetid* = *fetid* plus a "silent" *e*, or *demagogue* = *demagog* plus "silent" *ue* (this is, in fact, the interpretation placed on the spelling *catalogue* by librarians when they write it as *catalog* and the past tense of the verb as *cataloged*).

TABLE I. *Graphemic Representation of English Phonemes*

PHONEME	GRAPHEME	EXAMPLES
/iy/	ee	meet
	e	be
	e . . . e	mete
	ea	sea
	ae	Caesarian
	eo	people
	oe	amoeba

[2] Hall (*ibid.*, p. 24) lists the following works, which utilize the Trager-Smith approach to English phonemics:

Gleason, H. A. *An Introduction to Descriptive Linguistics*. Chapters 2–4, 13, 16. New York: Holt, Rinehart, and Winston, 1955.

Hockett, C. F. *A Course in Modern Linguistics*. Chapters 2–13. New York: The Macmillan Company, 1958.

Trager, G. L. and Smith, H. L., Jr. *Outline of English Structure*. Chapter 1. Norman, Okla.: Battenburg Press, 1951.

[3] Hall (*ibid.*, pp. 24–25) lists the following works which utilize the IPA-Kenyon-Pike approach to English phonemics:

Hall, R. A., Jr. *Introductory Linguistics*. Chapters 9–20. Philadelphia: Chilton Books, 1964.

Hall, R. A., Jr. *Linguistics and Your Language*. Chapters 3 and 11. New York: Doubleday Anchor Books, 1960.

Kenyon, J. S. *American Pronunciation*. 4th ed. Ann Arbor: Wahr, 1940, and later editions.

Pike, K. L. *Phonemics*. Ann Arbor: University of Michigan Press, 1947.

Thomas, C. K. *An Introduction to the Phonetics of American English*. New York: Ronald Press, 1947.

Thomas, C. K. *Handbook of Speech Improvement*. New York: Ronald Press, 1956.

TABLE I (continued)

PHONEME	GRAPHEME	EXAMPLES
	ei	*receive*
	ie	*believe*
	i	*machine*
	ey	*key*
	ay	*quay*
/i/	*i*	*hit*
	ie	*sieve*
	e	*England*
	ee	*been* (in American English)
	o	*women*
	u	*busy*
	y	*myth*
	ui	*build*
/ey/	*ei*	*veil*
	ea	*steak*
	ey	*obey*
	a . . . e	*gate*
	ai	*pain*
	ao	*gaol* (British spelling of *jail*)
	au	*gauge*
	ay	*ay*
/e/	*e*	*set*
	ea	*leather*
	ae	*aesthetic*
	ei	*heifer*
	ie	*friend*
	eo	*leopard*
	oe	*foetid* (alternative for *fetid*)
	ai	*said*
	a	*any*
	u	*bury*
/æ/	*a*	*hat*
	ai	*plaid*
	ay	*prayer*
	au	*laugh*
/a/	*a*	*father*
	e	*sergeant*
	ea	*heart*
	o	*hot*
/ə/	*u*	*cup*
	o	*son*
	ou	*couple*
	oo	*flood*
	oe	*does*

TABLE I (continued)

PHONEME	GRAPHEME	EXAMPLES
	a	along
	ai	mountain
	ia	parliament
	ei	villein
	eo	dungeon
	i	easily
	oi	porpoise
/o/	o	order
	oa	broad
	ou	ought
	a	tall
	ah	Utah
	al	talk
	au	fault
	aw	raw
/ow/	o . . . e	note
	oa	road
	oe	doe
	oh	oh
	ou	soul
	ow	flow
	eo	yeoman
	au	hautboy
	eau	beau
	ew	sew
/u/	u	put
	ou	should
	oo	book
	o	wolf
/uw/	u . . . e	rule
	ue	flue
	ui	fruit
	eu	maneuver
	ou	group
	ew	grew
	o . . . e	move
	oe	canoe
	wo	two
/i/ (for those who have this phoneme)	u	just (adv.)
	i	children
/y/	y	you
	i	union
	j	hallelujah

TABLE I (*continued*)

PHONEME	GRAPHEME	EXAMPLES
/w/	w	well
	u	quiet
/p/	p	pen
	pp	stopper
/t/	t	ten
	ed	walked
	th	thyme
	tt	bottom
/k/	c	cash
	cc	account
	cch	bacchanal
	ck	back
	ch	character
	cq	acquaint
	cque	sacque
	cu	biscuit
	k	keep
	q	barbeque (now the normal spelling of this word, by actual count)
	qu	liquor
/b/	b	bed
	bb	robber
/d/	d	den
	dd	ladder
	ed	pulled
/g/	g	give
	gg	egg
	gh	ghost
	gu	guard
/f/	f	feel
	ff	muffin
	gh	rough
	ph	physics
/θ/	th	thin
/v/	v	visit
	vv	flivver
	f	of
	ph	Stephen
/ð/	th	then
/s/	s	sit
	ss	loss
	sc	scene

TABLE I *(continued)*

PHONEME	GRAPHEME	EXAMPLES
	sch	schism
	c	city
/š/	sh	ship
	ce	ocean
	ch	machine
	ci	special
	s	sugar
	sch	schist
	sci	conscience
	se	nauseous
	si	mansion
	ss	tissue
	ssi	mission
	ti	mention
/z/	z	zone
	zz	dazzle
	s	has
	ss	scissors
	sc	discern
	x	Xenophon
/ž/	g	garage
	s	measure
	si	division
	z	azure
	zi	brazier
/č/	ch	church
	tch	patch
	t	natural
	te	righteous
	ti	question
/ǧ/	j	just
	d	graduate
	dg	judge
	di	soldier
	g	magic
	gg	exaggerate
/m/	m	mile
	mm	hammer
/n/	n	nail
	nn	banner
/ŋ/	ng	ring
	n	pink

TABLE I (continued)

PHONEME	GRAPHEME	EXAMPLES
/l/	l	love
	ll	call
/r/	r	red
	rr	carrot
	rh	rhesus
/h/	h	hit
	wh	who

In addition to the single phonemes listed, there are certain combinations of phonemes which have special graphemic representations in English spelling:

/ay/	i . . . e	bite
	i	high
	ai	aisle
	ay	aye
	ei	height
	ie	tie
	ey	eye
	uy	buy
	y	sky
/aw/	ou	out
	ow	now
/oi/	oi	boil
	oy	toy
/yuw/	u . . . e	use
	eau	beauty
	eu	feud
	ew	few
	ieu	adieu
	ue	cue
	iew	view
	yu . . . e	yule
	yew	yew
	you	you
/ər/	er	term
	ear	learn
	ir	thirst
	or	worm
	yr	myrtle
	ar	liar
/əl/	ul	cult
	ull	mull
	ol	pistol

TABLE 1 (continued)

PHONEME	GRAPHEME	EXAMPLES
	il	*pistil*
	el	*tinsel*
	le	*handle*
	al	*sandal*
/way/	*wi . . . e*	*wile*
	oi	*choir*
/wə/	*o . . . e*	*one*
/hw/	*wh*	*which*
/kw/	*qu*	*quick*
/ks/	*x*	*mix*

In addition to the individual correlations set forth above, there are certain patterns of representation which should be made evident at this point. Before a consonant, especially at the end of a word, as shown in Table II, certain vowel phonemes show parallelism in the way they are written. The first two sets of correspondences show, of course, the values for the vowel letters which, in traditional terminology, are called "short" and "long." There is a well-known correlation between the use of a single letter plus a following vowel letter (usually, though not always, "mute *e*") to indicate the "long" value of a preceding vowel letter (as in *bate, bating*); and the use of a single consonant letter at the end of a word or the use of two consonant letters in the middle of a word to indicate the "short" value of a preceding vowel letter (*bat, batting, basket*). The other three sets of correspondences shown in Table II exemplify less extensive but very widespread ways of representing the phonemes involved, which show a certain amount of parallelism in the graphemes used.

Our supra-segmental phonemes receive only a partial representation in writing. The period normally represents the "terminal contour" 2-3-1, the sentence-melody that tells us that an utterance is at an end; the comma, the 2-3-2 melody that tells us the speaker is not yet finished. The interrogation mark usually symbolizes, not only the 2-2-3 and 2-2-4 question melodies, but also various others. Colons, semi-colons and exclamation marks may or may not represent intonation contours; a good part of the time, they do not do so, and their use follows arbitrary rules of pseudo-"logic." Stress is not normally symbolized at all, except when emphatic stress on a syllable or a word is marked by italics or capital

TABLE II. Parallelism in Graphemic Representation

PHONEME	GRAPHEME	EXAMPLES
/i/ + consonant	*i* + consonant letter (single or double)	*bit; bitten*
/e/ + consonant	*e* + consonant letter (single or double)	*bet; better*
/æ/ + consonant	*a* + consonant letter (single or double)	*bat; batting*
/a/ + consonant	*o* + consonant letter (single or double)	*hot; hotter*
/ə/ + consonant	*u* + consonant letter (single or double)	*nut; nutty*
/iy/ + consonant	*e* + consonant letter + e	*mete*
/ey/ + consonant	*a* + consonant letter + e	*bate*
/ay/ + consonant	*i* + consonant letter + e	*bite*
/ow/ + consonant	*o* + consonant letter + e	*mote*
/yuw/ + consonant	*u* + consonant letter + e	*cube*
/iy/	*ee*	*beet*
/uw/	*oo*	*boot*
/iy/	*ea*	*beat*
/ow/	*oa*	*boat*
/ay/	*ie*	*tie*
/yuw/	*ue*	*cue*
/ow/	*oe*	*hoe*

letters ("You don't *say* so! How TER-ri-ble!"). Open juncture is repre-sented only in compound words and very haphazardly, by means of the hyphen: for instance, the compound /stríyt +kar/ may be written *street car, street-car,* or *streetcar.* The use of the hyphen in compounds or its absence is, in English orthography, quite capricious, and even different dictionaries give different prescription as to its use.

REGULARITY AND IRREGULARITY IN ENGLISH GRAPHEMICS

In the material presented in the preceding section, there is an interest-ing paradox. English has (according to which analysis we accept) be-tween nine and twelve vowel phonemes, two or three semi-vowels, and twenty-one consonant phonemes—somewhere between thirty-two and thirty-six phonemes in all; but the Roman alphabet has only twenty-six letters that can be used for symbolizing these thirty-two or more pho-nemes. Yet nevertheless, for almost every phoneme, there is a large num-ber of different ways of symbolizing it. That is to say, although there are not enough graphemes to "go around" in proportion to all the phonemes needing to be symbolized, there is a marked lack of economy—one might well go so far as to say that there is apparently a tremendous confusion—in the choice of graphemic representation for our English phonemes.

Most people, in their thinking about English spelling, get this far and no farther. It is very easy to observe the seeming confusion reigning in our orthography, and to conclude that it is a hopeless mess, out of which no order can ever be brought. From this, it is an easy step to the notion that each English word has its own spelling, and hence that, in effect, the spelling of each English word is like a Chinese character, unrelated in its structure to that of any other word, so far as its representation of sound is concerned. A further consequence of this notion is the idea that, in teaching children to read and spell English, we need pay no attention to the graphemic structure of a word's spelling, and that we can include words such as *laugh* or *choir* along with others like *fit* or *crab* from the very beginning.

Widespread though these notions may be, however, they are quite erroneous. Even though our English spelling system may seem capricious, it is by no means wholly so; there is a basic pattern to the way in which it symbolizes the language. Among the various graphemic representations shown in Table III, some are more consistent and more frequent than others: some spellings, that is, are *regular* and others are *irregular*. This basic fact needs to be more widely recognized than it is at present, and to be taken into account in teaching reading and spelling, if we are to avoid wasting time and energy on both teachers' and students' part.

In Table III we show what may be considered the regular graphemic representations of English phonemes, as determined by consistency and frequency.

There are, as can be seen from Table III, only a few instances in which an English phoneme does not have an independent regular representation of its own. The vowels /u/ and /uw/ are both represented most frequently by *oo*; the consonants /θ/ and /ð/ are both exclusively spelled *th*; and for /ž/ (which is relatively rare in any case) it is a toss-up whether its "regular" representation is to be considered as being *z* (as in *azure*), *s* (as in *measure*) or *si* (as in *division*). In general, however, English orthography does afford to each phoneme of the language at least one regular, clear and consistent alphabetic representation.

If anyone doubts this last statement, it is very easy to test it with nonsense syllables (as I have done in the last five minutes, with members of my family, before writing this!). Let us try and test the relationship in either direction—both going from pronunciation to spelling, writing down an unfamiliar syllable we hear spoken, or going from spelling to pronunciation, speaking a syllable to correspond to a sequence of letters we have not seen before. If we hear, say, /klǽb/, the spelling that comes most immediately and naturally to a writer of English is *clab;* for /glɔ́d/, *glud;* for /sméyt/, *smate;* for /háks/, *hox.* Try it the other way: how

TABLE III. Regular Graphemic Representations of English Phonemes

PHONEME OR COMBINATION OF PHONEMES	GRAPHEME	EXAMPLES
/i/	*i*	*hit*
/e/	*e*	*set*
/æ/	*a*	*bat*
/a/	*o*	*hot*
/ə/	*u*	*but*
/iy/	*e* + consonant letter + *e*	*mete*
/ey/	*a* + consonant letter + *e*	*hate*
/ay/	*i* + consonant letter + *e*	*kite*
/ow/	*o* + consonant letter + *e*	*mote*
/yuw/	*u* + consonant letter + *e*	*cube*
/o/	*aw*	*saw*
/u/	*oo*	*look*
/uw/	*oo*	*boot*
/oi/	*oi*	*boil*
/ər/	*ur*	*hurt*
/əl/	*ul*	*cult*
/p/	*p*	*lip*
/t/	*t*	*tip*
/k/	*c*	*can*
/b/	*b*	*bib*
/d/	*d*	*did*
/g/	*g*	*gag*
/f/	*f*	*fin*
/θ/	*th*	*thin*
/v/	*v*	*vim*
/ð/	*th*	*this*
/s/	*s*	*sop*
/š/	*sh*	*shop*
/z/	*z*	*zip*
/ž/	*z*	*azure*
/č/	*ch*	*church*
/ǧ/	*j*	*jam*
/m/	*m*	*man*
/n/	*n*	*nab*
/ŋ/	*ng*	*sing*
/l/	*l*	*lab*
/r/	*r*	*rot*
/w/	*w*	*wen*
/y/	*y*	*yet*
/h/	*h*	*ham*
/hw/	*wh*	*why*
/kw/	*qu*	*quick*
/ks/	*x*	*box*

would we pronounce, say, *shrump*? Normally, only /šrə́mp/. Similarly, we would pronounce *thrope* as /θrówp/, *nart* as /nárt/, *zebe* as /zíyb/, and so on.

By no means all of our words are written with these regular or consistent spellings, and there still remains a sizeable residue of words whose spelling is irregular. We must notice two essential points, however. The first is that very few words are wholly capricious in their spelling: most irregular spellings are irregular only in the representation of one or two of the phonemes contained in the word (usually, though not always, the vowels). Occasionally, some wag will present us with the sequence of letters *ghoti* and ask us how it is pronounced; the answer is /fiš/ *fish*, with *gh* = /f/ as in *tough*, *o* = /i/ as in *women*, and *ti* = /š/ as in *nation*. But such a monstrosity is so rare as to be virtually non-existent in normal English spelling; the closest thing to it is *choir*, with *ch* = /k/ (not a unique correspondence, since we have it in *chasm, chorus*, etc.) and with the really unique spelling of /way/ as *oi*.

The second thing to keep in mind is that even our irregular spellings are by no means wholly random; they fall, to a large extent, into certain sub-sets which are consistent within themselves. Table II above showed some of these sub-systems, which we might call "regular irregularities," such as *ee* and *ea* for /iy/, *oa* and *oe* for /ow/, etc. Another type of "regular irregularity," this time in the writing of consonants, is the use of double consonant letters at the end of words, and after vowel letters in their "short" values in the middle of words: e.g. *muff, till, mitt*, etc.; *sitting, hatter, kidded* and so on. With spellings of this type, their phonemic interpretation is still quite clear, and the normal speaker of English will read off *spreat* as /spriyt/, *toak* as /tówk/, of *diff* as /díf/. Going the other way, however, these "regular irregularities" offer alternate ways of writing down what one hears, and it is quite likely that a person who hears such a word as /níyk/ may write it as *neak* or *neek* instead of *neke*, or may write /lə́rt/ as either *lurt, lert*, or *lirt*. This type of alternate possibility, within the framework of our "regular irregularities," is responsible for a large proportion of the naive and harmless misspellings we get all the time from so many children (and adults), such as *dert* for *dirt, seperate* for *separate, speach* for *speech, vesuls* for *vessels, botes* for *boats*, or *skool* for *school*. Especially with the spelling of the vowel phoneme /ə/, there is inevitably a great deal of uncertainty in many people's minds, because of the existence of several reasonably frequent alternate spellings—*u, o*, and (before *r*) *e, a* and *i* as well. How do YOU spell /twə́rp/ "contemptible little person"—*twirp* or *twerp*?

When we have set up both the "regular" spellings of English phonemes, and the sub-systems of "regular irregularities," there is left a hard core of really irregularly spelled words. (The surprising thing, however, is how few these are in comparison to the great mass of regular and semi-regular spellings.) Under this heading come most of the numerous correspondences we listed under the vowel phonemes in Table I, and under /k g f š ž/. For a great many of these irregularities, there are only one or two examples, as in the case of *ay* for /iy/ in *quay*, *u* for /i/ in *busy*, *sch* for /s/ in *schism*, or *wh* for /h/ in *who*. Under this heading come also the "silent letters" like the *b* in *debt* or the *p* in *psychology*. These really irregular spellings do indeed have to be learned as such, but even in the case of *choir* or *quay* their irregular nature is not such that we should treat them as absolutely unique, after the fashion of Chinese characters.

This fundamental division of English spellings into three main types, the regular, the semi-regular and the downright irregular, has a highly important bearing on the way we present orthography to our students in teaching them to read and spell.

BIBLIOGRAPHY

HALL, FRANCES A., and ELEANOR H. BRENES. *Spelling Patterns, Teacher's Edition*. Ithaca, N.Y.: Linguistica, 1964.

MOULTON, WILLIAM G. "Introduction to *Teacher's Manual* for Frances A. Hall. *Sounds and Letters*. Rev. ed. Ithaca, N.Y.: Linguistica, 1964.

SOFFIETTI, JAMES P. "Why Children Fail to Read: a Linguistic Analysis." *Harvard Educational Review* 25.63–84, 1955. Most of the examples given in Table I are taken from this source, in somewhat rearranged and expanded form.

ADVANCED READING
Goals, Techniques, Procedures

WILLIAM E. NORRIS

Hearing before speaking, speaking before reading, reading before writing.
This prescription has dominated contemporary foreign-language teaching
in the United States at least since 1941, the year that marked the end of
our "linguistic isolation," as Moulton remarks in his excellent survey of
language teaching in the 1940s and 50s.[1] Since that time linguists have
been at work analyzing previously unfamiliar languages and designing
course material guided by such linguistic principles as these—principles
that have become, as Moulton puts it, language-teaching slogans of the
day—"Language is speech, not writing." "A language is a set of habits."
"Teach the language, not about the language."

Thus it was that the "oral approach" (or "audio-lingual method") got
its start with adult students. Quite clearly the emphasis was on spoken
language.

Influential publications of the period in which linguists set forth more
fully these "linguistic principles of language teaching" were these: L.
Bloomfield, *Outline Guide to the Practical Study of Foreign Languages*
(1942): C. C. Fries, *Teaching and Learning English as a Foreign Language* (1945); E. A. Nida, *Learning a Foreign Language* (1950); and E. T.
Cornelius, Jr., *Language Teaching: A Guide for Teachers of Foreign
Languages* (1953).

The sources of this oral-language influence can also, of course, be
traced back much farther than 1941 to the "phonetic method" introduced
in Europe and elsewhere in the late 19th century, which ultimately
evolved into the "direct method." But the direct method had relatively
limited success in the United States, and by the 1930s the emphasis in
the schools was on memorizing grammatical rules and reading by translation. Nevertheless, the direct method did influence intensive language
programs. Its heritage is reflected, for example, in the characterization
of one method as a "direct-structural-oral approach."

---

[1] William G. Moulton, "Linguistics and Language Teachings in the United States,
1940–1960," in *Trends in European and American Linguistics, 1930–1960,* ed. Christine Mohrmann (Utrecht and Antwerp: Spectrum, 1961).

READING AND THE ORAL APPROACH

The basic view of most linguists toward the teaching of reading in a foreign language during the 40s and 50s was summarized by Fries in this widely quoted remark: "Even if one wishes to learn the foreign language solely for reading, the most economical and most effective way of beginning is the oral approach." Nida put it even more strongly: "Listening, speaking, reading, then writing constitute the fundamental order in language learning. . . . The scientifically valid procedure in language learning involves listening first, to be followed by speaking. Then comes reading and, finally, the writing of the language." Although the actual "scientific validation" of this premise may not be easy to substantiate, its pedagogical effectiveness is now generally accepted in foreign-language courses for children and adults alike. At the beginning and intermediate stages of second-language teaching, the modern approach places emphasis primarily—and almost exclusively—on the spoken language.

Unfortunately, in many English-as-a-second-or-foreign-language programs, especially intensive courses for adult students, the written language has been de-emphasized almost to the point of extinction. Some students seem never to be *taught* how to read English at all. Apparently they are expected to pick up reading skills "automatically" along the way to oral mastery, or to develop them independently after completing oral language instruction. To be sure, many courses do not claim to go beyond the beginning or low-intermediate stages of instruction, but the neglect of reading seems not to be due simply to the fact that beginners outnumber advanced-level students. Witness, for example, the first two "principles of foreign-language teaching" listed by Cornelius in his *Language Teaching* (a book that, along with Fries's *Teaching and Learning English as a Foreign Language*, was one of the two most influential teacher guides in the early application of the oral approach to the teaching of English as a foreign language): "(1) The objective of a teacher of a foreign language is to expose students to the language as it is spoken. (2) The ability to read and write a language *may come as a by-product* of the process of learning the spoken language" (italics added).

Not all language teachers agreed, of course. Brooks, writing later, fixed the class time for teaching reading and writing skills in proportion to teaching oral skills at approximately 20% at the beginning level and 50% to 60% at the intermediate levels in the elementary and secondary school.[2] But by and large there has been little attention to the systematic teaching of reading in beginning and intermediate classes, especially the sort of

[2] Nelson Brooks, *Language and Language Learning*. New York: Harcourt, Brace, and World, 1960.

preparation that might be expected to facilitate the student's acquisition of reading fluency at the advanced level of instruction.

Practical considerations have also contributed to the de-emphasis on learning the written language. Many adult students, in particular, have an immediate need for spoken-language skills. Therefore, many beginning and intermediate courses have as a primary objective the development of aural comprehension and speaking ability, giving little attention to the written language.

Nevertheless, a careful consideration of the middle-range and long-range needs even of such students as these will usually reveal that an ability to read English is going to be very important. For many such students, in fact, reading skills will eventually be much more important than oral skills.

GOALS IN TEACHING ADVANCED READING

How do we define the specific tasks of a program for teaching reading for information? In focusing on the advanced level we will assume that our students have already, in the beginning and intermediate phases of their instruction, learned something about reading English—at least as a by-product of their oral language study. They know the English alphabet and the regular conventions and common irregularities of the spelling system. We also assume that the students are literate in their native language, although we cannot be sure that they are efficient readers in it. By the way, it would be interesting and useful to know whether reading efficiency in the native language has a bearing on acquiring reading efficiency in a foreign language. In any event, since our students are literate, it is not the process of reading as such that they must learn, but rather skills for reading a foreign language, English.

At the opposite extreme, we need not concern ourselves primarily with teaching appreciation or evaluation of literature. In most adult reading situations in English as a foreign language, literary worth is not relevant. Even among native speakers, after all, most purposeful reading is for information rather than enjoyment.

A third point: Our goals will not include the teaching of "speed reading" as that term is popularly employed today; however, reading rate is not unimportant for the student of English as a foreign language. As a matter of fact, the student who reads so slowly and laboriously that he can focus on just one word at a time—reading word by word—is not really reading at all. He will usually be unable to put the words together to understand the sense of the sentence, and he will certainly be unable to unite sentences into a full understanding of paragraph meaning. Ask him "What was the paragraph about?" and his only honest answer will be "About 75 words." Improving the student's reading rate in conjunction with, and in part as a result of, improving his other reading skills is an important goal. Harris says: "It has been our experience that even 'advanced' learners of English as a second language tend to be slow readers and that their slow reading speed constitutes a serious handicap when they commence their studies at our universities."[3]

Our goal, then, in the advanced reading course is to teach the student (who already has at least an "intermediate" mastery of spoken English) how to get information from the printed page efficiently, rapidly, and with full understanding. A more complete understanding of our task can be gained by listing the specific reading skills our students must develop or improve in order to achieve this goal.

FIVE AREAS OF SKILL

Advanced ability in reading English as a foreign language requires improvement in reading speed, vocabulary recognition, and the comprehension of sentences, paragraphs, and complete reading selections. These are not exclusive needs of the foreign learner of English, of course; they are the skills that native speakers must also develop in order to become efficient readers. We might delineate these five areas of skill as follows:

1. *Speed of recognition and comprehension*
   a) Word-recognition speed: improving eye movement, visual discrimination
   b) Word-comprehension speed: symbol-sound-meaning association
   c) Sentence-structure recognition: eye sweep, reading by structures

2. *Vocabulary recognition and comprehension*
   a) Word formation: derivation and compounding
   b) Lexical range: choices and restrictions
   c) Vocabulary in context: using context clues to meaning

3. *Sentence structure and sentence comprehension*
   a) Sentence structures: understanding advanced-level conjunction, nominalization, embedding, etc., and grasping the "main idea"
   b) Sentence comprehension: understanding the full meaning

4. *Paragraph structure and paragraph comprehension*
   a) Paragraph organization: the "central idea," paragraph development
   b) Scanning for specific information
   c) Full understanding: paragraph analysis

5. *Comprehension of the complete selection*
   a) Surveying for the main ideas
   b) Scanning for specific information
   c) Reading for full understanding

[3] David P. Harris, *Reading Improvement Exercises for Students of English as a Second Language* (Englewood Cliffs, N.J.: Prentice-Hall, 1966).

In a later section of this article, I give examples of techniques and exercises for the student of English as a second or foreign language in each of these five areas of reading skill.

READING COMPREHENSION VERSUS
ORAL COMPREHENSION

Teachers know that reading ability does not develop simply as a by-product of training in the spoken language. It is not easy for the foreign learner to transfer to visual symbols the comprehension he has already gained of auditory symbols. After all, not even native speakers of English find it easy to learn to read. Commonly, the difficulties of both native and foreigner have been attributed to the almost universally deplored "poor fit" between English pronunciation and orthography. English, it is complained, is not spelled "phonetically" (or "phonemically"), and that is quite true; but it is at the same time an unfair charge, since the English spelling system was probably never intended to be more than superficially phonemic. Contemporary linguistic investigation suggests that, all things considered, the present system may be hard to improve on for its intended users: competent speakers and readers of English. On the other hand, the system certainly was not designed to make things easy for the learner, whether native or foreign.

Aside from English orthography, there is another major problem in learning to read: written English differs considerably from spoken English in many features of structure and style. Thus, we cannot assume that the student who has been taught authentic oral English will be able to cope automatically with authentic written English. Yet neither should we assume that *all* differences between speech and writing will make for learning difficulties. In fact, reading is in some respects easier for the student than oral comprehension, as the second of the two comparisons that follow will illustrate.

FEATURES OF DIFFICULTY IN READING AS
COMPARED TO SPEECH

1. Words and phrases known orally may not be recognized in print (/maĵəl/—*module*, /kænt/—*cannot*), or may be confused with homographs (*bow, read*) or words spelled similarly (*strap—strip, through—thorough*).

2. Vocabulary and usage not commonly heard in speech are encountered often in reading (*manifest; ambivalence. This fact is nowhere better illustrated than in the . . .*).

3. Writing uses word order, lexical variation, and other signals to make distinctions signaled in speech by sentence stress, pause, and intonation.

4.   Writing uses long complete sentences—sentences that employ complex embedding, nominalization, and other syntactical devices. (*The executive turns to the party for personnel to man the top jobs in the administrative agencies, and a further relationship is established through which the party makes a contribution to the organization and action of government.*)

5.   Contextual clues to meaning are necessarily limited to the written text; unlike speech, clues cannot be derived from the non-verbal situation.

FEATURES OF EASE IN READING AS COMPARED TO SPEECH

1.   Written forms often differentiate homophones (*seed—cede*), inflections (*miss time—missed time*), and word junctures (*a nice house—an ice house*) that are obscured in speech.

2.   Dialectal variations in spelling (*labor—labour*) and syntax (*does not have—has not got*) are few and minor. Nor is it necessary for the reader to know the pronunciation in order to understand a new word through analysis or association with known words (*fragmentation, avionic*).

3.   Expository writing makes use of a more limited range of sentence types than speech. Statements predominate; questions are rarer, especially the Yes-No type; and short answers and reduced forms are uncommon. Further, the sentence fragments, redundancies, false starts, gaps, and hesitations so common in informal speech are almost entirely lacking. In other words, edited written English is more regular and "correct," employs complete and well-formed sentences, and is free of grammatical errors and misspellings.

4.   Writing is permanent, not transient in time. Hence the reader can proceed at his own pace, pausing to puzzle out word formations and syntactical constructions, to consult his dictionary, to re-scan and reread.

5.   Written English provides more background information than does informal speech; good expository writing, especially technical writing, does not require that we "read between the lines" to find the meaning.

6.   Finally, in contrast to oral dialogue, writing does not distract the reader by requiring him to formulate a verbal response. He can devote all his efforts to understanding what he reads.

TEACHING ADVANCED-LEVEL READING

The principal methods of reading improvement, for both the native language and a foreign language, have been known and in use for some time. Teachers of reading and authors of textbooks for English as a foreign language have borrowed many ideas from materials for native-language reading improvement, revising and adapting them to the needs of the non-native speaker. To these they have added a few other devices particularly suited to foreign-language teaching.

We have learned something about the teaching of reading, mainly from the three disciplines of education, psychology, and linguistics; but there appear to be almost no new developments with special reference to *second-* or *foreign-language* reading except for some influence from current theories of transformational grammar. A check on current research by reading specialists and projects by TESOL specialists does not turn up any work concerned specifically with second-language reading for adult students. The main sources to which we must look for new and improved ideas are recent reading textbooks in English as a foreign language.

TECHNIQUES AND EXERCISES TO IMPROVE READING SKILLS

The types of exercises in widest use are not new or novel, nor are they unique to the teaching of reading. They employ the well-known techniques of matching, multiple choice, true/false, same/different or same/opposite, filling blanks, rearrangement, transformation, summary, outline, and paraphrase. The examples I present below, illustrating typical improvement techniques and exercises for each of the five areas of reading skill described, are drawn from seven college-level reading tests.

1. Improving Speed. Timed reading puts pressure on the student to read faster. In some courses all reading is timed, even directions and exercises. Students convert their times to word-per-minute rates and keep a record of progress. Some textbooks give the word count for each selection and provide words-per-minute conversion tables. None of the texts I examined suggested using mechanical pacing devices, but one recent article recommends the use of a metronome. To what extent do students transfer their ability to read faster under pressure to normal, untimed reading situations? This is a crucial but unresolved question.

a)   Speed in Recognizing Words

Word Matching. Underline the word that is the same as the given word:

1.	**got**	get	pot	hot	god	got
2.	**home**	whom	hone	hum	home	some

Word Pairs. Indicate whether the members of the pair are the same or different by underlining S or D:

1.	doesn't know	doesn't show	Same	Different
2.	have time	have time	S	D
3.	poor day	poor pay	S	D

b)   Speed in Understanding Words

One-Word Definitions. Underline the word that has the same meaning as the given word:

1.	**shut**	watch	close	sleep	need
2.	**speak**	point	talk	hope	see
3.	**purchase**	step	buy	listen	dream

Sames and Opposites. Indicate whether the members of the pair are the same or opposite by underlining S or O:

1.	stop	go	Same	Opposite
2.	speak	talk	S	O
3.	dirty	clean	S	O

c)   Recognizing Sentence Structure

Reading by Structures

> People in the United States
> are always talking
> about the weather.
> It's a kind of habit
> with them.
> When they . . .

2. Improving Vocabulary.

a)   Word Formation

Negative Prefixes. Use the correct prefix (*dis-, im-, in-, mis-, un-*) to make negative forms of the following words from the essay:

1. appear: _____
2. just: _____
3. personal: _____

Fill the blank with the proper negative prefix:

1. He always _____ connects the wires.
2. He always _____ pronounces the words.
3. His work is completely _____ satisfactory.

Derived Words. Fill the blanks with a noun (plural form) related to the underlined noun in the sentence:

1. Our interest was in art and (*artists*).
2. Our interest was in crime and _____.
3. Our interest was in music and _____.

Complete the following table:

	ADJECTIVE	NOUN	ADVERB	VERB
1.	original	(originality)	(originally)	(originate)
2.	_____	evolution	XXX	_____
3.	_____	_____	_____	brighten

b) Lexical Range

Which sentence illustrates the same use of the word (or idiomatic or figurative expression) as in the reading selection?

1. There are bound to be regional differences.
    a) The book is *bound* in leather.
    b) Children are *bound* to have some accidents as they grow up.
    c) The prisoner's hands were *bound*.

c) Vocabulary in Context

Using Context Clues. A *dynamic* person can keep Washington affairs from becoming boring. Often, through his activity, he can become well known in a short time.

> The best synonym for *dynamic* is:
> _____ powerless   _____ forceful
> _____ athletic   _____ cheerful

Paired Responses Using Semantic Equivalents. The instructor gives the cue orally; the student reads aloud, recites, or writes his response:

Cue: They are trying to fire MacDonald as president.
Response: They are trying to get rid of MacDonald as president.

d) Other Techniques to Improve Vocabulary

Recalling Words from Their Definitions. Fill in the missing letters in words from the reading selection:

1. Able to be depended on: rel _ _ _ le
2. Too many to be counted: inn _ _ _ _ able

Using Words in Sentences (orally or in writing). Use in one sentence each pair or group of words from the reading listed together:

1. anthropologist, cultures
Example: An anthropologist is a person who studies different cultures.
2. borrow, inventions
3. technology, slow, past

Vanishing Cues and Alternative Word Glosses. From a partially obliterated version of a previously read selection the student reconstructs the original, first using glosses and then without them:

>   *wonderful*   *period*
> Less thXn twenty XXXXX XXX, a XXXXXXXX "new XXX" XX medXcine—
>   *introduced*
> or so XX was supXoXed to XX—was XXXXXXX XX by the "wonder XXXXX," the germ-XXXXXXs extrXXrdinary. Here, XX seemed, were the . . .[4]

[4] The original version, which the student is to reconstruct, reads as follows: Less than twenty years ago, a fabulous "new era" of medicine—or so it was supposed to be—was ushered in by the "wonder drugs," the germ-killers extraordinary. Here, it seemed, were the . . .

3. Sentence Structure and Comprehension

a) Sentence Structure and the Main Idea

Grammatical Details. Supply the appropriate preposition for each blank in these sentences from the essay:

1. All cultures seem to be _____ a continuous state _____ change.

Supply the structure words that have been omitted:
1. Two women who meet _____ the first time often do _____ shake hands unless one is _____ especially honored guest.

Complex Sentence Structure. Combine each group of statements into a single coherent sentence:
1. All cultures change. Some cultures change at a slower rate than others.

Drill on embedded relative clauses and prenominal modifiers:

> *Cue:* The arbitration settled the issue.
> The arbitration was compulsory.
> *Response:* *a)* The arbitration, which was compulsory, settled the issue.
> *b)* The compulsory arbitration settled the issue.

General Syntactical Meaning: the Main Idea. Put a check mark before each statement that suggests approval. Put a circle before each statement that seems to show disapproval:

_____ 1. It is difficult to see how anyone could find Professor Baker's latest book anything but completely satisfying.

_____ 2. Although I have the highest personal regard for Professor Baker, I must confess that I find few major points in this book on which he and I agree.

b) Sentence Comprehension: Getting the Full Meaning

Logical Completion. Complete the sentence in a logical way, using one of the four words:

1. You can trust Henry to take good care of your money, for he is very

_____.

(honest, angry, evil, distant)

2. We had hoped that Robert would agree to help us, but he has _____ to.

(desired, promised, refused, intended)

Comprehension Questions. See "Types of Comprehension Questions," below.

4. Paragraph Structure and Comprehension.

a) Paragraph Organization

Reading for the Central Idea
What single word expresses the central idea of paragraph 16?
Read the paragraph quickly to determine the central idea. Then turn

the page and choose one statement that best expresses the central idea. Do not look back at the paragraph.

Paragraph Development
Paragraph 9 uses examples. Find another paragraph in the reading developed in this same way.
Paragraph 10 explains a reason for a condition. What other paragraph uses this same method of development?
Create a coherent paragraph by placing the sentences below in logical order. (Five sentences from the reading are given.)
b)   Scanning for Specific Information
Scan the following paragraph to answer this question: How did the college get its name?
c)   Reading for Full Understanding: Paraphrase and Analysis

Paraphrasing. Fill the blanks on the basis of the selection just read:
Much instructional material . . . is "busy work." Generally, such materials _____ comprehension; they do not _____ it. With practice on them we learn to _____ the examiner.

Paragraph Analysis. Use the following strategy to determine what a paragraph is about:

> (a) *Gather evidence:* Read the first sentence. (b) *Establish a hypothesis:* That the first sentence is the main idea. (c) *Check the hypothesis:* Read the second sentence. (d) *Revise the hypothesis*—if necessary to include new ideas. *Continue.*

Comprehension questions. See "Types of Comprehension Questions," below.

5. Comprehension of Complete Selection.

a)   Surveying for Main Ideas and Organizational Pattern
Outlining. The main ideas are given below in mixed-up order. Arrange them in the order in which the author discusses them: (*a*) early settlers, (*b*) need for water, (*c*) major industries . . .
Outline the thesis and main supporting ideas in conventional outline form. (A preceding exercise has identified the central ideas of the separate paragraphs.)

Paraphrasing and Summarizing the Main Ideas (orally or in writing).

Organizational Pattern. Check whichever of the following statements best expresses the organizational pattern of this essay. (Some editors make general or specific comments on the organizational pattern and style of the essay. These appear either before or after the selection, or in the exercises.)

b)   Scanning for Specific Information
Skim quickly to find the number of the paragraph in which each of the following topics is mentioned or discussed.

c) Reading for Full Understanding

Discussion or Summary of the Reading (oral or written)

Comprehension Questions. See "Types of Comprehension Questions," below.

TYPES OF COMPREHENSION QUESTIONS

Questioning for comprehension deserves further description, because it is a technique of wide usefulness for teaching other language skills besides reading and because it is used extensively in almost all reading texts. (In some materials well over half of the exercises are comprehension questions of various kinds.)

Five types of questions for comprehension can be described and graded according to (*a*) the linguistic form of the required response, and (*b*) the relation between the information that is needed to answer correctly and the information provided in the reading selection.[5] I list the five types here in order of increasing difficulty for the student.

Type 1:   Information from the reading sufficient for the answer is contained in the question itself.

a) Answerable simply Yes/No or True/False

Before Frank left for town, did his wife hand him an umbrella?
Before Frank left for town, his wife handed him an umbrella. (True or False)

b) Multiple choice of answers is given with the question.

What did Frank's wife hand him before he left?
_____ an umbrella, _____ a piece of cloth, _____ a letter

Type 2:   Answerable with information quoted directly from the reading selection. (*Wh-* questions—*who, when, where, what*—usually not *why* or *how* questions.)

What did Frank's wife hand him before he left for town? *Answer:* (She handed him) a piece of cloth (before he left for town).

Type 3:   Answerable with information acquired from the reading selec-

[5] These types of questions are suggested in part by Fe Dacanay in *Techniques and Procedures in Second Language Teaching* (Quezon City: Phoenix Publishing House, 1963). The illustrative examples are adapted from Kenneth Croft's *Reading and Word Study for Students of English as a Second Language* (Englewood Cliffs, N.J.: Prentice-Hall, 1960).

tion, but not by direct quotation from a single sentence. (Usually *why* or *how* questions.)

> How did Frank explain his difficulties to his wife? *Answer:* First, Frank told her . . . Then he said . . .

Type 4: Answerable from inference or implication from the reading; the information is not stated explicitly in the selection.

> How do you suppose Frank's wife felt about his explanation? *Answer:* Well, since she looked cross, I suppose that she . . .

Type 5: The answer requires evaluation or judgment relating the reading selection to additional information or experience of the reader.

> What would *you* have done in Frank's place?

The five types of questions described above are used in reading comprehension tests at various levels of difficulty. The construction of tests is ably surveyed by Paul Pimsleur in his article "Testing Foreign Language" (in Albert Valdman, ed., *Trends in Language Teaching,* New York: McGraw-Hill, 1966). A more detailed analysis of the problems of testing reading comprehension will be found in Robert Lado's *Language Testing* (New York: McGraw-Hill, 1964). Pimsleur points out various pitfalls to avoid in test construction—pitfalls which the exercise writer should also be wary of—and warns in conclusion that "tests are the truest reflections of the teacher's pedagogical aims: he should beware of his tests, for they tell the truth about his objectives as a teacher." This statement is equally true if we substitute the word *exercises* for *tests.*

ANALYSIS OF WORD FORMATION

It is a commonplace to say that words derive their meanings from the context in which they occur. In the case of complex words, the derivational processes by which they are formed also contribute meaning. One feature of reading-improvement courses for native speakers of English is training in the use of context clues and the use of word analysis as an aid to determining meaning. Word analysis is also introduced in some reading texts for English as a second language (see sample exercises under "Vocabulary Improvement," above). These usually focus on the most frequent and productive prefixes and suffixes, in contrast to texts for native speakers, which concentrate on detailed analysis (that is, definition) of less common Greek and Latin affixes and bound bases. The difference in emphasis is understandable; native speakers do not usually have difficulties with more productive forms, but non-native students do.

On the other hand, some non-native students find Greek and Latin components relatively easy to understand because they are common in the student's native language. Word-analysis exercises for native speakers of English deal with roots and affixes such as those is capital letters in the following sentence, but in teaching English as a *second or foreign* language we need to develop the student's ability to recognize and understand such derivational elements as are illustrated by the *italicized* forms. There is some overlap, as, for example, in the prefix *CON-*, the overlap being indicated here by the use of italic capitals (capitals for root and affix, italics for derivational element):

There are abundant examples of this institution to be observed in *CON*-TEMPOR*ary* societies, yet certain values of our own culture PRECLUDE its accept*ance*.

Neither native-language nor foreign-language reading improvement texts give direct instruction in the analysis of word compounds, although words such as *network, outlying, underlie,* and *headlong* are frequent in all types of writing. Analyzing them is probably unnecessary for native speakers, but the student of English as a foreign language might well benefit from systematically organized exercises.

Word compounds can be understood in part by analyzing syntactically the underlying constructions from which they are derived, but such an analysis frequently reveals only a "literal" meaning, and context clues or other information must still be used to gain full understanding. Advanced students will have little difficulty with, for example, compounds of the types Adjective + Noun (*highbrow*) or Noun + Noun (*network*), which reflect the syntax of basic modification patterns in English. But the syntactical analysis of other types may be beyond the student's English competence, or in any event may result in an ambiguous, misleading, or non-sensical interpretation. For example, the student may consider such possibilities as:

stronghold	the hold is strong / it holds strongly
withhold	with a hold / it holds with X
headlong	his head is long / with a long head / he longs in his head

Verb + Adverbial constructions are particularly troublesome because no predictable order of compounding is apparent: *layout—outlying, breakup—upswing, runaway—outran, handout—offhand.* Exercises for teaching the most productive types of compounds, based on accurate classification and description, are presently lacking in reading texts for English as a foreign language. (An exception is Croft and Brown, 1966 —see *Bibliography*.)

At best, word analysis can only be partly effective: the meaning of the base itself cannot be determined through internal examination.

CONTEXT CLUES TO VOCABULARY MEANING

A more direct means than word analysis for determining the meaning of a word is to look for clues to the meaning elsewhere in the sentence or in adjacent sentences. Five types of context clues can be described: *definition, experience, comparison and contrast, synonym,* and *summary.* The examples of each type that follow were carefully selected (from English-as-a-foreign-language texts) to illustrate a single type of clue, but clear-cut examples are not very common. For any given word in context, there may be more than one type of clue present—or there may be none at all.

1. *Definition.* The word is defined or explained by the writer:
A number of languages of South Africa have *clicks,* a variety of popping sounds made by forming vacuums between the tongue and the hard or soft palate.

. . . result of *natural turnover*—the departure of workers through death, retirement, or voluntary decision to seek a job somewhere else, without any forced layoffs.

2. *Experience.* The meaning is clarified from direct or indirect experience of the reader; the situation is familiar to him or he can imagine it:

The *sweat* rolled down his face. His entire body was wet, as if he had fallen into a spring. . . . The heat was terrible.

3. *Comparison and Contrast.* The context compares the word with a familiar word or, negatively, tells what it does not mean:

Although he was accustomed to life in the desert, he could not *endure* the heat of this valley very long. . . . Two more hours of such heat would finish him.

4. *Synonym.* The same ideas are expressed by two or more different words or phrases, one of which may be familiar to the reader:

When it comes to manufactured goods there is actually more *diversity* in this country than Europe has ever known. The *variety* of goods carried by our stores is the first thing that impresses any visitor from abroad.

5. *Summary.* An idea or situation expressed in different ways is summed up in one word or expression:

The Spanish word *ni* means "nor," but the closest equivalent combination of sounds in English is *knee.* In Congo Swahili *ni* is a prefix to affirmative verbs and means "I," while in Navajo it is a suffix to verbs and indicates completed action. . . . It is entirely ARBITRARY which sounds are employed to express particular ideas.

The student who learns how to determine the meaning of an unknown word by means of word analysis or context clues whenever the situation permits can minimize his dependence on the dictionary and at the same time gain a more precise understanding of the word's meaning in the particular sentence. Training in the use of context clues does not appear to have been developed in an organized way in texts presently available. The trend in recent materials for native speakers has been toward programed texts using the familiar fill-the-blank and multiple-choice devices. Some of these texts have been used with adult students of English as a foreign language.

PROCEDURES FOR CONDUCTING THE LESSON

Most advanced reading lessons are developed around a reading selection varying in length from a short paragraph to several pages of text. Three stages in teaching the lesson are: (1) pre-reading preparation, (2) reading the selection, and (3) follow-up activities based on the selection. Stage 1 focuses the student's attention on the main objectives of the assignment. It may also provide information designed to minimize incidental problems that might otherwise be an obstacle to the main objectives. Stage 3 provides the drill necessary to achieve the objectives of the lesson.

STAGE 1: PRE-READING PREPARATION

In choosing items for pre-reading preparation the teacher must consider the purpose of the lesson. For example, if the objective of a particular lesson is training the student to use context clues, the teacher should not at stage 1 give definitions of the words the student will encounter in the lesson. He might, rather, start out the lesson with a warm-up practice in the use of context clues. At another time, however, he may wish to define new vocabulary in advance if its lack would be a barrier to the aim of reading quickly for the central idea. Sometimes the only preparation needed will be a brief instruction: "Try to read this selection faster than the last one," or "Read the next paragraph to find the central idea." But at other times fuller development will be needed in order to motivate the student and prepare him for linguistic problems.

Preparing for Vocabulary, Syntax, and/or Other Difficulties. (1) List new or difficult vocabulary items or idioms, with or without definitions, and give sentences from the reading plus additional sentences that show the meaning in context. (2) Present new or difficult grammatical structures. Give examples from the selection, supplemented by other examples if necessary, illustrating the meaning of the construction. (3) Explain items which may be difficult because the cultural or technical meaning is unfamiliar.

Motivating the Reading. (1) Give purpose to the reading. Tell the students that they are to read, for example, in order to summarize the main ideas, or find specific information, or do a vocabulary exercise. (2) Outline or paraphrase the selection for the students. (3) Relate the selection to the students' own experience, interests, or needs by means of questioning and discussion.

STAGE 2: READING THE SELECTION

Two suggested procedures for conducting this stage are outlined below, the second more "intensive" than the first. They are merely examples of how classroom reading of a selection might be carried on at a relatively early level of the course. At the later, more advanced, levels of the course most classroom reading will be done silently.

Suggested Procedure A. The teacher reads each sentence or phrase ("thought group")—the class repeats orally in chorus, books open—individuals repeat the same sentence. The teacher checks for pronunciation, rhythm, and intonation. After the entire selection has been read aloud, the class reads it silently for comprehension. The silent reading may be timed.

Suggested Procedure B. The teacher reads each sentence aloud—the class or individuals repeat. Each sentence is immediately followed by one or more comprehension questions of types 1, 2, 3 (described above), depending on the students' language ability. Each paragraph may also be followed by comprehension questions. Next, the teacher, class, or individuals read the whole selection through again orally. Silent reading may follow.

STAGE 3: FOLLOW-UP ACTIVITIES

In the Classroom. The teacher selects, according to the aims of the lesson, exercises of the types described in "Techniques and Exercises," above. He may conduct the session orally or in writing, or may use a combination of oral and written procedure: the teacher asks questions orally—the class responds in writing—individuals are called on to read answers orally.

As Homework. The teacher may assign written exercises developed out of the day's classroom work. *For example:* Write out full answers to comprehension questions done orally in class. Or write a paraphrase, summary, or outline of the reading selection. Or use the new vocabulary in additional sentences.

Homework assignments also carry the student into the preparation stage of the next lesson. He may be instructed to study new vocabulary in context, or to survey the selection for main ideas, or to scan it for specific information. At the earlier levels of instruction, however, reading for full understanding will be done only in the classroom under the teacher's supervision. At the most advanced levels, on the other hand, much of the reading might be done outside the class, with the class period devoted to follow-up exercises and preparation for the next selection.

OUT-OF-CLASS READING

Out-of-class *extensive* reading for expansion of reading skills, in contrast to intensive in-class drill in these same skills, should make use of relatively easier reading materials. Completely new vocabulary and grammatical patterns should be minimized if not avoided altogether—since the purpose is to provide a wide range of use and meaning contexts for known vocabulary and patterns. The student thus develops his skills in deducing meanings of new words and in extending the lexical range of known items.

Even though there may be no specific exercises correlated with the out-of-class reading selections, student motivation and follow-up are still important. Reading matter that appeals to student interests or needs, and which is somewhat less difficult than the classroom readings, helps encourage students to read on their own. Additional motivation can be provided by having the student read with the aim of using the information gained for some purpose, such as solving a problem, forming a judgment or opinion, or making an evaluation, etc., all of which can be reported to the teacher or the class orally or in writing.

A NOTE ON MECHANICAL AIDS TO READING IMPROVEMENT

The common classroom aids—chalkboard, pictures, charts—may be supplemented in reading instruction by greater use of duplicated handouts than is usual in the oral-language class. Examples of vocabulary in context and collections of sentences illustrating structural patterns can be presented orally, but in a reading class they also ought to be *read*, and duplicating them is much more efficient and less fatiguing than writing examples on the chalkboard.

The overhead projector can also be used effectively to present examples, and it has the advantage of limiting student attention to the particular items the teacher wants him to read; pointer, mask, or marker is used to pin-point the problem. A student with his nose in a book or handout may or may not be looking at the appropriate example—a teacher never knows for sure. A further use of the projector is for pacing reading speed: a selection or exercise is flashed on the screen for a limited time only.

Special mechanical aids have been developed for teaching reading improvement to native speakers—principally the various *pacer* devices and the *tachistoscope*. Pacers are designed to increase reading speed by forcing the student to read faster under pressure. Tachistoscopes and reading films are used to improve eye span and eye movement and thus increase reading efficiency. There are no reports I know of that such devices have been employed to any extent in foreign-language teaching, and in fact, their value in native-language situations has been questioned. Certain individual students do show improvement as a result of such external pressure, and the use of machines may encourage more effort from some students. But machine-induced skills must be transferred to reading that is not machine-assisted if they are to be of any real value to the reader.

SUMMARY

There are many more aspects of the teaching of reading than have been discussed here—including such topics as the selection of reading materials, adaptation and construction of texts and exercises, the relationship between reading and composition, teaching reading to special groups for particular purposes, and underlying linguistic factors in second language reading. This article has concentrated on matters of immediate and practical classroom application by focusing on three primary aspects of the teaching task: (1) definition of advanced-level reading goals, (2) varied techniques and exercises for achieving improvement in five reading skill areas, and (3) suggested classroom procedures for conducting the reading lesson. The material gathered together here represents a compilation of goal definitions, exercise techniques, and suggested teaching procedures drawn from a wide variety of sources. I have tried to present it in a context broad enough so as not to obscure its relevance and applicability in the majority of teaching situations.

BIBLIOGRAPHY

REFERENCES

BROOKS, NELSON. *Language and Language Learning.* New York: Harcourt, Brace and World, 1960.

DACANAY, FE R. *Techniques and Procedures in Second Language Teaching.* Quezon City: Phoenix Publishing House, 1963.

LADO, ROBERT. *Language Testing.* New York: McGraw-Hill, 1964.

MOULTON, WILLIAM G. "Linguistics and Language Teaching in the United States 1940–1960." *Trends in European and American Linguistics* 1930–1960, ed. Christine Mohrmann, pp. 82–109. Utrecht and Antwerp: Spectrum, 1961. (Available as an offprint from the U.S. Government Printing Office, Washington, D.C.)

PIMSLEUR, PAUL. "Testing Foreign Language Learning." *Trends in Language Teaching,* ed. Albert Valdman. pp. 175–214. New York: McGraw-Hill, 1966.

PLAISTER, TED. "Reading Instructions for College Level Foreign Students." *TESOL Quarterly* (September 1968), 164–68.

SMITH, DONALD E. P., ed., *Learning to Learn.* New York: Harcourt, Brace and World, 1961.

SELECTED READING TEXTS FOR ADVANCED LEVEL AND ADULT STUDENTS

BAUMWOLL, DENNIS, and ROBERT L. SAITZ. *Advanced Reading and Writing: Exercises in English as a Second Language.* New York: Holt, Rinehart and Winston, 1965.

BIGELOW, GORDON E., and DAVID P. HARRIS. *The United States of America: Readings in English as a Second Language.* New York: Holt, Rinehart and Winston, 1965.

CROFT, KENNETH. *Reading and Word Study for Students of English as a Second Language.* Englewood Cliffs, N.J.: Prentice-Hall, 1960.

CROFT, KENNETH, and BILLYE WALKER BROWN. *Science Readings for Students of English as a Second Language.* Washington, D.C.: Educational Services, 1966.

DOTY, GLADYS, and JANET ROSS. *Language and Life in the U.S.A.* Second ed. New York: Harper and Row, 1968.

HARRIS, DAVID P. *Reading Improvement Exercises for Students of English as a Second Language.* Englewood Cliffs, N.J.: Prentice-Hall, 1966.

IMAMURA, SHIGEO, and JAMES W. NEY. *Readings on American Society.* Waltham, Mass.: Blaisdell, 1969.

NEWMARK, LEONARD, JEROME R. MINTZ, and JAN LAWSON HINELY. *Using American English.* New York: Harper and Row, 1964.

SECTION FIVE
WRITING

Writing skills, like reading skills, are usually developed at the
advanced level of English instruction. Skill in writing, even more so
than in reading, depends heavily on a solid foundation in listening and
speaking skills. Throughout the beginning and intermediate states,
the student ordinarily learns something of the process of writing—as a
"by-product" or in support of oral language study—but actual skill
in writing only comes with concentrated practice and guidance.

The authors in this Section deal with writing at progressively higher
levels. Dykstra's programed techniques could be put into operation
at a fairly low level. Dictation, as described by Sutherland, could
begin at about the same level, perhaps a little higher. Slager's
controlled composition would have to start not lower than the intermediate level—probably high intermediate. Kaplan's expository
writing, mostly without controls, could only apply at the advanced
level.

PROGRAMED WRITING

The programs being prepared by Dykstra and his colleagues at the
Hawaii Curriculum Center enable the student to gain writing
competence rapidly and systematically. They are not designed simply to
reinforce oral competence, although they undoubtedly do that, too.
Dykstra points out that there are many steps leading through gradual
approximations to the goal of free writing. First the student observes
others' writing and he examines models; later he copies a word
from a model paragraph, then the title of a paragraph, and finally one
entire title and paragraph. "The program from this point on," he
continues, "can be seen as one of changing models into products
that are less and less like the models, until they are, in effect, new
creations, and until the models are no longer directly or consciously
used. . . . The steps include substitutions, transformations, reductions,
expansions, completions, additions, revisions, commentary and

creations." From the point of view of procedure, many of the steps parallel audiolingual pattern practice devices.

In regard to the effectiveness of this kind of program, Dykstra says "it is an excellent way to elicit large quantities of completely acceptable writing practice at each student's approximately best level of contributing ability. The sub-goals are always very explicit—to produce a completely acceptable product at whatever level the student is working. If he should fail, he tries again at that same level with a new model. If he fails repeatedly, he stays at one contributing level and the source of his difficulty should be pinpointed. In general, he clearly recognizes the goal and it is within his grasp." Concerning the transition from manipulation to communication, he mentions that "The top levels of the program request substantiation of the model, argument with the model, and various types of free writing. . . ."

Sutherland views dictation also as programed activity. "Dictation," he explains, "is the transference, by a second person, of primary auditory language symbols (speech) into secondary graphic ones (writing). He considers two main purposes for dictation: "[it] promotes the ability to decode sequences of oral symbols into written ones . . . [and it] serves as a testing device to check on student progress." He proceeds to point out that "the basic elements in programing— the idea of breaking up the material into small steps, asking the student to respond to each item, and rewarding him for correct answers —have been practiced by good teachers for centuries. . . . We can see that in dictation . . . the student is immediately reinforced by his own—and frequently the teacher's—observation that his sentences correspond to the ones dictated." Sutherland discusses several important principles relating to classroom dictation activities: specific objectives, appropriate practice, individual differentiation, immediate reinforcement, and graduated sequence.

SOME SPECIAL PROBLEMS

In the usual sequence of skills development—understanding, speaking, reading, and writing—we notice that reading and writing occupy positions three and four. According to an older point of view, listening and speaking skills should be developed to the point of fluency, and then the same techniques for teaching reading and writing to native speakers could be employed for teaching reading and writing to the non-native speaker. This idea has largely been abandoned, but it still persists in some quarters. Generally the demands for learning to read and write are too great to be ignored. Consequently, we work on all four skills, almost from the beginning —not simultaneously, but in the sequence noted. Then we apply more concentrated attention to reading and writing at the advanced level.

Slager concerns himself with the writing of paragraphs and of compositions consisting of several paragraphs. He describes and illustrates with model assignments "some of the techniques that have developed for guiding the students so carefully that they will leave the composition classroom with a sense of achievement rather than a feeling of frustration." He notes that "Students . . . need to start an assignment with more than blank paper, a sharpened pencil, and a dictionary. They must also have a subject about which all of them can write, a subject in common, so that they can begin with a repertory of relevant words and sentences. Since this common subject is usually provided by way of readings, the use of readings is assumed as background to most of the writing assignments . . . [he has selected]." In the end Slager points out that "Students who can do all these exercises are still a long way from free composition, which implies the ability to develop a well-organized theme on any subject that might be assigned. I have a suspicion that this kind of activity is never completely successful in the classroom. It requires a situation all too rare in the crowded schools of today—one in which there can be frequent individual conferences between the highly motivated student and the skillful teacher."

In our society we attach great importance to correctness of form in writing: margins, paragraph indentation, correct spelling, appropriate use of punctuation, complete sentences, unity, coherence, and the like. It was noted earlier (in Section Four) that we devote huge amounts of time in our school years to reading, spelling, and writing— so much so that we tend to consider language as something graphic. This emphasis on proper form is a particular focus of American education—it is by no means universal. As ESOL teachers we some- times face a serous problem in regard to the teaching of writing— not one of mechanics, though this may be serious, too, at times— but one of attitude. Many students find it difficult to believe that correctness in form deserves so much importance. Some students will never be convinced of it, and their writing reveals their attitude accordingly.

EXPOSITORY WRITING

Kaplan deals with problems of rhetoric. "The English language and its related thought patterns," he points out, "have evolved out of the Anglo-European cultural pattern. The expected sequence of thought in English is essentially a Platonic-Aristotelian sequence, descended from the philosophers of ancient Greece and shaped subsequently by Roman, Medieval European, and later Western thinkers. It is no better nor worse than any other, but it is different." In regard to paragraph development, he notes that "The thought patterns which speakers and readers of English appear to expect as an integral part of their communication is a sequence that is dominantly linear. An English expository paragraph usually begins with a topic statement, and then, by a series of subdivisions of that topic statement, each supported by example and illustrations, proceeds to develop that central idea and relate that idea to all the other ideas in the whole essay, and to employ that idea in its proper relationship with other ideas, to prove something, or perhaps to argue something."

After presenting a model English paragraph, Kaplan proceeds to contrast English paragraph development with paragraph development in other linguistic systems. He uses student compositions and translations into English as examples to demonstrate that "each language and each culture has a paragraph order unique to itself, and that part of the learning of a particular language is the mastering of its logical system." He provides some graphic sketches to show the direction followed in paragraph movement in the English, Semitic, Oriental, Romance, and Russian languages.

Kaplan suggests that the contrastive analysis of rhetoric is one possible answer to certain needs of advanced-level foreign students in learning to write themes, theses, essay examinations, and dissertations. "Such an approach," he continues, "has the advantage that it may help the foreign student to form standards of judgement consistent with the demands made upon him by the educational system of which he has become a part. At the same time, by accounting for the cultural aspects of logic which underlie the rhetoric structure, this approach may bring the student not only to an understanding of contrastive grammar and a new vocabulary, which are parts of any reading task, but also to grasp the idea and structure in units larger than the sentence. . . . The foreign student who has mastered the syntax of English may still write a bad paragraph or a bad paper unless he also masters the logic of English."

SELECTED READINGS

ARAPOFF, NANCY. "Writing: A Thinking Process." *TESOL Quarterly* 1(1967): 33–39.

———. "Discover and Transform: A Method of Teaching Writing to Foreign Students." *TESOL Quarterly* 3(1969):297–304.

DYKSTRA, GERALD. "Eliciting Language Practice in Writing." *English Language Teaching* 19(1964):23–26.

ERAZMUS, EDWARD T. "Second Language Composition at the Intermediate Level." *Language Learning* 10(1960):25–31.

KAPLAN, ROBERT B. "Contrastive Rhetoric and the Teaching of Composition." *TESOL Quarterly* 1(1967):10–16.

KNAPP, DONALD. "A Focused, Efficient Method to Relate Composition Correction to Teaching Aims." In *Teaching English as a Second Language: A Book of Readings.* Edited by Harold B. Allen. New York: McGraw-Hill Book Company, 1965.

LADO, ROBERT. *Language Teaching: A Scientific Approach.* Chapter 14: "Writing." New York: McGraw-Hill Book Company, 1964.

————. *Linguistics across Cultures: Applied Linguistics for Language Teachers.* Chapter 5: "How to Compare Two Writing Systems." Ann Arbor: The University of Michigan Press, 1957.

MOULTON, WILLIAM G. *A Linguistic Guide to Language Learning.* Chapter 8: "Writing." 2d ed. New York: The Modern Language Association, 1970.

PAULSTON, CHRISTINA BRATT. "The Use of Model Passages in a Program of Guided Composition." In *On Teaching English to Speakers of Other Languages, Series III.* Edited by Betty Wallace Robinett. Champaign, Ill.: National Council of Teachers of English, 1967.

RIVERS, WILGA M. *Teaching Foreign-Language Skills.* Chapter 10: "The Writing Skill." Chicago: The University of Chicago Press, 1968.

ROJAS, PAULINE. "Writing to Learn." *TESOL Quarterly* 2(1968):127–29.

SAWYER, JESSE O. and SILVER, SHIRLEY KLING. "Dictation in Language Learning." *Language Learning* 11(1961):33–42.

BREAKING DOWN
YOUR WRITING GOALS

GERALD DYKSTRA

Are you happy with the goals you have for your high school writing program? The majority of teachers feel their goals are satisfactory. They see the problem as one of method. They would prefer to ask instead, "How can we get high school students . . . to attain the desirable goals we have set?"

I would like to persist with the first question. I believe that by doing so we can get much farther than we can by directing our attention immediately to the second question. I believe that if you know where you want to go you can set up many ways to get there. And if you have more than one student you will need more than one way to get to any goal. Even if you had only one student, he would be likely to need differing approaches at different times. I believe that goals are often too large, too remote, or too amorphous. They can be broken down into components that are small enough, immediate enough, and sharp enough to be readily attained by the student. The question of "how" then begins to lose some of its magnitude.

WHAT ARE YOUR GOALS?

The question that must directly follow our opening question, especially if you answered that question with a "Yes," is "What are your goals?" Determining basic goals in high school writing programs is always a thorny problem. . . . One of the first concerns is that English is not in most cases the students' native language. A study commissioned by the Bureau [of Indian Affairs] recommended an experiment in which the teaching of reading in the native language would precede the teaching of reading in English.[1] Beyond this, should the students also have an opportunity to write first in their native language? What would the interference effects be, if any, when they subsequently write in English? What special difficulties are there in any case because of their non-

---

[1] Sirarpi Ohannessian, ed., *The Study of the Problems of Teaching English to American Indians: Report and Recommendations* (Washington, D.C.: Center for Applied Linguistics, 1967), p. 30.

English language and culture background? How do these factors affect establishment of a basic goal?

These and many other questions need to be answered before fully realistic goals can be formulated. Some teachers who answer "Yes" to the first question are unable to communicate clearly, even to another teacher, what these goals are. It is easy to understand why these teachers fail to communicate the goals to their students. Many others give an answer like "To write well." We can grant the legitimacy of this answer, but we still have to follow it up with the further question, "What do you mean by good writing?" This may be answered by a description of some kind, but the description will commonly fail to communicate meaningfully to most people. Teachers may feel that they will know good writing when they see it, but it is not easy to describe. A much easier and generally more successful approach is to provide samples that illustrate what you call good writing.

If you select samples with your students in mind, they should illustrate what can reasonably be expected from the student after a period of training. Ultimately, classroom goals depend primarily on what the teacher wants or expects with the "givens" he has. The teacher can make these goals relatively explicit by selecting models of student or professional writing as examples of goal attainment.

The opening question may take on special meaning in this context. The selections that you have, or have in mind, represent what you can now reasonably expect at least some of your students to attain. If you are not happy with these selections as representative of the ultimate goals you have for your students, you may nevertheless be happy with them as representative of the immediate goals you have. You may feel they represent a clear advancement in a student's ability during the time he is with you.

HOW DO WE GET THERE?

Surely the next question is, "How do we get there?" Yes, that is in one sense the next question, but I would prefer to ask, "Can you set up sub-goals that will take the student to the ultimate goal?" That is, can you ultimately break the goal down into moment-by-moment sub-goals? And will these sub-goals lead to closer and closer approximations to the ultimate goal? Can the student achieve successfully all along the way so that difficulties can be reasonably well pinpointed before he founders, trying unsuccessfully to reach the big conglomerate goal for the high school program?

There are many ways to break a goal down into smaller parts. Let me illustrate with a parable. A certain man decided to do 50 consecutive deep knee bends within one minute as part of his exercise routine. After 4 bends, the strength of his right knee gave way and though he fought valiantly, without the supporting lift from his right leg, he was unable to do more than 7 deep knee bends. Undaunted, he continued trying. For 17 successive days the same thing happened. Then his right knee began giving way after only 3 deep knee bends. He was, of course, crestfallen, not to say daunted.

He resolved, however, to attain his goal by trying one or more programs of sub-goals which he could invent in quantity. The following are only a few samples:

(1) He could start the first month with a goal of only one deep knee bend per day. Then he could try adding only one per day with each new month.

(2) He might be able to *start* with 50 bends if he allowed more time between each two, such as a full minute instead of only about one second. He could then gradually reduce the interval between bends from one minute to 59 seconds and eventually to one second.

(3) He could do 50 full bends from the start by pushing himself up with his arms or with the aid of a mechanical lift. Then he could gradually reduce his reliance on such help until he was finally doing 50 unaided bends.

(4) He could avoid an approach that required any form of full bends right from the start, and begin with 50 partial bends, flexing his knees just slightly at first, then increasingly until finally he would again be doing full bends. Or he could do the reverse, starting from the full bent position, and do partial "ups."

(5) He could, of course, do any of the dozens of kinds of knee and leg strengthening exercise programs that you can find in any professional gymnasium without specific reference to knee bends.

When last heard of, the certain man of our parable was progressing well, by his own account, doing partial knee bends as in the first part of the fourth alternative above with occasional forays into the others, largely to test his progress. In tests, he had attained 20 successive full bends after three months of his new regimen. He expects to attain 50 within the first year.

WORKING WITH SUB-GOALS

This parable is not intended to indicate a desirable way to physical development, nor to suggest that knee bends can contribute to composition writing. The point is that goals have many dimensions, and that a series of successively closer approximations to a big goal can be stated in many different ways once that larger goal is rather clearly indicated. When a goal is sufficiently broken down into sub-goals, sometimes referred to as objectives within goals, any further question of method usually becomes quite tractable. "Just show him" or "Tell him" or "Give him one to look at" are normal responses when someone needs to know how to do some small or simple thing. Essentially the same can be true of most big goals, whether in space exploration or in oral language learning or in writing, if the sub-goals are "moment-by-moment" enough.

The model of the goal, you will remember, is in the form of samples of good writing. How can we break down our goal of good writing into sub-goals of (or successive approximations to) this goal? It will mention one traditional and partial breakdown and then go into a little more detail on one alternative that has proved successful in providing clearly defined goals, and that is instrumental in eliciting large quantities of completely correct writing with degrees of student contribution up to a level that is effective in nearly every instance.

The writing breakdown that we are most accustomed to includes component goals of basic handwriting ability, skill with placement of punctuation, and other matters of form like margins and spelling, and ability to form grammatical sentences and paragraphs. We also ask for unity, coherence and organization. In the high school program, we assume that work toward each of these sub-goals is a part of the student's prior heritage, and we give him assignments that require him to perform well in all of them at a somewhat advanced level, like the man setting out to do 50 deep knee bends a minute the first day he began this exercise. Indeed, when the student was learning the component goals listed here there were probably times when limited parts of his writing program seemed to have relatively well-defined goals, as when he had to make the letters of the alphabet. But, for example, he may never have attained the stage of writing grammatical sentences with regularity. The goals involved here were mostly too big and too amorphous for him. Now we have him write, and we proceed to apply rather haphazard corrective procedures. We find out where his errors are, point them out to him, and give him some extra work. Then we go on our way. The student can rarely, if ever, predict that he has hit the target. The goal and all the sub-goals are too amorphous for that. Even the collection of acceptable samples is no help to him. These simply illustrate the level of the big goal, which is not directly attainable. Even if we give him work with one or another of the constituent components, it is like asking our certain man to begin with a small number of full knee bends, say ten—even that may be too difficult for him at the beginning.

It would certainly be possible to refine the traditional goal statements. But as a conclusion to this paper, I would like to look at an alternative— one among many—this one resembling in a way a combination of approaches 3 and 4 to the problem of deep knee bends above.

USING MODELS

Assume that you have the many models or samples of good writing that we mentioned earlier. Assume at least a hundred or two such models. Let the student observe these products as long and as often as he likes. This is all right. It should be condoned, even encouraged. That kind of product is the goal for your student. And he must surely be able to read with comprehension what you are realistically going to expect of him in the form of writing at some reasonable future time. A further program of observation, if it is necessary, can consist of watching the teacher or a student in the process of writing the early steps (and later the advanced ones) that will be mentioned shortly. Still, observation and reading won't produce a product like the samples. Eventually the student must write something. Must he jump from observation to free writing?

The answer is "No." There are any number of intervening small steps, like the aided knee bends in number 3, or the partial knee bends in number 4, which can lead the student through gradual approximations to the larger goal of free writing. The first step for a high school student may consist of moving from adequate observation to writing one word or a title from a model onto his own paper and keeping it for his own observation. A larger step consists of writing only that and then handing it to someone else for review and evaluation. Another type of larger step consists of writing more than just a title or a word.

A very large step for almost all high school students everywhere is, believe it or not, copying one entire title and paragraph without error. When given as the first step in the writing program I am now describing, it is the cause of more errors than any other single step on the whole route to acceptable free writing.

If your students succeed early in copying an acceptable selection completely to your satisfaction—and I would urge the highest of standards at this point—then you are on the way to success with them.

At this stage we have attained the corollary of simple repetition in oral work. In a sense it is only an active equivalent of observation. A critically important start has been made, but now there is a long road to travel.

PROCEEDING BY SMALL STEPS

There is not space in this paper to give detailed information about the many steps used in gradually reducing the student's dependence on the model. Representative examples and categories, however, will suffice to illuminate the principle, and there are an infinite number of variations possible.

The program from this point on can be seen as one of changing models into products that are less and less like the models until they are, in effect, new creations, and until the models are no longer directly or consciously used. The reworked models have sometimes been called transformations but they are not uniformly to be related to transformational grammar. The steps include substitutions, transformations, reductions, expansions, completions, additions, revisions, commentary and creations. The transformations include types that might be called applications of transformational grammar, but they are not limited to this.

Remember, getting on the road is a big step or series of steps. Once you are on the road—that means demonstrated ability to convert a printed product into a handwritten sentence, paragraph, or essay—it is not a very big step to move to substitution of one word in the model by another word in the student's completed version if that word occurs only once. This is still just a little way beyond observation. It is another small step if the word to be substituted occurs repeatedly. It is another small step if two or more different words are to be substituted. And, provided the grammar is known or taught just before, it is once more a small step if one word that is substituted requires a small grammatical change elsewhere. For example, a part of the model reads "He is here" and the assignment calls for changing "he" to "they." The small additional change that is required is a substitution of "are" for "is." Such assignments are built upon a host of changes of gender, number, tense, etc. These simple grammatical terms, often so frightening to the student, need not be used at all.

The assignments can become very complex if multiple types of changes are required simultaneously, but fortunately this does not seem to be a necessary stage. Students learn to go on to small changes in topic which require minimal meaning change elsewhere and this serves as a base for greater topic changes later. They can also move into the "free-addition" steps by, for example, adding another person and making all appropriate changes elsewhere. "His horse watered, Ben is ready . . ." may become "Their horses watered, Ben and Larry are ready . . ." Obviously if "Ben" is changed to "the kitten" it is instead a more advanced topic substitution and a possible production is "Its fur dried, the kitten is ready . . ." If this change is combined with free addition of a subject, you can get "Their coats dried, the kitten and the puppy were ready for . . ." Other types of additions, generally more advanced, include the options for adding modifiers of many kinds, time expressions, reasons, phrases and clauses of a wide variety of types, complete sentences, paragraphs, endings, beginnings, etc. These are intermediate steps among hundreds that can lead to higher goals.[2]

---

[2] A sample program, in a format designed for materials developers only, is a revision of a mimeographed paper formerly entitled "Worksheet No. 3, Expanding the Writing Horizons" by Gerald Dykstra, Richard Port and Antonette Port. For students, an early

ELICITING WRITING PRACTICE

It is important at this point to make both a disclaimer and a "claimer." When there is a mistaken expectation, the most common one is to expect a program like this to teach basic grammar, or even pronunciation, or other aspects of the oral base, necessary parts of which are assumed prerequisites in this program for successful writing at the upper levels. This type of program will effectively provide little, or nothing, that it is not designed to provide. On the other hand, it is an excellent way to elicit large quantities of completely acceptable writing practice at each student's approximately best level of contributing ability. The sub-goals are always very explicit—to produce a completely acceptable product at whatever level the student is working. If he should fail, he tries again at that same level with a new model. If he fails repeatedly, he stays at one contributing level and the source of his difficulty should be pinpointed. In general, he clearly recognizes the goal and it is within his grasp. If it is not, he is probably not ready to proceed much farther in writing without relevant basic instruction in points of the language as indicated by the type of problem he cannot overcome.

The top levels of the program request substantiation of the model, argument with the model, and various types of free writing including such advanced steps as the following which require the student:

—to write on the topic given. (A related model has been read previously.) He must write a paragraph for each key sentence and he may use the key word given as a clue or suggestion for each sentence in each paragraph;

—to write a paragraph following each (key) sentence given under the topic heading (no key words given);

—to write on the topic with a paragraph on each sub-topic given to guide organization. (No related paragraph has been seen previously.)

After other intermediate steps we come to the assignment that is so commonly the first assignment in many classes: Choose a topic and write (to the extent requested by the teacher or the materials writer or to the extent the student feels qualified).

A student can reach this level quickly if he is qualified. If he can't do it, the program provides an alternative of a sequence of sub-goals that

---

model with a very small selection of steps, by the same authors, was *A Course in Controlled Composition: Ananse Tales*, 2 vols., New York: Teachers College Press, 1966. And the newest version is *Guided Writing: Controlled—Free*, Programs 1–12, New York: McGraw-Hill, forthcoming. [Some sample pages from the latter are reproduced at the end of this article.]

will give him many successful writing experiences at his own best level of contribution. It is surprising to note the definable progress when there are enough definable sub-goals. It is not necessary to teach without seeing progress. But there is no alternative when the overall goals or the sub-goals are too big and too amorphous for the students to grasp.

Your goals may need breaking down in order to build up your students. Consider breaking them down to moment-by-moment goals.

A BRAVE HERO

Mr. Worm crawls into a jar. The bugs push it into the pond. He floats out in the water. He is able to see things through the glass. He sees the bottom of the pond. He sees many hungry fish. The fish see him.

Step 5. Write the story pretending you are Mr. Worm. Begin *I crawl into a jar.*

Step 6. Write the story changing the first sentence to *Mr. Worm crawled into a jar.* Be sure to change words like *push* and *floats.*

Step 11. Write the story changing all the sentences to questions. Begin *Does Mr. Worm crawl into a jar?* Be careful of this mark . and words like *floats* and *is.*

Step 16. Write the story taking this mark . out after the word *jar* and putting in this mark ; and the word *then.* Be sure to change the *T* in the word *The.* Also take this mark . out after the word *fish* and put in this mark ; and the word *likewise.* Be sure to change the *T* in the word *The.*

Step 21. Write the story putting a word of your own in front of *jar.* Now put different words of your own in front of *bugs, things* and *bottom.*

Step 31. Write the story putting two or more new sentences of your own after the word *water.* Tell how Mr. Worm feels as he floats out in the water.

Gerald Dykstra, Richard Port, Jan V. Prins

PROGRAM 4

JOHNNY APPLESEED

An old woman in Pennsylvania talks about a wanderer named John Chapman. She calls him Johnny Appleseed. She says that Johnny Appleseed carried a bag full of apple seeds and planted them wherever he went. She tells her children that apples are nutritious and taste good.

Step 30. Write this story putting the word *often* in front of *talks.* Also put the word *always* in front of *carried, usually* in front of *tells* and *very* in front of *nutritious.*

Step 44. Write this story adding two or three sentences of your own after sentence 3. Tell what happened after he planted the seeds.

Gerald Dykstra, Antonette Port, Carol A. Janowski

PROGRAM 5

HORSES IN THE WEST

It is absolutely necessary to have a horse out here in the West. Places are very far apart from each other. There is no other form of transportation. You can't go anywhere if you don't have a horse. Horses are usually kept in a stable. They are fed oats. They should be washed often and given plenty of water. They should be taken to the veterinarian for an examination when something is wrong. If a horse gets a broken leg, the horse must be shot. Some families have more than one horse in the stable.

Step 68. Write this story in an up-to-date way. Change the first sentence to *It is absolutely necessary to have a car out here in the country.* Change all words about horses, like *stable,* and *oats,* to words about cars.

Step 85. Find the words *if you don't have a horse* and put *because* and some words of your own after *if you don't have a horse.* Find the word *wrong* and put *because* and some words of your own after *wrong.* Find the word *shot* and put because and some words of your own after *shot.*

Gerald Dykstra, Richard Port, Lois Morgan

PROGRAM 6

HOMES FOR DIFFERENT PEOPLE

A person may call many different types of dwellings home. A man uses available materials to erect a shelter suitable to his environment.

An Eskimo uses a knife to build an igloo of ice to protect him from the arctic winds and cold. When an Eskimo moves he can easily build a new home.

A South Pacific islander weaves the leaves of a coconut palm and plaits its fiber to hold his house together. With a grass or fern roof the hut protects him from the hot sun and the heavy rains. If a hurricane blows his house away, an islander can rebuild from a coconut palm which sways with the strong winds and survives the storm.

Step 13. Change the underlined nouns from singular to plural and change the determiners, verbs and pronouns where necessary. Begin *People may call many different types of dwellings home. Men often use available materials to erect shelters suitable to their environment* . . .

Step 108. Describe your home, stating the kind of materials used, where it is located and who built it. How did your family afford it? Could it be replaced easily?

Step 109. Compare these homes with those found in a large city.

Step 110. Write about other types of homes.

Gerald Dykstra, Richard Port, Alice C. Pack

PROGRAM 10

DICTATION
IN THE LANGUAGE CLASSROOM

KENTON K. SUTHERLAND

For a long time now, language teachers have made extensive use of dictation as a teaching device. Indeed, many teachers almost always reserve a portion of class time for this activity, rarely questioning its validity as an effective language-teaching technique. In observing and consulting with language teachers over the past decade, I have been surprised to find that a majority of them have been unable to tell me why they use dictation—except that they and other language teachers have always done so—or exactly what their students learn from it. The purpose of this article, then, is to examine critically the possible uses of dictation as a language-learning activity, and to point out several parallel pedagogical principles.

THE PURPOSE OF DICTATION

The past abuses of dictation, it seems to me, have occurred mainly because instructors have, more often than not, used the technique incorrectly and at the wrong time. While I would agree that dictations *can* on occasion be used effectively in most language classrooms, such effectiveness depends to a large extent on (*a*) when it is used, i.e., at what stage in the sequence of language-learning activities, and (*b*) how it is handled. These two important considerations can be discussed only if we agree on the purposes of dictation which, in my mind, are at least two:

1) Dictation is the transference, by a second person, of primary auditory language symbols (speech) into secondary graphic ones (writing). It would seem to follow that one purpose of this activity is to serve as a learning device that promotes this ability to decode sequences of oral symbols into written ones.

2) A concurrent pedagogical purpose would be to serve as a testing device to check on student progress. Dictation exercises, it would seem, ought to help an instructor identify specific problems in the student's ability to comprehend, to retain briefly, and immediately to write down

brief stretches of language, on the assumption that such ability is closely related to general language performance—though this assumption has not to my knowledge been scientifically proved. Indeed, many of my colleagues, in their enthusiasm for a total aural-oral, or audio-lingual, approach, have questioned the usefulness of the activity—and perhaps not without reason. The only answers I can give such critics are necessarily impressionistic ones: It has been my observation that students who are exposed to properly handled dictation exercises not only learn to recognize the relationship of speech to writing at an earlier stage, but that such students also improve more rapidly in their ability to comprehend stretches of spoken material—their ears, so to speak, become more sensitive and discriminating.

FROM PRIMARY TO SECONDARY FORMS

The ability to write and compose in a foreign language also improves, I have found, from the experience and practice of having copied down good, clear models. As an important side result, students with exposure to dictation activities also learn to be more at ease with such graphic landmarks as capitalization, punctuation, spelling, and contractions. Perhaps more important, however, many students begin to realize—after a short exposure to dictated material—that the omission or misuse of small function words is a serious error, since such devices are highly important to the grammatical signalling system of the language. Many students actually never hear certain unstressed syllables and one-syllable function words and, according to the authors of one article on the subject of dictation, they "never fully realize their problems in incorrectly identifying what they hear. They may be able to read and spell a word, but they don't recognize it when it is spoken, or they confuse different words or phrases with the ones they are hearing."[1] The student, in other words, according to the same article, "discovers the things he doesn't hear" via dictation exercises. In short, dictation activities seem to help students to become more conscious of the structure of the language, and as teachers point out how function words are being obscured and compressed, they teach their students to hear them better.

Since dictation employs a secondary graphic form of language, it would follow that effective utilization of the activity as a teaching-learning device would necessarily proceed from primary to secondary forms, from speech to writing. What this means it that students should

---

[1] J. Sawyer and S. Silver, "Dictation in Language Learning," as given in the list of references. This worthwhile article contains a discussion of several types of dictation activities, e.g., phonemic text vs. orthographic text dictation, as well as good suggestions for handling them in the classroom and for marking dictation papers. The article is reprinted in *Selected Articles from Language Learning No. 2*, Univ. of Michigan, Ann Arbor, 1963.

not be given dictation until they have had plenty of practice with the spoken form of language. To be sure, dictation can be used occasionally to provide a change of pace, a new focus, for students who have become weary of oral drilling, but it is important that the activity follow—rather than precede—oral practice of the patterns to be dictated. Dictation should provide the students with additional practice in using language correctly rather than with a tricky guessing game in which they mostly make mistakes. As for the place of dictation in the manipulation-communication scale of classroom activities, Clifford Prator has pointed out that "it is chiefly a manipulation activity, involving decontrol of all the mechanical elements of writing but preserving strict phonological and grammatical controls."[2] As such, dictation would certainly be one of the first writing activities that we would want to have students engage in. The suggestion that "dictation should be substituted for composition, largely if not wholly, during the earlier stages of instruction" is not a new idea, for Edward S. Joynes' article in which it was made (in the list of references) appeared in 1900.

THE REINFORCEMENT FACTOR

In considering the classroom mechanics of dictation, we can derive some valuable pedagogical insights from looking at the activity from the point of view of programed instruction—the theory upon which "teaching machines" are based. Most readers will probably recall that programed learning owes its existence mainly to Harvard University's brilliant behavioral psychologist, B. F. Skinner. His life work has been an investigation of the learning process and an attempt to pin-point the "laws" that govern it. While experimenting with pigeons, Skinner discovered that his birds could be taught to accomplish many astonishing feats—such as whirling in a circle or pecking out a tune on a toy piano—providing each step of their behavior was rewarded with a grain of corn. Psychologists call this process of rewarding "reinforcement," and reinforcement is central to Skinner's theories about programed instruction. In 1954 Skinner published an article in which he argued that people could be taught the same way he had taught his pigeons—that is, they

[2] In a personal letter and notations on my previous article on this subject, January 10, 1966. Professor Prator is vice-chairman of the Department of English, University of California, Los Angeles, and head of the Certificate Program for Teachers of English as a Second Language of the same institution. For a discussion of the manipulation-communication scale, see his "Development of a Manipulation-Communication Scale," given in the list of references. Professor Prator is currently at work on a book to be entitled tentatively *The Three M's of TESOL: Matter, Methods and Materials for Teaching English to Speakers of Other Languages,* which can be expected to contain additional references to the manipulation-communication scale.

could be "reinforced" each time they took a correct step toward mastering a subject. The article signaled the birth of programed instruction.

In a program for people, the reinforcement factor is not corn but a more oblique kind of encouragement. The student is "rewarded" at each step by being told instantly this his answer is correct. That is why a programer arranges his material in a tightly graded series of small steps so as always to invite a correct response. Getting things right, says Skinner, is a pleasant experience that will encourage him to learn more.

If a student commits an error on a program, it is considered the fault of the program, not of the student. "There are no wrong answers," runs the programer's slogan—"only wrong questions."[3]

Certainly the basic elements in programing—the idea of breaking up the material into small steps, asking the student to respond to each item, and rewarding him for correct answers—have been practiced by good teachers for centuries. And it is precisely these elements that will produce results in language classrooms as well as in self-instructional teaching-machine programs. We can see that in dictation, for example, the student is immediately reinforced by his own—and frequently the teacher's—observation that his sentences correspond to the ones dictated. As the teacher observes the ability of his students to perform this task, he is able to adjust his instructional program—by speeding up or slowing down, jumping ahead or going back to review previous material—according to the performance of the group, perhaps better than a machine can.

IMPORTANT PRINCIPLES

In order to take advantage of programed learning techniques in classroom dictation activities, it seems to me that language instructors need to keep several important principles in mind:

The Principle of Specific Objectives. This principle tells us that a dictation exercise should be planned as an activity which involves specific structures and vocabulary—and possibly even special sounds—for specific purposes (at least two of which were stated earlier in this article).

The Principle of Appropriate Practice. In dictation, this means that the students must have had sufficient previous practice with the elements that enter into the sentences to be dictated, including written practice, before they can be expected to perform acceptably, and that they must

[3] This discussion of programed instruction is taken from the article by Richard Margolis given in the list of references.

receive, via the dictation activity, plenty of additional practice with correct forms. A dictation exercise, therefore, should never be used as a way to catch students in as many errors as possible, but rather as another way to provide them with as many successful language experiences as possible.

The Principle of Individual Differentiation. In giving dictation, a language teacher needs to recognize that the speed and performance of the students will vary greatly. He should not attempt, therefore, to dictate another phrase or sentence until he has observed that all (or nearly all) of the students have written down the preceding one. Careful observation of the performance of the students is also necessary so that future classwork and dictations will reflect the various observed weaknesses and strengths in their performances. Recurring errors and problems should be pointed out to the class, and persistent individual problems should be dealt with through individual conferences, planned review sessions, and special assignments.

The Principle of Immediate Reinforcement. This is perhaps the most crucial principle to the effective outcome of dictation and the one most commonly violated by language teachers. If we can learn anything at all from Skinner's work, it is that a student, if he is to learn from his performance, must do so *right away* and not an hour or a day or a week later. As Goodwin Watson points out in "What Do We Know about Learning?" (see list of references):

> Behaviors which are rewarded (reinforced) are more likely to recur. This most fundamental law of learning has been demonstrated in literally thousands of experiments. It seems to hold for every sort of animal from earthworms to highly intelligent adults. The behavior most likely to emerge in any situation is that which the subject found successful or satisfying previously in a similar situation. No other variable affects learning so powerfully. The best-planned learning provides for a steady, cumulative sequence of successful behaviors. Reward (reinforcement), to be most effective in learning, must follow almost immediately after the desired behavior and be clearly connected with that behavior in the mind of the learner. The simple word 'right,' coming directly after a given response, will have more influence on learning than any big reward which comes much later or which is dimly connected with many responses so that it can't really reinforce any of them. Much of the effectiveness of programed self-instruction lies in the fact that information about success is fed back immediately for each learner response. A total mark on a test the day after it is administered has little or no reinforcement value for the specific answers.

Except in testing situations, then, dictations should be *corrected immediately by the student himself*. If the teacher wants to pick up the papers for his own information, he should do so only after the students have had the chance to learn from their own responses. Indeed, most dictation activities would probably be even more effective as "reinforcement" if the students were allowed to check their work as soon as they had copied down a sentence, rather than waiting until the end of the entire dictation, since the learner cannot improve until he has been informed whether or not each effort has been successful.

The Principle of Graduated Sequence. As in oral drilling, dictation exercises will proceed most effectively from simple to gradually more complex forms, and to progressively more and more effort on the part of the students. The teacher needs to pace the increase in the speed and size of graduation so that it is consistent with the student's ability to perform, never, of course, breaking up phrases more than in normal speech. Although most students would probably like their teachers to slow down on dictations—some would even prefer to have them dictate word by word—it is important that the teacher keep the students reaching ahead by dictating larger and larger portions of material in a series of continuous sequences, allowing as much time between word groups as may be needed for writing. While the speed of dictation should always be "normal," most language teachers would probably agree that beginning students should be dictated to in a "slow-normal" speed rather than in a super-fast speed that would be more appropriate for a trained stenographer taking dictation in his own language. Earl Stevick suggests here that "dictating this way without distortion is a valuable skill that requires practice and, for most people, some coaching—that it is not just something that comes naturally to any native speaker."[4]

SUMMARY

In summary, I suggest that these five educational principles can direct language teachers toward the more effective use of dictation in their classrooms. The actual way that dictations are handled will, of course, have a great deal to do with the level of instruction and with the ages of the students, as well as with the personality and cleverness of the individual instructor. I think it is safe to say, however, that as long as these principles are incorporated into a dictation activity, positive results will follow for any level and for any teacher.

[4] In a January 1966 notation on my previous version of this article. Dr. Stevick is a resident linguist and specialist in African languages at the Foreign Service Institute. He has published several works in the teaching of English as a second language, including the two in the list of references.

An interesting final suggestion for the use of dictation as a self-instructional device is made by Leonard Newmark, who, in commenting on an earlier version of this article, wrote the following:[5]

> Since you talk about dictation in terms of programed instruction, why not talk about it as a device that lends itself well to self-instruction with a tape-recorder? Nothing about the technique you describe requires a live teacher and certain of the principles you mention—e.g. "The Principle of Individual Differentiation"—are better served by a tape-recorder, which allows the slow student to play the dictation over as many times as he needs, without forcing the good student to listen to unneeded repetitions. The poor student also benefits by not being forced to compete in the exercise against the good student. Correcting the dictation against the original script can be done in the laboratory as well as in the classroom. Of course, the teacher *can* be used as an expensive substitute for a machine, but I don't quite see why he should be so used. If you feel that visual cues (lip movement and hand gestures, for example) are necessary for optimal dictation training, I suggest you consider the possibilities now made available by videotape-recorders.

This should prove to be an interesting experiment for those readers who have access to tape- and/or videotape-recorders. Anyone care to try it?

In conclusion, here are six dictation techniques suggested by Earl Stevick in his *Workbook,* arranged in approximate order of difficulty. "Which are suitable for your group?" he asks:

Dictation with Key Words Written on Blackboard

1. Each phrase or sentence repeated without limit
2. Each phrase given only twice
3. Each phrase given only once

Dictation Without Key Words Given

4. Unlimited repetition
5. Each phrase given twice
6. Each phrase given once

---

[5] In a personal letter, January 12, 1966. Professor Newmark is chairman of the Department of Linguistics, University of California, San Diego. He is one of the co-authors of *Using American English,* given in the list of references, a highly teachable approach to dialogues and written material from an entirely fresh viewpoint—the learning and use of language *wholes* rather than the learning of a patchwork of individual features.

REFERENCES

Joynes, Edward S. "Dictation and Composition in Modern Language Teaching," *Modern Language Association Publications*, Vol. XV, App. I, 1900, pp. xxv–xxx.

Mager, Robert F. *Preparing Objectives for Programed Instruction*. San Francisco: Fearon Publishers, 1962.

Margolis, Richard. "Programed Instruction: Miracle or Menace?" in *Revolution in Teaching: New Theory, Technology and Curricula*, Alfred de Grazia and David A. Sohn, editors. New York: Bantam Books, 1964, pp. 108–20.

Newmark, Leonard, Jerome Mintz and Jan Ann Lawson. *Using American English*. New York: Harper and Row, 1964.

Popham, James W. *The Teacher-Empiricist: A Curriculum and Study Supplement*. Los Angeles: Aegeus Press, 1965.

Prator, Clifford H., Jr. "Development of a Manipulation-Communication Scale," in *The 1964 Conference Papers of the Association of Teachers of English as a Second Language of the National Association for Foreign Student Affairs*, Robert P. Fox, editor. New York: N.A.F.S.A., 1965, pp. 57–62.

Sawyer, J., and S. Silver. "Dictation in Language Learning," *Language Learning* (XI, 1–2, 1961).

Stevick, Earl. *Helping People Learn English*. New York and Nashville: Abingdon Press, 1958.

———. *A Workbook in Language Teaching with Special Reference to English as a Foreign Language*. New York and Nashville: Abingdon Press, 1963.

Watson, Goodwin. "What Do We Know about Learning?" in *Revolution in Teaching: New Theory, Technology and Curricula*, Alfred de Grazia and David A. Sohn, editors. New York: Bantam Books, 1964, pp. 82–87.

CLASSROOM TECHNIQUES
FOR CONTROLLING COMPOSITION

WILLIAM SLAGER

Let me begin by defining composition as writing beyond the sentence level. This will enable me to dispose of the very necessary first steps of copying English and of writing it down from dictation—in other words, of becoming accustomed to the physical act of writing English. It will also enable me to pass over the important exercises in sentence building that must precede what I have here defined as composition. I would like to concentrate, then, on the writing of paragraphs and of compositions of several paragraphs in length.

The assumption, by now basic to the profession, is that composing—writing beyond the sentence—must be guided or controlled. But unfortunately we have not until recently been very specific about ways in which control can be accomplished. What I intend to do here, therefore, is sketch some of the techniques that have been developed for guiding the students so carefully that they will leave the composition classroom with a sense of achievement rather than a feeling of frustration.

This sense of achievement is the goal toward which all composition teachers work. When we receive a set of compositions that we must cover with red marks—when we must spend hours correcting a single assignment—then we can be certain that we have not been teaching the students but merely punishing them. We have obviously asked them to do something they are not yet ready to do or have given them a vague assignment. The best procedure in such a case is to throw away the papers and begin again—this time with a detailed assignment that conscientious students *can follow with reasonable expectation of success.*

Another comment is necessary by way of introduction. Students beginning composition in English as a second language need to start an assignment with more than blank paper, a sharpened pencil, and a dictionary. They must also have a subject about which all of them can write, a subject in common, so they can begin with a repertory of relevant words and sentences. Since this common subject is usually provided by way of readings, the use of readings is assumed as background to most of the writing assignments described in this article.

Now for the assignments themselves. The list is by no means complete, but I have tried to give examples that range from strict control to "freer" writing, and from the single paragraph to the whole composition. These ideas have been gathered from a number of texts, which I acknowledge in the accompanying bibliography. They also come from experience in our classrooms in Utah.

ANSWERING QUESTIONS, OR TURNING QUESTIONS INTO STATEMENTS

For answering questions or turning questions into statements, possibly the simplest introduction to paragraph writing, the teacher gives the students three or four sequential questions that, when answered, form a coherent paragraph. Three examples follow, the first two from Book V of the *English for Today* series and the third adapted from Lois Robinson's article on composition in Harold Allen's anthology *Teaching English as a Second Language*.

Two kinds of questions can be used here—*yes-no*-questions and *or*-questions. The exercise on *yes-no*-questions is easier, but artificial, since the students are asked to do no more than a mechanical operation. *Or*-questions are more "natural," since they require the students to decide on the correct answer. If they are to make this decision, the questions must either be based on a reading that the students are familiar with or carefully phrased to rely on general knowledge common to all the students.

a) Yes-No-*Questions*. INSTRUCTIONS: Turn the following *yes-no*-questions into statements:

Are movies just a little over fifty years old? Have they grown to be the most popular form of entertainment in the world? Have people who have never seen a stage play seen movies? Have people who have never attended an opera or a concert seen movies?

b) Or-*Questions*. INSTRUCTIONS: Answer the following *or*-questions (based on a reading):

Were the early movies skillful or crude? Was the photography poor or good? Did the people in the film move naturally and smoothly, or did they move in a fast and jerky way? Were the pictures steady, or did they flicker?

c) Or-*Questions*. INSTRUCTIONS: Answer the following *or*-questions (based on general knowledge):

Is the Atlantic Ocean east or west of the United States? Is Mexico north or south of the United States? Is Canada north or south of the United States?

One slight variation on these exercises is useful in showing the students ways to strengthen paragraph coherence by the use of connectors:

d) *Combination.* INSTRUCTIONS: Refer to the paragraph of statements that you have constructed from the set of questions in section *a* above. Combine your first two statements by using a *though*-clause and your last two by using *and*.

e) *Further Combination.* INSTRUCTIONS: Refer to the paragraph of statements that you have constructed from the set of questions under section *b* above. Combine your last three statements by presenting them as three items in a series. You will separate the first two with a comma and the second and third by a comma plus *and*.

REORDERING SENTENCES

Baumwoll and Saitz, in *Advanced Reading and Writing*, make extensive use of exercises in *reordering* sentences, which involve the scrambling of the sentences of a carefully constructed paragraph. The students' assignment is to write the sentences out in correct order. In this way they become keenly aware of the sequence required of the sentences in a well-written paragraph. The problem for the teacher, of course, is to choose paragraphs in which the order is clear and the sequence obvious. Here is one example from Book V of *English for Today:*

INSTRUCTIONS: Write out the following sentences in the order that makes of them a well-constructed paragraph:

1) The reason Hollywood was a natural place for making movies was that the sun shines there every day.

2) In the early years, most movies were made outdoors with natural light.

3) A suburb of Los Angeles, California, named Hollywood started to become the center of the film industry.

FILLING IN BLANKS WITH
CONNECTING WORDS AND PHRASES

Exercises that call for supplying connecting words teach the students the grammatical connectors used to show relationships of ideas in a paragraph or a larger composition—for example, subordinating conjunctions such as *although* and conjunctive adverbs such as *nevertheless*. Many texts present lists of such words, but as far as I know the teaching of connectors has not been incorporated into meaningful exercises. A few representative examples follow, which also come from Book V of *English for Today*. The idea is suggested in Miss Robinson's article referred to above, and elsewhere.

a)   A Random List of Connecting Words. INSTRUCTIONS: Write out the paragraph below, filling in the blanks with the appropriate connecting words chosen from the following: *though, whom, but, what.*

> Shakespeare's art is English, _____ it is also international. _____ his characters act out upon the stage are universal human problems. Hamlet, Macbeth, and many other characters from Shakespeare's plays are timeless creations, in _____ people everywhere recognize themselves. _____ they may speak English, Shakespeare's characters can be understood in any language.

b)   Contrasting Important Connecting Words in Contexts that Establish Their Meaning. INSTRUCTIONS: *Consequently* means something like "as a result of this." *Furthermore* means something like "in addition to this." Decide what the relationship is between the two parts of each sentence below, then write out the paragraph, supplying for each blank the one of these two connectors that establishes the proper relationship.

> Americans today are marrying at an earlier age than their parents and grandparents did; _____, they are required to assume heavy responsibilities when they are still very young. Many college students are holding down all-day jobs; _____, they are helping their wives at night and on weekends in the care of the children. Young men must assume responsibility early; _____, there is no longer much chance for "youthful pranks" or youthful experimentation.

c)   A Variation with Connectors. A useful variation of the above exercise requires the students to supply connectors but does not tell them precisely where the connectors are to go. INSTRUCTIONS: Make the following paragraph read more smoothly by connecting two of the sentences with *but* and two of them with *so*. Decide what the relationship between the sentences is, then write out the paragraph and insert in the proper place the one of these conjunctions that expresses the proper relationship:

> I have always wanted to see a skyscraper. I never had the opportunity to visit a big city like New York or Chicago. I probably won't have the opportunity to visit the United States for a long time. I suppose the next best thing is to go to the library and find out if it has any books about skyscrapers.

d) Another Suggestion. Another variation suggests certain sentence types that can be used in a connected paragraph. The following exercise is a modification of an idea from Lois Robinson:

Instructions: Write a paragraph with the title "A Skyscraper I Read About," incorporating in successive sentences the groups of words given below. Begin sentences 1, 3, and 5 with *There is/There are* and sentences 2, 4, and 6 with *It is/They are:*

1) skyscraper on 42nd street
2) one hundred stories tall
3) fountain at the entrance
4) made of marble
5) twelve elevators in the lobby
6) very busy all day

USING SUBSTITUTION TABLES

Substitution tables have been used extensively for written exercises on the sentence level. In fact, F. G. French's *English in Tables* (Oxford University Press) employs this device exclusively. Here is an example from Book IV of *English for Today:*

Because / Since	the highways are crowded, there is no parking space, gas is expensive, the traffic is heavy,	Dick takes the train to work. Dick doesn't drive to work. Dick leaves his car at home. some commuters prefer trains.

Such tables can easily be extended to include sentences in sequence—that is, they can easily be extended to provide exercises in writing on the paragraph level. The use of this technique has been reported in a magazine published in East Nigeria. In Ethiopia, John Rodgers of the British Council has used substitution tables on the paragraph level. The example that follows is adapted from a handout prepared by Mr. Rodgers for English teachers in Ethiopia:

Two of our students My uncle A friend of mine	went to	England the U.S. New York	last year. two days ago. last week.

They He	went there	to inspect a new factory, to study at the university, to see Mr. _____,	which who

produces teaches works	in the office of a big company. chemicals. students from many countries.	They He	went by

sea air train	because	they he	couldn't get space on a ship. couldn't afford an air ticket. couldn't get there by train.

While such exercises are purely manipulative, they at least demand that the students keep track of the meaning. They should teach the students something, also, of the way in which sentences are related to each other in a well-organized paragraph. One variation that has been suggested in using these tables is to remove gradually certain frames with the information they provide—for example, it is possible to remove from the table above the place visited and the time. If this procedure is followed in detail, the students will gradually be able to write the paragraph without the table.

SUPPLYING A TOPIC SENTENCE THAT LIMITS THE VERB FORM OR THE SENTENCE PATTERN

The following four examples are adapted from sentence-building exercises in Ross and Doty, *Writing English*. I have changed them slightly by adding a topic sentence, so that the result in each case will be a simple paragraph instead of merely a series of sentences:

a)   *Simple Present Tense. My friend (Jim) spends his money cautiously.* INSTRUCTIONS: Start with this as a topic sentence and add three sentences of your own about your friend, using in each the *-s* form of the verb.

b)   *Present Perfect Construction. My friend (Tom) has tried to save money ever since he decided to go to college.* INSTRUCTIONS: Start with this as a topic sentence and write a paragraph by adding three sentences of your own, each beginning with *He/She has. . . .*

c)   *Modal Perfect Construction. I don't know how (Jane) saved her money.* INSTRUCTIONS: Start with this as a topic sentence and write a paragraph by adding three sentences beginning with *She might have. . . .*

d)   *Object Complement Pattern. Yesterday we had a meeting of our club.* INSTRUCTIONS: Begin with this topic sentence and add three sentences of this type: *We (elected) (Tom) (president).* Choose from this list of verbs and nouns: VERBS: *choose, name, call, make, consider;* NOUNS: *chairman, treasurer, secretary.*

MORE ABOUT THE USE OF TOPIC SENTENCES

Another way in which topic sentences can be used systematically in the composition class is presented in the guide for English teachers prepared by the Salt Lake Public Schools. To practice the writing of well-constructed paragraphs, the guide suggests, the teacher can write on the chalkboard every day for several weeks three topic sentences from which the students can choose. Here are some examples of the kind of topic sentence that might be used:

I prefer	romances comedies travel films	to any other type of movie.
I prefer	milk lemonade coffee	to any other drink.
I prefer	cake pie ice cream	to any other dessert.

Each student writes a short paragraph beginning with the topic sentence he selects, after which the teacher examines and discusses what the students have written. Often the teacher can write some of the better paragraphs on the chalkboard or read them to the class. During these practice periods, the paragraphs are criticized and discussed, but they are not graded. Grading comes later, after most of the students have reached the point where they fully understand what is expected of them and can write a short paragraph in class with little hesitation and few false starts. As in all teaching, careful *development of the skill* must precede *testing:* The two steps cannot be confused.

FINISHING SENTENCES THAT ARE CAREFULLY ORDERED TO PRODUCE A COHERENT PARAGRAPH

The following examples of completing carefully ordered sentences are adapted from Book V of *English for Today*. Notice that this method of paragraph control also provides practice in using a selected verb structure.

a) Paragraph with "If—Might." INSTRUCTIONS: Write a paragraph on the suggested subject by starting with the first sentence and completing each of the following *if*-clauses by adding a main clause containing the modal *might:*

A TRIP TO NEW YORK

If I had enough money, I might take a trip to New York. If I went to New York, ... If I passed a skyscraper, ... If I went to the 100th floor, ... If the elevator broke down, ...

b) *Paragraph with "If—Would."* INSTRUCTIONS: Write a paragraph on the suggested subject by completing each of the following *if*-clauses by adding a main clause with *would:*

IF I WERE AN ENGLISH TEACHER

If I were an English teacher, ... If I were teaching pronunciation, ... If I were teaching grammar, ... If I were asked to explain the difference between British and American English, ...

WRITING SUMMARIES OF PARAGRAPHS

Summaries of paragraphs can be handled in a variety of ways. It is important to emphasize here that beginning and intermediate students should not be inhibited by undue emphasis on paraphrasing. Rather, they should be encouraged to stay close to the reading itself in paraphrasing and development, using their own sentences whenever it seems necessary for them to shorten or to make clearer connections.

Providing a topic sentence, by the way, is frequently essential with the beginning composition student. A sentence like the one in assignment *a* below suggests the development that is to follow—in this case, a listing of the ways in which the talkies differ from the silent movies.

a) *A Modified Dictation Exercise.* First introduce orally the paragraph with which the students will work—in this case, a paragraph on silent and talking movies. Explain as necessary the vocabulary and the grammar, and then make the students thoroughly familiar with the contents by means of intensive questioning and other kinds of discussion. Then you are ready to use successfully an assignment like the following, based on a paragraph you have already worked with:

INSTRUCTIONS: I am going to read this paragraph aloud three more times. Listen carefully each time. Then see if you can summarize it in writing. You are free to use as much of the original wording as you can remember. Begin your summary with the following topic sentence: *The silent movies were very different from the talkies.* (You might write this sentence on the board or let the students write it down from dictation, but be sure that they lay down their pencils and listen only, not try to write, as you read the paragraph through three times.)

b) *A Summary in Which Questions Provide the Clues.* INSTRUCTIONS: Read the paragraph through three more times. (Or *you* may read the paragraph three times.) Then see whether you can write a similar paragraph. Remember that the paragraph should contain answers to the following questions: *When and where was Shakespeare born? What kind of education did he receive? How old was he when he married? What were the names of his wife and children?*

c) *Writing One-Sentence Summaries.* INSTRUCTIONS: Notice that the first two paragraphs can be summarized in a single sentence. Give similar one-sentence summaries of the other paragraphs. (The assignment is adapted from Book V of *English for Today.*)

Paragraph 1. Jazz had its beginnings in the folk songs of the southern Negro.

Paragraph 2. Band instruments extended the human voice, thus opening the way to jazz.

Paragraph 3. _____

Etc.

SUPPLYING TOPIC SENTENCES FOR A COMPOSITION LONGER THAN A PARAGRAPH

This exercise is adapted from Book V of *English for Today.* INSTRUCTIONS: Add three more sentences to develop each of the following topic sentences:

1) Once I visited a village that was located . . . .

_____

_____

_____

2) The people of the village had their own distinct customs.

_____

_____

_____

3) The people of the village spoke a distinctive dialect.

(used a different word for . . .)

(used a different pronunciation for . . .)

(used a different grammatical construction for . . .)

4)   The people of the village made their living by . . . .

_____

_____

_____

WRITING SUMMARIES OF WHOLE COMPOSITIONS

The student who is learning about organization for the first time must see it on two levels. On the paragraph level, he looks for a topic sentence that summarizes the content of the paragraph—or he learns to supply one if the topic sentence is implied rather than stated. On the level of the whole composition, he looks for the central thought, which again may be stated or implied. Thus he gradually develops an awareness of organization by being led from the paragraph and its topic sentence to the larger composition with its central thought. At first it is best to give the students the central thought and ask them to add sentences that show the development of the reading. (Adapted from Book V of *English for Today*.)

a)   Developing the Central Thought. INSTRUCTIONS: The central thought of the reading can be stated as follows:

From their crude beginnings, motion pictures have developed into an art that is the most widespread form of entertainment in the world.

List the ways in which movies have developed from their crude beginnings. Use complete sentences, and follow the time order of the reading.

b)   Noting Certain Kinds of Organization. In a sense, this is a kind of modified outline that requires the students to work out—with very specific guidance—the development of the essay.

INSTRUCTIONS: In paragraphs one and two, the author calls attention to the increase in the number of automobiles (the cause) and says that this increase has brought about a change in living habits (the effect). In the rest of the reading he discusses the effects in detail. One effect (paragraph three) is the development of the motorized suburb. List in complete sentences the other effects that the automobile has had on American life.

(moving businesses to the suburbs) _____

(parking problems) _____

(American farmers) _____

c)   Writing an Organized Paragraph. If the goal is composition, such careful attention to organization can be justified only when it is applied to the students' own writing. Here is an assignment that asks for exactly the same kind of organization.

INSTRUCTIONS: Write a composition of three or four paragraphs with a cause-and-effect organization. Choose one of the following topics:

1) The Effect of the (Telephone) on Our Family

2) The Effect of the (New Highway) on Our City

3) The Effect of the (Radio) on Our Country

DERIVING A COMPOSITION FROM A MODEL

Elsewhere (*The Florida FL Reporter*, Spring 1965) I have listed the characteristics of models that can be used successfully for student imitation: They must be short (not too much longer than the compositions the students will eventually be expected to write); they must be contemporary and reasonably simple (not too far beyond the style the students themselves should be expected to reach); and they should have an organization that is careful and obvious.

The following assignment is based on the first reading in Book III of the *English for Today* series. Called "In a Small Town," it is a short sketch of the daily routine in Fairfield, a typical small town in the Middle West of the United States. The time sequence is obvious (from morning to night on weekdays, etc.), and the paragraphs often begin with time expressions (*It's early morning . . . . At eight o'clock . . . . At three-thirty . . . .*). The assignment is made after the students are thoroughly acquainted with the reading. At this intermediate stage of language learning, such acquaintance assumes previous oral introduction, intensive questioning, dictation, etc.

INSTRUCTIONS: Write a composition on life in a small town in your own country. Begin by making changes within the sentences: For example, *It's early morning in Fairfield* becomes *It's early morning in (Pana)*. Your teacher will help you supply new words when you need them.

Decide what examples you want to use. For instance, in Fairfield, people are awakened when the newsboy throws the paper at the front door. How are people awakened in the small town you want to describe? By bells? By whistles? By the noises of the tradesmen?

The composition that results from this assignment is often very close to the model, although the more advanced and creative students might depart quite far from it. In no event will the composition be in the strictest sense original. The students are still depending on the model and the teacher while they are beginning to express their own ideas in compositions longer than a single paragraph.

MOTIVATING A COMPOSITION BY SHOWING PICTURES AND SUPPLYING PATTERNS OF MODIFICATION

The following assignment is adapted from a much more detailed one presented by Adelaida Paterno in "A Lesson on English Modification," originally published in the *Manila Secondary Teachers' Quarterly* and reprinted in Harold Allen's anthology, given in the bibliography. The composition follows an elaborately developed lesson that reviews modifiers. The first exercise is preparatory work for the second, which calls for the writing of a composition.

a) INSTRUCTIONS: Here are some pictures of La Mesa Dam. What objects do you see in the pictures? How can you describe the objects?

(The teacher writes both nouns and the modification structures on the board: for example, *fields, green fields, fields along the highway, fields that are yellow with ripening grain.*)

b) INSTRUCTIONS: You went on an excursion to La Mesa Dam. Write a three-paragraph composition on your excursion.

Paragraph 1. You went on an excursion. What did you see on the way?
Paragraph 2. When you arrived at your destination, what did you see and what did you do?
Paragraph 3. How did you feel at the end of the day?

In the assignments as given by Miss Paterno, topic sentences are provided, and the students are also given key words and phrases for the sentences that are to be developed.

Students who can do all these exercises accurately are still a long way from free composition, which implies the ability to develop a well-organized theme on any subject that might be assigned. I have a suspicion that this kind of activity is never completely successful in the classroom. It requires a situation all too rare in the crowded schools of today—one in which there can be frequent individual conferences between the highly motivated student and the skillful teacher.

BIBLIOGRAPHY

TEXTS WITH MANY IDEAS FOR GUIDED WRITING

BASKOFF, FLORENCE. *Guided Composition Writing.* New York: American Language Institute, New York University, 1969.

BAUMWOLL and SAITZ. *Advanced Reading and Writing.* New York: Holt, Rinehart and Winston, 1965.

DYKSTRA and PORT. *A Course in Controlled Composition: Ananse Tales.* New York: Teachers College Press, 1966. 2 vols.

National Council of Teachers of English. *English for Today.* New York: McGraw-Hill.
> Book III, *The Way We Live,* 1964.
> Book IV, *Our Changing World,* 1966.
> Book V, *Life in English-Speaking Countries,* 1967.

NEWMARK, MINTS, and HINLEY. *Using American English.* New York: Harper and Row, 1964.

NICHOLS, ANN E. *English Syntax: Advanced Composition for Non-Native Speakers.* New York: Holt, Rinehart and Winston, 1965.

ROBINSON, LOIS. *Guided Writing: A Sub-Freshman Composition Text for English as a Second Language.* New York: Harper and Row, 1967. (See also Miss Robinson's article on composition in Harold Allen's anthology, below.)

ROSS and DOTY. *Writing English: A Composition Text in English as a Foreign Language.* New York: Harper and Row, 1965.

WISHON and BURKS. *Let's Write English.* New York: American Book Company, 1968. 2 vols.

JOURNALS THAT SOMETIMES CARRY ARTICLES ON COMPOSITION

Language Learning (Ann Arbor, Michigan).

TESOL Quarterly (Washington, D.C.)

English Language Teaching (London).

Manila Secondary Teachers' Quarterly (Manila).

English: A New Language (Sydney).

ANTHOLOGY WITH SEVERAL ARTICLES ON COMPOSITION

ALLEN, HAROLD B., ed. *Teaching English as a Second Language.* New York: McGraw-Hill, 1965.

CULTURAL THOUGHT PATTERNS IN INTER-CULTURAL EDUCATION

ROBERT B. KAPLAN

The teaching of reading and composition to foreign students does differ from the teaching of reading and composition to American students, and cultural differences in the nature of rhetoric supply the key to the difference in teaching approach.

> . . . Rhetoric is a mode of thinking or a mode of "finding all available means" for the achievement of a designated end. Accordingly, rhetoric concerns itself basically with what goes on in the mind rather than with what comes out of the mouth. . . . Rhetoric is concerned with factors of analysis, data gathering, interpretation, and synthesis. . . . What we notice in the environment and how we notice it are both predetermined to a significant degree by how we are prepared to notice this particular type of object. . . . Cultural anthropologists point out that given acts and objects appear vastly different in different cultures, depending on the values attached to them. Psychologists investigating perception are increasingly insistent that what is perceived depends upon the observer's perceptual frame of reference.[1]

Language teachers, particularly teachers of English as a second language, are late-comers in the area of international education. For years, and until quite recently, most languages were taught in what might be called a mechanistic way, stressing the prescriptive function of such teaching. In recent years the swing has been in the other direction, and the prescriptive has practically disappeared from language teaching. Descriptive approaches have seemed to provide the answer. At the present moment, there seems to be some question about the purely descriptive technique, and a new compromise between description and prescription seems to be emerging. Such a compromise appears necessary to the adequate achievement of results in second-language teaching. Unfortunately, although both the prescriptivists and the descriptivists have recognized the existence of cultural variation as a factor in second-language teaching, the

[1] Robert T. Oliver, "Foreword," *Philosophy, Rhetoric and Argumentation*, ed. Maurice Nathanson and Henry W. Johnstone, Jr. (University Park, Pennsylvania, 1965), pp. x–xi.

recognition has so far been limited to the level of the sentence—that is, to the level of grammar, vocabulary, and sentence structure. On the other hand, it has long been known among sociologists and anthropologists that logic *per se* is a cultural phenomenon as well.

> Even if we take into account the lexical and grammatical similarities that exist between languages proceeding from a common hypothetical ancestor, the fact remains that the verbal universe is divided into multiple sectors. Sepir, Whorf, and many others, comparing the Indian languages with the Occidental languages, have underlined this diversity very forcefully. It seems, indeed, as if the arbitrary character of language, having been shown to be of comparatively little significance at the level of the elements of a language, reasserts itself quite definitely at the level of the language taken as a whole. And if one admits that a language represents a kind of destiny, so far as human thought is concerned, this diversity of languages leads to a radical relativism. As Peirce said, if Aristotle had been Mexican, his logic would have been different; and perhaps, by the same token, the whole of our philosophy and our science would have been different.
>
> The fact is that this diversity affects not only the languages, but also the cultures, that is to say the whole system of institutions that are tied to the language . . . [and] language in its turn is the effect and the expression of a certain world view that is manifested in the culture. If there is causality, it is a reciprocal causality. . . .
>
> The types of structures characteristic of a given culture would then, in each case, be particular modes of universal laws. They would define the Volksgeist. . . .[2]

LOGIC AND RHETORIC

Logic (in the popular, rather than the logician's sense of the word) which is the basis of rhetoric, is evolved out of a culture; it is not universal. Rhetoric, then, is not universal either, but varies from culture to culture and even from time to time within a given culture. It is affected by canons of taste within a given culture at a given time.

> Every language offers to its speakers a ready-made *interpretation* of the world, truly a Weltanschauung, a metaphysical word-picture which, after having originated in the thinking of our ancestors, tends to impose itself ever anew on posterity. Take for instance a simple sentence such as 'I see him. . . .' This means that English and, I might say, Indo-European, presents the impressions made on our senses predominantly as human *activities*, brought about by our *will*. But the Eskimos in Greenland say not 'I see him' but 'he appears to me. . . .' Thus the Indo-European

[2] Mikel Dufrenne, *Language and Philosophy,* trans. Henry B. Veatch (Bloomington, 1963), pp. 35–37.

speaker conceives as workings of his activities what the fatalistic Eskimo sees as events that happen to him.[3]

The English language and its related thought patterns have evolved out of the Anglo-European cultural pattern. The expected sequence of thought in English is essentially a Platonic-Aristotelian sequence, descended from the philosophers of ancient Greece and shaped subsequently by Roman, Medieval European, and later Western thinkers. It is not a better nor a worse system than any other, but it is different.

> . . . As human beings, we must inevitably see the universe from a centre lying within ourselves and speak about it in terms of a human language by the exigencies of human intercourse. Any attempt rigorously to eliminate our human perspective from our picture of the world must lead to absurdity.[4]

A fallacy of some repute and some duration is the one which assumes that because a student can write an adequate essay in his native language, he can necessarily write an adequate essay in a second language. That this assumption is fallacious has become more and more apparent as English-as-a-second-language courses have proliferated at American colleges and universities in recent years. Foreign students who have mastered syntactic structures have still demonstrated inability to compose adequate themes, term papers, theses, and dissertations. Instructors have written, on foreign-student papers, such comments as: "The material is all here, but it seems somehow out of focus," or "Lacks organization," or "Lacks cohesion." And these comments are essentially accurate. The foreign-student paper is out of focus because the foreign student is employing a rhetoric and a sequence of thought which violate the expectations of the native reader.

> A personality is carved out by the whole subtle interaction of these systems of ideas which are characteristic of the culture as a whole, as well as of those systems of ideas which get established for the individual through more special types of participation.[5]

The fact that sequence of thought and grammar are related in a given language has already been demonstrated adequately by Paul Lorenzen. His brief paper proposes that certain linguistic structures are best com-

---

[3] Leo Spitzer, "Language—The Basis of Science, Philosophy and Poetry," *Studies in Intellectual History*, ed. George Boas *et al.* (Baltimore, 1953), pp. 83–84.
[4] Michael Polanyi, *Personal Knowledge: Towards a Post-Critical Philosophy* (Chicago, 1958), p. 9.
[5] Sapir, "Anthropology and Psychiatry," *Culture, Language and Personality* (Los Angeles, 1964), p. 157.

prehended as embodiments of logical structures.[6] Beyond that, every rhetorician from Cicero to Brooks and Warren has indicated the relationship between thought sequence and rhetoric.

> A paragraph, mechanically considered, is a division of the composition, set off by an indentation of its first sentence or by some other conventional device, such as extra space between paragraphs. . . . Paragraph divisions signal to the reader that the material so set off constitutes a unit of thought.
>
> For the reader this marking off of the whole composition into segments is a convenience, though not a strict necessity. . . . Since communication of one's thought is at best a difficult business, it is the part of common sense (not to mention good manners) to mark for the reader the divisions of one's thought and thus make the thought structure visible upon the page. . . .
>
> Paragraphing, obviously, can be of help to the reader only if the indicated paragraphs are genuine units of thought. . . . For a paragraph undertakes to discuss one topic or one aspect of a topic.[7]

PARAGRAPH DEVELOPMENT IN ENGLISH

The thought patterns which speakers and readers of English appear to expect as an integral part of their communication is a sequence that is dominantly linear in its development. An English expository paragraph usually begins with a topic statement, and then, by a series of subdivisions of that topic statement, each supported by example and illustrations, proceeds to develop that central idea and relate that idea to all the other ideas in the whole essay, and to employ that idea in its proper relationship with the other ideas, to prove something, or perhaps to argue something.

> A piece of writing may be considered unified when it contains *nothing* superfluous and it omits nothing essential to the achievement of its purpose. . . . A work is considered coherent when the sequence of its parts . . . is controlled by some principle which is meaningful to the reader. Unity is the quality attributed to writing which has all its necessary and sufficient parts. Coherence is the quality attributed to the presentation of material in a sequence which is intelligible to its reader.[8]

Contrarily, the English paragraph may use just the reverse procedure; that is, it may state a whole series of examples and then relate those examples into a single statement at the end of the paragraph. These two

[6] *Logik und Grammatik* (Mannheim, Germany, 1965).
[7] Cleanth Brooks and Robert Penn Warren, *Modern Rhetoric,* 2nd ed. (New York, 1958), pp. 267–68.
[8] Richard E. Hughes and P. Albert Duhamel, *Rhetoric: Principles and Usage* (Englewood Cliffs, New Jersey, 1962), pp. 19–20.

types of development represent the common *inductive* and *deductive* reasoning which the English reader expects to be an integral part of any formal communication.

For example, the following paragraph written by Macaulay demonstrates normal paragraph development:

> Whitehall, when [Charles the Second] dwelt there, was the focus of political intrigue and of fashionable gaiety. Half the jobbing and half the flirting of the metropolis went on under his roof. Whoever could make himself agreeable to the prince or could secure the good offices of his mistress might hope to rise in the world without rendering any service to the government, without even being known by sight to any minister of state. This courtier got a frigate and that a company, a third the pardon of a rich offender, a fourth a lease of crown-land on easy terms. If the king notified his pleasure that a briefless lawyer should be made a judge or that a libertine baronet should be made a peer, the gravest counsellors, after a little murmuring, submitted. Interest, therefore, drew a constant press of suitors to the gates of the palace, and those gates always stood wide. The King kept open house every day and all day long for the good society of London, the extreme Whigs only excepted. Hardly any gentleman had any difficulty in making his way to the royal presence. The levee was exactly what the word imports. Some men of quality came every morning to stand round their master, to chat with him while his wig was combed and his cravat tied, and to accompany him in his early walk through the Park. All persons who had been properly introduced might, without any special invitation, go to see him dine, sup, dance, and play at hazard and might have the pleasure of hearing him tell stories, which indeed, he told remarkably well, about his flight from Worcester and about the misery which he had endured when he was a state prisoner in the hands of the canting meddling preachers of Scotland.[9]

The paragraph begins with a general statement of its content, and then carefully develops that statement by a long series of rather specific illustrations. While it is discursive, the paragraph is never digressive. There is nothing in this paragraph that does not belong here; nothing that does not contribute significantly to the central idea. The flow of ideas occurs in a straight line from the opening sentence to the last sentence.

CONTRAST WITH OTHER SYSTEMS

Without doing too much damage to other ways of thinking, perhaps it might be possible to contrast the English paragraph development with paragraph development in other linguistic systems.

[9] From *The History of England from the Accession of James the Second* (London, 1849–61).

For the purposes of the following brief analysis, some seven hundred foreign student compositions were carefully analyzed. Approximately one hundred of these were discarded from the study on the basis that they represent linguistic groups too small within the present sample to be significant.[10] But approximately six hundred examples, representing three basic language groups, were examined.[11]

In the Arabic language, for example (and this generalization would be more or less true for all Semitic languages), paragraph development is based on a complex series of parallel constructions, both positive and negative. This kind of parallelism may most clearly be demonstrated in English by reference to the King James version of the Old Testament. Several types of parallelism typical of Semitic languages are apparent there because that book, of course, is a translation from an ancient Semitic language, a translation accomplished at a time when English was in a state of development suitable to the imitation of those forms.

1. Synonymous Parallelism:	The balancing of the thought and phrasing of the first part of a statement or idea by the second part. In such cases, the two parts are often connected by a coordinating conjunction.
Example:	His descendants will be mighty in the land *and* the generation of the upright will be blessed.
2. Synthetic Parallelism:	The completion of the idea or thought of the first part in the second part. A conjunctive adverb is often stated or implied.
Example:	Because he inclined his ear to me *therefore* I will call on him as long as I live.
3. Antithetic Parallelism:	The idea stated in the first part is emphasized by the expression of a contrasting idea in the second part. The contrast is expressed not only in thought but often in phrasing as well.
Example:	For the Lord knoweth the way of the righteous: But the way of the wicked shall perish.

[10] The following examples were discarded: Afghan–3, African–4, Danish–1, Finn–1, German–3, Hindi–8, Persian–46, Russian–1, Greek–1, Tagalog–10, Turk–16, Urdu–5; Total–99.

[11] The papers examined may be linguistically broken down as follows: Group I—Arabic–126, Hebrew–3; Group II—Chinese (Mandarin)–110, Cambodian–40, Indo-chinese–7, Japanese–135, Korean–57, Laotian–3, Malasian–1, Thai–27, Vietnamese–1; Group III–(Spanish-Portugese) Brazilian–19, Central American–10, South American–42, Cuban–4, Spanish–8 (French) French–2, African–2 (Italian) Swiss–1. Group I total–129; Group II total–381; Group III total–88; TOTAL–598. These papers were accumulated and examined over a two year period, from the beginning of the Fall 1963 semester through the Fall 1965 academic semester.

4. Climactic Parallelism: The idea of the passage is not completed until the very end of the passage. This form is similar to the modern periodic sentence in which the subject is postponed to the very end of the sentence.

         Example: Give unto the Lord, O ye sons of the mighty,
Give unto the Lord glory and strength[12]

The type of parallel construction here illustrated in single sentences also forms the core of paragraphs in some Arabic writing. Obviously, such a development in a modern English paragraph would strike the modern English reader as archaic or awkward, and more importantly it would stand in the way of clear communication. It is important to note that in English, maturity of style is often gauged by degree of subordination rather than by coordination.

The following paper was written as a class exercise by an Arabic-speaking student in an English-as-a-second-language class at an American university:

> The contemporary Bedouins, who live in the deserts of Saudi Arabia, are the successors of the old bedouin tribes, the tribes that was fascinated with Mohammad's massage, and on their shoulders Islam built it's empire. I had lived among those contemporary Bedouins for a short period of time, and I have learned lots of things about them. I found out that they have retained most of their ancestor's characteristics, inspite of the hundreds of years that separate them.
>
> They are famous of many praiseworthy characteristics, but they are considered to be the symbol of generosity; bravery; and self-esteem. Like most of the wandering peoples, a stranger is an undesirable person among them. But, once they trust him as a friend, he will be most welcome. However, their trust is a hard thing to gain. And the heroism of many famous figures, who ventured in the Arabian deserts like T. E. Lawrence, is based on their ability to acquire this dear trust!
>
> Romance is an important part in their life. And "love" is an important subject in their verses and their tales.
>
> Nevertheless, they are criticized of many things. The worst of all is that they are extremists in all the ways of their lives. It is there extremism that changes sometimes their generosity into squandering, their bravery into brutality, and their self-esteem into haughtiness. But in any case, I have been, and will continue to be greatly interested in this old, fascinating group of people.

Disregarding for the moment the grammatical errors in this student composition, it becomes apparent that the characteristics of parallelism do occur. The next-to-last element in the first sentence, for example, is

---

[12] I am indebted to Dr. Ben Siegel for this analysis.

appositive to the preceding one, while the last element is an example of synonymous parallelism. The two clauses of the second sentence illustrate synonymous parallelism. In the second "paragraph" the first sentence contains both an example of antithetic parallelism and a list of parallel nouns. The next two sentences form an antithetic pair, and so on. It is perhaps not necessary to point out further examples in the selection. It is important, however, to observe that in the first sentence, for example, the grammatical complexity is caused by the attempt to achieve an intricate parallelism. While this extensive parallel construction is linguistically possible in Arabic, the English language lacks the necessary flexibility. Eight conjunctions and four sentence connectors are employed in a matter of only fourteen "sentences." In addition, there are five "lists" of units connected by commas and conjunctions.

Another paper, also written by an Arabic-speaking student under comparable circumstances, further demonstrates the same tendencies:

At that time of the year I was not studying enough to pass my courses in school. *And* all the time I was asking my cousin to let me ride the bicycle, *but* he wouldn't let me. *But* after two weeks, noticing that I was so much interested in the bicycle, he promised me that if I pass my courses in school for that year he would give it to me as a present. *So* I began to study hard. *And* I studying eight hours a day instead of two.

My cousin seeing me studying that much he was sure that I was going to succeed in school. *So* he decided to give me some lessons in riding the bicycle. After four or five weeks of teaching me and ten or twelve times hurting myself as I used to go out of balance, I finally knew how to ride it. And the finals in school came *and* I was very good prepared for them *so* I passed them. My cousin kept his promise *and* give me the bicycle as a present. *And* till now I keep the bicycle in a safe place, *and* everytime I see it, It reminds me how it helped to pass my courses for that year.

In the first paragraph of this example, four of the five sentences, or 80% of the sentences, begin with a coordinating element. In the second paragraph, three of the six sentences, or 50% of the total, also begin with a coordinating element. In the whole passage, seven of the eleven sentences, or roughly 65%, conform to this pattern. In addition, the first paragraph contains one internal coordinator, and the second contains five internal coordinators; thus, the brief passage (210 words) contains a total of thirteen coordinators. It is important to notice that almost all of the ideas in the passage are coordinately linked, that there is very little subordination, and that the parallel units exemplify the types of parallelism already noted.

Some Oriental[13] writing, on the other hand, is marked by what may

13 *Oriental* here is intended to mean specifically Chinese and Korean but not Japanese.

be called an approach by indirection. In this kind of writing, the development of the paragraph may be said to be "turning and turning in a widening gyre." The circles or gyres turn around the subject and show it from a variety of tangential views, but the subject is never looked at directly. Things are developed in terms of what they are not, rather than in terms of what they are. Again, such a development in a modern English paragraph would strike the English reader as awkward and unnecessarily indirect.

The following composition was written, as a class exercise, by a native speaker of Korean, under the same circumstances which produced the two previous examples. Obviously, this student is weaker in general English proficiency than the students who produced the two prior examples.

DEFINITION OF COLLEGE EDUCATION

College is an institution of an higher learning that gives degrees. All of us needed culture and education in life, if no education to us, we should to go living hell.

One of the greatest causes that while other animals have remained as they first man along has made such rapid progress is has learned about civilization.

The improvement of the highest civilization is in order to education up-to-date.

So college education is very important thing which we don't need mention about it.

Again, disregarding the typically Oriental grammar and the misconception of the function of "parts of speech," the first sentence defines college, not college education. This may conceivably be a problem based upon the student's misunderstanding of the assignment. But the second sentence appears to shoot off in a totally different direction. It makes a general statement about culture and education, perhaps as *results* of a college education. The third sentence, presented as a separate "paragraph," moves still farther away from definition by expanding the topic to "man" in a generic sense, as opposed to "non-man." This unit is tied to the next, also presented as a separate paragraph, by the connecting idea of "civilization" as an aspect of education. The concluding paragraph-sentence presents, in the guise of a summary logically derived from previously posited ideas, a conclusion which is in fact partially a topic sentence and partially a statement that the whole basic concept of the assignment is so obvious that it does not need discussion. The paper arrives where it should have started, with the added statement that it really had no place to go to begin with.

The poorer proficiency of this student, however, introduces two other considerations. It is possible that this student, as an individual rather than as a representative native speaker of Korean, lacks the ability to abstract sufficiently for extended definition. In the case under discussion, however, the student was majoring in mathematics and did have the ability to abstract in mathematical terms. While the demands of mathematics are somewhat different from the demands of language in a conventional sense, it is possible to assume that a student who can handle abstraction in one area can also probably handle it at least to some extent in the other. It is also possible that the ability to abstract is absent from the Korean culture. This appears quite unlikely in view of the abundance of Korean art available and in view of the fact that other native speakers of Korean have not demonstrated that shortcoming.

The examples cited so far have been student themes. The following example is from a professional translation. Essentially, the same variations can be observed in it. In this case, the translation is from French.

> The first point to which I would like to call your attention is that nothing exists outside the boundary of what is strictly human. A landscape may be beautiful, graceful, sublime, insignificant, or ugly; it will never be ludicrous. We may laugh at an animal, but only because we have detected in it some human expression or attitude. We may laugh at a hat, but we are not laughing at the piece of felt or straw. We are laughing at the shape that men have given to it, the human whim whose mold it has assumed. *I wonder why a fact so important has not attracted the attention of philosophers to a greater degree. Some have defined man as an animal that knows how to laugh. They could equally well have defined him as an animal which provokes laughter;* for if any other animal or some lifeless object, achieves the same effect, it is always because of some similarity to man.[14]

In this paragraph, the italicized portion constitutes a digression. It is an interesting digression, but it really does not seem to contribute significant structural material to the basic thought of the paragraph. While the author of the paragraph is a philosopher, and a philosopher is often forgiven digressions, the more important fact is that the example is a typical one for writers of French as well as for writers of philosophy. Much greater freedom to digress or to introduce extraneous material is available in French, or in Spanish, than in English.

Similar characteristics can be demonstrated in the writing of native French-speaking students in English. In the interests of keeping this report within some bounds, such illustrations will be inserted without comment. The first example was written under circumstances similar to

---

[14] From *Laughter, An Assay on the Meaning of the Comic,* Trans. Marcel Bolomet (Paris, 1900).

those described for the preceding student samples. The writer is a native speaker of French.

AMERICAN TRAFFIC LAW AS COMPARED WITH
TRAFFIC LAW IN SWITZERLAND

At first glance the traffic law in United States appeared to me simpler than in Switzerland.

The American towns in general have the disposition of a cross, and for a driver who knows how to situate himself between the four cardinal points, there is no problem to find his way. Each street has numbers going crecendo from the center of the town to the outside.

There are many accidents in Switzerland, as everywhere else, and the average of mortality comparatively to the proportion of the countries is not better than in United States. We have the problem of straight streets, not enough surveillance by policemen on the national roads, and alcohol. The country of delicious wines has made too many damages.

The following illustration, drawn from the work of a native speaker of Latin American Spanish, was produced under conditions parallel to those already cited:

THE AMERICAN CHILDREN

In America, the American children are brought differently from the rest of the children in other countries. In their childhood, from the first day they are born, the parents give their children the love and attention they need. They teach their children the meaning of Religion among the family and to have respect and obedience for their parents.

I am Spanish, and I was brought up differently than the children in America. My parents are stricter and they taught me discipline and not to interrupt when someone was talking.

The next and last example is again not a piece of student writing, but a translation. The original was written in Russian, and the translation attempts to capture the structure of the original as much as possible, but without sacrificing meaning completely.

On the 14th of October, Kruschev left the stage of history. Was it a plot the result of which was that Kruschev was out of business remains not clear. It is very probable that even if it were anything resembling a plot it would not be for the complete removal of Kruschev from political guidance, but rather a pressure exerted to obtain some changes in his policies: for continuations of his policies of peaceful co-existence in international relations or making it as far as possible a situation to avoid formal rupture with the Chinese communist party and at any rate not to go unobstructed to such a rupture—and in the area of internal politics, especially in the section of economics, to continue efforts of a certain softening of "dogmatism," but without the hurried and not sufficiently reasoned experimentation, which became the characteristic traits of Kruschev's politics in recent years.[15]

Some of the difficulty in this paragraph is linguistic rather than rhetorical. The structure of the Russian sentence is entirely different from the structure of the English sentence. But some of the linguistic difficulty is closely related to the rhetorical difficulty. The above paragraph is composed of three sentences. The first two are very short, while the last is extremely long, constituting about three quarters of the paragraph. It is made up of a series of presumably parallel constructions and a number of subordinate structures. At least half of these are irrelevant to the central idea of the paragraph in the sense that they are parenthetical amplifications of structurally related subordinate elements.

There are, of course, other examples that might be discussed as well, but these paragraphs may suffice to show that each language and each culture has a paragraph order unique to itself, and that part of the learning of a particular language is the mastering of its logical system.

> . . . One should join to any logic of the language a phenomenology of the spoken word. Moreover, this phenomenology will, in its turn, rediscover the idea of a logos immanent in the language; but it will seek the justification for this in a more general philosophy of the relations between man and the world. . . . From one culture to another it is possible to establish communication. The Rorschach test has been successfully applied to the natives of the island of Alor.[16]

This discussion is not intended to offer any criticism of other existing paragraph developments; rather it is intended only to demonstrate that paragraph developments other than those normally regarded as desirable in English do exist. In the teaching of paragraph structure to foreign students, whether in terms of reading or in terms of composition, the teacher must be himself aware of these differences, and he must make these differences overtly apparent to his students. In short, contrastive rhetoric must be taught in the same sense that contrastive grammar is presently taught. Now not much has been done in the area of contrastive rhetoric. It is first necessary to arrive at accurate descriptions of existing paragraph orders other than those common to English. Furthermore, it is necessary to understand that these categories are in no sense meant to be mutually exclusive. Patterns may be derived for *typical* English para-

---

[15] From S. Schwartz, "After Kruschev," trans. E. B. Kaplan, *The Socialist Courier* (April, 1965), p. 3.
[16] Dufrenne, pp. 39–40.

graphs, but paragraphs like those described above as being atypical in English do exist in English. By way of obvious example, Ezra Pound writes paragraphs which are circular in their structure, and William Faulkner writes paragraphs which are wildly digressive. The paragraph being discussed here is not the "literary" paragraph, however, but the expository paragraph. The necessities of art impose structures on any language, while the requirements of communication can often be best solved by relatively close adhesion to established patterns.

Superficially, the movement of the various paragraphs discussed above may be graphically represented in the following manner:

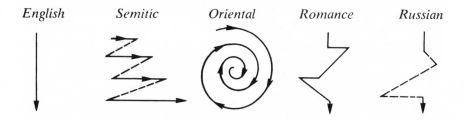

| English | Semitic | Oriental | Romance | Russian |

Much more detailed and more accurate descriptions are required before any meaningful contrastive system can be elaborated. Nonetheless, an important problem exists immediately. In the teaching of English as a second language, what does one do with the student who is reasonably proficient in the use of syntactic structure but who needs to learn to write themes, theses, essay examinations, and dissertations? The "advanced" student has long constituted a problem for teachers of English as a second language. This approach, the contrastive analysis of rhetoric, is offered as one possible answer to the existing need. Such an approach has the advantage that it may help the foreign student to form standards of judgement consistent with the demands made upon him by the educational system of which he has become a part. At the same time, by accounting for the cultural aspects of logic which underlie the rhetorical structure, this approach may bring the student not only to an understanding of contrastive grammar and a new vocabulary, which are parts of any reading task, but also to a grasp of idea and structure in units larger than the sentence. A sentence, after all, rarely exists outside a context. Applied linguistics teaches the student to deal with the sentence, but it is necessary to bring the student beyond that to a comprehension of the whole context. He can only understand the whole context if he recognizes the logic on which the context is based. The foreign student who has mastered the syntax of English may still write a bad paragraph or a bad paper unless he also masters the logic of English. *"In serious expository prose, the paragraph tends to be a logical, rather than a typo-*

graphical unit."[17] The understanding of paragraph patterns can allow the student to relate syntactic elements within a paragraph and perhaps even to relate paragraphs within a total context.

Finally, it is necessary to recognize the fact that a paragraph is an artificial thought unit employed in the written language to suggest a cohesion which commonly may not exist in oral language. "Paragraphing, like punctuation, is a feature only of the written language."[18] As an artificial unit of thought, it lends itself to patterning quite readily. In fact, since it is imposed from without, and since it is a frame for the structuring of thought into patterns, it is by its very nature patterned. The rhetorical structures of English paragraphs may be found in any good composition text.[19] The patterns of paragraphs in other languages are not so well established, or perhaps only not so well known to speakers of English. These patterns need to be discovered or uncovered and compared with the patterns of English in order to arrive at a practical means for the teaching of such structures to non-native users of the language.

In the interim, while research is directed at the rhetorics of other languages, certain practical pedagogical devices have been developed to expedite the teaching of rhetorical structures to non-native speakers of English. An elementary device consists simply of supplying to the students a scrambled paragraph. A normal paragraph, such as the one cited from Macaulay above, may be arbitrarily scrambled, the sentences numbered, and the students asked to rearrange the sentences in what appears to them to be a normal order. Frequently, the results of such an assignment will demonstrate the diversity of views or cultures represented in the classroom. The exercise can be used effectively to point out the very disparity. The students must then be presented with the original version of the paragraph, and the instructor must be able to explain and justify the order of the original.

[INSTRUCTIONS: Arrange the sentences below into some normal order.]

Scrambled Order

1. A jackass brays; a turkey cock gobbles; a dog yelps; a church bell clangs.
2. The narrow streets and lanes leading into the market are crammed with Indians, their dark skins glistening like copper or bronze in the bright sun, their varicolored cloaks looking like a

[This is the order in which the author arranged his sentences. Can you detect his reason?]

Normal Order

The narrow streets and lanes leading into the market are crammed with Indians, their dark skins glistening like copper or bronze in the bright sun, their varicolored cloaks looking like a mass of palette colors smeared together. In the

---

[17] Hans P. Guth, *A Short New Rhetoric* (Belmont, California, 1964), p. 205.

[18] Edward P. J. Corbett, *Classical Rhetoric for the Modern Student* (New York, 1965), p. 416.

[19] Important work in the rhetoric of the paragraph is being done by Francis Christensen, among others. See especially "A Generative Rhetoric of the Paragraph," *College Composition and Communication* (October, 1965), pp. 144–56.

mass of palette colors smeared together.

3. There is the smell of animal dung mingled with the odor of carnations and heliotrope from the flower stalls.

4. In the open plaza outside the market the crowd mills about.

5. Mothers sit on the curb nursing their babies.

6. A kind of blending of Indian talk in various dialects creates a strange droning noise.

7. On the narrow sidewalks, merchandise is spread so haphazardly that in order to pass, pedestrians have to press against the wall or leap the displays.

8. Wrinkled old women squat over charcoal braziers cooking corn cakes, or black beans, or pink coconut candy.

open plaza outside the market the crowd mills about. A kind of blending of Indian talk in various dialects creates a strange droning noise. A jackass brays; a turkey cock gobbles; a dog yelps; a church bell clangs. On the narrow sidewalks, merchandise is spread so haphazardly that in order to pass, pedestrians have to press against the wall or leap the displays. Wrinkled old women squat over charcoal braziers cooking corn cakes, or black beans, or pink coconut candy. Mothers sit on the curb nursing their babies. There is the smell of animal dung mingled with the odor of carnations and heliotrope from the flower stalls.[20]

[This paragraph is descriptive, presented in the present tense, and arranged perceptually in the order of sight, hearing, and smell.]

A second device consists of giving the students carefully written topic sentences, arranged in some convenient way such as that suggested below, and then asking the students to fill out the subdivisions of the topic sentence with examples and illustrations chosen to support the point. Depending upon the relative difficulty of the topic, the examples may be supplied by the instructor in scrambled order.

AMERICAN TELEVISION

American commercial television appears to consist of three principal classes of material: programs of serious interest, such as news broadcasts and special features; programs intended primarily as entertainment, such as variety shows, situation comedies, and adventure tales; and the advertisements which link all of these.

I. Programs of serious interest:
   A. News Broadcasts:

     1. _____

     2. _____

   B. Special Features:

     1. _____

[20] Hudson Strode, "The Market at Toluca," *Now in Mexico* (New York, 1947).

2. _____

II. Programs intended primarily as entertainment:
   A. Variety Shows:

      1. _____

      2. _____

   B. Situational Comedies:

      1. _____

      2. _____

   C. Adventure Tales:

      1. _____

      2. _____

III. Advertising:

   A. _____

      1. _____

      2. _____

   B. _____

      1. _____

      2. _____

IV. [Conclusion:]

[INSTRUCTIONS: The student is to supply contrasting examples for each of the spaces provided under items I and II. In item III the student must also supply the main subdivisions, and in item IV the point of the whole essay must also be supplied by the student. Obviously, item IV will vary considerably depending upon the kinds of illustrations selected to fill the blanks.]

The illustration constitutes a very simple exercise. Greater sophistication may be employed as the student becomes more familiar with the techniques. Obviously, too, the outline must be introduced and taught simultaneously. A simple technique for teaching the outline may be found illustrated in a number of texts for both American and foreign students.[21]

It is important to impress upon the student that "A paragraph is *clear* when each sentence contributes to the central thought . . . [and that] clarity also demands coherence, that is, an orderly flow of sentences marked by repetition of key ideas."[22]

While it is necessary for the non-native speaker learning English to master the rhetoric of the English paragraph, it must be remembered that the foreign student, ideally, will be returning to his home country, and that his stay in the United States is a brief one. Under these circumstances, English is a means to an end for him; it is not an end in itself. Edward Sapir has written:

An oft-noted peculiarity of the development of culture is the fact that it reaches its greatest heights in comparatively small, autonomous groups. In fact, it is doubtful if a genuine culture ever properly belongs to more that such a restricted group, a group between the members of which there can be said to be something like direct intensive spiritual contact. This direct contact is enriched by the common cultural heritage on which the minds of all are fed. . . . A narrowly localized culture may, and often does, spread its influence far beyond its properly restricted sphere. Sometimes it sets the pace for a whole nationality, for a far flung empire. It can do so, however, only at the expense of diluting the spirit as it moves away from its home, of degenerating into an imitative attitudinizing."[23]

He is absolutely correct in pointing out the dangers of spreading a culture too thin and too far from home. However, in the special case of the foreign student learning English, under the conditions stipulated above, the imitation which would be an error in most cases is the sought aim. The classes which undertake the training of the "advanced" student can aim for no more. The creativity and imagination which make the difference between competent writing and excellent writing are things which, at least in these circumstances, cannot be taught. The foreign student is

[21] At the risk of being accused of immodesty, I would recommend in particular the section entitled "Outlining" in Robert B. Kaplan, *Reading and Rhetoric* (New York, 1963), pp. 69–80.
[22] Francis Connolly, *A Rhetoric Casebook* (New York, 1953), p. 304.
[23] Edward Sapir, "Culture, Genuine and Spurious," *Culture, Language and Personality* (Los Angeles 1964), pp. 113–14.

an adult in most cases. If these things are teachable, they will already have been taught to him. The English class must not aim too high. Its function is to provide the student with a form within which he may operate, a form acceptable in this time and in this place. It is hoped that the method described above may facilitate the achievement of that goal.

SECTION SIX
VOCABULARY

The papers in this section take the form of surveys or reviews. Twaddell deals with various factors affecting an intermediate phase of massive and rapid vocabulary expansion. He reviews the knowledge concerning the nature of the vocabulary part of language that linguists have contributed, and he looks to the application of linguistic findings to enable us to teach vocabulary more efficiently in the future. Lado outlines and classifies many of the problems of vocabulary learning largely in terms of contrastive analysis. Higa reviews the psycholinguistic concept of "difficulty" and identifies some important variables in regard to the learning of vocabulary.

At the beginning stages of second-language instruction we place much more emphasis on the structural signals and grammatical patterns of the language than on vocabulary. We do have to have enough vocabulary to operate the patterns and illustrate the pronunciation, but we concentrate on habit formation—making the use of the language patterns automatic. At this level we are primarily concerned with structural matters: word forms, function words, word order, and the like. Vocabulary building at the same time would be an extra burden.

As a rule vocabulary expansion gets under way at the intermediate level, and the student's vocabulary continues to grow as long as he continues to use the language through listening, speaking, reading, and writing. Moving up the scale from language manipulation to communication new vocabulary items are introduced at a faster pace. With the study of word derivation patterns the student increases his vocabulary progressively. The process of reading generally promotes vocabulary growth more than anything else.

Both Lado and Twaddell make a distinction between two levels of vocabulary control: these are sometimes referred to as "active" and "passive" vocabularies. Lado labels them "vocabulary for production and vocabulary for recognition." He also points out that our recognition vocabulary is much larger than our production vocabulary. Twaddell notes "that reading per se involves greater demands on our vocabulary resources than conversation: there is no actual environmental situation to provide clues, and there is no opportunity for emergency feedback questions as in conversation. (Listening to a lecture involves the same demands as reading, plus the additional handicaps of inability to reread and the probability of some acoustic noise interference.)"

CONTEXT CLUES

At the intermediate level, where massive vocabulary expansion should begin, Twaddell points out that "the learner is faced with a disastrous shortage of vocabulary resources . . . . We simply cannot predict *which* vocabulary items the learner will need for the next page of reading or the next minute of listening: the fact is that he will encounter very-low-frequency items, including some that he cannot possibly have encountered before. It is futile to select in advance the, say, 6000 words to be learned during the intermediate level as being the most useful for his future listening and reading . . . . The resources are scanty; they must be compensated by skills."

The basic skill, he continues, "is the habit of guessing from context, using both grammatical and pragmatic clues. This habit appears to be normal in listening to and reading the native language, for those who really listen and read. It is not automatic in dealing with a foreign language, especially in the transition from the introductory level (with its necessarily controlled vocabulary) to and through the intermediate levels toward real use of the foreign language. On that introductory level . . . the skill of sensible guessing was not called into play. But as the learner moves . . . into something like a real use of the foreign language, the skill of sensible guessing becomes a major teaching objective."

In the development of this basic skill, Twaddell makes these suggestions: "Do not focus on words that are likely to be unfamiliar; do not punish guesses which are vague; punish guesses which are purely random, and then practice correctively with guided guessing . . . [funneled by grammatical possibility and pragmatic probability].

Politzer (in Section Three) also emphasizes the importance of context clues to meaning. He notes that "Once you have acquired a knowledge of structure and a limited vocabulary, you can use this knowledge to help you understand new words and to comprehend sentences that are— partially at least—made up of unknown words."

INTERFERENCE FROM THE NATIVE LANGUAGE

Lado points out that "Similarity and difference to the native language in form, meaning and distribution will result in ease or difficulty in acquiring the vocabulary of a foreign language. Comparing the foreign language vocabulary with that of the native language we will find words that are (1) similar in form and in meaning, (2) similar in form but different in meaning, (3) similar in meaning but different in form, (4) different in form and in meaning, (5) different in their type of construction, (6) similar in primary meaning but different in connotation, and (7) similar in meaning but with restrictions in geographical distribution." In regard to predicted level of difficulty, he classifies each of these groups as easy, normal, or difficult.

Concerning his pattern 3, "Words that are similar in some of their frequent meanings but different in form," he notes that "This kind of vocabulary learning is naively taken by many to represent all vocabulary learning. Such an oversimplification fails to account for the various vocabulary groups which appear when we have looked closer and have considered the native language. It is also important to note that although certain meanings of a word in one language are sometimes translatable into a word in another language there are very few if any words in two languages that are the same in all their meanings . . . . It is these content words . . . , however, that decisions can and should be made as to vocabulary size on the basis of frequency lists for recognition and adequacy for expression on a productive level."

Lado's pattern 5, "Words that are different in their morphological construction," includes most of the so-called "idioms," though we might apply the label "idiom" to some of the items in pattern 4, "Words that are different in form and represent meanings that are 'strange' to speakers of a particular native language, that is, meanings that represent a different grasp of reality." He notes that " 'idioms'—expressions peculiar to a language—are identifiable as we compare two languages . . . . An expression which may seem peculiar to native speakers may be quite natural to speakers of another language and would therefore not be an 'idiom' to them. On the other hand, an expression which seems quite natural to native speakers may be strange to foreign speakers of a particular language background. If we should find on comparing the expression with a variety of languages that it is strange to all or nearly all of them, we would be justified in calling it an idiom in general, but even then the statement would be meaningless in those cases in which the other language had a parallel expression."

Croft (in Section Nine) deals with interference from language categories—the structuring of the way that people habitually think about and understand phenomena they deal with in their everyday lives. He discusses the work of linguists in mapping out grammatical categories and the work of linguistic anthropologists in mapping out categories of (other) cultural phenomena utilizing theories, research methods, and analytical devices that are similar to those of the linguist.

PSYCHOLOGICAL FACTORS

Higa points out that "The most common practice of arranging learning materials today is to order them from the simple to complex or from the concrete to abstract. The assumption underlying this practice is that complex or abstract materials are more difficult than simple or concrete ones. A corollary derived from this assumption is that learning materials should be organized from the easy to the difficult in sequence . . . . What is problematic is that judgments are often made subjectively as to which materials are simple and easy and which are complex and difficult." His paper treats "the psycholinguistic concept of 'difficulty' in relation to the semantic (as opposed to phonetic or grammatical) aspect of foreign language vocabulary . . . ."

He notes that "From the psycholinguistic viewpoint the 'difficulty' of foreign language vocabulary seems to consist of five factors which reflect the relationships between and among words already learned and words to be learned. These factors are: (1) the 'intrinsic difficulty' of a word to be learned, (2) the interaction between previously learned words and a new word to be learned, (3) the interaction within a group of words to be learned at the same time, (4) the interaction between groups of words to be learned in sequence, and (5) the effect of repeated presentation of words to be learned. A great number of psychological experiments have been conducted on these factors, and successful control and prediction of the 'difficulty' of verbal learning materials are now possible in a laboratory situation."

Many of the points brought out in Higa's discussion of the five factors mentioned above have a direct bearing on our work as classroom teachers. These points are too numerous to list here, but you will find on reading his paper that there are quite a few discrepancies between our "logical" thinking about language teaching matters and what has been discovered through psychological research.

SELECTED READINGS

ANTHONY, EDWARD M. "The Teaching of Cognates." *Language Learning* 4 (1952–1953):79–82.

BROOKS, NELSON. *Language and Language Learning: Theory and Practice.* 2d ed. Chapter 13: "Vocabulary." New York: Harcourt Brace Jovanovich, 1964.

FRIES, CHARLES C. *Teaching and Learning English as a Foreign Language.* Chapter 4: "The Words: Mastering Vocabulary Content." Ann Arbor: The University of Michigan Press, 1945.

FRIES, CHARLES C., and TRAVER, A. AILEEN. *English Word Lists: A Study of Their Adaptability for Instruction*. Ann Arbor: George Wahr, 1950.

HADLICH, R. L. "Lexical Contrastive Analysis." *Modern Language Journal* 49(1965):426–29.

JONES, R. M. "Situational Vocabulary." *IRAL* 4(1966):165–73.

LADO, ROBERT. *Language Teaching: A Scientific Approach*. Chapter 12: "Live Words and Their Meanings." New York: McGraw-Hill, Inc., 1964.

————. *Linguistics across Cultures: Applied Linguistics for Language Teachers*. Chapter 4: "How to Compare Two Vocabulary Systems." Ann Arbor: The University of Michigan Press, 1957.

MOULTON, WILLIAM G. *A Linguistic Guide to Language Learning*. 2d ed. Chapter 6: "Words." New York: The Modern Language Association, 1970.

OLOROSO, LAURA S. "Types of Exercises for Doing Vocabulary Study." *MST English Quarterly* 12(1962):40–43, 49.

PALMER, ADRIAN. "A Classroom Technique for Teaching Vocabulary." *TESOL Quarterly* 2(1968):130–133.

PETTY, WALTER T., CURTIS P. HEROLD, and EARLINE STOLL. *The State of Knowledge about the Teaching of Vocabulary*. Champaign, Ill.: National Council of Teachers of English, 1968.

POLITZER, ROBERT L. *Foreign Language Learning: A Linguistic Introduction*. Chapter 9: "Vocabulary Problems"; Chapter 13: "Learning Words and Their Meanings." Englewood Cliffs, N.J.: Prentice-Hall, Inc., 1970.

THORNDIKE, EDWARD L. and IRVING LORGE. *The Teacher's Word Book of 30,000 Words*. New York: Bureau of Publications, Teachers College, Columbia University, 1944.

WEST, MICHAEL. *A General Service List of English Words: With Semantic Frequencies and a Supplementary Word-List for the Writing of Popular Science and Technology*. London: Longmans, Green, 1953.

LINGUISTS
AND LANGUAGE TEACHERS

W. FREEMAN TWADDELL

LINGUISTS ON THE NATURE OF LANGUAGE

Let us begin with some professional history: about a quarter of a century ago, some linguists came out of the woodwork and made some comments about foreign language teaching. They reported that a language is a set of habits—a complex set of complex habits. Within a language, these habits interlock and largely reinforce each other. The reinforcement is considerable but not total: there are idioms which are not reinforced by other grammatical and vocabulary habits, and there are grammatical structures which are ambiguous as to analysis or indeterminate as to synthesis. But predominantly, there is a high degree of orderliness about the interlocking of habits within a language.

As between the habits of two languages, the non-reinforcements and downright conflicts are considerable. Comparison of two linguistic structures pinpoints the conflicts and reveals that they are often deeper than even an experienced foreign language teacher might have realized.

But more than any specific instances of such conflicts, the contribution of linguistic analysis to foreign language teaching was the revelation of the *fact* of conflict of habits and the *nature* of language as habits rather than intellectual manipulation. The complexity of those habits is such that it is impossible for a naive expert speaker to be aware of them, and the habits of listening and speaking are the deepest and most unconscious.

The evidence presented by linguistics during the past decades has been convincing. That evidence has pointed to the first stage of language teaching as a habit forming program. It was for the linguists to present the facts about language, then for language teachers to translate those insights and the inferences from them into practicable procedures and materials for habit forming practice.

LANGUAGE TEACHING ON THE INTRODUCTORY LEVEL

The result has been that today we are in possession of fairly successful devices and procedures for teaching the introductory level of a foreign language. The teachers have applied the linguists' diagnosis and developed ways to assure overlearning of model samples through mimicry-memorizing, dialogue practice, and short question-answer drills. The formation of habits of structural control is guided by pattern practices of several sorts, directed oral reports, and enactment of situationally varied conversations.

VOCABULARY LEARNING ON THE INTRODUCTORY LEVEL

Throughout that introductory level the focus is on the truly systematic features of a language: the pronunciation system, the major grammatical structures as exemplified in word formation, phrase formation, and the basic sentence types. There is a general consensus in the profession that during this phase of habit formation the vocabulary[1] is to be rigorously limited. For vocabulary is the least systematic component of a language, and any increase of the learning burden during the habit forming stage would be an unwelcome distraction.

All very true. But our gratifying success on the introductory level has certainly outrun our performance at later stages of language teaching. Oral practice, we assert, provides a basis for good reading habits, by building habits of word grouping corresponding to the intonation stretches of speech and by assuring familiarity with the basic sentence types and the clues to grammatical functions (nouns, verbs, adjectives, etc.). But one essential device during this process, the limitation on vocabulary, leaves our students with the serious deficit of hopelessly inadequate vocabulary resources for any kind of real use of the language they are learning. Especially when the foreign language is to be used as a second language in educational experience, there is a need for an intermediate phase of massive and rapid vocabulary expansion, to meet the minimum requirements of reading and listening to lectures.

VOCABULARY NEEDS FOR USE IN READING (AND AUDIENCE-LISTENING)

We note that reading per se involves greater demands on vocabulary resources than conversation: there is no actual environmental situation to provide clues, and there is no opportunity for emergency feedback questions as in conversation. (Listening to a lecture involves the same demands as reading, plus the additional handicaps of inability to reread and the probability of some acoustic noise interference.)

---

[1] Since the term "vocabulary" is used with a variety of meanings, some linguists nowadays are using "lexis" to refer to a stock of words. It is usually easy to understand this technical usage in any given technical context.

LINGUISTS ON THE NATURE OF VOCABULARY

If history is to repeat itself, with experienced foreign language teachers finding devices and procedures to apply the findings of linguists, let us first ask what the linguists can report on the nature of the vocabulary part of a language. Then we may hope that pedagogical applications may be found in due time. Whatever due time may be, it will be none too soon. When we foreign language teachers are being honest with ourselves and each other, we admit that somehow our more successful students have learned to read, but we don't know how to teach them to read.

"MEANING"—POLYSEMY AND HETEROSEMY

The linguists report qualitatively on the nature of the relationship between words and meanings. A slogan which is both catchy and deeply true is "Words don't have meanings; people have meanings for words." Linguists have insisted on the arbitrary nature of any language: the relation between a linguistic signal and its meaning is a matter of habitual association by speakers and listeners between that signal and something meaningful in the situations in which that signal is used. (This is not a modern heresy; since Plato's *Kratylos* there has been no informed contradiction of this formulation.)

Indeed, for our purposes we may expand the slogan to say: "People don't have a meaning for a word; people have meanings for words." We are able to cope with the word *table* in "She looked at the table and decided it wouldn't go well with her other furniture." "She looked at the table and quickly found the square root." In so doing, we are also coping with "go, well, square, root" for some of the meanings we have for each of those words. This phenomenon—having meanings and very often very different meanings for a word—is *polysemy*, multi-meaningness. Polysemy is extensive, even within one language. Not only does one person have different meanings for one word, but different persons will have different meanings for a word. (For a group concerned with English as a second or foreign language, the problem of polysemy has a special urgency because of the increasing modern English trend toward two-part verbs like "carry on, carry out, pick out, pick on, pick up, go with, go on, go down the line, go through with the job, see through [in at least two senses], make out, make up.")

Just as important as polysemy for our purposes is the profound *heterosemy* when the vocabularies of two languages are compared. Except for deliberately monosemic inventions like "volt, CO_2, GNP, $\sqrt{-1}$ " there is very little one-to-one correspondence between the meanings speakers of one language have for any one of their words and the meanings speakers of another language have for any one of theirs. Both linguists and thoughtful foreign language teachers know that memorizing matched pairs of words in two languages is an educational atrocity, inhibiting the development of reading and speaking, and of use only as preparation for tests designed to check on such preparation for such tests.

Yet we know no complete escape from the device of glossing—supplying a word or words in a familiar language as a guide to understanding a passage in a less familiar one. This glossing may be in the form of a marginal or footnote gloss, or in an alphabetical end-vocabulary or bilingual dictionary. In any case, it is an emergency clue to the comprehension of a phrase or sentence, and at most a beginning of the learner's developing meaning for a word. A gloss is better than nothing, but no more than a starting point. The least valuable information about a word is a word in another language. To treat pair-matching as a learning objective or as a testing device violates what we know about polysemy and heterosemy.

Linguists are quite secure in reporting that polysemy and heterosemy are realities, and that they obviously bear on the pedagogy of massive vocabulary expansion. It is for language teachers to devise procedures in accordance with these realities and meanwhile to at least avoid rewarding the wrong kind of vocabulary learning—pair-matching between languages.

THE FREQUENCY-STRUCTURE OF A VOCABULARY

Less familiar to language teachers than these qualitative aspects is the quantitative structure of a vocabulary. At one time or another, foreign language teachers have examined frequency lists with a view to pedagogical applications. Almost exclusively their attention has been fixed on the upper end of the frequency list—those words (or stems, or roots) which occur most frequently. Lists of the 600 most frequent, the 1500 most frequent, the 3,000 most frequent words have been taken as guides for the construction of introductory and even intermediate materials.

There has been very much less attention to the other end of the list, the low-frequency words. Yet this low end is vitally significant in any consideration of massive vocabulary expansion. It is a matter not so much of *which* words occur with low frequency as of the shape of the frequency distribution, so to say. Most foreign language teachers to whom I have put the question of frequency distribution have made the natural guess that there would be a bell-shaped curve representing a few very-high-frequency words, a large number of medium-frequency words, and a few low-frequency words. This guess is natural, but it is quite wrong.

Actually, the shape of frequency distribution is like a ski jump: a very few very-high-frequency words, a small number of medium-frequency words, and a very large number of very-low-frequency words.[2] Depending on the criterion for "word," the slope of the ski jump curve will vary, but it is always very steep at the high end and very extensive at the low end. A great majority of the vocabulary items in any body of natural speech or writing will occur very infrequently. We may paraphrase the remark attributed to Lincoln: "Speakers must love the low-frequency words, because they use so many of them."

If we define "word" as being a sequence of letters or sounds which is different from any other sequence, then we will find that a few dozen such words at the top account for a sizable fraction of the total text; these are the very few very-frequent words. At the other end, we find that nearly one half of such "different words" occur *once and only once* in the text. This tapering off of the vocabulary is a thoroughly attested fact, based on scores of statistical examinations of many kinds of materials in many languages.

What is significant for our problem of massive vocabulary expansion on the intermediate levels is how early in the list this tapering off sets in. Consider some recent frequency counts:

In the text referred to in footnote 2, the ten most frequent words (*the, of, and, to, a, in, that, is, was, he*) account for 246,114 of the 1,014,235 words of text. The most frequent word, *the*, has a frequency of 69,970: i.e., it occurs on the average about once every 15 words. The tenth most frequent word, *he* (frequency 9544), occurs once every 106 words. The fiftieth, *if* (frequency 2199), occurs once every 461 words. By the time we reach the one hundredth word, *down*, we find a frequency of 895: i.e., *down* occurs on the average of once every 1133 words. Thus, even this close to the top of the frequency list, we are already noting a sharp tapering off.

J. A. Pfeffer has recently reported on a frequency count of modern

---

[2] For example, some statistics of a modern English text are described in a forthcoming Brown University Press publication, *Computational Analyses of Present-Day American English*, edited by Henry Kučera and W. N. Francis. The text is 1,014,235 words in length. Its total vocabulary (i.e., different words) amounts to 50,457, of which a great majority—42,540—occur only ten times each or less. (N.B. that a frequency of ten in this text corresponds to an average occurrence less than once every hundred thousand words of text.) The figures for this low end of the frequency list are:

FREQUENCY	NUMBER OF WORDS WITH THAT FREQUENCY	FREQUENCY	NUMBER OF WORDS WITH THAT FREQUENCY
10	561	5	1822
9	694	4	2464
8	826	3	3946
7	1118	2	7231
6	1280	1	22598

spoken German.[3] His list uses a broad definition of "word," including as one item all forms of any noun, adjective, or verb. Even so, we note the same tapering off very close to the top. His one hundredth most frequent word occurs once every 772 words of text; the six hundredth occurs once every 10,258 words of text.

Pfeffer's data cover a text over 595,000 words in length, in which nearly 25,000 different "words" appeared. A text of this size is not enormous; probably any educated person hears and reads many times this amount every year. How has he acquired the 25,000-word vocabulary to do it? How can a learner of a foreign language be guided to acquire even a fraction of this vocabulary?

THE VOCABULARY OF A LANGUAGE LEARNER ON THE INTERMEDIATE LEVEL

The relevant conclusion from these quantitative properties of a vocabulary is the hard saying that at the beginning of intermediate language study the learner is faced with a disastrous shortage of vocabulary resources, and this shortage will continue through and beyond the intermediate level. And we simply cannot predict *which* vocabulary items the learner will need for the next page of reading or the next minute of listening: the fact is that he will encounter several very-low-frequency items, including some that he cannot possibly have encountered before. It is futile to select in advance the, say, 6,000 words to be learned during the intermediate level as being the most useful for his future reading and listening. At the level of the 6,000th most frequent word in a frequency list, we are far far out on the low-frequency end of the list, where the predictability of occurrence or recurrence is very small indeed.

RESOURCES AND SKILLS

However grim this picture is, it is real. We have to face the fact that our students will not have adequate vocabulary resources until after many many hours of conversation and many hundreds of pages of reading. The resources are scanty; they must be compensated for by skills. Skills can be taught; resources must be acquired. The record of thousands of learners who have somehow acquired the vocabulary resources needed for using a foreign language shows that it can be done. But we may as well honestly admit that it is the students who have acquired the resources through developing their own skills, without too much effective help from us. And the other thousands of learners who have not devel-

---

[3] *Grunddeutsch. Basic (Spoken) German Word List* (New York: Prentice-Hall, Inc., 1964).

oped the skills or acquired the resources are on our conscience. It is wholesome to consider that possibly the successful ones succeeded without essential guidance from us—perhaps in some cases despite misguidance from us.

What are the skills which compensate for a lack of resources, in vocabulary expansion? Clearly not a gift for memorizing definitions in one's native language, nor bilingual glossings in a foreign language. Those processes would have been far too time-consuming to provide us with our vocabulary resources in our native language or in any foreign language in which we have become competent.

We must have acquired our meanings for words in other ways. What the two relevant findings of linguistics—the qualitative fact of polysemy and the quantitative fact of very numerous low-frequency items—point to is a skill in reading and listening. Possessors of this skill are those who are somehow adjusted to encounter low-frequency (often quite unfamiliar) vocabulary items and to somehow have a meaning for them in the context in which they are encountered.

PANIC OR INFER!

Clearly, that last phrase is the crucial one. The reader or listener encountering a "new word" can panic, especially if he has been trained to panic. Or he can have acquired the skill of inference from context. In the latter case, he uses what is not unfamiliar in the context to convey a meaning (not necessarily complete or precise) of the phrase or sentence. Whatever meaning he attributes to that phrase or to that sentence determines a meaning he can begin to have for that new word.[4]

GRAMMATICAL AND PRAGMATIC INFERENCES FROM THE CONTEXT

If a reader or audience-listener habitually controls the basic grammatical structures (as he very effectively does in his native language and as he does to some extent in a foreign language he is studying), the sheer grammar of the text environment of a "new" word significantly restricts the kind of meaning he can have for it in that context. If the grammatical environment is most appropriate for a noun, it is inefficient for him to consider a meaning appropriate to an adverb. If the new word, probably a noun, is probably the subject of a verb normally used with animate-human subjects, the scope of inference is further narrowed,

---

[4] In an earlier passage, the reader encountered: . . . deliberately monosemic inventions like "volt, CO_2, GNP, $\sqrt{-1}$." The reader had to make an inference about "monosemic" from context, including earlier "polysemy, heterosemy"; and probably every reader did.

and it is unlikely that the new word belongs in a meaning class with such nouns as "logarithm, prayer, bilabial, autumn."

In short, the basic skill in vocabulary expansion is the habit of guessing from context, using both grammatical and pragmatic clues. This habit appears to be normal in listening to and reading the native language, for those who really listen and read. It is not automatic in dealing with a foreign language, especially in the transition from the introductory level (with its necessarily controlled vocabulary) to and through the intermediate levels toward real use of the foreign language. On that introductory level the learner had been given every help to have meanings for the new words as they were introduced cautiously and underwent saturating recurrence. The skill of sensible guessing was not called into play. But as the learner moves from the protection of a rigorously controlled vocabulary into something like a real use of the foreign language, the skill of sensible guessing becomes a major teaching objective.

LINGUISTIC FINDINGS AND VOCABULARY-BUILDING PEDAGOGY

Here, I would suggest, lies the present gap between linguistic insights and pedagogical procedures. Just as the experienced teachers were able to translate the reports about the habitual nature of language into habit forming overlearning on the introductory level, they are now called on to apply the consequences of polysemy and the frequency distribution on the intermediate level of language learning. The targets are clear: learners must develop skills to compensate for scanty resources. The skills involve freedom from panic at encountering an unfamiliar vocabulary item. Ergo, the teacher must not pounce upon such items; a pouncing teacher produces panic or defensive boredom.[5] The skills involve sensible guessing at a useful meaning for the item in its context; this sensible guessing is funneled by grammatical possibility and pragmatic probability. The guessing must tolerate vagueness and the chance of misunderstanding. (How many native speakers of English have guesses at "osprey" that are vague as to color and size and shape, and perhaps as to membership in the animal, vegetable, or mineral kingdoms—without any calamitous impairment of their listening and reading ability?) Ergo, a teacher must not institute searching inquiries designed to punish vagueness or even misunderstandings in a learner's buildup of meanings for words.

These negative teaching procedures do not take us very far, but they are likely to be hard sayings for teachers at the intermediate level of

---

[5] There are implications here for any attempt to design programed learning courses to develop reading ability. Prompt correction of every "mistake" is just what the vocabulary-expanding learner should not experience.

foreign language instruction. "Do not focus on words that are likely to be unfamiliar; do not punish guesses which are vague; punish only guesses which are purely random, and then practice correctively with guided guessing using the available grammatical and pragmatic clues in the context." But a hard saying is not an invitation to abdicate responsibility. Many foreign language teachers have made the difficult transition from a grammar-translation method to habit forming teaching on the introductory level, with materials and procedures developed by their colleagues in response to the challenge of linguistic findings. Everybody knows that it is a more strenuous kind of teaching. But our students learn more. Thirty years ago foreign language learners spent years and semesters in classrooms and were unable to speak, understand, read, or write in the foreign language. Now those who have been guided through a modern introductory level are able to do some speaking and understanding.

The time has come to move up one level and guide an increasing proportion of learners at the intermediate level to an ability to read and to understand speech of a considerably more sophisticated kind, approximating a genuine use of the foreign language.

Pessimism is not in order. The language teaching profession has done it before on the introductory level, and we can do it again. Teachers of the "commonly taught languages" are beginning to produce materials to reward the virtue of sensible guessing and tolerable vagueness and to punish (or at least not reward) the vices of panic and slavish dependence on word matching. But it is only a beginning; and once again we need an application of linguistic findings. We need practical classroom procedures and devices, practical teaching materials on the intermediate level, to develop the skills for massive vocabulary expansion.

PATTERNS OF DIFFICULTY IN VOCABULARY

ROBERT LADO

1. WORDS

1.1 Undue emphasis on words as words to the neglect of pronunciation and grammatical structure is not in keeping with modern linguistic thinking. Sapir says bluntly in talking about linguistic study, "The linguistic student should never make the mistake of identifying a language with its dictionary."[1] On the other hand, one cannot deny or ignore the existence of the word as a tangible unit of language. Sapir again, with characteristic insight, puts it thus:

> No more convincing test could be desired than this, that the naïve Indian, quite unaccustomed to the concept of the written word, has nevertheless no serious difficulty in dictating a text to a linguistic student word by word; he tends, of course, to run his words together as in actual speech, but if he is called to a halt and is made to understand what is desired, he can readily isolate the words as such, repeating them as units. He regularly refuses, on the other hand, to isolate the radical or grammatical element, on the ground that it "makes no sense."[2]

1.2 The word has been defined for scientific linguistic study by Bloomfield:

> A free form which consists entirely of two or more lesser free forms, as, for instance, *poor John* or *John ran away* or *yes, sir*, is a *phrase*. A free form which is not a phrase, is a *word*. A word, then, is a free form which does not consist entirely of (two or more) lesser free forms; in brief, a word is a *minimum free form*.[3]

[1] Edward Sapir, *Language* (New York, 1921), p. 234.
[2] *Ibid.*, pp. 34–35.
[3] Leonard Bloomfield, *Language* (New York, 1933), pp. 177–78. For a more complete discussion of the word see also pp. 178–83 and 207–46. For a mechanical procedure that shows word and morpheme boundaries see the recent article by Zellig S. Harris, "From Phoneme to Morpheme," *Language*, XXXI (1955), pp. 190–222.

1.3 A clear insight into the way words are used by the speakers of a language is given by Fries. He says,

> For us, a *word* is a combination of sounds acting as a stimulus to bring into attention the experience to which it has become attached by use. . . .[4]
>
> More than that, while the experience that is stimulated by the sound combination is a whole with a variety of contacts, usually only one aspect of this experience is dominant in attention—a particular aspect determined by the whole context of the linguistic situation. When one uses *head* in such a context as "a *head* of cabbage," it is the shape which is the dominant aspect of the experience that has made a connection with the material unit, a cabbage. When one uses head in such a context as "the *head* of a department," it is the head as the chief or dominating part of the body. When it is used in "the head of the river," another aspect of the relation of head to the body is important in attention. From a practical point of view, the various separate dictionary meanings of a word are the particular aspects of the experience stimulated by a word that have been dominant in the attention of users of the word as these aspects may be inferred from the context of a large number of quotations in which the word appears. For the native user of a language, the symbol, with the wide range of experience it stimulates, is so much a part of the very texture of his thought that he exercises great freedom in turning upon any aspect of this experience in line with the pressing needs of his thinking. The "meanings" of words are, therefore, more fluid than we realize. For the foreign speaker of a language who learns this new language as an adult, the words as stimuli probably never function with anything like the same fullness and freedom as they do for a native.[5]

1.4 Three aspects of words concern us here: (1) their form, (2) their meaning, and (3) their distribution.

1.41 Form. In most languages the form of words consists of sound segments, stress, and, in tone languages such as Chinese and Thai, pitch. The form of the Spanish word *jugo* 'juice' is made up of four significant sound segments (phonemes) /xúgo/ and stress—primary stress on the first syllable. If we change one of the sound segments, *j*, to *y*, a new word results, *yugo* 'yoke.' If we change the position of the primary stress, a new word results, *jugó* 'he played.' The Thai word อม̃ [ma:ʔ] 'horse' is made up of certain sound segments and a high, level pitch. The same segments with a rising pitch would mean 'dog.'

---

[4] Charles C. Fries, with the cooperation of A. Aileen Traver, *English Word Lists, A Study of Their Adaptability for Instruction*, Washington, D.C., American Council on Education. Reprinted Ann Arbor, 1940, p. 87.
[5] *Ibid.*, p. 88.

The form of words varies according to the formality of the situation, speed of talk, position in the sentence, position as to stress, etc. For example, the English word *and* varies from three segmental phonemes /ænd/ through intermediate degrees of reduction, /ənd/, /æn/, /ən/, to one segmental phoneme, /n/. The word *not* occurs as /nat/ and /nt/; *will* as /wɪl/ and as /l/; *is* as /ɪz/ and /s/ or /z/. Naïve speakers of a language find it difficult to believe that the words they use vary so much in form.

Another relevant feature of form is that of the parts of words. English *observational* is made up of a stem *observ-* (compare *observe*),[6] a suffix *-(a)tion,* and another suffix *-al.* Other languages, on the other hand, permit more complex combinations than those of English. As something of a linguistic curiosity, but definitely a form of the language, Sapir mentions the example from Paiute, *wii-to-kuchum-punku rügani-yugwi-va-ntü-m(ü)*, meaning 'they who are going to sit and cut up with a knife a black cow (or bull).'[7]

The frequency of the parts of words may counteract the lack of frequency of the total word. If we use the word *observational*, it will probably be understood by elementary students of English as a foreign language even though it appears among the 1,358 least frequent words in Thorndike's list.[8] The parts *observe + (a)tion + al* are much more frequent than the word itself. The word *observe* is listed by Thorndike among the 2,000 most frequent words in English. The suffix *-tion* is used in so many words in English that its total frequency must be very high. I found examples of *-tion* in every page of a random ten page sample of Bloomfield's *Language* and in a similar spot-check of ten random pages of the lighter style of *The Art of Plain Talk* by Rudolf Flesch.[9] The suffix *-al* is less frequent than *-tion*, but it is still frequent enough to occur on practically every page of text.

English has lexical forms made up of patterns of separate words, for example *call up* 'to phone.' Many languages do not permit such units or do not permit the same types of formal patterns. Compare for example Spanish *telefonear* 'to telephone' or *llamar por teléfono* 'call by telephone' but nothing like the construction *call up.*

1.42 Meaning.   It is quite an illusion to think as even literate people sometimes do that meanings are the same in all languages, that languages differ only in the forms used for those meanings. As a matter of fact the meanings into which we classify our experience are culturally determined

---

[6] It is doubtful that native speakers break this form further into *ob + serve*.

[7] Edward Sapir, *Language*, p. 31.

[8] Edward L. Thorndike and Irving Lorge, *The Teachers' Word Book of 30,000 Words* (New York, 1944).

[9] Rudolf Flesch, *The Art of Plain Talk* (New York, 1946).

or modified and they vary considerably from culture to culture. Some meanings found in one culture may not exist in another. The meaning, 'horse' did not exist in American Indian languages until the Spanish conquest and colonization brought horses to America. Similarly, the meanings 'corn' (in the sense of maize) and 'potatoes' did not exist in Europe until the same people took those products from America to Europe in their ships. But even when the reality is available to the culture, the meanings will differ, or not exist in some cases. The Eskimos have many meaning distinctions correlating with different types of snow and use separate words to express those distinctions, whereas other cultures that have considerable experience with snow simply do not have as many meaning distinctions. These meaning differences are seldom as forcefully noticeable as when one attempts to translate accurately a text from one language to another.

Meanings can be classified according to the forms they attach to. Meanings that attach to words as words are lexical meanings, for example the meaning, 'a building for human habitation,' that attaches to the form *house* is a lexical meaning in English. The meaning 'two or more; plural' that attaches to the bound form *-s* [s] in *books, cats, maps,* can be called a morphological meaning, while the same meaning 'plural' that attaches to the word form *plural* is a lexical meaning. The meaning 'question' attached to the word arrangement in the sentence, *Is he a farmer,* is a syntactic meaning, but the meaning 'question' attached to the word form *question* is a lexical one.

At the moment, we are primarily concerned with lexical meanings, but different languages classify their meanings differently, that is, what is habitually a lexical meaning in one language may be a morphological meaning in another. Speakers of one language who have not come in meaningful contact with other languages assume not only that the meanings are the same but that they will be classified the same way. Speakers of English find it difficult to imagine a language in which the singular-plural distinction in *book:books* is not made morphologically. "How else can you communicate that idea?" they are apt to ask. In Chinese, for example, that distinction is not made, that is, it is not made morphologically, by a bound form such as *-s* in English. In Chinese, the meanings 'two' 'three' 'more than one' etc. are lexical meanings; those meanings attach to words. When the meaning is relevant to the message, the words are included, and when the meaning is not relevant, the words are left out. Greek had the meanings 'singular' 'dual' and 'plural' as morphological meanings. We can assume that Greek speakers wondered how languages that have only singular and plural could express the meaning 'dual; two.' That distinction is a lexical one in English.

The matter of the frequency of the various meanings of a word is relevant to us. If one uses the word *get*, which appears among the 500 most frequent ones in Thorndike's list, in the context, *We did not want to overdo the thing and get six months,* meaning 'suffer imprisonment by way of punishment,' we would find that some fairly advanced students of English as a foreign language would not 'know' the word. Yet we could not convincingly assume that they did not really know one of the 500 most frequent words in English. That particular meaning of *get* is so infrequent that it was not reported as having occurred at all in a sample of over half a million running words.[10] The *Oxford English Dictionary* lists 234 meanings for the word *get* and obviously one can know a good many of those meanings and still miss the word in the particular context used as an example above.

The meanings discussed are usually part of the intended message in communication. These meanings are more or less consciously intended by the speaker and may be called primary meanings. In actual use, however, other meanings are conveyed by words, for example, if a word is restricted in use to a given social class, its use by a speaker may give the listener the meaning of social class identification. Similarly if a word is restricted to a geographical area, its use by a speaker will convey a locality meaning, also.

1.43   The distribution of words is important to us because at any given moment in the history of a language the speakers of that language carry with them the habits of the restrictions in distribution and because different languages have different restrictions. There are grammatical restrictions so that in English, *water* may be a noun as in *a glass of water,* a verb as in *water the garden,* a noun adjunct as in *water meter,* but not an adjective without some change in form, e.g. *watery substance.* In other languages the restrictions may be greater; for example in Spanish, *agua* 'water' as a word may only be a noun unless its form is changed.

The fact that words may show different geographic distribution, falling in or out of this or that dialect area of a language is important. And, as already indicated, distribution in the various social class levels also has to be considered because of the secondary meanings such distribution conveys. Statements of raw frequency alone leave these matters unresolved. Thorndike's list gives *ain't* among the 2,000 most frequent words in English, but the list does not say if *ain't* is typical of Standard English or of the speech representing certain other dialects.

Words are not only restricted geographically and socially; they are often restricted as to styles of speaking and writing. For example, many words found in poetry will not be found in ordinary conversation or in ordinary prose; and vice versa, some words used in prose will not be found in poetry.

[10] Estimated from data supplied in Irving Lorge.

1.5 Classifications.   It should be abundantly clear from the above brief discussion if not previously so that the words of a language are more than merely a list of lexical items. The words of a language are a highly complex system of classes of items—interlocking classes as to meaning, form, grammatical function, distribution, etc.

1.51   Fries[11] classifies English words into four groups that seem relevant to us. They are (1) function words, (2) substitute words, (3) grammatically distributed words, and (4) content words. The function words primarily perform grammatical functions, for example, *do* signalling questions. The substitute words, *he, she, they, so,* etc. replace a class of words and several sub-classes. Grammatically distributed words, *some, any,* etc. show unusual grammatical restrictions in distribution. The number of words in the first three groups is rather small, say 200 in round numbers in English.[12] The fourth group, content words, constitutes the bulk of the vocabulary of the language. In English and in many other languages the content words are subdivided into items treated as things, as processes, as qualities, etc.

1.52   Two further distinctions in vocabulary are required to complete our model. We need to distinguish between a common core vocabulary known to all the members of a language community, and specialized vocabularies, known only to special groups. We are of course primarily interested in the common core vocabulary, because specialized vocabularies have to be learned by native as well as non-native speakers. We are interested primarily in the special problems of the latter.

1.53   The other distinction is that between vocabulary for production and vocabulary for recognition. As a rule our recognition vocabulary is much larger than our production vocabulary. Various estimates have been made of the minimum necessary vocabulary for a student to be able to communicate in ordinary situations. Basic English uses approximately 1,000 words for that purpose.[13] Michael West considers a vocabulary of 2,000 words "good enough for anything, and more than enough for most things."[14] Obviously these are minimum production vocabularies. For recognition, larger minimum vocabularies are necessary.

---

[11] Charles C. Fries, *Teaching and Learning English as a Foreign Language* (Ann Arbor, 1945), pp. 44–50.
[12] Estimated from data supplied in Fries, *The Structure of English* (New York, 1954), Ch. VI.
[13] C. K. Ogden, *The System of Basic English* (New York, 1934).
[14] Michael West, "Simplified and Abridged," *English Language Teaching*, V, No. 2, p. 48.

2. THE NATIVE LANGUAGE FACTOR

2.1 Ease and difficulty.   Given the above model and making use of available vocabulary studies one might attempt to select a sample vocabulary for teaching or for testing. Such attempts have been made and have received wide circulation. C. K. Ogden's Basic English list and West's *A General Service List of English Words*[15] are well known examples in an active field. Nevertheless, in spite of the care and experience that has gone into the preparation of such lists, they cannot give us a vocabulary sample graded as to difficulty because by their very nature they fail to take into account the most powerful factor in acquiring the vocabulary of a foreign language, namely, the vocabulary of the native language.

If in a test of English vocabulary for Spanish speakers one uses the words *machete, suppuration,* and *calumniator* which appear among the 1,358 least frequent words in Thorndike's 30,000 word list, one would find that practically all the students knew them. Could we then assume that those students possessed a vocabulary of over 28,642 words in English? Obviously not. Spanish has the words *machete, supuración* and *calumniador,* similar in form and meaning to the English words, and Spanish-speaking students will know those words by the mere fact of knowing Spanish. We simply cannot ignore the native language of the student as a factor of primary importance in vocabulary, just as we cannot ignore it in pronunciation and grammatical structure.

Another example arguing for the importance of the native language has to do with grammatical distribution of two very simple words. The words *fire* and *man* will probably be more difficult for Spanish speakers in the contexts, *Fire the furnace,* and *Man the guns,* than in *Open fire* 'start shooting' and *A man broke his leg.* The difference is more subtle than in the previous example, but it is there nevertheless. Spanish has a noun, *fuego,* 'fire' used in *Abran fuego,* 'Open fire' but not used as a verb as in *Fire the furnace.* Similarly, a Spanish noun, *hombre,* 'man,' is used in *Un hombre se rompió una pierna,* 'A man broke his leg,' but is not used as a verb as in *Man the guns.* There are other elements involved in these examples to be sure, but grammatical distribution is definitely a factor.

2.2 Difficulty patterns.   Similarity and difference to the native language in form, meaning and distribution will result in ease or difficulty in acquiring the vocabulary of a foreign language. Comparing the foreign language vocabulary with that of the native language we will

---

[15] Michael West, *A General Service List of English Words with Semantic Frequencies and a Supplementary Word-List for the Writing of Popular Science and Technology.* (New York, 1953).

find words that are (1) similar in form and in meaning, (2) similar in form but different in meaning, (3) similar in meaning but different in form, (4) different in form and in meaning, (5) different in their type of construction, (6) similar in primary meaning but different in connotation, and (7) similar in meaning but with restrictions in geographical distribution.

Since some of these groups overlap, with the result that some words will fall into more than one group at the same time, the difficulty will vary somewhat. Nevertheless, we can predict general level of difficulty on the basis of these groupings, and will classify each group into one of three levels of difficulty; (1) easy, (2) normal, and (3) difficult.

The term *similar* is restricted here to items that would function as "same" in the other language in ordinary use. We know that complete sameness is not to be expected in language behavior. The actual behavioral boundaries of similarity depend on the items that persons of one language "identify" or "translate" as same from and into the other language. References to form are to the sounds of the words, not to the spelling, even though spelling is used to represent the words in this paper.

Pattern 1, Cognates:[16] Words that are similar in form and in meaning. English and Spanish have thousands of words that are reasonably similar in form and in meaning, for example *hotel, hospital, calendar.*[17] Some of these were kept in Spanish as it evolved from Latin and were borrowed into English from Latin or French. Some go back to earlier forms presumably found in Indo-European, the common ancestor of English and Spanish in what is known as the Indo-European family of languages. Whatever the cause of the similarity, these words usually constitute the lowest difficulty group—they are *easy*. In fact, if they are similar enough, even students who have never studied English at all will recognize them. These words are of value at the very elementary level.

Even though there are thousands of words that are similar in English and Spanish these similarities can be classified into a relatively small number of sub-patterns, for example, English *-tion* is similar to Spanish *-cion,* and hundreds of words can be classified as similar under that sub-pattern.[18] When using such words in teaching and testing beginning

[16] Cognates here mean words that are similar in form and meaning regardless of origin. The usual meaning of cognate is "related in origin." For us even if two words are not related in origin they will be called cognates if they are similar in form and meaning. Similarly, if two words have the same origin but are now so different that speakers do not identify them as similar, they will not be considered cognates for our purpose.

[17] For a list of Spanish-English cognates see Marshall E. Nunn, and Herbert A. Van Scroy, *Glossary of Related Spanish-English Words,* University of Alabama Studies, Number 5.

[18] For a brief account of nine patterns of Spanish-English cognates see *Lessons in Vocabulary,* from *An Intensive Course in English* by the Research Staff of the English Language Institute, Charles C. Fries, Director (Ann Arbor, 1954). Compare also E. M. Anthony "The Teachings of Cognates," *Language Learning,* IV (1952–53), pp. 79–82.

students we will do well to sample them as sub-patterns rather than as independent items.

Vigorous discussion often results when cognate words are mentioned in connection with teaching. We do not need to get involved in such discussions since cognates are presented here for recognition rather than for production. There can be little quarrel with having the student recognize them when they are used by others.

It is sometimes falsely assumed that cognates are to be found only between two related languages such as English and Spanish, not between unrelated languages such as English and Japanese, Chinese and English. In actual fact, numerous cognates can be found between English and Japanese and between English and Chinese, and many other languages which are quite unrelated to each other. There are many words which have circled the globe, and many more that have extended far beyond the boundaries of any one language or any one culture.

Pattern 2, Deceptive Cognates:[19] Words that are similar in form but represent meanings that are different. Words that are similar in form in two languages may be only partly similar in meaning, they may be altogether different in meaning but still represent meanings that exist in the native language, or they may be different in meaning and represent meanings that are not grasped as such in the native language. Japanese borrowed the word *milk* from English but restricted its meaning to 'canned milk.' The form of the word in Japanese is similar to English but the meaning is only partly similar since it does not include fresh milk, for example. Spanish has a word, *asistir*, which is similar in form to English *assist*, but the meaning is practically always different. Spanish *asistir* is similar in meaning to English *attend*, while English *assist* carries with it the feature of helping, of supporting. As a result of this difference in meaning, Spanish speakers learning English say they *assisted a class* when meaning they *attended* 'were present.' English *in the table* and *on the table* are similar in meaning to Spanish *en la mesa* in ordinary conversation. Only under very special circumstances will a Spanish speaker make a meaning distinction between *in* and *on* the table, and then it will not be only an *in:on* contrast but a *table* vs. *drawer* contrast as well. Spanish speakers will say *en el cajón* 'in the drawer' and *sobre la mesa* 'on the table.' The problem here is not simply attaching a familiar meaning to a new form but also grasping a new meaning distinction, a different way of classifying reality.

These words that are similar in form but different in meaning constitute

---

[19] "Deceptive cognates" as used here refers only to similarity in form and difference in meaning; it does not refer to the origin of the words. In usual linguistic terminology deceptive cognates would refer to words in two languages that because of their form would seem to be related by origin but are not so related. For us such a case would be classed as a cognate provided the meanings are also similar.

a special group very high on a scale of difficulty. We will label them *difficult*. They are not adequately sampled on frequency criteria alone because their similarity in form to words in the native language raises their frequency in student usage above normal for the language. In other words, they are more important than their frequency rating might indicate. They are sure-fire traps.

Pattern 3, Different Forms: Words that are similar in some of their frequent meanings but different in form. Difficulty level: normal. Example: English *tree* in the context, *The leaves of that tree are falling,* is similar in its primary meaning to Spanish *árbol* in a comparable context. The learning burden in this case is chiefly that of learning a new form, *tree,* for a meaning of *arbol* already habitually grasped by Spanish speaking students. This kind of vocabulary learning is naïvely taken by many to represent all vocabulary learning. Such an oversimplification fails to account for the various vocabulary groups which appear when we have looked closer and have considered the native language.

It is also important to note that although certain meanings of a word in one language are sometimes translatable into a word in another language there are very few if any words in two languages that are the same in all their meanings. It is difficult for example to realize that the words *tree* and *arbol* of our example are similar in only about four out of their twenty or more meanings and uses. Only the poorest two-language dictionaries will show numbers of words in a one-to-one meaning correspondence in the two languages. Only words such as *penicillin,* which are borrowed into many languages simultaneously, can be considered equivalent in all their meanings, and even then if such words gain any currency at all they soon develop new meanings that are not parallel in different languages.

It is in these content words that are different in form but similar in some meanings, however, that decisions can and should be made as to vocabulary size on the basis of frequency lists for recognition and adequacy for expression on a production level.

Pattern 4, "Strange" Meanings: Words that are different in form and represent meanings that are "strange" to speakers of a particular native language, that is, meanings that represent a different grasp of reality. Difficult. In American English, *first floor* is different in form from Spanish *primer piso* and different in its grasp of what constitutes "first." Spanish *primer* "first" in this case does not mean number one at ground level but number one above ground level, and so *primer piso* refers to what in Am. English is called *second floor* and not *first floor,* which would be the literal translation.

These cases constitute special problems in the vocabulary of a foreign language. Obviously it is not enough merely to teach a new form; the strange meaning must be made familiar. Some of the instances covered by this pattern—the instance in which the form in the two languages is similar—fall also under pattern 2, *deceptive cognates*. Pattern 4, however, includes all those in which there is no particular similarity in the form of the words in the two languages.

There is every reason to believe that the same kind of distortion that we can observe in the sounds of the speech of a non-native speaker also occur in the meanings he is trying to convey. In both cases he is substituting sounds and meanings of his native language and culture. In the case of sounds the untrained person hears a vague "foreign" accent and the trained person hears specific distortions. In the case of meanings the distortions go largely undetected by the observer or listener because the native meanings stimulated in him by the speech forms may not be accompanied by outwardly observable behavior. It is only when a word form is used in an "unusual" way that our attention is drawn to possible meaning differences. Similarly, when the non-native speaker of a language listens to the language as spoken by natives, the meanings that he grasps are not those that the native speakers attempt to convey, but those of the system of the language of the listener.

Pattern 5, New Form Types: Words that are different in their morphological construction. Difficult. When the speakers of various Romance languages and of Japanese, Chinese and other languages learn English they have great trouble learning such lexical items as *call up* 'to telephone,' *call on* 'to visit,' and *run out of* 'to exhaust the supply of.' If in the native language of the student there are no lexical items made up of two otherwise separate words in patterns like the one illustrated, he will not easily grasp these "two-word verbs" in the foreign language. The difficulty is increased when the elements can be separated by other words as in the example, *Did you call the boy up?* These two-word verbs constitute a difficulty group all its own for speakers of various languages.

"Idioms"—expressions peculiar to a language—are identifiable as we compare two languages rather than within the language itself. An expression which may seem peculiar to native speakers may be quite natural to speakers of another language and would therefore not be an "idiom" to them. On the other hand, an expression which seems quite natural to native speakers may be strange to foreign speakers of a particular language background. If we should find on comparing the expression with a variety of languages that it is strange to all or nearly all of them, we would be justified in calling it an idiom in general, but even then the statement would be meaningless in those cases in which the other language had a parallel expression. As a matter of fact, the idiom counts made in the wake of the Modern Foreign Language Study were two-language studies. The *Spanish Idiom List* by Keniston[20] lists expressions in Spanish that are strange to English speakers. In all of the counts the compilers looked at expressions in the foreign language with English as their frame of reference.

Pattern 6, Different Connotation: Words that have widely different connotations in two languages. Difficult. A special difficulty group is represented by words that are harmless in connotation in the native language but offensive or taboo in the foreign language, or vice versa. When they are harmless in the native language the student will use them in the foreign language without realizing their effect. When they are harmless in the foreign language the student will avoid using them for fear of setting off the same reactions they produce in his native language. In either case they are important on the level of social acceptability of words. A few examples will show how important these connotation differences can be.

In Spanish the expression *Díos mío* meaning literally 'My God' is often used as an appeal to the Almighty in matter-of-fact conversation. Even those Spanish speakers who have progressed considerably in their control of English will sometimes use the expression with the same feeling and intent in English, but the effect on English listeners is of course different. The name *Jesús* is often used as a given name in Spanish. Parents who thus name their children may actually feel they are honoring Christ, or at least do not feel any lack of respect. In English, however, people find it difficult to call a person by that name. It seems to smack of irreverence to English speakers to use the name for a human being, a radically different connotation from that in Spanish. In whistling at sports events or political rallies the difference is in the opposite direction: Spanish speakers may be shocked to hear a speaker whistled at and applauded at the same time. They believe the whistles indicate disapproval and they wonder why disapproval is expressed so openly as it appears to them. In Spanish the applause indicates approval, and whistling, a vulgar form of disapproval. Some youthful students of foreign languages delight in learning certain unprintable expressions not approved in polite company. When they ask for translations they get colorless renderings which when uttered leave us wondering why they are uttered at all.

The differences in connotation sometimes develop between dialects of the same language. In Cuba the familiar form of the second person pronoun, *tú*, is more widely used than in Mexico for example. A Cuban young man was rebuked by two Mexican young ladies because he used

[20] Hayward Keniston, *Spanish Idiom List Selected on the Basis of Range and Frequency of Occurrence*. Publications of the American and Canadian Committees on Modern Languages. XI (New York, 1929).

the familiar *tú*, which sounded a bit too bold to them. No amount of explaining was enough to completely convince the girls that the young man actually meant no disrespect. The word *grueso* 'fat' is used as a compliment at least in some dialects of present day Spanish. On a visit to Spain I was greeted repeatedly with "flattering" expressions of how "fat" I was. Being aware of the favorable connotation I appreciated the remark, but many an American young girl may not have felt flattered.

These have been obvious, even coarse examples of wide differences in connotation. More subtle differences exist and remain in the speech of speakers of foreign languages through the advanced stages of control of the language. We cannot do much to teach or to test these subtle differences specifically and completely, but it is possible to sample the more frequent and obvious cases of wide discrepancy in connotation.

Pattern 7, Geographically Restricted: Words that are restricted as to the geographic areas in which they are used in the foreign language. Difficult, because the restrictions must be learned also. Restrictions in geographic distribution of words are important to the selection of words for teaching and for testing. Unless we are interested in teaching or testing a particular geographic dialect of a language we will choose forms that are part of the standard language if there is one, and words that are common to the major dialects if there is not a standard language. If we are interested in English without regard to whether it is Standard British or Standard American English we would avoid such words as *petrol* and *gasoline* in testing because they are typical of British and American usage respectively. If on the other hand we are interested in Standard American English as distinct from British English, we would use *gasoline*. Within American English, if we are not interested in any one dialect, we would use *dragon fly* for the insect known by that name, because that term is more general than Northern *darning needle* and Midland *snake feeder* for the same insect.[21]

Although part of what has been said about pattern 7 seems not to apply directly to the definition of a pattern of difficulty, it is an important consideration. The matter of geographic distribution fits more neatly into a difficulty pattern when we consider that a student who has learned a geographically restricted form must learn another for the same meaning if he is to communicate with speakers from geographic areas where the form he learned has no currency. Hence, the label "difficult" we have given the pattern.

.   .   .

[21] Hans Kurath, *A Word Geography of the Eastern United States.* (Ann Arbor, 1949). p. 14.

There has been on the whole much superficial oversimplified thinking about the vocabulary of languages, and a great deal of vocabulary research such as word frequency lists and simplified vocabularies suffers from that oversimplification. In dealing with vocabulary we should take into account three important aspects of words—their form, their meaning, their distribution—and we should consider the various kinds or classes of words in the operation of the language. If these things are important in understanding the vocabulary system of a language, they become even more important when one learns the vocabulary of a foreign language since the forms, meanings, distribution, and classifications of words are different in different languages. Out of these differences arise vocabulary problems and difficulty levels that constitute teaching and learning problems and are telltale matters for vocabulary tests. The patterns of difficulty described above are an attempt to clarify and classify the problems involved.

REFERENCES

Bloomfield, Leonard. *Language*. New York: Henry Holt and Company, 1933.

Bongers, Herman. *The History and Principles of Vocabulary Control*. Woerden, Holland: Wocopi. Three volumes in two, 1947.

Flesch, Rudolf. *The Art of Plain Talk*. New York and London: Harper & Brothers Publishers, 1946.

Fries, Charles C., with the cooperation of A. Aileen Traver. *English Word Lists*. A Study of Their Adaptability for Instruction. Washington, D.C.: American Council on Education, 1940. Reprinted 1950 by The George Wahr Publishing Co., Ann Arbor.

Fries, Charles C. *Teaching and Learning English as a Foreign Language*. Ann Arbor: University of Michigan Press, 1945.

Fries, Charles C. *The Structure of English*. New York: Harcourt, Brace and Co., Chapt. VI, 1954.

Keniston, Hayward. *Spanish Idiom List*, Selected on the Basis of Range and Frequency of Occurrence. New York: Publications of the American and Canadian Committees on Modern Languages. Vol. XI, 1929.

Kurath, Hans. *A Word Geography of the Eastern United States*, Ann Arbor: University of Michigan Press, 1949.

Lorge, Irving. *The Semantic Count of 570 Commonest English Words*. New York: Bureau of Publications, Teachers College, Columbia University, 1949.

Nunn, Marshall E., and Van Scroy, Herbert A. *Glossary of Related*

Spanish-English Words. University, Alabama: University of Alabama Studies, Number 5, 1949.

Ogden, C. K. *The System of Basic English.* New York: Harcourt, Brace and Company, 1934.

Ogden, C. K. *The Oxford English Dictionary.* Vols. I–XII and Supplement (Corrected Reissue). Oxford University Press, 1933.

Rodríguez Bou, I. *Recuento de vocabulario español.* Río Piedras, Peurto Rico: Universidad de Puerto Rico. Two volumes in Three, 1952.

Sapir, Edward. *Language.* New York: Harcourt, Brace and Co., 1921.

Thorndike, Edward L., and Lorge, Irving. *The Teacher's Word Book of 30,000 Words.* New York: Bureau of Publications, Teachers College, Columbia University, 1944.

West, Michael. "Simplified and Abridged," *English Language Teaching* 5, no. 1 (Nov. 1950):48–52.

West, Michael. *A General Service List of English Words,* with Semantic Frequencies and a Supplementary Word-List for the Writing of Popular Science and Technology. London; New York; Toronto: Longmans, Green and Co., 1953.

THE PSYCHOLINGUISTIC CONCEPT OF "DIFFICULTY" AND THE TEACHING OF FOREIGN LANGUAGE VOCABULARY

MASANORI HIGA

I. INTRODUCTION

On the basis of classroom observation in foreign language teaching, teachers have come to assume that success in teaching a foreign language, as in teaching other subject matters, is partly a function of how learning materials are presented to the learner. They have long been aware that differently organized materials have different effects on learning, but, at the same time, they have a feeling of helplessness because the variables affecting the organization of learning materials are not very well known. This feeling is shared by both textbook writers and educational research-ers. The ideal in textbook writing, as expressed by the American Text-book Publishers Institute (1949, p. 9), is to "organize learning materials so ingeniously, so tightly that each lesson applies what has been taught before and prepares for what is to follow . . . ," but the ideal still remains unrealized. According to Fattu (1960, p. 1533), an educational researcher, "The writing of textbooks and preparation of films, as well as classroom presentation of content, today is largely an art. Very few variables are identified, and the interaction of these is unexplored terri-tory.

The most common practice of arranging learning materials today is to order them from the simple to complex or from the concrete to abstract (Herrick, 1960). The assumption underlying this practice is that complex or abstract materials are more difficult than simple or concrete ones. A corollary derived from this assumption is that learning materials should be organized from the easy to difficult in sequence. As will be explained later in this paper, the assumption, together with its corollary, seems to be valid. What is problematic is that judgments are often made sub-jectively as to which materials are simple and easy and which are com-plex and difficult. Much improvement might be achieved in curriculum preparation, if we had a clear understanding of what "difficulty" is and how it may be measured.

This paper reviews the psycholinguistic concept of "difficulty" in rela-tion to the semantic (as opposed to phonetic or grammatical) aspect of

292

foreign language vocabulary with a hope that such a review will assist teachers and textbook writers in their attempt to organize foreign language learning materials for effective teaching and learning.

II. THE DEFINITION OF "DIFFICULTY"

As Skinner (1953) has pointed out, we have a tendency to label behavior using adjectives such as *intelligent* and *aggressive*, then coin nouns like *intelligence* and *aggressiveness* from such adjectives, and begin to assume that there exist such entities or traits as intelligence and aggressiveness. Because of this tendency there is a danger of circular argument when behavior is described. We observe a man devouring food and then infer that the man is hungry. At the next moment, in an attempt to attribute his behavior to some cause, we are likely to say that the man is eating voraciously *because* of hunger. Skinner appropriately warns that we should be cautious in using coined abstract terms such as *hunger, intelligence, anxiety,* etc.

The term "difficulty" seems to be another abstract noun coined from an adjective. The adjective in this case is, of course, *difficult.* In general we label learning material as difficult, if it is not learned in a short time. This is labeling learning material on the basis of the learner's behavior. A possible circular argument here would be to say that the learner takes much time to learn certain material because it is difficult or because it is not well-presented.

Just as a man's hunger may be described operationally in terms of duration of food deprivation, so may the "difficulty" of learning material be described in terms of time or number of trials needed to learn it by one person or a given group of persons. In fact, this is how "difficulty" is defined in psychology. When person A takes more time to learn item X than item Y, we may say that item X is more difficult for person A than item Y. However, if person B takes more time to learn item Y than item X, then Y is more difficult than X for person B. This means that there is no such thing as "difficulty" in the absolute. *It is chiefly the learner's past and present learning experience that makes any learning material easy or difficult.*

III. THE "DIFFICULTY" OF FOREIGN
LANGUAGE VOCABULARY

From the psycholinguistic viewpoint the "difficulty" of foreign language vocabulary seems to consist of five factors which reflect the relationships between and among words already learned and words to be learned. These factors are: (1) the "intrinsic difficulty" of a word to be learned, (2) the interaction between previously learned words and a new word to be learned, (3) the interaction within a group of words to be learned at the same time, (4) the interaction between groups of words to be learned in sequence, and (5) the effect of repeated presentation of words to be learned. A great number of psychological experiments have been conducted on these factors and successful control and prediction of the "difficulty" of verbal learning materials are now possible in a laboratory situation. Of the many variables manipulated in experimentation this paper treats only those that seem to be directly related to the "difficulty" of the meanings of foreign words. Such variables as the age, aptitude, and motivation of the learner and modes of practice, which are also important in language learning, are omitted because they seem to be only peripherally related to the organization of learning materials.

1. THE "INTRINSIC DIFFICULTY" OF A WORD TO BE LEARNED

It is often said that an "abstract word" is more difficult than a "concrete word" because the former is "intrinsically" more complex than the latter. However, in language learning the complexity of a word seems to be more psychological than logical. A word may be logically complex because of its structure and meaning, but psychologically it may be simple. For this reason the problems of simplicity versus complexity and codability are examined below.

Simple vs. Complex. Ever since Hume (1739) defined *simple* and *complex* in terms of "distinguishable parts," no new definition seems to have been formulated by either philosophers or psychologists. Dictionaries of philosophy and psychology (e.g., Baldwin, 1901; Fleming, 1866; Runes, 1942) give definitions similar to those given by Hume. The following are typical:

Complex: made up of components that are either interdependent or in a relationship of subordination to other components.
Simple: elementary, not further analyzable, easy to understand or do.
(English and English, 1958)

According to Hume, an apple is a complex thing because it has several distinguishable attributes: the color, the taste, and the smell. This is a logical analysis of complexity, but from the psychological viewpoint how complex anything is depends on how the learner recognizes its attributes rather than on how many attributes it has. A number of studies on concept formation indicate that when a person hears a new word, he associates the word with some, but not necessarily all, of the attributes of what he thinks is its referent (Bruner *et al.*, 1956; Brown, 1956; Chomsky, 1959). For instance, an apple is shown to a child and he is told that it is a McIntosh. Then the child hypothesizes that the attributes of a McIntosh are its red color and round shape. Later he sees a different kind of red apple and calls it a McIntosh. He is told it is not and his hypothesis regarding the attributes of a McIntosh receives a negative confirmation. He keeps forming and testing new hypotheses until he receives a positive confirmation.

The implication of the above analysis for the language teacher is that a word which may be associated with only a few tangible attributes is relatively easy to learn in the sense that the learner may need only one trial of hypothesis formation and testing. So-called "abstract words" are relatively difficult because they must be often associated with multiple intangible attributes. Some "concrete words" are also difficult because the attributes of their referents are inconspicuous, though tangible. The point to be emphasized here is that *simple, concrete,* and *easy* are not necessarily synonymous and that the "intrinsic difficulty" of a word may be considered in terms of the number and conspicuousness of the attributes with which it is to be associated.

Codability. A foreign word may be "intrinsically" difficult for the learner, if its referent is not linguistically coded in the lexicon of his mother tongue. How well coded a thing is, i.e., its codability, in a given language may be estimated by how fast and how succinctly the thing may be named or described by the speakers of that language. According to one investigation (Brown and Lenneberg, 1954), differences in the codability of colors in English are significantly related to differences in the recognition of colors by English-speaking people.

Based on the above experiment, one might predict that foreign words whose referents are highly codable in the learner's language would be learned more easily than those whose referents are low in codability. For example, Zuni-speaking persons would probably take more time to learn English words such as *yellow* and *orange* than words such as *black* and *white,* since the colors yellow and orange are given just one name in Zuñi (Lenneberg and Roberts, 1956). For English-speaking students the distinctly different Spanish verbs *ser* and *estar,* both of which are translated as *to be* in English, should be more difficult than words like *mano* (hand) and *casa* (house) due to the differences in their codability in the English lexicon.

2. THE INTERACTION BETWEEN PREVIOUSLY LEARNED WORDS AND A NEW WORD TO BE LEARNED

In psychology it is assumed that in general the learner finds learning material difficult to learn, if it has no relation, association, or similarity to any of the materials he has already learned. This sort of interaction between new and previously learned materials is studied in verbal learning experimentation in terms of meaningfulness and familiarity.

Meaningfulness. When Ebbinghaus (1913) used nonsense syllables in place of prose or poetry materials for the first time in memory experiments, he assumed that they were homogeneous in their meaninglessness. The fallacy of his assumption has since been pointed out by many (e.g., Glaze, 1926; Hull, 1933; Witmer, 1935). It is now established that even nonsense syllables are differentially learned, depending upon their meaningfulness which is measured in terms of association value. The usual method of measuring the meaningfulness of a nonsense syllable is to present the syllable to a given group of subjects and ask them if the syllable arouses any "ideas." If 75% of them say yes, then the syllable is determined to be 75% meaningful. The consensus of many experimental results is that the higher the meaningfulness of a nonsense syllable, the faster it is learned (e.g., Dowling and Braun, 1957; Morikawa, 1959; Noble and McNeely, 1957; Underwood and Richardson, 1956).

There seems to be no question about the significance of meaningfulness in foreign language learning. But the meaningfulness of a foreign word to be learned depends on its accidental phonetic similarity in whole or part to some word in the learner's native language. In this situation what the textbook writer may do is to arrange learning materials systematically so that words taught earlier will increase the meaningfulness of words to be introduced later. One crude example is that by introducing words like *mean, meaning, meaningly, meaningful, meaningless, meaninglessly,* and *meaningfulness* in sequence at different intervals, the preceding one can increase the meaningfulness of the following one.

Another aspect of meaningfulness that must be considered is that it has two sources in second language learning, foreign words and their translated meanings. A foreign word may have high meaningfulness phonetically but its translated meaning in the learner's mother tongue may have low association value and vice versa. The few experimental reports available on the effects of such possible pairs of different degrees of meaningfulness (e.g., Sheffield, 1946; Noble and Stockwell, 1957) would suggest that the "difficulty" of a foreign word depends not so much on how it sounds as on how meaningful and familiar its translated meaning is to the learner.

Familiarity. A number of experimental studies (e.g., Bousfield and Cohen, 1956; Noble, 1955; Solomon and Postman, 1952) have shown that familiarity is a significant variable in recognition, learning, and recall. The familiarity value of a word is measured by the frequency of its usage which is found in word counts such as *The Teacher's Word Book of 30,000 Words* by Thorndike and Lorge (1944).

All foreign words are supposed to be unfamiliar to the learner at their first learning. Only their translated equivalents can have familiarity value. According to a study conducted by Chapman and Gilbert (1937), foreign equivalents of frequently used vernacular words are learned faster and retained better than those of less frequently used vernacular words. This phenomenon is understandable in the sense that familiarity is very closely related ($r = .92$) to meaningfulness (Noble, 1953). The more frequently a word is used, the more association value it acquires and the faster it is learned. A practical question for the language teacher is how to increase the familiarity value of unfamiliar words. As our common sense tells us, the best answer available is to expose unfamiliar words frequently to the learner. This matter will be further treated later under the topic of repetition.

3. THE INTERACTION WITHIN A GROUP OF WORDS TO BE LEARNED AT THE SAME TIME

When only one word is taught, we have to consider its "intrinsic difficulty" and its interaction with previously taught words. However, if several words are taught simultaneously, in addition to those factors, we must consider the interaction among them. This interaction is reviewed in terms of serial position, semantic relationship, amount of intake, and context.

Serial Position. In verbal learning, when the learner is asked to learn a list of words or nonsense syllables, he learns the first and the last items on the list faster than those in the middle (Hovland, 1938; Ward, 1937). Psychologists have given the names of "primacy effect" and "recency effect" to those phenomena. Between these two, recency effect is known to be far stronger than primacy effect. Interestingly enough, the most difficult item is not the one which is exactly in the middle of the list. According to the data obtained by Hovland (1940), in a list of eight items the point of maximum difficulty was the sixth position; in a list of eleven items, the seventh position; in a list of fourteen items, the eighth position.

The above results apply where words are presented in a list, but it is not clear whether or not primacy and recency effects can be observed even when new words to be learned are presented in sentential context. It would seem that the effects are as significant in the latter case as in the former.

Semantic Relationship. Words can be related to each other in terms of their meanings and such relationship can have differential effects on word learning. In one study (Higa, 1963) six kinds of semantic relationships were investigated regarding their effects on learning. These relationships were: (a) synonymity where words are related to each other because of their synonymous meanings; (b) antonymity where words are related because of their opposite meanings; (c) free association where words are free associates like *bed-sleep;* (d) partial response identity where words are similar in terms of their free associates; (e) connotation where words are related in their connotative meanings; (f) category coordinate where words such as apple-pear are related for being coordinates in the same category. The degrees of relationships were measured using various association norms (e.g., Carroll *et al.,* 1962; Cohen *et al.,* 1957; Jenkins, *et al.,* 1959; Russell and Jenkins, 1954).

The results showed that of the six lists of related words the lists of free associates, synonyms, and antonyms were found to be significantly more difficult to learn compared to the list that contained semantically dissimilar words. One may infer from these experimental results that the present-day textbook writer's practice of introducing semantically closely related words in the same lesson is causing more "difficulty" than facilitation. Perhaps the textbook writer today is too theme-oriented, i.e., to every lesson, regardless of its length, he has a tendency to give a title such as "In a Restaurant," "Family," or "School" and attempts to tell some kind of story. In a lesson titled "Family," for instance, many kinship terms are introduced all at once such as *father, mother, brother, sister, uncle,* and *aunt* in their foreign equivalents. It would seem that, in order to reduce the amount of interference in word learning, this practice may be corrected in favor of teaching words of little semantic relationship in the same lesson.

Amount of Intake. The commonly accepted method of deciding the amount of intake, i.e., the number of words to be taught, is for some authority to select so-called minimum essential words on the basis of usefulness and frequency of usage and for the teacher or the textbook writer to divide the words into a given number of years and lessons. In Japan, for example, the Ministry of Education issues courses of study. The course of study for English (Ministry of Education, 1959) clearly states, in addition to objectives and methods, a minimum number of words, idiomatic phrases, and sentence patterns to be taught. According to this, 300 words are to be taught in the first year of junior high school, 400 in the second year, and 500 in the third. Of these 1200 words the course of study specifically lists 300 "basic" words. The job of the textbook writer is to select the other 900 words and determine the frequency of their appearance and the order and context in which they are to appear in a textbook. A survey of several popular English textbooks used in Japan shows that this task is done apparently on an intuitive rather than a systematic basis (Ministry of Education, 1958).

Although experimenters on the effect of amount of intake on verbal learning agree that as the number of words to be learned increases, the amount of time that must be spent per word also increases (e.g., Carroll and Burke, 1965; Thurstone, 1930), there has been no conclusive statement as to what the optimum number of words is for a given amount of time or for one lesson in foreign language teaching. Teaching too many words at the same time may cause "difficulty" but, on the other hand, teaching too few or repeating the same too frequently may be a waste of time.

Studies on memory span (Lumley and Calhoun, 1934; Miller, 1956; Young and Supa, 1941) offer some suggestion concerning the above problem. These studies would indicate that the span of one's immediate memory imposes severe limitations on the number of words one can learn at a time without interference and that the optimum number is about five for the average high school student and seven for the average college student and adult. This would mean that the number of new words to be taught should be between five and seven in one lesson period depending upon the age of the learner.

Context. It appears that these investigators (e.g., Briones, 1937) who favor the teaching of words in sentential context are suggesting that word association is important in vocabulary learning and that sentential context provides more word association than a mere word list. However, there are some experimental reports (e.g., Morgan and Bailey, 1943; Morgan and Foltz, 1944) which deny the advantage of such contextual learning. From the realistic viewpoint of the classroom teacher these opposing results may not be so meaningful, since the learning of a foreign language involves the coordinated acquisition of vocabulary, pronunciation, and syntax. If in any given situation the learning of words *per se* is the only purpose, then contextual learning may not be an effective method. On the other hand, if there is a need to review and exercise previously taught words and sentence patterns, it is impractical to separate vocabulary and syntax and the teacher should use the contextual method of teaching new words.

4. THE INTERACTION BETWEEN GROUPS OF WORDS TO BE LEARNED IN SEQUENCE

Under the topic of the interaction between groups of words to be learned, the fundamental question is: Which should be taught first, easy material or difficult material? In one verbal learning experiment (Higa, 1963) it was found that, even after taking into account such factors as familiarity and learning-to-learn effects, the easy-to-difficult order is significantly more facilitative in learning words than the difficult-to-easy order. This is also understandable in terms of sustaining interest and motivation.

5. THE EFFECT OF REPETITION

Once the relative "difficulties" of words have been estimated on the basis of the variables mentioned above, words may be taught in the easy-to-difficult order. Since difficult words require, of necessity, more time to learn, what the textbook writer should do is to give them more time by means of exposing them to the learner more frequently than easy words. The studies cited below have shown that repetition has a positive effect on learning, but the optimum number of repetitions and the optimum interval between repetitions are not clearly known.

In a typical experiment on the effect of exposure frequency (Noble, 1955), eight groups of students were exposed to six relatively unfamiliar verbal items of low meaningfulness at the frequencies of 0, 1, 2, 3, 4, 5, 10, and 20, respectively. After the exposure, the students were asked to learn the same items in a certain serial order. The results showed that the amount of time needed to learn the serial list was negatively correlated to the frequency of exposure. However, the effect of exposure frequency was significant only between 0, 10, and 20 frequencies and little effect was observed between 1 and 5 frequencies. It is now concluded that a relatively large number of repetitions is necessary to produce significant effects in verbal learning (Underwood and Schulz, 1960).

IV. BY WAY OF SUMMARY

The above review of the psycholinguistic concept of "difficulty" indicates that, although there is still much left to be investigated, various experimental studies have identified some important variables in terms of which the organization of foreign language teaching materials and the writing of a foreign language textbook may be considered. For many years foreign language teachers and textbook writers have concerned themselves more with the selection of so-called minimum essential words and with the introduction of foreign culture and less with the organization of materials for optimum learning (cf., Reports of Northeast Conference on the Teaching of Foreign Languages).

In addition to vocabulary "difficulty" we must have an understanding of syntactic "difficulty." At present, the latter is much less well known than the former. Applied linguists judge the "difficulty" of the syntax of a given language on the basis of its similarity to the syntax of the learner's first language, but their measurement of syntactic similarity is still qualitative using two dichotomous similar and dissimilar categories. What we now need is a quantitative, psycholinguistic measure of syntactic similarity and "difficulty" so that an effective control of vocabulary and syntax may be achieved in the teaching of a second language.

REFERENCES

AMERICAN TEXTBOOK PUBLISHERS INSTITUTE. *Textbooks in Education*. New York: American Textbook Publishers Institute, 1949.

BALDWIN, I. M. (ed.). *Dictionary of Philosophy and Psychology*. New York: Macmillan, 1901.

BOUSFIELD, W. A., and COHEN, B. H. "Masculinity-feminity in the Free Recall of a Categorized Stimulus Word List." *Percep. Mot. Skills* 6(1956):159–65.

BRIONES, I. T. "An Experimental Comparison of Two Forms of Linguistic Learning." *Psychol. Rec.* 1(1937):205–11.

BROWN, R. W., and LENNEBERG, E. H. "A Study in Language and Cognition." *J. abnorm. soc. Psychol.* 49(1954):454–62.

BROWN, R. W. "Language and Categories." In *A Study of Thinking*, J. S. Bruner, *et al.* New York: Wiley, 1956. Pp. 247–312.

BRUNER, J. S., GOODNOW, J. J., and AUSTIN, G. A. *A Study of Thinking*. New York: Wiley, 1956.

CARROLL, J. B., KJELDERGAARD, P. M., and CARTON, A. "Number of Opposites vs. Number of Primaries as a Response Measure in Free Association Tests." *J. verb. Learn. verb. Behav.* 1(1963):22–30.

CARROLL, J. B., and BURKE, M. L. "Parameters of Paired-associate Verbal Learning: Length of List, Meaningfulness, Rate of Presentation, and Ability." *J. exp. Psychol.* (1965):543–53.

CHAPMAN, F. L., and GILBERT, L. C. "A Study of the Influence of Familiarity With English Words Upon the Learning of Their Foreign Language Equivalents." *J. educ. Phychol.* 28(1937):621–28.

CHOMSKY, N. Review of *Verbal Behavior* by B. F. Skinner. *Language* 39(1959):26–58.

COHEN, B. H., BOUSFIELD, W. A., and WHITMARSH, G. A. *Cultural Norms for Verbal Items in 43 Categories*. Tech. Rep., No. 22, ONR Contract Nonr-631 (00), University of Connecticut, 1957.

DOWLING, R. M., and BRAUN, H. W. "Retention and Meaningfulness of Material." *J. exp. Psychol.* 54(1957): 213–17.

EBBINGHAUS, H. *Memory: a Contribution of Experimental Psychology*. Translated by H. A. Ruger and C. E. Bussenius. Columbia Univ. Coll. Educ. Reprints, No. 3, New York: Teachers College, Columbia University, 1913. (Reprinted as a Dover paperback in 1964.)

English, H. B., and English, A. C. *A Comprehensive Dictionary of Psychology and Psychoanalytic Terms.* New York: Longmans, Green, 1958.

Fattu, N. A. "Training Devices." In *Encyclopedia of Educational Research,* 3d ed. Edited by C. W. Harris. New York: Macmillan, 1960. Pp. 1529–35.

Fleming, W. *The Vocabulary of Philosophy, Mental, Moral, and Metaphysical.* New York: Sheldon, 1866.

Glaze, J. A. "The Association Value of Nonsense Syllables." *J. genet. Psychol.* 35(1928):255–69.

Herrick, V. E. "Elementary Education." In *Encyclopedia of Educational Research,* 3d ed. Edited by C. W. Harris. New York: Macmillan, 1960. Pp. 430–42.

Higa, M. "Interference Effects of Intralist Word Relationships in Verbal Learning." *J. verb. Learn. verb. Behav.* 2(1963):170–75.

Hovland, C. I. "Experimental Studies in Rote-learning Theory. III. Distribution of Practice With Varying Speeds of Syllable Presentation." *J. exp. Psychol.* 23(1938):172–90.

Hovland, C. I. "Experimental Studies in Rote-learning Theory. VII. Distribution of Practice With Varying Lengths of List." *J. exp. Psychol.* 27(1940): 271–84.

Hull, C. L. "The Meaningfulness of 320 Selected Nonsense Syllables." *Amer. J. Psychol.* 45(1933):730–34.

Hume, D. *A Treatise of Human Nature.* Edited by L. A. Selby-Bigge. Oxford: Clarendon Press, 1888.

Jenkins, J. J., Russell, W. A., and Suci, C. J. "A Semantic Table of Distances for the Semantic Atlas." *Amer. J. Psychol.* 72(1959):623–25.

Lenneberg, F. H., and Roberts, J. M. "The Language of Experience." *Memoir of the International Journal of Linguistics* 12(1956: No. 13.

Lumley, F. H., Calhoun, E. W. "Memory Span for Words Presented Auditorily." *J. appl. Psychol.* 18(1934):773–84.

Miller, G. A. "The Magical Number Seven, Plus or Minus One or Two: Some Limits on Our Capacity for Processing Information." *Psychol. Rev.* 63(1956): 81–97.

Ministry of Education. *Summary of the Textbook Surveys.* Tokyo: Ministry of Education, 1958.

Ministry of Education. *Teacher's Guide to Foreign Language Instruction in Junior High School.* Tokyo: Ministry of Education, 1959.

Morgan, C. L., and Bailey, W. L. "The Effect of Context on Learning a Vocabulary." *J. educ. Res.* 34(1943):561–65.

Morgan, C. L., and Foltz, M. C. "The Effect of Context on Learning a French Vocabulary." *J. educ. Res.* 38(1944):213–16.

Morikawa, Y. "Studies in Paired-associate Learning of Stimulus and Response on Learning and Recall." *J. exp. Psychol.* 30(1959):166–75.

NOBLE, C. E. "The Meaning-familiarity Relationship." *Psychol. Rev.* 60(1953): 89–98.

NOBLE, C. E., and MCNEELY, D. A. "The Role of Meaningfulness (m) in Paired-associative Verbal Learning." *J. exp. Psychol.* 53(1957):16–22.

NOBLE, C. E., and STOCKWELL, F. E. "Stimulus vs. Response Meaningfulness in Paired-associate Verbal Learning." *Amer. Psychol.* 12(1957):425.

NORTHEAST CONFERENCE ON THE TEACHING OF FOREIGN LANGUAGES. *Reports of the Working Committees*. Annual publication.

RUNES, D. D. *The Dictionary of Philosophy*. New York: Philosophical Library, 1942.

RUSSELL, W. A., and JENKINS, J. J. *The Complete Minnesota Norms for Response to 100 Words from the Kent-Rosanoff Word Association Test*. Tech. Rep., No. 11, ONR Contract N8 onr-66216, University of Minnesota, 1954.

SHEFFIELD, F. D. *The Role of Meaningfulness of Stimulus and Response in Verbal Learning*. Ph.D. dissertation, Yale University, 1946.

SKINNER, B. F. *Science and Human Behavior*. New York: Macmillan, 1953.

SOLOMON, R. L., and POSTMAN, L. "Frequency of Usage as a Determinant of Recognition Thesholds for Words." *J. exp. Psychol.* 43(1952):195–201.

THORNDIKE, E. L., and LORGE, I. *The Teacher's Word Book of 30,000 Words*. New York: Teachers College, Columbia University, 1944.

THURSTONE, L. L. "The Relation Between Learning Time and Length of Task." *Psychol. Rev.* 37(1930):44–58.

UNDERWOOD, B. J., and RICHARDSON, J. "The Influence of Meaningfulness, Intralist Similarity, and Serial Position." *J. exp. Psychol.* 52(1956):119–26.

UNDERWOOD, B. J., and SCHULZ, R. W. *Meaningfulness and Verbal Learning*. New York: Lippincott, 1960.

WARD, L. B. "Reminiscence and Rote Learning." *Psychol. Monogr.*, 1937, 49, No. 220.

WITMER, L. R. "The Association Value of Three-place Consonant Syllables." *J. Genet. Psychol.* 47(1935):337–59.

YOUNG, C. W., and SUPA, M. "Maemonic Inhibition as a Factor in the Limitation of the Memory Span." *Amer. J. Psychol.* 54(1941):546–52.

SECTION SEVEN
TESTING

Testing is closely allied to teaching in several ways. First of all, many classroom activities we commonly label "teaching" are actually "testing." When we call on students to demonstrate by their performance in the classroom that they have mastered certain material or that they have acquired a given language habit, we are, in a sense, testing them. Paulston (in Section Three) mentions two kinds of language drills—for teaching and for testing. "What is involved," she says, "is the difference between drills that serve primarily to help the student memorize a pattern with virtually no possibility for mistake and drills which test or reinforce the learning of the pattern."

Formal testing may provide feedback on teaching and learning. We need to know from time to time how effective our teaching has been or how much progress our students have made. We prepare and administer *achievement* tests to find out. The same tests or similar ones may indicate certain weak points in our teaching effectiveness or areas where the students do not perform as well as expected. We call these *diagnostic* tests: they tell us which areas require more concentrated teaching and study.

When a new student with prior English training comes to our school, we do not require him to start all over at the beginning. By means of a *placement* test we determine his appropriate level of study, and he joins a class with other students at approximately the same level. At times we need to know whether a student is proficient enough in English to perform certain tasks or undertake a training program where English is the language of instruction. We prepare or select a *proficiency* test to help make this determination. The score on a proficiency test is an indicator of English ability. To that extent it can be considered a *predictive* test, but it provides no guaranteee that the student will be able to perform the tasks required or be successful in a training program conducted in English. Predictions of success must take into account other factors besides English proficiency. Another kind of predictive test is the *aptitude* test which indicates probable success or failure in certain kinds of study. Aptitude tests have been developed for speakers of English contemplating the study of a foreign language, but to my knowledge none have been prepared for English as a second language.

In this section, Spolsky describes and discusses the various kinds of tests in detail. With the exception of aptitude tests, we usually group all tests into two classes on a functional basis: achievement tests and proficiency tests. Achievement and diagnostic tests go together. And placement tests, noted above, are kinds of proficiency tests: they measure the proficiency level a student has reached for a placement decision to be made.

PROFICIENCY TESTING

There are several large-scale programs for the testing of English-language proficiency. The largest by far is TOEFL—*Test of English as a Foreign Language,* administered jointly by the College English Examination Board and Educational Testing Service, and made available on a worldwide basis to foreign students who plan to enter a school, college, or university in the United States. The test allows non-native speakers of English to demonstrate their English proficiency at the advanced level required for study in American institutions of higher learning. TOEFL is, for the most part, an objective-type test measuring listening comprehension, English structure, vocabulary, reading comprehension, and writing ability. Scores are given for each of the five skills tested, along with an overall performance score. The institution to which the student applies for admission receives a copy of the score report for consideration together with the student's application. Administered three times a year, TOEFL supplies a new test form for each administration.

The *Michigan Test of English Language Proficiency* is a similar testing program administered from the University of Michigan. It has three forms—A, B, and C—which may be used alternately to guard against compromise. ALIGU—the American Language Institute, Georgetown University—has prepared and published a battery of tests for use in screening the English proficiency of applicants for training grants, scholarships, and fellowships made available to foreign nationals by U.S. government agencies. ALIGU tests have a number of alternate forms, and new ones are continually being developed. Similarly, the English Language School of the Defense Language Institute (DLI) at Lackland Air Force Base, Texas, has developed a battery of tests for use in English programs conducted by the military. New forms of DLI tests, like ALIGU tests, are continually being produced. Actually, Educational Testing Service, the University of Michigan, Georgetown University, and Lackland maintain testing centers, where research and experimentation in the field of testing are carried on.

Cambridge University (in England) and the University of Michigan have certification programs which involve English proficiency testing. On the basis of satisfactory performance on a comprehensive examination, Cambridge and Michigan award certificates of proficiency in English to overseas students. Usually such students take the certification examination in their own countries, and if they demonstrate that their proficiency is equal to or surpasses the required minimum standard, they receive certificates—similar in appearance to diplomas. These present evidence that a fairly high proficiency level has been attained, and in some countries it is necessary to obtain such a certificate in order to qualify as a teacher of English.

A new certification program, based on proficiency testing, has been announced by Southern Illinois University (SIU) in cooperation with Litton Educational Publishing International. As a means of preparing for the *Certificate Level Examination*, SIU offers two other examinations to certificate candidates—an *Intermediate Examination* and a *Preparatory Examination*—in accordance with the level of English competence the candidate has reached.

Many large-scale teaching programs have their own proficiency tests which are "guarded" carefully to prevent compromise. Commercially-available tests, by no means numerous, are listed in the Ohannessian and Pedtke bibliographies noted in the Introduction to this book.

GENERAL INFORMATION

The authors in this section provide information of a general nature on types of tests, the mechanics of test construction, and a classification of item types used in the construction of tests. There is also a discussion of validity in testing.

Sako describes and gives examples of many item types employed in testing the four skills—listening comprehension, reading comprehension, speaking production, and writing production—separately and in various combinations: listening-reading comprehension, speaking production with listening comprehension, writing production with listening comprehension, speaking production with reading comprehension, and writing production with reading comprehension. He also recommends the best possible use for each of the different types.

Harris treats the different aspects of test construction with considerable thoroughness: planning the test, preparing the test items and directions, submitting the test material to review and revising it, pretesting the material and analyzing the results, assembling the final form, and reproducing the test. In his section on planning the test, he follows a step-by-step procedure in setting up a sample achievement test—a final examination for an intensive intermediate course for secondary-school students. The remainder of his paper has to do with general principles of test construction.

Spolsky deals with the matter of validity. He points out that "The central problem of foreign-language testing, as of all testing, is validity. With tests of the first class [achievement tests], used by classroom teachers in the control of instruction, this problem is not serious, for the textbook or syllabus writer has already specified what should be tested. With tests of the second class [proficiency tests], it remains a serious difficulty, for we have not yet found a way to characterize knowledge of a language with sufficient precision to guarantee the validity of the items we include or the types of tests we use."

Instead of attempting to measure language ability in linguistic terms, that is, as mastery of a criterion percentage of items in a grammar or lexicon, he suggests "A more promising approach might be to work for a functional definition of levels: we should aim not to test how much of a language someone knows but test his ability to operate in a specified socio-linguistic situation with specified ease or effect. The preparation of proficiency tests like this would not start from a list of language items, but from a statement of language function; after all, it would not be expected to lead to statements like 'He knows sixty percent of English,' but 'He knows enough English to shop in a supermarket.'" Spolsky proceeds to explain how tests might be developed "which would permit of greater confidence in use, greater possibility of improvement . . . , and greater refinement in their interpretation"—a rather ambitious and costly project.

There are three books now available on language testing, designed to assist teachers and program administrators in the preparation of language tests for various purposes: Lado's *Language Testing*, Valette's *Modern Language Testing*, and Harris' *Testing English as a Second Language*. (See *Selected Readings*.) These are excellent reference works, which bring together a huge amount of information on the subject of language testing.

SELECTED READINGS

BRIÈRE, EUGÈNE J. "Are We Really Measuring *Proficiency* with Our Foreign Language Tests?" *Foreign Language Annals* 4(1971):385–91.

———. "Current Trends in Second Language Testing." *TESOL Quarterly* 3(1969):333–40.

BROOKS, NELSON. *Language and Language Learning: Theory and Practice,* 2d ed. Chapter 15: "Tests and Measurements." New York: Harcourt Brace Jovanovich, 1964.

CARROLL, JOHN B. "Fundamental Considerations in Testing for English Language Proficiency of Foreign Students." In *Testing the English Proficiency of Foreign Students*. Washington, D.C.: Center for Applied Linguistics, 1961.

COLLEGE ENTRANCE EXAMINATION BOARD and EDUCATIONAL TESTING SERVICE. *Test of English as a Foreign Language: Handbook for Candidates*. Princeton, N.J.: Educational Testing Service, 1969.

————. *Test of English as a Foreign Language: Interpretive Information*. Princeton, N.J.: Educational Testing Service, Revised January, 1968.

COOPER, ROBERT L. "Testing." In *Preparing the EFL Teacher: A Projection for the '70's*. Edited by Robert C. Lugton. Philadelphia: The Center for Curriculum Development, Inc., 1970.

DAVIES, ALAN, ed. *Language Testing Symposium*. London: Oxford University Press, 1968.

HARRIS, DAVID P. *English Testing Guidebook*. Washington, D.C.: The American University Language Center, 1960–1961. Parts I and II.

————. *Interpretive Manual for the Tests of English as a Second Language of the American Language Institute, Georgetown University*. Washington, D.C.: The Institute, 1967.

————. *Testing English as a Second Language*. New York: McGraw-Hill Book Company, 1969.

ILYIN, DONNA. "Structure Placement Tests for Adults in English-Second-Language Programs in California." *TESOL Quarterly* 4(1970):323–30.

LADO, ROBERT. *Language Teaching: A Scientific Approach*. Chapter 16: "Language Testing." New York: McGraw-Hill, Inc., 1964.

————. *Language Testing; The Construction and Use of Foreign Language Tests: A Teacher's Book*. New York: McGraw-Hill Book Company, 1964.

PATERNO, ADELAIDA. "Foreign Language Testing." *MST English Quarterly* 10(1960):14–31, 269.

PIMSLEUR, PAUL. "Testing Foreign Language Learning." In *Trends in Language Teaching*. Edited by Albert Valdman. New York: McGraw-Hill Book Company, 1966.

RIVERS, WILGA M. *Teaching Foreign-Language Skills*. Chapter 12: "Testing: Principles and Techniques." Chicago: The University of Chicago Press, 1968.

UPSHUR, JOHN A. "Objective Evaluation of Oral Proficiency in the ESOL Classroom." *TESOL Quarterly* 5(1971):47–59.

UPSHUR, JOHN A., and JULIA FATA, eds. *Problems in Foreign Language Testing. Language Learning*. Special Issue Number 3, 1968.

VALETTE, REBECCA M. *Modern Language Testing: A Handbook*. New York: Harcourt Brace Jovanovich, 1967.

WRITING PROFICIENCY
AND ACHIEVEMENT TESTS

SYDNEY SAKO

Teachers of English to speakers of other languages are often confronted with the problem of writing good test items both for the proficiency-type test and the achievement-type test. The technique of writing test items for the achievement test is similar to that for the proficiency test in that both are designed to measure the amount of skill in speaking and writing the language, and the level of listening and reading comprehension of the language.

Test items designed to measure the four different types of language skills as well as five different combinations or integration of these skills will be presented in this article. Various presentations of item types are also illustrated, such as the question, statement, sentence completion, short dialog forms, and their combinations. Also the best possible uses will be brought out for each of the different types.

Test items can be written for each of the separate language skills as well as their combinations, such as:

1. Listening comprehension

2. Reading comprehension

3. Speaking production

4. Writing production

5. Listening-reading comprehension

6. Speaking production with listening comprehension

7. Writing production with listening comprehension

8. Speaking production with reading comprehension

9. Writing production with reading comprehension

1. LISTENING COMPREHENSION

Items of listening-reading comprehension are often mistaken for items of pure listening comprehension. In order to test for straight listening comprehension there should be no reading involved; consequently, determination of a person's listening comprehension should be made through the use of pictures or movement of the body. The stem or lead can be presented in different forms, such as questions, statements, or their combinations. Examples of a picture test are shown as follows:

a.   Question Form: Objective, listening comprehension of *comb*.
Which person has a comb in his hand?

b.   Statement Form: Objective, listening comprehension of *on his back*.
Joe is using both hands to carry the load on his back.

c.   Statement-Question Combination: Objective, Listening comprehension of *level*.
Bill is riding on a level street. Which street is he using?

Some points to keep in mind when writing test items for listening comprehension are:

a.   Does the stem present a clear, central problem?

b.   Does the stem avoid giving away the correct answer by extra clues?

c.   Is only the single objective being tested?

Examples of body motion test for listening comprehension:

1.   Place your right hand on your forehead.
2.   Wink your left eye.
3.   Walk around the chair twice.
4.   Open your book to page fifteen.
5.   Pick up a red pencil with your left hand.

The stems which are in command or request form are presented orally in an interview type situation. If the person responds appropriately, he is given credit for the item. The body motion test should contain at least 60 items to produce a comprehensive and reliable test. The response should be limited to actions that can be performed within the testing area.

The picture test and the body motion test measure the listening comprehension of an individual. These tests can be used for testing pupils and adults whose reading ability is limited; they can be used as sub-tests of a more comprehensive proficiency-type language test; or they can be used as an external criterion test for validation of other types of listening and reading comprehension tests.

The difficulty level of these items can be increased by adding action verbs of a more complicated nature, by adding idiomatic expressions, or by using symbols and objects which are more difficult for the examinee.

2. READING COMPREHENSION

The problems of constructing items for reading comprehension take on a different nature from those for listening comprehension. In the listening-type items the problems of pronunciation and controlled speed must be taken into consideration. Usually these items consist of conversational material. On the other hand, reading items usually represent samplings taken from the reading material found in textbooks, manuals, newspapers, magazines, technical books, and other sources. The vocabulary used, therefore, covers a wider range and the structure is more complex than that for the listening comprehension test. The stem may be presented in question form, statement form, incomplete sentence form, dialog, or in any of their combinations. Structure and vocabulary meanings are thus being tested. Examples of these items are as follows:

Lexical Items:

  a. Question form:
     What is a center of gravity?
        a. the midway point of any part of a body
        b. the point where the weights are equal
    x c. the point about which all parts are balanced

  b. Words in context:
     The lever *oscillated* rhythmically.
        a. jumped in and out
    x b. swung back and forth
        c. turned completely around

  c. Statement form:
     The enemy finally gave up.
    x a. They surrendered.
        b. They attacked fiercely.
        c. They retreated.

  d. Sentence completion:
     He missed the question by giving the _____ answer.
    x a. wrong
        b. correct
        c. complete

  e. Statement-question combination:
     The survivors were located yesterday. Who were they?
        a. those missing
    x b. those living
        c. those dead

Structural Items:

  a. Sentence completion form:
     Mr. Jones had thought that he _____ next month.
    x a. might arrive
        b. had arrived
        c. did arrive

  b. Paragraph form:
New Orleans is located on the Mississippi River. At its numerous wharves, we can see the loading and unloading of large quantities of cotton, rice, sugar, and coffee. Because of its early history, it is one of the most distinctive cities in the USA. The oldest section is the French Quarter, where Bienville founded the city of New Orleans in 1718.

    The city of New Orleans _____.
        a. was originally called Bienville

    b. is in the French Quarter
x c. is situated on a river

One of the important uses of the reading test is to ascertain the degree of reading comprehension of selected material by individuals regardless of their speaking ability or listening comprehension. A person at the elementary level will be able to understand only the basic structures and vocabulary limited to the basic needs, while a person at the professional competence level will be able to understand complex structures and vocabulary of a fairly sophisticated nature. If a person is required to pursue academic studies, instructor training, intelligence work, etc., he should have a high level of reading comprehension.

When writing test items for reading comprehension it has been proven valuable to consider the following questions:

a. Is the item, taken as a whole, specific?

b. Is the problem stated briefly?

c. Are the distracters important, plausible answers rather than obviously wrong?

d. Are all alternatives as well as the correct responses parallel in structure?

3. SPEAKING PRODUCTION

A speaking test proposes to determine how well a person can speak the foreign language. In order to elicit oral responses, the directions or questions should be stated in simple terms. Stimuli to induce speech may take on the nature of a picture stimulus or perhaps the native language. For a speaking test, items are needed that will test the individual's pronunciation, fluency, vocabulary knowledge, and grammatical control.

Examples of types of items for a speaking test are as follows:

OBJECTIVE	TYPE OF STIMULI	TYPE OF RESPONSE
a. Pronunciation	Written sentences	Reading sentences aloud
b. Retention and repetition	Sentences on tape	Repeating sentences aloud
c. Vocabulary and grammatical control	Picture	Description of the picture
d. Fluency	Interview or questions	Answer to questions

Specific segmental phonemes within each sentence should be evaluated for correctness in pronunciation, intonation, rhythm, and stress. The sentences on tape should be short and relatively simple at the beginning and longer and more complex toward the end. Students with low speaking proficiency may be able to remember and repeat the short sentences but not the long complicated ones. Students with high proficiency will be able to remember and repeat both. Simple sentences should be used in interviews so the student will not be penalized for failure to understand the directions or questions.

The student responses can be rated by the examiner by conducting individual interviews or by checking the recorded material. It is preferable to have a check list prepared in advance so that rating can be performed more objectively.

To rate the pronunciation the following rating scale may be used:

P–1 Mispronounces significant phonemes to such an extent as to be often incomprehensible.

P–2 Speech contains errors in some significant phonemes to the extent of requiring repetition, but is generally comprehensible. Accent very noticeable.

P–3 Student's accent is noticeable but not disturbing. His mispronunciation contains few irregularities in significant phonemes.

P–4 Student's pronunciation is adequate for immediate comprehension in normal conversation or situations.

P–5 Student pronounces clearly and distinctly and should be understood well over telephone as well as in face-to-face conversation. Has no peculiarities of accent or intonation which prevent immediate understanding.

To rate the fluency, vocabulary, and grammatical control, the following rating scale may be used:

E–1 Can formulate only simple phrases. Vocabulary and structure very limited.

E–2 Can formulate complete sentence structures within limited vocabulary. Can make himself understood in conversation of limited range.

E–3 Student's speech can be understood, but listener must pay closer attention than normal. Does not express himself easily, and must repeat or reword some statements to make them comprehensible. Sentence structure shows variations which hinder immediate comprehension.

E–4 Handles the standard speech patterns and structures with few significant variations.

E–5 Student's speech generally follows the normal English patterns and structures.

These ratings may be averaged, and then checked against the overall rating or against the rating done by another person. This will serve as a cross validation which tends to improve the reliability of the rating. Description of these ratings will help the test writer determine the difficulty level of the oral questions so he can write questions which would be appropriate for the desired level of the test.

4. WRITING PRODUCTION

In testing an individual's writing skill, elements such as vocabulary, structure, accuracy and speed of script writing, spelling, punctuation, content, and organization of material can be evaluated; however, the emphasis placed on testing the writing skills is usually on lexical and structural items, and on the accuracy and speed of script writing.

The stimuli used for eliciting writing production are similar to those prepared for eliciting oral production. They may be presented in picture form, in the native language, or in the target language in simplified form.

The grading of the written responses, like those of the oral responses, is also subjective. To improve the objectivity of scoring, graded samples of student's written material of the various levels can be used for comparison. The determination of the levels of these written materials may be made by individual teachers or by a panel of raters. A description of the different levels of the writing skills is presented below:

DESCRIPTION	LEVEL
Elementary proficiency. Can write simple statements and questions using a very limited vocabulary. Errors in spelling and structure frequently obscure meaning.	1
Limited working proficiency. Can write sentences on familiar topics using non-technical vocabulary and basic structural patterns. Errors in spelling and structure occasionally obscure meaning.	2
Minimum professional proficiency. Can write paragraphs on familiar topics using basic structural patterns. Errors seldom obscure meaning.	3
Full professional proficiency. Can write prose with sufficient structural accuracy and sufficient vocabulary to satisfy professional requirements.	4
Native or bilingual proficiency. Can write with a proficiency equivalent to that of an educated native speaker.	5

The following is a sample listing of objectives, and types of stimuli and responses for the writing test:

OBJECTIVE	TYPE OF STIMULI	TYPE OF RESPONSE
1. Accuracy and speed of script writing	Dictation (live or taped)	Writing dictated material
2. Vocabulary	Incomplete sentences	Writing the correct response which completes the meaning of the sentence correctly
3. Vocabulary and grammatical structure	Picture stimuli, or instructions in the native language	Writing sentences or paragraphs

The following are sample pictures and simple directions for eliciting the writing responses:

a.   Write what you see in the pictures shown below. Make complete sentences.

b.   Write a paragraph on the topic "Why I want to study a foreign language."

c.   Write an autobiography of at least one full page.

5. LISTENING AND READING COMPREHENSION

The listening and reading comprehension test is probably used more than any other combination to measure the integrated language skills. This type of test produces scores that correlate highly with success of predicting students' ability to acquire instruction in English. It lends itself well to the use of multiple-choice test items and therefore to the use of standard answer sheets which can be machine scored. The aural or listening portion is usually recorded on tape, while the reading portion is printed in the test booklet. The stem is presented orally in different forms, such as question, statement, incomplete sentence, or dialog form, or any combination thereof. The written responses provide stimuli for reading comprehension. The aural stems with the alternatives in written forms are illustrated as follows:

a. Statement form:
   Mr. Jones took a bus to town. (Aural)
   x a. He rode the bus.
     b. He put the bus away.
     c. He pulled the bus to town.

b. Question form:
   Did all the students do their homework last night? (Aural)
   x a. Yes, they completed their homework.
     b. Yes, they will do their homework.
     c. Yes, they are working on their homework.

c. Dialogue form:
   "Was Tom driving a car when you saw him yesterday?" (Aural)
   "Yes, he was." (Aural)
   x a. Tom drove a car yesterday.
     b. Tom didn't drive a car yesterday.
     c. Tom was riding in a taxi yesterday.

d. Incomplete sentence form:
   The telephone is out of order. It is _____. (Aural)
     a. working
   x b. not working
     c. not installed

e. Statement-question combination:
   The weather is variable. What kind of weather is it? (Aural)
     a. cold weather
     b. hot weather
   x c. changeable weather

Care must be taken that items do not test memorization of facts, but mainly knowledge of the language:

Testing Memorization:
The President is elected for_____.

    a. three years
  x b. four years
    c. five years

Testing Language:
The President is elected for four years.

    a. He is appointed.
    b. He is nominated.
  x c. He is chosen.

6. SPEAKING PRODUCTION WITH LISTENING COMPREHENSION

When a language teacher rates students by asking them questions and having them respond orally, he is testing listening comprehension and speaking production. The listening portion of the test should be designed so that very simple questions are asked at the lower level, and progressively more difficult questions at the higher level. Two methods can be used to determine the levels of difficulty of questions asked of the students:

1. Content determined by three variables: vocabulary, structure, and concept. The difficulty level of vocabulary can be obtained by frequency count, origin of word, and differences in meaning. The difficulty level of structure can be determined by the complexity of patterns used, by the tenses, by the modes, and other grammatical usages. The difficulty level of concepts may range from the simple (concrete concepts) to the complex (abstract concepts).

2. Item analysis using the ease index will reflect the percentage of the population answering the questions correctly. The questions comprising the lower level should have high ease indices, and those of the higher level should have low ease indices.

In other words, questions used in Level 1 should have very simple structure with basic vocabulary within the first 200 words and ease indices of .90 or over. Concepts used should be concrete in nature. Questions used in Level 5 should use complex structure, idiomatic expressions, and ease indices of .25 or less. They should consist of cultural items with abstract concepts, since this type of item requires greater knowledge of the language and culture, and a higher proficiency level.

Some sample questions which can be used in this test are listed under the five levels:

Level 1. Elementary Proficiency

1.   Hello, how are you? (or Good Morning).
2.   What is your name?
3.   Where are you from?
4.   Why did you come here?
5.   What things do you see in this room?
6.   Where do you eat lunch?
7.   What time is it?
8.   How do you go to town from here?
9.   Do you drive a car?
10. Why do you go to the laundry?

Level 2. Limited Working Proficiency

1. Where did you go to school?
2. What are some of your work experiences?
3. What do you want to do in the future?
4. If you were very sick, what would you do?
5. How do you like to travel best?
6. What kind of climate do you have in your hometown?
7. What are some of the popular sports you like?
8. Do you plan to buy a car? What kind?
9. Who is your favorite movie star?
10. What is the meaning of the following paragraph?
(Read a paragraph and see if the student can explain it. Pick an easy one from a newspaper or magazine.)

Level 3. Minimum Professional Proficiency

1. Describe the furniture you see in this room.
2. What are some activities you like to do best?
3. What is your specialty or profession?
4. Discuss your plans for the future.
5. Compare the weather here with that of your hometown.
6. What kind of tools or books do you use in your work?
7. How do you start your automobile?
8. What do you do when you put on the brakes?
9. What would you do if the lights would not work?
10. Listen to the following paragraph and explain the main points.
(Choose a paragraph from his field of interest and read it in a normal way.)

Level 4. Full Professional Proficiency

1. Describe your educational background.
2. What do you like to do best when you are not busy?
3. Tell one of the most exciting experiences you have ever had.
4. Describe the person whom you admire most.
5. Tell of an emergency situation you have encountered in the past.
6. Have you ever run out of gas? What did you do?
7. Do you think there is a good chance of a hard freeze tonight?

8. Why is weather a common topic of conversation?

9. Have you ever broken in a pair of shoes?

10. Describe the kind of work you do?

Level 5. Bilingual or Native Proficiency

1. How long have you studied your second language?

2. What were your major courses in school?

3. Describe your work experiences in civilian life.

4. What do you like to do best on weekends?

5. What was one of the most pleasant moments of your life?

6. What do you mean by "home run" in a baseball game?

7. What would you do if you were told to cut in on Mr. Jones?

8. Did you ever back out of a bargain? Explain.

9. Did you ever get stuck on a purchase? Explain.

10. Why do we say that communication is a basic human activity?

The oral responses of different proficiency levels would also parallel the description just related. The same rating form used in the speaking production test will apply here. If a student answers the questions adequately, it is assumed that he understands the listening portion of the test. A student who answers the questions in an excellent manner will receive a plus to the rating (1–5). If he answers poorly, he will receive a minus to his rating. Rating students for listening comprehension and oral production is rather subjective, but a person can become more objective in rating through experience.

7. WRITING PRODUCTION WITH LISTENING COMPREHENSION

The purpose of the test of writing production with listening comprehension is to check both the aural comprehension and the writing proficiency of the student. The main elements of writing that are usually tested are the proper choice of vocabulary and the correct usage of grammatical structure. Testing for the organization of content and the style of writing is usually made at the higher level of proficiency.

To check the aural comprehension and to elicit the written responses, the same types of questions mentioned in the aural-speaking test can be used, and these can be pre-recorded on tape.

Another type of oral presentation is the sentence completion form. This method of presentation requires the students to write the words or phrases which will complete the meaning of the sentence correctly. Examples of the sentence completion type are shown as follows:

1. A goat is a kind of _____.   (animal)
2. When water freezes, it turns into _____.   (ice)
3. A group of sheep is called a _____.   (flock)
4. A dull movie is one that is not _____.   (interesting)
5. If sugar is put in the coffee, the coffee is
said to be _____.   (sweetened)

This type of test item requires greater skill in construction than others. There must be just enough information presented to elicit the required response. If not enough information is given, the examinee will not be able to come up with the intended correct answer. If too much information is given, the item will be a give away.

Not enough information: Improved:
    A sheep is _____.   A sheep is a kind of _____.

If an item can elicit several responses which can be correct semantically and syntactically, credit should be given to the student when he responds to any of the possible correct answers.

8. WRITING PRODUCTION WITH READING COMPREHENSION

Some of the quizzes used in the classrooms or portions of the proficiency tests may be classified as tests of writing production with reading comprehension. The purpose of this type of test is to determine how well a person can understand the reading material and at the same time to determine how well he can write the answers. The same type of topics or directions used in the reading-speaking test may be used for this test. If a student has had the same amount of training in oral as well as in writing skills, he should do just about as well in one test as the other. However, if the writing symbols of the student's native language are drastically different from those of the language he is learning, such as a Chinese speaker who is learning English, but is accustomed to writing ideographs that show no phonemic contrasts, then such students may do better in the speaking test than in the writing test.

Two types of criteria may be used to determine the levels of reading and writing proficiency. One criterion is to use the rating scales, and the other is to compare the student's written material against a graded sample. The grading of this type is subjective. We can make this test semi-objective by using incomplete sentences. We find more freedom in the placement of blanks in the incomplete sentence form in this test than in those used in the listening-speaking test.

The following are some examples of the completion type sentences that may be used in the reading-writing test:

1. Mary read the letter carefully, didn't _____? (she)
2. He is _____ most likeable person I know. (the)
3. What time _____ he get up yesterday? (did)
4. Do you mind _____ I smoke here? (if)
5. It's very stuffy in here; please turn _____ the fan. (on)

Some other examples of test items which can be used in this type of test are as follows:

Change the statements to questions. Keep the same tense.

STATEMENTS	QUESTIONS
1. This is your book. _____	(Is this your book?)
2. He was not in class today. _____	(Wasn't he in class today?)

Change the sentences to negative sentences:

SENTENCES	NEGATIVES
1. This is my pen. _____	(This is not my pen.)
2. He saw an accident yesterday. _____	(He didn't see an accident yesterday.)

9. SPEAKING PRODUCTION WITH READING COMPREHENSION

When a written topic is presented to a student and he is required to tell something about it, or when he has to read a passage and then say something about it, we have a speaking test with reading comprehension. The student must be able to understand the written portion and at the same time be able to respond orally. The same questions used in the speaking test with listening comprehension may be used here. Of course, the students will read the questions instead of listening to them. Examples of other topics or directions which can be presented to the students are as follows:

a.   My favorite food.

b.   My most embarrassing moment.

c.   My earliest recollections.

d.   Describe one of the largest cities you have lived in. What things interested you the most?

e.   Describe a method of transportation you like the best. Why do you pick this method?

f.   Tell something about your favorite sports. Why do you like them?

g.   Talk about some interesting things concerning your home town, including the location, historical events, people, culture, educational system, and industries.

h.   Talk about your interests in life, including such things as your family, educational experiences, work experiences, hobbies, and future plans.

i.   Talk about the climate of the place you came from, temperature range, rainfall, extreme fluctuations of the weather.

j.   Talk about some interesting people you know, including your friends, favorite movie stars, former teachers, and some outstanding scientists or political figures.

CONCLUSION

The use of the different types of items for testing proficiency and achievement presented here will depend upon the objectives of the training course. If the student is expected to use his speaking ability rather than his writing ability, the speaking production test or the speaking production test with listening comprehension will be used almost exclusively. If the student is expected mainly to understand the lectures and reading material, it is recommended that a listening-reading comprehension test be used. Thus the selection of the types of items and their use will ultimately be based on the objectives of training and the needs of the student; and teachers of English to speakers of other languages will play a vital role in checking these objectives and needs, and finally in constructing the proper instrument for evaluation.

CONSTRUCTING THE TEST

DAVID P. HARRIS

The construction of an educational test includes the following steps:

1. Planning the test

2. Preparing the test items and directions

3. Submitting the test material to review and revising on the basis of review

4. Pretesting the material and analyzing the results

5. Assembling the final form of the test

6. Reproducing the test

   . . . We shall briefly describe each step in the process of test construction as applied to the testing of English as a second language. . . .

PLANNING THE TEST

Effective testing requires careful planning. Yet as reasonable and obvious as that statement may sound, all too many educational measures—and particularly those prepared by classroom teachers—are constructed without sufficient forethought. It is just too easy for the amateur test writer to take pen in hand and turn out items without much consideration of the balance or adequacy of the resulting test content. Except by chance, such a test will not prove a very valid measure of the specific skills that the testing situation calls for.

The following steps provide a brief guide to the planning of tests of English as a second language. We have arbitrarily chosen to describe the planning of a final achievement test in a hypothetical course of study. Very similar procedures would be followed in the planning of a general proficiency test, except that the test outline would have to be built on a broader base than simply the content of a single course. Probably in this case the test writer would wish to seek the advice of a panel of subject-matter experts or analyze the content of a cross section of widely used and well-regarded textbooks to establish the topics of his test outline and the emphasis to be given to each.

STEP 1: DETERMINING THE GENERAL COURSE OBJECTIVES

In the preparation of an achievement test, one may base the test objectives directly on the objectives of the course. Sometimes such objectives have been carefully formulated by the teacher or his department, and in other cases they are implicit in the methods and materials of the course. Let us suppose, for example, that our task is to prepare a final examination in an intensive intermediate-level course in English as a second language for secondary-school students. We find that the course content is as follows:

1. Textbook lessons, each consisting of
   a. Short reading selection (simple description or exposition)
   b. Dialogue
   c. Pronunciation drill
   d. Grammar drill
   e. Word study
   f. Homework grammar exercise
2. Laboratory practice, including drill on dialogue and pronunciation points keyed to the textbook
3. Weekly compositions based on topics related to the textbook readings

From the course coverage it is clear that the general objectives of the course are:

1. To increase skill in listening comprehension
2. To increase skill in oral production
3. To develop skill in reading simple descriptive and expository prose
4. To develop skill in writing simple description and exposition

Our basic objectives, then, are to measure the extent to which students have acquired or improved their control of these skills.

STEP 2: DIVIDING THE GENERAL COURSE OBJECTIVES INTO THEIR COMPONENTS

The objectives we defined in step 1 were extremely broad. As our next step, then, we need to break them down into their specific components, after which we may determine which of these components we shall measure in our final examination.

. . . Listening, speaking, reading, and writing each include four elements:

1.   Phonology/orthography: the sound system (in listening and speaking) and graphic system (in reading and writing), which seem sufficiently parallel to be treated in a test outline as a single "either-or" component of language.

2.   Grammatical structure: the system of grammatical signaling devices. Not all grammatical patterns are equally common in the written and spoken forms of the language. Many, however, are; and it is probable that in our intermediate-level materials use is made of structure points that are equally appropriate in the exercise of all four skills.

3.   Vocabulary: the lexical items needed to function effectively in each of the four skills. The advanced-level learner of a language has several "word stocks": (a) the items that he uses in speech but not in writing, and vice versa; (b) words that he recognizes in listening and/or reading but does not himself employ in his speaking and writing. Such differences are probably not great at the intermediate level of instruction, however. We may assume that the course materials utilize much the same stock of lexical items in the reading selections, dialogues, and writing exercises—that the various types of activities are designed to reinforce the learning of a controlled vocabulary.

4.   Rate and general fluency: the speed and ease with which the user of a language can decode and encode messages. In intermediate-level courses we ordinarily put a good deal of time and effort into increasing students' aural/oral facility but do not concern ourselves much with the sheer rate of reading and writing—linguistic activities that are perhaps being introduced (as skills in themselves) for the first time and where, therefore, the emphasis is simply on developing the students' control of the basic signaling devices.

STEP 3: ESTABLISHING THE GENERAL DESIGN OF THE TEST

Our two preliminary steps have established the objectives of our hypothetical course in sufficient detail to enable us now to decide upon the general design of the final achievement test. At this point two extremely important factors must be considered: the time to be provided for testing, and the degree of speededness we wish to build into our test.

Let us assume that a maximum of two hours has been scheduled for the final examination. Of the total 120 minutes, we should reserve *at least* 10 minutes for administrative procedures: seating the students and handing out the materials, giving general directions, collecting the materials at the end of the testing period, handling unanticipated problems, etc. We are thus left with 110 minutes for actual testing.

The issue of whether or not tests of English as a second language should be highly speeded is somewhat complex. As already noted in this book, speed of performance is unquestionably an important aspect of language proficiency. On the other hand, slow *test* performance may be due to the foreign students' unfamiliarity with certain test techniques (particularly the multiple-choice types) which are relatively uncommon in many parts of the world, where examinations may still consist of fairly leisurely grammar-translation exercises. It would probably be fairest and safest in most common testing situations (e.g., in general screening tests or final examinations in English courses) to time the tests so that all but the slowest 10 or 15 percent of the subjects—those most likely to have severe rate-of-performance problems—are able to attempt all the items. Such a compromise should not seriously impair the validity of our test for foreign students, and it may quite possibly increase the reliability of the measure. Let us agree, then, to provide fairly liberal time allotments for the achievement test we shall now begin to design.

Our earlier determination of course components would suggest that two parts of the test should be devoted to *structure* and *vocabulary*, two basic components of all four skills taught in the course. For each of these parts we should make immediate decisions about the type and number of items, bearing in mind our overall limit of 110 minutes for testing. Because our test will be administered to a rather small number of examinees and can be scored more or less at leisure, we can safely use supply types of items for at least some portions of our test. As we noted in earlier chapters, supply (short-answer) items require less preparation time and somewhat less test-writing proficiency than multiple-choice items and would therefore be appropriate for the kind of teacher-made test we are considering.

. . . The fill-in item type is particularly useful in informal classroom situations. Such items require the examinee to complete or rewrite sentences in a prescribed manner. Although the time required to complete these items will vary somewhat according to the complexity of the tasks, we may suppose that in general the reasonably proficient student can answer fill-in problems at the rate of about 1½ per minute, including time for the reading of the directions and the mental adjustment that will accompany each new section (for we must assume that the various types of structure problems will have to be grouped into several sections). Reasonable test coverage can probably be achieved with 70 structure items, for which we shall allow forty-five minutes.

For the vocabulary part of our test, we may use the supply item type termed the paraphrase. . . . This item type, it will be remembered, consists of a sentence with an underlined test word; the examinee is to rewrite the sentence, substituting other words for the underlined portion. Such items go quite slowly; we shall have to allow about one minute per item. Let us plan on 40 items to be answered in another forty-five minute period.

Including the time reserved for administrative procedures, we have now accounted for 100 of our allotted 120 minutes, and so far we have made no provision for the testing of *phonology,* which is clearly an important component of our course. As we observed in earlier chapters, the testing of listening ability is relatively easy, while in contrast the testing of oral production is both difficult and inexact. For our teacher-made test, therefore, it would be prudent to settle for an objective measure of sound discrimination and general auditory comprehension. The two sections might be planned as follows:

Section One: Sound Discrimination. The examinee hears sets of three words and is asked to indicate which two are the same. Twenty items.

Section Two: Auditory Comprehension. The examinee hears a series of questions and for each question indicates which one of four printed choices would make a logical answer. Twenty items.

The 40-item objective test outlined above can be administered easily in twenty minutes.

Our test outline is now complete:

PART	ITEM TYPE	NUMBER OF ITEMS	MINUTES
1. Listening	Multiple-choice	40	20
2. Structure	Short-answer	70	45
3. Vocabulary	Short-answer	40	45
		150	110
		Administration:	10
			120

We should now check our test content against the detailed course outline we prepared earlier. Figure 3 plots the test content on a grid showing the principal components of the four skills areas of the course. The checkmarks indicate the components which our proposed test will measure. As we see from the chart, our test measures most of the goals of instruction; we would not suppose that this or any other single test could measure *all* the objectives that the teacher has tried to achieve.

COMPONENTS	LANGUAGE SKILLS			
	LISTENING	SPEAKING	READING	WRITING
Phonology/orthography	✓			
Structure	✓	✓	✓	✓
Vocabulary	✓	✓	✓	✓
Rate and general fluency	✓		▓	▓

Check marks indicate components measured by the final examination.
Shaded areas indicate components not emphasized in the course.

FIGURE 3. The Components of an Intermediate-level ESL Course Used as a Checklist for the Design of the Final Examination

Quite probably the teacher would add other criteria to the final examination in making his final evaluation of the students. For example, we noted earlier in our description of the course content that there were weekly compositions, and the teacher would almost surely wish to include the scores or grades on these in his final evaluation of student achievement. In addition it would be possible to give a general rating of the student's progress in oral production on the basis of his daily class performance.

The next step in the construction of our test would be the selection of the specific problems on which to base our test items. . . . The content of an achievement test should directly reflect the course content. Our procedure would therefore be to prepare an inventory of the phonological points, grammatical structures, and lexical items treated in the class textbook and to make a note of the emphasis given to each. Quite probably we would find that our list contained more items than we could possibly cover in a two-hour examination, and some types of problems would have to be eliminated. As a starting point, we might feel justified in omitting some of the material from the earlier chapters if it were clearly a review of what our students had mastered at a previous stage of learning. We could thus concentrate on those matters that were new to most of the students when introduced during the course of our instruction. But even then we might be left with more problem types than could be included in 120 test items. We might then proceed to reduce our list on the basis of our answers to the following questions:

1. Which phonemic contrasts presented major difficulties to our students?

2. Which grammatical structures received the most emphasis in the course and required continued review?

3. Which vocabulary items would seem to have the greatest utility value to our students?

If some decisions about test content proved especially difficult, we could at least console ourselves by remembering that *all educational testing is a sampling process* and that our final examination would probably be only one of several measures that would be taken into account in our final evaluation.

With these remarks we shall leave our consideration of what might go into one specific examination and return to the discussion of general principles of test construction.

PREPARING THE TEST ITEMS AND DIRECTIONS

ADDITIONAL NOTES ON THE PREPARATION OF ITEMS

In the preparation of multiple-choice or short-answer (supply) items, it is always necessary to write more items than will be needed in the final form of the test. In the first place, a careful review of the complete collection of items will almost surely disclose flaws in individual items that were not apparent at the time of writing, and some material will therefore have to be discarded. Secondly, if the material is submitted to a full-fledged pretesting, still more items will be found inappropriate or defective, and a further reduction will be necessary. It is never possible to predict exactly what proportion of the original items will survive item review and pretesting; however, a reasonable rule of thumb is to begin with at least 30 to 40 percent more material than will finally be required. To ensure that the reduction of items does not leave important problems untested in the final form, one may wish to begin with two or three items testing the same general point. Very often one such item will do well in pretesting while another will, for any of a variety of reasons, prove ineffective.

As items are written, it is a good procedure to type each one on a separate slip of paper (5- by 8-inch size is recommended), with the answer on the back. Slips are much more convenient to work with than sheets: items can easily be added or deleted, and the material can be reordered without the necessity of recopying. The answer should be put on the back of the slip so that an outside reviewer will not be influenced before he makes his own decision as to the correct response.

WRITING TEST DIRECTIONS

Test directions should be brief, simple to understand, and free from possible ambiguities. They should be accompanied by sufficient examples to ensure that even the slow learner or least skilled examinee understands the problem type. Clear instructions on whether or not examinees are to guess at answers should be provided. It is usually advisable, too, to indicate the length of time which will be allowed for the test or its several parts. If the test is highly speeded, examinees should be prepared for this in the directions so that they will not become unnerved by their inability to finish.

In short, the purpose of test directions is to allow all examinees to begin the problems on an equal footing. If the language of the directions is difficult or confusing, one cannot be sure that poor test performance indicates low proficiency in the skills area being tested. If the number or the explanation of the examples is inadequate, what was designed as a proficiency or achievement test may become partly an intelligence test instead. Note the following:

> . . . final punctuation has been omitted to eliminate orthographic clues to the answers.

It is doubtful whether this "explanation," taken from the directions to an English test for foreigners, will be understood by more than a small portion of the examinees. The others may quite possibly waste valuable time trying to puzzle out the meaning of such language and, failing in their efforts, become unduly anxious and upset over their failure.

REVIEWING THE ITEMS

When the items have all been written, they should be set aside for a few days before being reviewed by the writer. Once he is satisfied with his material, it should be submitted to at least one colleague with experience in the subject-matter field—as, in this case, a teacher of English as a second language. Comments by the outside reviewer can be put on the back of the item slips; items judged satisfactory can be marked "O.K." with the reviewer's initials. Careful review will often identify items which otherwise would be lost later in pretesting or would arouse the criticism of the subject-matter specialists were they to appear in the final version of the test. Very often minor defects in items can be corrected and the items salvaged.

PRETESTING THE MATERIAL

Standard objective tests consist of pretested materials. That is to say, all the items have first been tried out on a fairly large number of subjects of the same kind as those for whom the test is being designed. Only those items which prove statistically satisfactory in the pretest are included in the final version of the test. Items are said to be statistically satisfactory if they meet two requirements:

1. If they are of a suitable level of difficulty—neither too hard nor too easy for the population being tested
2. If they discriminate between those examinees who know the material or have the skills or abilities being tested, and those who do not

Pretesting also provides an opportunity for the test maker to try out the test directions and to check the estimated time required for examinees to work the items of the test. If the directions are not clear to the subjects, this should certainly be noted at the time of pretesting so that the instructions can be clarified in the final form. If a large number of subjects are unable to answer items at the anticipated rate of speed, the test maker may wish to reduce the number of items or increase the time allowance on the final form of the test.

Effective pretesting requires, above all, that the pretest subjects be as similar as possible to the kind of examinees for whom the final form of the test is intended. The closer the two groups are to each other, the more meaningful will be the pretest data. In addition, however, some test writers like to administer their tests of English as a second language to a sample of native speakers of English as a form of item validation: items which cause difficulty for subjects who use English natively perhaps do not belong in a test for foreign learners. (As we have noted in earlier chapters, however, this principle would not necessarily apply to some kinds of advanced-level tests, such as those of reading comprehension or writing ability, which are skills in which native speakers of English show a wide range of ability.)

A second important point in pretesting is to allow sufficient time for all, or nearly all, examinees to attempt every item, for if a substantial number do not reach the end of the pretest, there will be insufficient data on the last items in the pretest. It is common, therefore, to allow more generous time limits for pretests than for the final form of a test. If the test writer needs to determine the speed at which most subjects can work the problems, he can call time at an appropriate point in the pretest and have the subjects mark the item they have reached. Those who have not completed the test can then be allowed to proceed to the end.

In the case of informal classroom tests, pretesting is seldom practicable, and in the preparation of such tests this step, and item analysis, may need to be omitted.[1] Pretesting is, however, essential for any test that is to be administered to large numbers of examinees and used to make im-

[1] Even with these tests, however, item analysis conducted after the testing is useful in determining which items worked more effectively; these may be put into an "item pool" for reuse at a later date.

portant decisions about these subjects—as, for instance, a test designed to screen university applicants or to place such students in appropriate classes.

ANALYZING THE PRETEST RESULTS (ITEM ANALYSIS)

After the pretest answer sheets have been accumulated (and there should be a safe number of these—generally at least 100 completed papers), the items should be analyzed to determine their effectiveness in terms of the two criteria listed in the preceding section.

DETERMINING ITEM DIFFICULTY

The first step is to determine the difficulty level of each item. Though much more sophisticated techniques have been developed, a very satisfactory method is simply to ascertain the percent of the sample who answered each item correctly. Multiple-choice items that are excessively easy (say, those correctly answered by at least 92 percent of the examinees) or unreasonably difficult (perhaps those answered correctly by less than 30 percent of the sample group) will generally be discarded as not contributing significantly to the measurement function of the test.[2] Those which remain must still meet the second of the two requirements, that is, discrimination.

DETERMINING ITEM DISCRIMINATION

The second step, then, is to determine how well each item discriminates between high- and low-level examinees, for each item in a test should help to separate the proficient subjects from those who lack the tested skills or learnings.

The usual method is to assume that an examinee's performance on the total test will provide a reasonably good indication of his level of achievement or proficiency. Therefore, the test analyst will first separate the highest and lowest papers in terms of the total scores on the test. He will then determine how the two groups did on each item; the discriminating items will be those answered correctly by more of the high group than the low group.

[2] There will occasionally be exceptions. For instance, if a test is of a highly unusual nature, it may be felt desirable to begin with several "giveaway" items—those which are exceptionally easy—in order to start all the candidates out on the right track. The same results, however, may be achieved more efficiently by including a sufficient number of sample items, and it is usually preferable to include in the actual test only items which make a real contribution to the measure.

Of the several statistical techniques that have been devised for calculating item discrimination, the following is one of the simpler methods that can be recommended to the classroom teacher.[3]

Step 1.   Separate the highest and the lowest 25 percent of the papers.

Step 2.   For each item, subtract the number of "lows" who answered the item correctly from the number of "highs" who answered correctly. (If more "lows" than "highs" get an item right, the result of this calculation will of course be negative and should be marked with a minus sign.)

Step 3.   Divide the result of step 2 by the number of papers in each group, "highs" and "lows," to obtain the "item discrimination index."

For example, if one has a sample of 100 completed papers, he should separate the highest and the lowest 25 papers. Let us then say that the first item was answered correctly by 22 "highs" and 10 "lows." Subtracting 10 from 22, we obtain +12, which, divided by 25 (the size of each group of papers), gives an item discrimination index of +.48. We would conclude that this item has satisfactory discriminating power. Items showing negative discrimination or low discrimination (discrimination much below .30) should be either revised or discarded.

DETERMINING THE EFFECTIVENESS OF DISTRACTERS

One further step in the analysis of multiple-choice items is highly desirable, and that is to inspect the way each item distracter functioned. If an item contains a distracter which attracted no one, not even the poorest examinees, it is a nonfunctioning choice which will increase the chances that some examinees will get the item right by guessing between or among the remaining two or three possibilities. Again, an inspection of the performance of distracters will sometimes show that a "wrong" answer attracted more high than low scorers. Retaining such a distracter will actually harm the test. Nonfunctioning and malfunctioning distracters should be replaced, but the revised items should then be pretested again, for the original statistics will almost always be affected by alterations.

---

[3] Other techniques are described in the standard texts on educational measurement. Frequently these are based on the analysis of the top and bottom 27 percent of the papers, the proportion found most effective in determining the discriminative power of an item. Some techniques make use of conversion tables such as the familiar one developed by J. C. Flanagan to obtain a "normalized biserial coefficient of correlation" between the performance of the "highs" and "lows." (Such a table will be found in Henry E. Garrett, *Statistics in Psychology and Education,* 5th ed. New York, London, and Toronto: Longmans, Green & Co., 1958, p. 366.)

RECORDING ITEM ANALYSIS DATA

It is most convenient to record item analysis data on an "item analysis slip" which contains (1) the item, written out in full, (2) an identification of the pretest in which the item was tried out, (3) the position of the item in the pretest, (4) the item difficulty and discrimination indices, and, in the case of multiple-choice items, (5) a tabulation of how the "highs" and "lows" responded to the several choices. (Some test writers like to include the performance of the "mid" group of examinees as well.) A sample item analysis slip is shown in Figure 4.

Pretest _X-β (vocab)_				
Item No. _40_				
		a brief, light sleep		
		A. yawn		C. nap
		B. stroll		D. hug
Choices	Highs	Mids	Lows	
A	1	4	5	Difficulty: _.66_
B	2	6	5	Discrimination: _.48_
C	22	34	10	
D	0	4	4	
Omit	0	2	1	

FIGURE 4.   Sample Item Analysis Sheet

The use of item analysis slips will greatly simplify the preparation of the final form of a test, for they are easy to work with during the assembly of the test and need merely be reordered to provide the material for the typist.

ASSEMBLING THE FINAL FORM

On the basis of pretesting, any necessary changes in the directions can be effected, and the selection of usable items can be made. In part the choice of items will depend upon the overall level of difficulty desired. In most testing situations it is advisable to begin with rather easy items, lead gradually to more difficult problems, and end with those items which only the best candidates can answer correctly. For a language test intended to discriminate well at various levels of competence, a wide range of item difficulty with a mean between 60 and 70 percent is recommended. Such a test will challenge most of the students yet will not include many items so difficult as to discourage large numbers of the less proficient subjects.

In assembling multiple-choice items in the final form, the test maker must take care not only to order the items according to increasing level of difficulty but also to ensure that (1) each answer position is used about the same number of times and (2) the answer positions do not form any observable pattern. For example, if we have a test consisting of one hundred 4-choice items, each answer position, A, B, C, and D, should occur about twenty-five times, the answers having the appearance of a completely random sequence (BDACDBAACBDCADA, etc.)

REPRODUCING THE TEST

1. It is essential that test materials be reproduced as clearly as possible, for poor reproduction of a test will almost certainly affect student performance. For large-scale testing, photo-offset or letter-press printing is customary; such methods provide the sharpest text and also the greatest number of good copies. For local, small-scale tests, duplication may be by mimeograph, multilith, or a similar process. Ditto (spirit carbon) processes are the least satisfactory, both because the copies often lack clarity and because only a limited number of copies can be made per master.

2. Test material should be spaced so as to provide maximum readability. With most multiple-choice item types, two columns per page will make the reading task easiest. On the other hand, with short-answer (supply) items it is generally best to extend the text the full width of the paper.

3. No multiple-choice item should be begun on one page and continued on the next, for such a break in the text will disrupt the reader's train of thought.

4. When blanks are left for the completion of short-answer items, a guideline should be provided on which the examinee may write his response. Guidelines should be of sufficient length that even the examinees with large handwriting will not have to crowd their answers.

5. It is advisable to indicate at the bottom of each page whether the examinee is to continue on to the next page or stop his work. In the former case, a simple instruction such as "Continue on the next page" should be given. If each part of the test is separately timed, the last item in each part should be followed by instructions such as: "STOP. Do not go on to the next part of the test until you are told to do so. If you finish this part before time is called, you may check your work on this part only."

6. If each part of the test is separately timed, the directions for each part should occupy a right-hand page of the book so that examinees cannot see the next set of items until the examiner gives instructions to turn the page.

7. The use of a separate cover sheet will prevent examinees from looking at the test material before the actual administration begins. If the responses are to be made in the test book, the cover sheet can include

spaces for the examinee's name, class, the date, etc. The cover sheet is also the best place for giving general information and instructions about the test, such as:

a. The general purpose of the test
b. The method of recording responses
c. The method of changing answers if the examinee changes his mind
d. Information on whether or not guessing is penalized
e. In the case of reusable test books, an admonition not to write in the book

8. The pages of the test book should be stapled together with great care so that the back pages will not become detached in the course of handling. Moreover, the staples should be so placed that the book can be opened wide enough for the text on the stapled side of the pages to be read with ease.

USING SEPARATE ANSWER SHEETS FOR MULTIPLE-CHOICE TESTS

In large testing programs where the scoring of multiple-choice tests is done by machines, the use of separate answer sheets is mandatory. But even when the tests are hand scored, it is usually economical to have answers recorded on separate answer sheets rather than in the test books themselves. Not only may the books then be used again, but a great deal of time will be saved in scoring, for the various types of keys can be applied much more easily to single-page answer sheets than to test books.

It must be remembered, however, that separate answer sheets always complicate the mechanics of test-taking, and particularly so in the case of foreign examinees, who quite likely have had little or no previous experience with such devices. The most serious dangers are two in number: (1) that the examinee will not understand how the answer sheet is to be used; (2) that he will lose his place on the answer sheet and record his answers on the wrong lines.

The first danger may best be avoided, or at least substantially reduced, by including examples of correctly marked answers on the answer sheet and referring to these in the general test directions:[4]

. . . and thus the answer to Example Number 1 is choice A. Look on your answer sheet and see how choice A has been marked for you.

It is also advisable for the examiners to circulate among the examinees at the commencement of the test to see that each one is marking his answers in the proper way.

[4] Another related technique is to have the examinees do a number of sample problems themselves, which the examiners should then check on.

The danger of the examinee's losing his place is a more difficult one to eliminate, and even the most practiced test-taker occasionally makes errors of this sort. One form of help is the use of letters rather than numbers to indicate choices:

> 3. affluent
> A. quick
> B. sharp
> C. noisy
> D. wealthy

It will be easier for the examinee to remember and mark 3-D as his answer than 3-4, which might get reversed in the recording process. Sometimes this device is carried one step further and alternating sets of letters are used with the choices; thus odd-numbered items might have A, B, C, D for the choices, and even-numbered items have E, F, G, H, thereby reducing the possibility of an examinee's skipping one line on the answer sheet and consequently mis-keying the rest of his answers.

Figure 5 shows part of a homemade answer sheet which can be used in local testing. Special long-handled hole punches can be purchased for the preparation of a *stencil key* for such answer sheets. The key is made by first marking the correct answers on an answer sheet and then punching out these correct responses. When the key is placed over an examinee's answer sheet, only his correct responses will appear, and the scorer can make a mark with a colored pencil in the holes which contain no response. By counting up the colored marks, the scorer obtains the number of incorrect items and omits.

If the proper kind of punch is not available, one can prepare a *fan* or *accordion key,* which is simply a correctly marked answer sheet folded so that each vertical column of keyed answers can be placed directly beside the same column on the examinee's answer sheet.

Score_____

Vocabulary Test for Students of English as a Second Language

Name _____ Date_____

Native language_____ Country_____

1. ( ) ( ) ( ) ( )	21. ( ) ( ) ( ) ( )	41. ( ) ( ) ( ) ( )
A B C D	A B C D	A B C D
2. ( ) ( ) ( ) ( )	22. ( ) ( ) ( ) ( )	42. ( ) ( ) ( ) ( )
A B C D	A B C D	A B C D
3. ( ) ( ) ( ) ( )	23. ( ) ( ) ( ) ( )	43. ( ) ( ) ( ) ( )
A B C D	A B C D	A B C D
4. ( ) ( ) ( ) ( )	24. ( ) ( ) ( ) ( )	44. ( ) ( ) ( ) ( )
A B C D	A B C D	A B C D

FIGURE 5. Part of a Homemade Answer Sheet

PREPARING EQUIVALENT FORMS

It is sometimes advisable to prepare more than one form of a test that is going to be used repeatedly. *Equivalent*, or *parallel*, forms are useful for a number of purposes, of which the following are the most common.

1. To provide for pre- and post-testing. One form may be used at the beginning of a course of study or training program, and another form at the conclusion of the program to determine degree of improvement. It is better to use two equivalent forms for this purpose than to repeat the same form, for some examinees may remember specific item content.

2. To decrease the chance of "test compromise." Two or more forms of a test, administered alternately according to an irregular schedule, will help reduce the temptation on the part of examinees to memorize test content and pass it on to their friends.

By far the simplest way to construct equivalent forms is to pretest sufficient material to assemble two forms on the basis of a single item analysis. The two forms should have similar item-difficulty distributions and follow the same *general* content-area specifications. Thus, for example, both forms of a structure test should have the same number of items testing word order, tense of verbs, etc. The *specific* content of the items in the two forms, however, should be different so as to constitute two samplings of word-order problems, verb-tense problems, etc.

Constructing two or more forms of a test simultaneously of course requires a good deal of pretesting: if a final form of 70 items is required, one will have to prepare and pretest a minimum of about 180 items (70 X 2 + 30 percent extra to allow accurate matching and to compensate for pretest item casualties). The best procedure would be to organize the material into two 90-item pretests and to administer these to the same pretest group(s) on two days within the same week. Where practicable, the pretests should be administered in opposite order to the two halves of the pretest population in order to neutralize the "practice effect."

Once the two forms have been prepared, it is important to try them out on other examinees to ensure that the forms really are equivalent in difficulty, for the difficulty of individual items may change when they are moved to different positions in the tests.

There are also statistical methods for preparing a second form of a test after the first form has been in use for some time, but these techniques are considerably more complicated.[5]

---

[5] For a discussion of procedures for constructing equivalent forms or obtaining equivalent test scores, see John C. Flanagan, "Units, Scores, and Norms," in E. F. Lindquist (ed.), *Educational Measurement*, Washington: American Council on Education, 1951, pp. 749–760.

LANGUAGE TESTING—
THE PROBLEM OF VALIDATION

BERNARD SPOLSKY

Foreign-language tests fall naturally into two classes according to the purposes for which they are used. In the first class are tests used for the control of instruction. They are the concern of the classroom teacher who wishes to find out how effective his teaching and the students' learning have been or to discover what needs to be taught. The second class are tests used in the control of a person's career. Used by administrators or counsellors, they are intended to help make decisions about someone's qualifications for a given task or about the type of training he should follow.

Each of these classes may be further divided according to the temporal relation of the test to its goal. Tests of the first class concerned with testing what has been taught are achievement tests; those concerned with what is about to be taught are diagnostic tests. Tests of the second class concerned with what the subject can do now are achievement tests; those concerned with what he should be able to do in the future are predictive tests. But this temporal distinction is less important than the major functional one; exactly the same test can serve as a diagnostic test before some material is taught and as an achievement test after it. Similarly, proficiency tests are generally used as predictors of future performance.

This functional classification agrees with one that can be made on operational grounds: tests of the first class are relatively simple to prepare and straightforward to interpret, while tests of the second class involve serious theoretical and practical difficulties in preparation, interpretation, and especially, in validation. Why this is so becomes clear if we consider the steps to be followed in preparing a test.

ACHIEVEMENT AND DIAGNOSTIC TESTS

Take the preparation of a test of the first type, an achievement or diagnostic test, to be used by a classroom teacher either before she starts a unit or chapter in the textbook or after she has finished. The starting point is the syllabus, with its list of items to be learned in the unit. The purpose of the test will be to decide how many of the items on the list have been mastered by the students. For our example, let us assume that we have an elementary class in English as a second language; we wish to test their knowledge of vocabulary, and our syllabus is defined by Lesson Eleven of Book One of *English for Today*.[1] Notice that the first, and in many ways, most important task of test writing has been done: the syllabus (or textbook in this case) gives us a list of the sixteen new words in the lesson. There is no point in our going beyond the list unless of course we wish to test words previously taught. From it, we select the words to be tested. If we have time, we can put every word in the test, but there is no need, for using some appropriate techniques, we can choose a representative sample. Next, we have to decide on the testing technique we are going to use. It is here that we are called on to define more precisely what it means to "know vocabulary"; we need to translate the general term into a more precise one. Here are some possible operational definitions, each describing a possible technique:

(a)   When presented with a word on the list, the student taking the test should say, "I know it" or "I don't know it."

(b)   When presented with a word on the list, he must select which one of a group of definitions is appropriate:

> glass—something you drink out of
> something you paint with
> something you draw with

(c)   When presented with a picture of the object named by a word on the list he indicates its name:

> glass
> cup
> bottle

(d)   When presented with a picture, the student must write down what it is.

There are of course many other techniques,[2] but these may be considered a representative sample. Of course, they each raise minor problems. The first, (a), might not be considered a normal sort of test, but it is likely to be a most useful technique with teachers and students who are cooperating closely in the learning process. The second and third raise a special problem: when multiple choice items are given, the student should know the meaning of the incorrect answers as well as the correct one; otherwise, the choice is unduly limited. For example, in (c) above,

---

[1] *English for Today*, ed. William R. Slager (New York: McGraw-Hill, 1962).
[2] See, for details, Robert Lado, *Language Testing* (New York: McGraw-Hill, 1961), or Rebecca Valette, *Modern Language Testing: A Handbook* (New York: Harcourt, Brace and World, 1967).

bottle would be a bad distractor, for the word is not introduced in Lesson Eleven (or in fact in Book One). Similarly, (b) has a bad definition; the word *drink* comes in Lesson Sixteen; in Lesson Eleven, all you do with glasses is wash them. A more serious problem in choosing a test technique is deciding whether it is a valid representation of the skill we want to test. Is there a serious difference between being able to recognize a definition and being able to give a definition? The former technique is easy to mark, the latter takes much longer. But it is quite easy to try out all the different techniques, and decide for ourselves whether they correlate so well that we only need to use one in the future.[3] Once we have decided on the items and technique, the rest of the task of preparation is simple. And interpretation is straightforward, too. As long as the test is a representative sample of items, its result will say, "This student scored sixty percent on the test; he knows sixty percent of the words on the list." If the test is a diagnostic test, we will know what words need be taught; if an achievement test, we will know how effective our teaching has been. What has made test preparation and interpretation so simple has been that we have been able to ask a question to which there is a quantifiable answer. We have not asked whether or not the student knows English vocabulary, but rather how many of the words on this list he knows. Our results are clear, for they say he knows a given percentage of the words in Lesson Eleven of the textbook.

Basic to this relative simplicity was the existence of a list of items to be tested. Clearly, such lists are not available for all tests used in control of instruction. But it is equally clear that effective teaching depends on the availability of clear specifications. Normally, we have a syllabus or textbook or both, with lists of vocabulary, grammatical structures, etc. With such a syllabus or textbook, test making is straightforward. A control of instruction test is concerned with the question, "Have the items listed in the syllabus or textbook been learned to some criterion level?" It is not concerned with what should be learned. It would be wrong to include in a test of this class items that are not included in the syllabus.

PREDICTIVE AND PROFICIENCY TESTS

When we say then that an achievement test is not a good one, we are referring to its inability to test a defined body of material; we are not

[3] *The Interpretive Information for the Test of English as a Foreign Language* (Educational Testing Service, 1967, revised January 1968) for example describes an interesting comparison of the scores on the "writing" section (a set of multiple-choice questions) with the scores of the same students on a set of essays graded by a team of examiners. The correlation is .74, which is close enough to suggest that the saving in time is worthwhile, unless of course we are planning to interpret the scores as though they had 100 percent validity. And on this see Paul Holtzman's paper in *NAFSA Studies and Papers,* English Language Series, Number 13: ATESL Selected Conference Papers (1967).

saying anything about what should constitute that material. That is the task of the syllabus or textbook writer. Now, there are clearly cases when the distinction between test writer and textbook writer are blurred. One such case is when the test writer is trying to evaluate achievement in something that has not in fact been specified. He then has to do the textbook writer's job of specification before he can prepare an achievement test. This happens when one has a set of materials that can be listed as items and patterns, but one wishes to test the ability of the students to know more than the items or patterns they have been taught. For example, one may wish to find out about a student's ability to speak naturally on a topic other than those he has been trained for in memorized dialogues, or to use patterns with words other than those included in the pattern drills. But in such cases, we are really moving out of the realm of achievement tests, and into the area of proficiency, the second class of tests. These cases in fact set the limit; the first class in its purest form consists of tests defined not only functionally but also operationally—functionally, in that they are used in the control of instruction, and operationally, in that they are tests prepared on the basis of specifications of behavior or items that have been prepared, independently of the test, as part of the development of materials, textbooks, and syllabus.

The second class of foreign-language tests is defined functionally as tests used primarily in the control of a subject's career. They serve to make judgments possible on such questions as:

1. How well will the subject do at learning foreign languages in general, or one foreign language in particular? Should he be advised (permitted, encouraged) to study a language? Should his employer (or the government, or the armed forces) invest time and money in his studying a language?

2. How well does the subject perform in the given foreign language? If he needs to use the language in government or other service, will he be successful? If he is a graduate student in a given field, will he be able to read books in the foreign language?

Tests aimed to handle the first set of questions are predictive tests; their task is to make some sort of judgment possible on the question of the student's language-learning aptitude, and will need to make available information on any factors that will be relevant to language learning. This type of test sets many basic problems about the nature of second language acquisition, but will be left out of consideration in this paper.[4] Here, we shall be concerned with tests intended to answer questions of the second sort, proficiency tests.

[4] For a discussion of this problem, see Paul Pimsleur, "Testing Foreign Language Learning," *Trends in Language Teaching*, ed. Albert Valdman (New York: McGraw-Hill, 1966).

KNOWING A LANGUAGE

Fundamental to the preparation of valid tests of language proficiency is a theoretical question of what it means to know a language. There are two ways in which this question can be answered. One is to follow what John Carroll[5] has referred to as the integrative approach, and to accept that there is such a factor as overall proficiency. The second is to follow what Carroll called the discrete-point approach: this involves an attempt to break up knowing a language into a number of separate skills, and further into a number of distinct items making up each skill. We are using the overall approach when we give a subjective evaluation of the proficiency of a foreign speaker of our language. In such cases, we usually do not refer to specific items that he has or hasn't mastered but to his ability to function in a defined situation. We do not say, "He is unable to distinguish between the phonemes /i/ and /iy/," but rather something like "He doesn't know enough English to write an essay, but he seems to be able to follow lectures and to read his textbooks without much trouble." The key assumption of the discrete-point approach is that it is possible to translate sentences of the second type into a list of sentences in the first, and the key requirement for discrete-point testing is that we could quantify "He knows the words on this list."

Detailed instructions on how to prepare tests like this are given in the books by Lado and Valette referred to earlier. Drawing in particular on the powers of techniques developed by taxonomic linguistics to describe in detail the surface structure of languages, Lado shows how it is possible to construct tests that permit very fine discrimination of the strengths and weaknesses of foreign-language learners. Basic to Lado's approach is a theory calling for systematic description of the surface structure of the language being learned, combined with comparison with the language of the learner; it leads to a notion that tests as well as teaching material should be based on contrastive analysis, and prepared accordingly. Using these techniques, it is possible to develop tests that may be scored objectively (although some studies have raised some questions about the type of question used)[6] and the results of which lead to such precise interpretation as "the subject confuses medial /l/ and /r/." Tests of this nature are obviously of very great value in the control of instruction, whether as diagnostic or achievement tests.

But we must ask whether such an approach, assuming that all we have to do is to list all the items, permits us to characterize overall proficiency. If so, overall proficiency could be considered the sum of the specific items

[5] John B. Carroll, "Fundamental Considerations in Testing for English Language Proficiency of Foreign Students," *Testing* (Center for Applied Linguistics, 1961).
[6] See for instance, Eugène Brière, "Testing the Control of Parts of Speech in FL Compositions," *Language Learning*, XIV, 1 & 2 (1964).

that have been listed and of the specific skills in which they are testable. To know a language is then to have developed a criterion level of mastery of the skills and habits listed. There are rather serious theoretical objections to this position. First, a discrete-point approach assumes that knowledge of a language is finite in the sense that it will be possible to make an exhaustive list of all the items of the language. Without this, we cannot show that any sample we have chosen is representative and thus valid. We must then argue for selection on the basis of functional necessity. This involves defining the functional load of the ability to distinguish between a pair of phonemes or of the ability to recognize the appropriateness of a given verb form. To do this, we would have to collect a list of minimal pair utterances in which the distinction is vital, but there turn out to be very few real minimal-pair situations, that is, situations where a single linguistic difference in a given situation will lead to complete misunderstanding. I have been told for instance the true story of a foreign lady speaking to her Italian maid: she asked to have the meat (*carne*) brought to the table, but had it given to the dog (*cane*) instead; rather strong punishment for speaking an r-less dialect. The rarity of such situations is a result (and theoretical cause) of the redundancy of natural languages.[7] Thanks to redundancy, we can communicate satisfactorily without knowing any given item in a language. This is most obvious in the area of vocabulary, where it is quite clear how many of the words in the dictionary are unknown to the average native speaker; it is true also in the area of phonology, otherwise speakers of different dialects of the same language would never be able to understand each other. It is probably not true in the case of many syntactic rules, but many of these are likely to turn out to be universal, and so irrelevant to foreign-language testing. More important, though, is the fact that syntactic rules are untestable unless fleshed out with vocabulary and phonology or spelling.

FUNCTIONAL STATEMENTS OF PROFICIENCY

All of this suggests the impossibility of characterizing levels of knowing a language in linguistic terms, that is, as mastery of a criterion percentage of items in a grammar and lexicon. A more promising approach might be to work for a functional definition of levels: we should aim not to test how much of a language someone knows, but test his ability to operate in a specified sociolinguistic situation with specified ease or effect. The preparation of proficiency tests like this would not start from a list of language items, but from a statement of language function; after all, it would not be expected to lead to statements like "He knows sixty percent

[7] For a brief account of this, see John B. Carroll, *Language and Thought* (Englewood Cliffs: Prentice-Hall, Inc., 1964).

of English," but "He knows enough English to shop in a supermarket."

Functional statements of language proficiency may take various forms. One of the most thorough examples of a fairly complete scale is that prepared by the Foreign Service Institute for the classification of officers of the U.S. State Department. These Absolute Language Proficiency Ratings, as they are called, involve a division into language skills (reading, writing, speaking, and comprehending) and a numerical rating for each. The numerical ratings are generally described by a brief title, and range from "elementary," through "working" and "professional" to "native or bilingual." For each level of each skill there is a short description, again emphasizing skill. For example, to receive the rating S-3, one must be "able to speak the language with sufficient structural accuracy and vocabulary to satisfy representation requirements and handle professional discussions within a special field." There is then a longer description, suggesting the type of language-learning experience that is associated with the level.[8]

Starting with functional statements of this sort (and there should be little problem in preparing such descriptions for each of the situations in which proficiency tests are used), the language tester's problem is to find a reliable, valid, and economical method of rating a subject's proficiency in these terms. The first question is one of strategy. The discrete-point approach implies that it is possible to give a linguistic description of each level, to list the words and grammar needed to achieve this, but this is not possible either in theory or practice. The practical approach followed in the past has been to decide in some ad hoc way (the opinion of teachers, for instance) on the sort of items to be tested and the sort of test to use, but even though such a test can be made extremely reliable, it proves impossible to show its validity with sufficient precision to justify interpretations or improvements.[9] A more helpful strategy is to prepare proficiency tests in two stages. For the first stage one must forget considerations of expense and time. Expensive tests, using panels of trained judges, and having the subject function in situations of the sort described in the rating scales, should first be developed as yardsticks. The second stage then involves taking cheaper procedures, of whatever kind, and correlating them with the more expensive measures. The degree of correlation will show the value of the ad hoc tests and make clear the degree of doubt that must be kept in their interpretation.

The exact nature of these more practical tests is not important; one

[8] The Absolute Language Proficiency Ratings are described in a number of mimeographed circulars. Most accessible is the sample quoted by John Carroll in his article in *Foreign Language Annals* I, 2 (December 1967), and the description by Frank Rice in the *Linguistic Reporter* (May 1959).

[9] This problem has been discussed, among other places, at a seminar held at the 1967 Conference of the National Association for Foreign Student Affairs, the proceedings of which have been published in *ATESL Selected Conference Papers*.

would presume that they would be similar to many of the tests presently being used,[10] but they would permit of greater confidence in use, greater possibility of improvement (for we could then be in a position to speak about improving the validity of an object test), and greater refinement in interpretation. It is probable that we would be able to develop simpler tests (e.g., the overall proficiency test using redundancy I have been working on[11]), and so ultimately justify the expense of the validation procedures.

The central problem of foreign-language testing, as of all testing, is validity. With tests of the first class, used by classroom teachers in the control of instruction, this problem is not serious, for the textbook or syllabus writer has already specified what should be tested. With tests of the second class, it remains a serious difficulty, for we have not yet found a way to characterize knowledge of a language with sufficient precision to guarantee the validity of the items we include or the types of tests we use.

[10] John Carroll, for instance, has investigated the correlation between the FSI Absolute Language Proficiency Ratings and the MLA Foreign Language Proficiency Tests for Teachers and Advanced Students.
[11] Bernard Spolsky, Bengt Sigurd, Masahito Santo, Edward Walker, and Catherine Arterburn, "Preliminary Studies in the Development of Techniques for Testing Overall Second Language Proficiency," *Problems in Foreign Language Testing.* John A. Upshur and Julia Fata, eds. *Language Learning* (Special Issue Number 3, 1968).

SECTION EIGHT
TEACHING AIDS

A large number of teaching aids have proved to be very useful in second-language instruction. The most familiar to the classroom teacher are, of course, the textbook and the chalkboard. Other aids noted in this section include tape recorders, record players, movies, overhead projectors, gestures, charts, pictures, filmstrips, flannel boards, games, songs, and puppets. We usually group all of these together under the term *audiovisual aids.*

In teaching small children, where no reading or writing enters the instructional program, the teacher makes use of several of the devices mentioned: pictures, flannel boards, puppets, songs, games—and also realia. An excellent demonstration of this kind of program is the film *Starting English Early,* produced at the University of California, Los Angeles, under the supervision of Lois McIntosh. Aids enable the teacher to move from one activity to another in order to keep the pupils' interest and attention from lagging; they also provide settings and stimuli for reviewing or testing previously studied items and patterns.

Older students and adults welcome diversified classroom activities, too. The learning of another language involves a great deal of imitation, repetition, and manipulation—a considerable amount of sameness—and boredom almost invariably sets in at some point. Audiovisual aids can help to break the monotony by adding variety to classroom drills and exercises. In addition these aids make possible a number of activities that reinforce regular classroom studies.

The authors in this section deal with gestures, games, pictures, and the language laboratory. It should perhaps be noted that some of the devices mentioned can serve a learning purpose outside the classroom as well as inside. Tape recorders, for example, are key equipment in the language laboratory. But they may be used, too, for group practice in the classroom—in addition, students may own, rent, or borrow tape recorders for individual practice at home. Commercial movies in English provide excellent practice in listening to interpersonal dialogue and an opportunity to observe "authentic" gestures that accompany speech. Radio and television programs in English are also good for listening practice. Dobson suggests that games can be used at language clubs and parties as well as in the classroom: they tend to promote "fun and relaxation while remaining within the framework of language learning—and may reinforce that learning." The same would apply partly, at least, to singing. Many students enjoy learning to sing songs in English, especially popular songs.

GESTURES

Saitz considers gestures on a fairly broad basis. He recognizes gestures as a teaching aid in the classroom, but he is also concerned with the teaching of appropriate gestures to students along with the language. He points out that "systematic description of gestural habits are rare; contrastive studies of two gesture-systems are difficult to find and only recently have some textbooks (notably in Spanish) begun to include bits of such information. At present, for teachers of English as a second language, the best source of gestural information is the language teacher who is able to observe behavior in the two cultures, that of the native language and that of the target language."

Some gestures, or body movements, are presumably idiosyncratic. But others appear to be patterned—a particular gesture and a particular speech form go together. Saitz calls our attention to this in greetings, leave-takings, indicating directions, getting attention, and commands. We also notice, at times, that gestures take the place of speech. When a certain gesture ordinarily accompanies a given speech form, the gesture will convey the message whether the speech form occurs or not. The study of body motion and stance in communication is called *kinesics*. Our interest is not in kinesics as a whole, but only in gestures that regularly accompany speech forms and that sometimes replace speech forms. Just as speech habits differ from language to language, so do gestural habits. Since gestures form part of the total communication framework, they need to be learned along with the vocal symbols that they accompany (or replace).

Saitz discusses a number of situations in which gestures lead to misunderstanding in intercultural communication. He urges teachers to gather useful information on gestures from their own observations, and he suggests how the learning of gestural habits may be introduced into classroom activities. A similar matter should perhaps be introduced at the same time: interpersonal distance in speech communication. Speaker distance sometimes leads to awkwardness, discomfort, and misunderstanding. Students should at least be acquainted with the norms, and they should understand the cultural significance of being too far away from or too close to a person in direct conversation.

For classwork teachers usually develop a set of hand signals for students to follow in certain kinds of drills, especially choral drills. Classroom drills can proceed more smoothly if the teacher does not have to stop and give verbal instructions to the class. A particular hand movement on the part of the teacher instructs the students to "repeat in unison." Another indicates "listen"; another, "students on the teacher's left should respond only"; another, "students on the teacher's right should respond only"; etc. One of the ablest teachers I know has a repertory of about twenty such signals which he uses to guide his class in choral drills; by means of conventionalized hand movements, he gives directions to his students: voicing of a particular sound, more lip rounding, higher pitch, raise the front part of the tongue higher, and the like. The way he conducts his class reminds me of an orchestra conductor guiding musicians in the performance of a symphony.

PICTURES

What we say about pictures generally applies to other visual aids as well. Their principal value, I think, lies in recreating situations and environments that provide contexts for language lessons. We have already noted that such aids help the teacher maintain interest and attention and also that they enable the teacher to move from one context to another quickly and easily. Kreidler notes further that pictures make the association of ideas or concepts with their verbal symbolization much simpler, pictures save class time (avoiding verbalism), and pictures make exercises more meaningful, with a reduction of ambiguity.

She mentions that commercially available pictures for classroom drills are of two types: "context-oriented pictures and structure-oriented pictures. Context-oriented pictures are those with a context set by pictures, such as a home scene, beach scene, or sports scenes. Each picture includes several objects, or actions, or relationships which may be used to practice several types of structure. Structure-oriented pictures consist of actions, objects, or relationships also. In one set of commercially available aids the pictures are placed in chart form in groups of nine to twelve items chosen for the types of structures they will drill. In the other set of aids the pictures are on individual cards, color-keyed by grammatical category, but flexible enough to allow the teacher to construct his own drills. Although these pictures may be used for vocabulary or pronunciation drill, usually the items pictured are of such high frequency that the most effective use is for drilling points of grammar." She also points out that such pictures can be drawn by the teacher or taken from magazines.

Drills with the aid of pictures seem to be most useful at the early stages of learning a second language. "The most effective practice for automatic control . . . ," Kreidler says, "is varied, fast-moving, and related to a situation or environment." She notes that pictures lend themselves especially well to substitution and conversion drills and, in addition, to testing: "A picture may be used as the cue which provides the stimulus for rapid drill or as the context for testing practice." Prator (in Section Nine) suggests that picture cues in place of oral cues, add a measure of communication to certain kinds of classroom drills.

THE LANGUAGE LABORATORY

The language laboratory perhaps deserves more attention than a single general paper in this section. It is by far the most valuable supplementary aid to second-language instruction and also the most baffling to the average teacher. A few years ago there was a great deal of concern among language teachers that they would eventually be replaced by machines. But today I think it is abundantly clear that this will not come about for a long, long time, if ever. We still consider the teacher's role in language learning to be vital.

The subject of the language laboratory is very well treated in separate books, chapters in pedagogical handbooks, and hundreds of journal articles. I can best refer the reader to a few important works on the subject: Stack's *The Language Laboratory and Modern Language Teaching*, Hocking's *The Language Laboratory and Language Learning*, and Hayes' *Language Laboratory Facilities*. Lado and Rivers have chapters on the language laboratory, and Valdman's *Trends* contains a thoroughgoing treatment of laboratory equipment and utilization by Hutchinson. (See *Selected Readings* below for bibliographical information.)

A laboratory with tape recorders usually requires the services of a skilled technician. Relatively few teachers know enough about the maintenance of electronic equipment to keep the machines in working order. Another requirement is a tape library, the size determined largely by the size of the language program and the "mode" of laboratory activities. Commercially available tapes can fill part of the library's needs, but not nearly all of them. As a rule, teachers voice additional tapes to fill gaps in the tape collection. It has been well established that students make much better use of laboratory equipment and progress in learning when they are supervised and monitored. The teacher ideally plays this role, too. On the whole, laboratory operations are costly in both money and time.

Nevertheless, the evidence makes it amply clear that the language laboratory is, or can be, an extremely valuable supplement to classroom instruction, especially at the beginning and intermediate levels. A very large number of schools now have language laboratories. At some schools laboratory activities have been integrated into the language curriculum and the system works beautifully. At other schools laboratory activities leave much to be desired. The main problem, as revealed in evaluation studies, centers around making the best use of the equipment available. A variety of reasons are given to account for this situation, but one point seems to stand out clearly: most teachers still must be taught how to use laboratory facilities effectively.

SELECTED READINGS

BIRDWHISTELL, RAY L. *Kinesics and Context: Essays on Body Motion Communication.* Philadelphia: University of Pennsylvania Press, 1970.

DORRY, GERTRUDE NYE. *Games for Second Language Learning.* New York: McGraw-Hill Book Company, 1966.

FINOCCHIARO, MARY. "Visual Aids in Teaching English as a Second Language." *The ABC English as a Second Language Bulletin* 1(1966).

HAYES, ALFRED S. *Language Laboratory Facilities.* London: Oxford University Press, 1968.

HOCKING, ELTON. *The Language Laboratory and Language Learning.* Washington, D.C.: Department of Audiovisual Instruction, National Education Association, 1964.

HUTCHINSON, JOSEPH. "The Language Laboratory: Equipment and Utilization." In *Trends in Language Teaching.* Edited by Albert Valdman. New York: McGraw-Hill Book Company, 1966.

KREIDLER, CAROL J. "Effective Use of Visual Aids in the ESOL Classroom." *TESOL Quarterly* 5(1971):19–37.

LADO, ROBERT. *Language Teaching: A Scientific Approach.* Chapter 17: "The Language Laboratory," and Chapter 19: "Teaching Machines and Programmed Learning." New York: McGraw-Hill Book Company, 1964.

MATTHIES, BARBARA F. "TESOL at the '5 and 10'." *TESOL Quarterly* 2(1968): 280–84.

RAMIREZ, MAC M. "The Neglected Tools Can Work for You." *English Teaching Forum* 6(1968):10–15.

REES, ALUN L. W. "The Display Board in Language Teaching." *TESOL Quarterly* 4(1970):161–64.

RICHARDS, JACK. "Songs in Language Learning." *TESOL Quarterly* 3(1969): 161–74.

RIVERS, WILGA M. *Teaching Foreign-Language Skills.* Chapter 13: "Tape Recorders and Language Laboratories." Chicago: The University of Chicago Press, 1968.

SEBEOK, THOMAS A., ALFRED S. HAYES, and M. C. BATESON, eds. *Approaches to Semiotics.* The Hague: Mouton, 1964.

STACK, EDWARD M. *The Language Laboratory and Modern Language Teaching*. Rev. ed. New York: Oxford University Press, 1966.

TITONE, RENZO. "The Role of Audio-Visual Aids in Language Teaching." In *English as a Second Language: Current Issues*. Edited by Robert C. Lugton. Philadelphia: The Center for Curriculum Development, Inc., 1970.

GESTURES
IN THE LANGUAGE CLASSROOM

ROBERT L. SAITZ

Dialect comedians and experienced second-language teachers have always known the importance of gesture in communication. A language teacher who teaches Italian with his hands folded on the desk is as difficult to imagine as a Danny Kaye imitating a Frenchman without pursing his lips and lifting one eyebrow. In recent years, perhaps as a result of research in kinesics[1] and of the increasing use of "natural" contexts (such as dialogues, for example) in language teaching, more and more teachers want to introduce the gestures of the speakers of the target language along with the linguistic patterns being taught. Such teachers feel that it is more interesting for the student, and thus more effective pedagogically for the teacher, when the student who is learning a how-do-you-do greeting can be shown the appropriate handshake, handclasp, armclasp, etc., that usually accompanies such a greeting in the culture of the language being taught.

Yet systematic descriptions of gestural habits are rare; contrastive studies of two gesture-systems are difficult to find and only recently have some textbooks (notably in Spanish) begun to include bits of such information. At present, for teachers of English as a second language, the best source of gestural information is the language teacher who is able to observe behaviour in the two cultures, that of the native language and that of the target language. In this respect the overseas language-teacher who is a native of the target culture is often in an advantageous position; very likely he is already an observer of the customs of his students, and if not, it takes little effort to become such an observer. Once he has begun to note gestural habits his major task becomes one of comparison, as he contrasts local habits with his own or those of his compatriots, if any are available. The teacher who is not a native speaker of the language he

---

[1] The study of gestures, body movements, stances, etc., is called kinesics. *Approaches to Semiotics*, edited by Sebeok, Hayes, and Bateson, and published by Mouton, The Hague, in 1964, gives summaries and discussions of work in this field and provides a bibliography.

teaches must rely on his observation of native speakers, in person, if available, or through the media of the stage or film.[2]

GESTURES IN FIXED SOCIAL CONTEXTS

The kinds of gestures which are easiest to observe and which are frequently the easiest to incorporate into language teaching we might call the social gestures. These are the gestures used commonly in fixed social contexts such as greetings, leave-takings, getting attention, commands, etc. Although there is often variation in the individual performance of such gestures, there is also a significant configuration, an essential characteristic of the movement, which most "performers" within a culture will use. Thus an Englishman or an American who is indicating that he wants a subordinate (a child or a student in class, for example) in his culture to move in a particular direction will likely extend his index finger to indicate the direction. He may extend his arm fully or not; he may extend one or more other fingers as well; he may move his hand back and forth, etc., but the essential feature of the gesture remains the extended index finger. Similarly a common American and English gesture for warning someone (a mother saying "Don't do it!" to her child, for example) consists of extending the index finger from a fist, and then moving the hand back and forth with the index finger pointing towards the person being warned. The arm may be raised to different heights, the motion back and forth may be slow or fast, etc., but the essential elements of the gesture are the raised index finger and the movement toward and away from the person being addressed. (We should note that in a number of other cultures it is common for such a warning gesture to be made with the index finger moving from side to side, not pointing at the person being warned; in fact, the pointing of a finger at someone may be considered an extreme insult.)

Among the kinds of social gestures most significant for second-language teachers are those which are the same in form but different in meaning in the two cultures. These might be called the ambiguous gestures. For example, a Colombian who wants someone to approach him often signals with a hand movement in which all the fingers of one hand, cupped, point downward as they move rapidly back and forth. Speakers of English have a similar gesture (though the hand may not be cupped and the fingers may be held more loosely) but for them the gesture means *goodbye* or *go away*, quite the opposite of the Colombian gesture. Again, in Colom-

---

[2] Although film gestures are frequently exaggerated, and occasionally idiosyncratic, they remain one of the best sources of gesture. "Live" television, of course, is even better.

bia,[3] a speaker of English would have to know that when he indicates height he must choose between different gestures depending on whether he is referring to a human being or an animal. If he keeps the palm of his hand parallel to the floor, as he would in his own culture when indicating the height of a child, for example, he will very likely be greeted by laughter; in Colombia this gesture is reserved for the description of animals. In order to describe human beings he should keep the palm of his hand at right angles to the floor. Substitutions of one gesture for the other often create not only humorous but embarrassing moments. In both of the examples above, speakers from two different cultures have the same gesture, physically, but its meaning differs sharply. The inclusion of such information in the language classroom is surely as important as work on linguistic patterns, if not more so.

UNFAMILIAR GESTURES IN THE CULTURE OF THE TARGET LANGUAGE

A second category of social gestures which the language teacher should consider includes those which are common in the culture of the target language but unfamiliar in the native culture. For example, students of English should be aware that in a number of English-speaking cultures there is a gesture for indicating close friendship, in which the middle finger of one hand is crossed over the index finger of the same hand as the hand is held up. In some cultures this gesture is not used at all, while in others it has quite a different meaning. Similarly the American gesture for hitch-hiking, for stopping a car, in which the thumb is extended from a fist is not common in other cultures; South Americans, for example, usually extend their arms and all the fingers of one hand to stop a car. And in some countries the American gesture would be ambiguous, as there a waving, extended thumb means *pass on, do not stop*. The gesture for *all is well*, or *O.K.*, a circle formed by the thumb and index finger of one raised hand, is common in English-speaking countries; it exists elsewhere, of course, but in some places it has a different meaning, while in others it is unknown. The method of attracting the attention of waiters and waitresses in the U.S. and Great Britain often needs comment. In contrast to the table-tapping, glass-knocking, hissing, etc., that can be observed in other cultures, the unfortunate patrons of a restaurant in the U.S., for example, must rely on head and eye movements. Any sharp or hissing noises may result in an insulted waiter and the likelihood of a long wait for service.

[3] A specific comparison of Colombian and American gestures may be found in *Colombian and North American Gestures*, E. J. Cervenka and R. L. Saitz, published by the Centro Colombo-Americano, Bogota, Colombia (1962).

In addition, the language-teacher should consider those social gestures of the native culture which are not used or which have different meanings in the culture of the target language. The speaker of Spanish from South America must know that his gesture for indicating that a place is crowded, in which one or both hands form a teardrop shape, is not used in most English-speaking countries and that in some it has a crude connotation. Similarly, those who customarily purse their lips and then move them to the right or left to call attention to a person or thing in the direction indicated must know that this gesture, unknown in most English-speaking countries, might be interpreted as a nervous tic or as a vulgar invitation to a kiss. The Japanese student who touches his nose with his finger to indicate that he is not really sure that the teacher has called on him to recite should be informed that in the U.S., for example, such a gesture might well astonish his teacher.

There are many gestures and movements which it might not be useful to describe. Often the gestures which indicate temporary attitudes, such as anger and joy, exhibit such variation from individual to individual within a culture that careful description might not turn out to be pedagogically useful. However, even with such gestures there are often general statements which would be worth making: whether body position and stance are particularly significant in indicating attitude, as they are in southeast Asia, for example; how significant hand and arm waving might be when they accompany emotional utterances; etc.

By observing the kinds of gestures mentioned above, language-teachers can gather a great deal of useful information. Some may ask, however, how such information can be integrated into classroom activities.

GESTURES IN CLASSROOM ACTIVITIES

The teacher's discretion, of course, must dictate the choice of material: the culture, the level of the class, the age of the students, the social background of the students, etc., all will be important factors. But once the teacher has decided what to include, he might consider two methods of presenting the material. First, the most important kinds of gestures (that is, the ambiguous ones and the ones used in everyday activities) should be introduced in the contexts in which they normally occur. The teacher should provide the model, of course, and the students can be expected to use the appropriate gesture at the right spot in the dialogue. Gestures of this type, particularly those used for greetings, leave-takings, indicating directions, getting attention, etc., should be introduced in elementary classes, where it is likely that vocabulary and dialogues relevant to such situations are being presented. In addition, such habits as stance and speaker distance might profitably be demonstrated at this level. For example, when two Russian or two South American or two Italian speak-

DON'T DO IT

HE (SHE) IS THIS TALL

MANY PEOPLE

COME HERE

From Saitz, Robert L. and Edward J. Cervenka. *Colombian and North American Gestures: An Experimental Study.* Drawing by Renee Bigio. Bogotá: Centro Colombo Americano, 1962.

Some Colombian Gestures

ers are conversing they will stand much closer together than would two Americans or Englishmen. The speaker of Spanish who knows this will understand if the Englishman he is speaking to seems to be backing away from him across the room.

In addition to the gestures which might be taught as part of the dialogue, we have those gestures which the students need to recognize but which they need not attempt to produce. Such gestures may be described and discussed. In this category we might find the gestures that accompany emotional expressions and the gestures that refer to the character or characteristics of others (gestures indicating stinginess, thievery, garrulity, for example). Because of the difficulty in knowing when to use them, students should not be expected to produce them; however, the introduction of such gestures provides excellent stimuli for classroom discussion. These discussions lead to useful comparisons between cultures and form a good bridge to work on connotation. Discussion of such gestures serves best, therefore, in an advanced class.

Since we all use gesture quite unconsciously, it often comes as an interesting surprise when others describe our habits to us. Similarly, the introduction of gesture into the language class always brings forth humour and lively discussion from the students. The enthusiasm and interest thus generated by dramatization and discussion often carries over into the learning of the linguistic patterns of the target language. Thus not only does the use of gesture provide the students with information valuable in itself, but it insures an initial stimulus which the language-teacher should be able to take advantage of.

TRY ONE
OF MY GAMES

JULIA DOBSON

Do you ever use games in your classroom? Many teachers of English as a second or foreign language who use games with children and teenagers—and even adults—are extremely pleased with the results. I myself have found that a good language game is a wonderful way to break the routine of classroom drill, because it provides fun and relaxation while remaining very much within the framework of language learning—and may even reinforce that learning. Furthermore, a good language game provides excellent entertainment outside the class; such games are particularly good at language clubs and parties. But what exactly *is* a good language game?

To me, a good language game is one that (*a*) requires little or no advance preparation, (*b*) is easy to play and yet provides the student with an intellectual challenge, (*c*) is short enough to occupy a convenient space during the class period, (*d*) entertains the students but does not cause the class to get out of control, and (*e*) requires no time-consuming correction of written responses afterward.

After much experimenting with language games, I have collected 15 of my own favorites that I believe fit all of the requirements set forth above. I have found that these games, which are PRIMARILY FOR TEEN-AGERS AND ADULTS but often for children as well, are always successful. So I would like to share these tested favorites of mine with you.

I have grouped the games according to the size of the class for which I think each is best suited. Some of the games should be used only with small groups, while others can be successfully played in classes ranging up to 80 students (but heaven forbid that you should have a class that large!). So, as simple guidelines for you in choosing a game, I have set up the following classifications: large classes (40–80 students), medium-size classes (20–40 students), small classes (6–20 students), and very small groups (up to 6). Actually, these numbers are arbitrary, but I hope they will help you choose a game suitable for your own class.

You will note that each game carries an explanatory subtitle indicating the "language" nature of the game—whether it deals with pronunciation, vocabulary, grammar, spelling, numbers, or rhymes. In addition, each game carries an indication of the level of English proficiency for which I consider the game best suited. These levels are assigned the following symbols:

> Elementary Level: A
> Intermediate Level: B
> Advanced Level: C

The indication of proficiency level appears in parentheses after the explanatory subtitle. Thus, the first game presented, called Category Bingo, is identified as a "Vocabulary and Spelling Game," with the symbols *B, C* indicating that it is best suited to intermediate and advanced classes. To decide which game you would like to try first, turn to the class-size division that best fits your situation. From the games given there, select one with a symbol that indicates the proficiency level of the group with which you wish to use it—*and* that you think your students will enjoy.

To create the greatest success with the game you choose, you may find the following general suggestions helpful:

1. Before introducing a game to a class, ask the students if they think they would enjoy this kind of activity. Children and teen-agers usually delight in playing a language game—and most adults do, too. Occasionally, however, an adult class may express absolutely no interest in the prospect of playing a game. If this should happen, it would probably be the better part of wisdom not to use a game at all with this group—at least at this time.

2. Choose a game that will allow as many of your students as possible to participate. If you have a large class, there are some games where a number of students will of necessity sit as the audience. But even here, there are ways of having members of the "audience" keep score and in other ways take part in the game. In small classes, you should make sure that every student has an active role in every game played. Incidentally, some of the games described in the sections for medium-size classes and large classes are equally successful in smaller groups.

3. Be sure that the game you select is within the range of your students' ability. Although I have found that all the language games given here are easy for students of English to play, you must remember that the students will be greatly challenged by the simple fact that they are playing the game in a language other than their mother tongue.

4. Do not play a game at the beginning of the class hour. Save the game for use in the middle or toward the end of the hour, when the students need a break from tiring drills.

5. Give the directions to the game very clearly, so that everyone under-

stands exactly how to play. You may want to play a few "trial" games first, just to make sure that everyone knows the rules.

6. Direct the game yourself. Always stand in front of the class so the students can see you as you serve as the leader or referee.

7. Be sure to follow the rules of the game exactly. If you do not "stick to the rules" but permit even one student to break a rule, you will establish an unfortunate precedent that can lead to hostility among the students. It is always best, therefore, to prevent all problems of this kind, to play the game according to the rules.

8. Keep the game well under control. Even though you want your students to have a good time, you cannot allow class discipline to disintegrate. Establish a pleasant but firm tone, in order that the game can both amuse and teach the students.

9. In team games, try to have an equal number of more proficient students and less proficient students on each team, so that the teams will be balanced. This not only prevents embarrassment on the part of the weaker students but also makes the contest far more exciting.

10. Always stop playing a game before the students are ready to quit. In other words, never play a game so long that it begins to bore the participants. Similarly, do not play one game too often, causing it to lose its novelty.

As you read the directions to the games that follow, do not be discouraged by the length of some of the directions. Long directions might make you think that the game is a complicated one, but actually, as I have said, I have found all of the games here quite easy for students to learn and to play.

LARGE CLASSES
40–80 STUDENTS

1. CATEGORY BINGO—VOCABULARY AND
   SPELLING GAME (B, C)

I recommend this game highly—even though you will have to take time in advance to prepare lists of words in various categories. Once you have done this, however, you can make copies of the lists and save them for future games.

Take the category *Fruit*, for instance, and list various kinds of fruits— as many fruits as you can think of. Similarly, make another list called *Vegetables* containing only the names of vegetables. Other suggested categories for lists are: *Animals, Furniture, Languages, Countries, Sports, Relatives, Musical Instruments, Flowers, Trees*, etc. Be sure, when making these lists, that each one has 16 or more entries.

Now you are ready to play the game with your students. Ask each student to draw 16 squares on a piece of paper, like the example below. Then choose one of your categories—*Animals*, for instance—and tell each student to fill in each of his 16 squares with the name of a different animal, working as rapidly as he can. Give the signal to begin and allow exactly ten minutes for everyone to fill in the squares. You should stress, of course, that the words must be spelled correctly to count.

At the end of the time limit, a student's paper might look like this:

cat	horse	fox	tiger
giraffe	lion	sheep	cow
elephant	wolf	zebra	bear
ostrich	dog	camel	monkey

Now call out a word at random from your master *Animal* list. Be sure to cross this word off your list as you announce it. If a student hears a word that appears on his paper, he should draw a line through the word.

Just as soon as a student has four words crossed out in a line going up and down, across, or diagonally (Bingo-fashion), he shouts, "Bingo!" Then he brings his paper to you, so you can check it with your master list and make sure that you called out the words he has crossed out—and that the words are spelled correctly. If everything is correct, he is declared the winner of that game, and you can begin a new Bingo game in another category.

If your students have a limited vocabulary to draw on for this game, you can write all of the items from one of your master lists on the blackboard. Explain the meaning of each word, then have each student select any 16 of the words on the board to fill in the squares on his paper. Then erase the words from the blackboard and play the game as outlined above.

2. SPELLING BEE–SPELLING GAME (A, B, C)

Before you plan to play this enjoyable game with your students, make a list of words that the class has studied. Include in the list words that are particularly challenging to spell. Occasionally, you may find words on your list that sound alike but are spelled differently, such as *flower* and *flour*. Be sure to put a little mark beside these words to remind yourself that you will have to define these words when you give them out in class.

When your list is complete, choose 20 students and divide them into two teams of equal number. Have one team stand on one side of the room and the other team on the opposite side, so the two teams are facing each other. The remaining students will serve as the audience.

Explain to the students that you will "give" a word from your list to the first student on Team I. He must spell the word aloud. If he spells it correctly, he remains standing. You will then give a different word to the first student on Team II to spell. If this student spells his word correctly, you will give a new word to the second student on Team I—and so on, with the students on the two teams alternating turns in spelling the words.

Each person has only one chance to spell his word. If he misspells it, he must leave his team and sit down. Even if he spells it correctly, he must sit down if he mispronounces one of the letters. For instance, if a student spelling the word *boy* pronounces the letter *b* as he would in his native language and not as it sounds in English—as *be* (as in the verb to *be*)— he is disqualified.

Whenever anyone makes an error in a word—either a spelling or a pronunciation error—the word goes to the next player on the other team. Thus, a sample game might go something like this:

YOU: **clock**

TEAM I
STUDENT A: **c-l-o-c-k**

YOU: **knife**

TEAM II
STUDENT A: **k-n-i-f-e**

YOU: **yellow**

TEAM I
STUDENT B: **y-e-l-o-w**

This student has made an error, so he must sit down.

YOU: **yellow**

Team II
STUDENT B: y-e-l-l-o-w

YOU: **think**

Team I
STUDENT C: **t-h-i-n-k**

                                etc.

When the last player on a team has had his turn, the play returns to the first student on the team. The game can continue until only one player is left standing. If you do not have enough time for this, you may want to set a time limit before the game begins. When the time limit is up, the team with the most members left standing is declared the winner.

3. WHAT WOULD YOU DO IF. . . ?—GRAMMAR GAME (B, C)

This is such an amusing game that your class will probably want to play it often.

Begin the game by dividing the class into two teams of equal number. Designate one as Team I and the other as Team II.[1] Then, write the following on the blackboard:

> *Team I* (or Reds)   *Team II* (or Blues)
> What would you do if . . . ? I would . . .

Now give everyone on Team I a slip of paper and explain that each person on the team must write an imaginative question beginning with *What would you do if . . . ?* For example, someone might write *What would you do if an elephant walked into this room?* Someone else might write *What would you do if you found a fly in your soup?* etc.

While Team I is following these directions, give everyone on Team II a piece of paper. Explain that each member of this team must write an imaginative sentence beginning *I would. . . .* For instance, someone could write *I would buy a purple umbrella.* Another person might write *I would sing a happy song*, etc.

When everyone has finished writing his assigned sentences, collect all of Team I's question in one box and all of Team II's answers in another.

---

[1] Here, and in any other "team" games, you might want to "personalize" the game by having each side quickly choose a team name, such as a color or an animal or a bird—or the name of a local sports team currently in the news. Thus the "Reds" could play against the "Blues," or the "Cats" against the "Dogs" or the "Hawks" against the "Eagles." With such names as these, the students would be using English here, too. But here, as elsewhere in conducting the games, you would have to make sure this aspect of the game did not get out of control—or did not use up too much game time.

You, or students on the team (or in the audience), can now draw and read first a question and then an answer. This game is sometimes called "Cross Questions and Crooked Answers"; the fun comes from the fact that the questions and answers are so utterly and ridiculously unrelated. Some of the results will be very funny indeed!

4. ALPHABET SOUP–VOCABULARY GAME (A, B, C)

This is a game that 14 students at a time can play, with the other students serving as an interested participating audience.

First, select 14 students and divide them into two teams of equal number. Then have the students on each team line up one behind the other to form two rows facing the class.

Once the rows are formed, assign each student a number from 1 to 14. The first student in line on one team will be 1, the second 2, the third student 3, and so on up through 7. The first student on the other team will be 8, the second 9, and so on up through 14. Be sure that everyone knows what his number is, because the numbers are an important part of the game.

Next, choose two students from the audience—one to act as timekeeper and the other to record on the chalkboard the points the teams make, in large figures that everyone can see. If possible, equip the timekeeper with a watch having a "second" hand, so he can time 20-second intervals. (If no watch is available, the timekeeper should count to 20 quietly and then "call time.")

Now explain that you will call out a number belonging to someone on Team I. Along with the number, you call out a letter of the alphabet (any letter except x, y, or z).

For instance, you might call out, "3–s." At this moment, the timekeeper begins timing and the student who is 3 must immediately step to one side of the line so the audience can see him. Just as fast as he can, he must name all of the words beginning with s that he can think of before his 20-second limit is up. For example, he might say *see, shoe, sing, sell, snake, slow, shine, say. . . .* Just after *say*, the timekeeper indicates that his time limit is up, so he steps back to his place in line. Since the contestant called out 8 correct words, he chalks up 8 points for his team. The recorder notes these points on the board under the name of the proper team.

Now it's the turn of the other team. You call out a number belonging to a member of that team, along with another letter, and the appropriate person steps out of line and gives as many words as he can beginning with the designated letter. Of course, it is very important for everyone on the team to be alert, so that the correct player steps out as promptly as possible to start giving the words. Otherwise, any confusion will make the team lose precious seconds.

As the game continues, the teams alternate turns until each player has had a chance to win points for his team. At the end of the contest, the scorekeeper adds us the points for each team and declares the team with the most points the winner.

You may want to prepare a list in advance for calling out the numbers and letters, so there will be no duplication and everyone will have one chance. Such a list might look like this:

TEAM I	TEAM II
5 – B	8 – N
4 – G	10 – J
1 – A	9 – C
6 – R	11 – H
3 – L	14 – U
2 – S	13 – T
7 – I	12 – E

Also, you may want to make the game a continuing contest in which two new teams, composed of students who have not yet had a chance to play, compete each day or each week. A student can keep a record of the winning teams along with the names of the team members, so that eventually the winning teams can play each other to determine the winner of the class championship.

MEDIUM-SIZE CLASSES
20–40 STUDENTS

1. FAST THINKING—VOCABULARY GAME (B, C)

Before you play this game with your class for the first time, draw each letter of the alphabet clearly on a piece of stiff cardboard or heavy paper. Each of these "cards" should be . . . [8½ x 11 inches], with the letter large enough to be clearly visible to students in the back of the room. After you complete the front of a card, indicate lightly in pencil on the back the letter that appears on the front. This allows you to identify the letter readily when you show the card to the class. (You can make two sets of these alphabet cards if you wish.)

Now shuffle the cards thoroughly, so letters do not appear in alphabetical order. Next, divide your class into two teams of equal number. Have one team sit on one side of the room and the other team on the other side. Appoint a captain for each team and have the captains seated in the front row, so that each captain can easily collect the cards that his team wins.

Explain that you will draw one card at a time and hold it up chest-high with the letter facing the group. As you draw a letter, you will call out the name of a "part of speech," such as noun, adjective, verb, adverb, etc.

The first person who shouts a word (only words that are not capitalized are accepted) in the stated category and beginning with the letter on the card wins the card for his team. You will then give this card to the appropriate team captain.

For instance, if you hold up a card with the letter *B* and call out "Adjective," perhaps someone on Team II will quickly shout "Beautiful." Since this is a good answer, you will hand the *B*-card to the captain of Team II.

Sometimes several players may call out a word almost simultaneously. You will have to establish who was first and what his word was. In case of a tie (students from both teams calling out correct responses at exactly the same time), no one will win the card, and you will keep it as a bonus to be given with the next card.

It may be that occasionally none of the students can think of a word beginning with the specified letter in the required category. When this happens, you return the letter to the stack and draw another one.

When all of the cards have been given out, or when you reach the end of the time limit established at the beginning of the game, the team holding the most cards is declared winner. (Be sure to save the cards for future games.)

2. CHAIN SPELLING—SPELLING GAME (A, B, C)

This is a game that provides enjoyable practice in spelling. It is played as follows:

With the students standing beside their desks, have one student begin the game by pronouncing a word and spelling it. The next student must pronounce and spell a word that begins with the last letter of the first word spelled, and so forth.

For example, the first student might say, "Car—c-a-r." Then the next player must think of a word beginning with the final letter of *car*, which is *r*; so he might say "Read—r-e-a-d." The third student might say "Dog—d-o-g," and so on.

If a player cannot think of a word, or begins a word with the wrong letter, or misspells his word, or pronounces a letter in the word incorrectly, he must sit down and is out of the game. The game continues until only one student is left standing. If your students are fairly advanced, you may wish to limit the words to a special category, such as nouns, verbs, adjectives, etc. This makes the game even more challenging.

3. BUZZ–NUMBER GAME (A, B, C)

This game is always a great success and provides the students with excellent practice with numbers.

According to the rules of the game, 7, or any *multiple* of 7 (such as 14 or 35), or any number containing 7 (such as 17 or 47) is "forbidden" and must not be said during the course of counting.

One player begins by saying "One," the next player says "Two," the next player, "Three," and so on up through six. Then the player whose turn it is to say "Seven" must say the word *Buzz* instead. The game continues with the next player saying "Eight," the next "Nine," and so forth.

A sample game might go something like this:

STUDENT A:	One	STUDENT J:	Ten
STUDENT B:	Two	STUDENT K:	Eleven
STUDENT C:	Three	STUDENT L:	Twelve
STUDENT D:	Four	STUDENT M:	Thirteen
STUDENT E:	Five	STUDENT N:	**Buzz**
STUDENT F:	Six	STUDENT O:	Fifteen
STUDENT G:	**Buzz**	STUDENT P:	Sixteen
STUDENT H:	Eight	STUDENT Q:	**Buzz**
STUDENT I:	Nine	STUDENT R:	Eighteen

The game should be played as fast as possible—which means that the students have to think quickly. If a player completely forgets to say "Buzz" at the right moment, he is out of the game. Even if he starts to say "Sev-," for instance, and quickly adds "Buzz," he is out of the game.

Sometimes a player will mistakenly say "Buzz" for a number that does not contain a seven or is not a multiple of seven. When this happens, he, too, is eliminated from the game. In addition, any player who miscounts is out of the game. For example, if Student A says "Thirty-one," Student B says "Thirty-two," and Student C says "Thirty-four," Student C is out of the game.

When a player is eliminated from the game, the next player begins with "One" and the game starts over. If you ask your students to stand beside their desks while playing the game, you can easily handle the problem of eliminating players who make mistakes by simply asking them to sit down. The game continues until only one player remains standing. He then is declared the winner.

After your students have played the game a great deal, they may reach the 70s—where each number (71, 72, etc.) must be rendered as "Buzz." In later games you can vary the challenge by having either 4 or 6 as the "forbidden" number. Incidentally, even though "Buzz" can be played to good advantage in classes containing 20–40 students, it is also an excellent game in smaller classes.

4. VOCABULARY RACE—VOCABULARY GAME (B, C)

This game revolves around quick thinking. Have one student come to the front of the room and tell him to think of any three-letter word. When he has selected a word, he calls on someone in the class and announces his word clearly. The student called on must then give a word beginning with each of the three letters within a certain time limit or else he will have to take the first student's place in front of the class.

For example, if the first student says, "John Wilson—man," then John Wilson might say in rapid succession "Me—apple—new," within the time limit. Since John Wilson has won the race against the time limit, the student standing in front of the class has to think of another word. He calls out, "Mary Smith—old." Mary Smith says "Orange—little. . . ." But she cannot think of a third word in time, so she has to go to the front of the class.

To handle the problem of timing, you can ask one student to act as timekeeper and he can quietly start counting to ten just as soon as a student's name is called. If the student cannot think of three appropriate words by the time the timekeeper reaches ten, he loses the race.

It may be that someone in the room has a watch with a "second" hand; in this case a certain number of seconds can be established as the time limit, making timing considerably easier. You will, of course, adjust the time limit to the ability of your class. If you would like to make the game especially challenging, you can retain the same time limit but play the game with four- or even five-letter words.

You may find when playing the game that the student who stands in front of the class has a hard time thinking of a word with the specified number of letters. To avoid this problem, you can prepare a number of slips of paper in advance with a word written on each one. Simply hand one of these pieces of paper to the student and he will call on someone, reading the word that appears on the paper.

SMALL CLASSES
6–20 STUDENTS

1. PRONUNCIATION CONTEST—PRONUNCIATION GAME (A)

You have to prepare this game in advance but the preparations are really quite simple. They are as follows:

Make a list of the words that the students have studied but which they often mispronounce. If you are teaching Spanish-speaking students, for instance, you might include the following words in your list, since they pose special problems for Spanish speakers:

ice
very
three
ship
jet

If you are teaching students of another language background, you will, of course, choose words THEY find difficult to pronounce.

Once you have listed the words, print each word on a card. Then, in class, divide your students into two teams of equal number. Have one team stand on one side of the room and the other team on the opposite side.

Explain that you will walk over to the first student on one team and show him a card containing a word. When the student sees the word, he must say it aloud. (He is given only one chance to pronounce the word.)

If he pronounces the word correctly, he remains standing. If he mispronounces it, he must sit down—and you show the same word to the first student on the other team. If this player pronounces it correctly, you give a different word to the next player on the first team, and so on.

The game can continue until only one player is left. This player will then be declared the winner of the contest. If there is not enough time for a lengthy contest, you can set a time limit (such as five minutes) at the beginning of the game. Then, when the time is up, the team with the larger number of players still standing is declared the winner.

2. CLASSROOM "TWENTY QUESTIONS"—GRAMMAR GAME (B, C)

This is an excellent guessing game in which one person chooses a visible object in the room and the other students try to guess what it is by asking questions.

Suppose that you, for instance, begin the game by mentally selecting a green hair ribbon that one of the girl students is wearing. Tell the students that you have chosen an object and that each student in turn can ask one question about it. You will give a complete answer to the question.

After several questions have been asked, the person whose turn is next may think he knows what the object is. In this case, he can ask, "Is it a (the) . . . ? If he has guessed correctly, he wins the game and becomes the person who chooses the object in the second game. You will need someone to keep count of the number of questions asked. If no one has guessed the object after twenty questions, the person who selected the object wins the game and can choose another object for the second game.

The game might go something like this if the green hair ribbon is the object to be guessed:

STUDENT A: Is it as large as the map on the wall?
ANSWER: No, it isn't as large as the map.

STUDENT B: Is it made of metal or cloth?
ANSWER: It's made of cloth.

STUDENT C: Does it belong to a student?
ANSWER: Yes, it belongs to a student.

STUDENT D: Is it in front of me or behind me?
ANSWER: It's in front of you.

STUDENT E: Is it square?
ANSWER: No, it isn't square.

STUDENT F: Is it cheap or expensive?
ANSWER: It's cheap.

STUDENT G: What color is it?
ANSWER: It's green.

STUDENT H: Is it Mary's hair ribbon?
ANSWER: Yes, it is. You've won the game!

At this point, Student H comes to the front of the room and mentally selects a new visible object for the next game.

If your students are quite advanced, you may wish to play the original game of "Twenty Questions." In this form of the game, only questions that take a Yes or No answer are permitted, and objects not visible in the room may be chosen. Another variation of the game is to select a famous person, living or dead, to be guessed, instead of an object. This lends even more interest to the game.

3. GOSSIP—PRONUNCIATION AND GRAMMAR GAME (A, B, C)

Have your students sit in a circle. Whisper a phrase or sentence rapidly to one student. He then whispers what he has just heard (or thinks he heard) to the person on his right. This student repeats what he just heard to the third student, and so on all around the circle.

When the phrase or sentence reaches the last student, he says aloud the phrase or sentence as he heard it. Both you and the students may be surprised to see how much the phrase or sentence changed as it went around the group.

You can now begin a new game by having another person think of a new phrase or sentence. Remember to stress that in passing the utterance from one person to another, it must be said rapidly and ONLY ONCE. Otherwise, the game loses much of its fun.

4. SIMON SAYS—GRAMMAR GAME (B, C)

This is a good group game that provides your students with practice in forming and following commands.

The students can sit in their usual seats. Explain that one person will serve as Simon. (If you are introducing the game for the first time, you should serve as Simon for one or two games.)

Simon will give a series of commands, such as:

> Simon says, "Put your left hand up."
> Simon says, "Point to the blackboard."
> Simon says, "Clap your hands."

The person who is Simon will do all of the things he asks the group to do, and they will imitate him as he does each thing. Then, to trick the group (and this is the point of the game), Simon gives a command without first saying "Simon says." As before, Simon performs the act called for—but this time the group should NOT imitate him—they should not do anything at all. Anyone who does imitate Simon loses the game and must become the new Simon. If several persons are caught doing something that Simon did not say, Simon chooses one of them to take his place, and the game begins again.

You should constantly encourage the students to play the game fast to make it really enjoyable. A sample might go like this:

SIMON:　Simon says, "Nod your head."

GROUP:　Everyone nods his head.

SIMON:　Simon says, "Point to the door."

GROUP:　Everyone points to the door.

SIMON:　Clap your hands.

GROUP:　One student claps his hands. The other students sit still. At this point, the student who clapped his hands becomes Simon.

A variation of the game, making it more of a challenge, is to have Simon purposely confuse the players by giving the group a command which he does not obey. In other words, Simon might announce, "Simon says, 'Hands on your head' "—but at the same time he puts his hands on his shoulders. The students, of course, should do what Simon SAYS, not what he DOES.

VERY SMALL GROUPS
UP TO 6

1. WORD PSYCHOLOGY—VOCABULARY GAME (A, B, C)

Have the players sit at their desks in a circle or semicircle. Announce that during the game everyone will participate in the same rhythmic action pattern, which you will demonstrate as follows:

First, strike the top of your desk lightly twice with the palms of your hands; raise your hands and clap them twice; then snap your fingers twice. Do all three steps rhythmically and in equal time, and when you complete them, begin the pattern over again without a loss of the rhythmic beat. (It is best when playing the game for the first time to establish a relatively slow beat. As the players become more proficient, you can gradually adopt a faster beat.)

Once the students have mastered this pattern in unison, you can explain that everyone goes through the first two steps together. Then, during the third step, when everyone snaps his fingers, the first player says a word aloud—any word that comes to his mind.

The pattern begins over again; and the next player, striking the desk and clapping his hands in unison with the other players, must say another word aloud as he snaps his fingers. If he loses the beat of the rhythm as he says the word, or repeats a word that another player has said, or cannot think of any word at all, he is out of the game. The object of the game, thus, is to say a new word whenever it is your turn without losing the rhythm of the game.

You and your students will be surprised to see what fun this game can be, because frequently a player will lose the beat or repeat a word or say something so funny that the next player will not be able to think of a new word. One by one the players will be eliminated until one person wins the game. If your students are advanced, you can establish word categories that limit the words in one game to nouns, words in the next game to verbs, etc. This makes the game even more challenging.

2. FUN WITH RHYMES—RHYMING GAME (A, B, C)

Before you introduce the game, write down a list of words that the students know. These should be words that have rhyming counterparts also familiar to the students.

Now tell your students that you will read a word from the list. The first player must give a word that rhymes with the word you have given.

The second player must give another word that rhymes with the word you gave—and so on, around the class. If a player cannot think of a word or if he gives one that does not rhyme, or makes any other sort of mistake, he is out of the game. At this point, you give a new word, and the game continues until there is one winner.

A sample game might go like this:

YOU:	though
STUDENT A:	know
STUDENT B:	show
STUDENT C:	sew
STUDENT D:	_____

Since Student D cannot think of another word that rhymes, he is out of the game, and you begin with a new word as follows:

YOU:	tree
STUDENT E:	he
STUDENT F:	key
STUDENT A:	see

This game can turn into an excellent contest if your students have good vocabularies, but it is fun for beginning students as well.

3. GHOST–SPELLING GAME (B, C)

Have the students sit in a circle or semicircle. Explain that the object of this spelling game is to avoid being the person who completes a word as one letter is added to another letter around the group.

One student (number 1) begins the game by thinking of a word. (Any word is acceptable except proper nouns.) When the student has a word, he announces THE FIRST LETTER of the word. (Perhaps he thinks of *books* and announces *B*.) The next student (number 2) thinks of a word beginning with the letter just announced. He tries to discard all words that might end on him as the game progresses. (Say, for example, that six are playing. *Blow* would be a good word, for it would end on number 4. *Babies* would end on number 6. *Believe* would end on number 1 in the second go-around. But *beautify*, with eight letters, would in the second go-around end on number 2. So number 2 avoids *beautify*.)

For example, the game might go like this if six students are playing:

FIRST STUDENT:	p (thinking of *pie*)
SECOND STUDENT:	l (thinking of *place*)

THIRD STUDENT: a (thinking of *play*)

FOURTH STUDENT: n (thinking of *plane* and forgetting that p-l-a-n spells *plan*.)

Because the fourth student has ended a word, he becomes "one third of a ghost." The game begins again, this time with the fifth student announcing the first letter of his new word. The sixth student continues and is followed by the first student, etc.

If during the game any player completes a word of three letters or more, he is automatically "one third of a ghost"; if he completes a second word, he becomes "two thirds of a ghost"; if he completes a third word, he is a "full ghost"—and is out of the game. The game continues until everyone becomes a "full ghost" except one player, who is declared the winner.

There are two additional rules that you should keep in mind. First, in this version of "Ghost," players may make two-letter words without penalty. For instance, if the first player says "s," and the second player says "o," the second player does not become "a third of a ghost." A three-letter or longer word, however, gets an immediate penalty—changes the player into "a third of a ghost."

The second rule is that if a player cannot think of a word containing the letters he has been given—or if he doubts that the preceding player is actually spelling a word—he can say to the preceding player, "I challenge you." The preceding player must then announce the word he had in mind. If the player has in mind a real word and is spelling it correctly, then the person who challenged him becomes "a third of a ghost"—or increases his ghostly status by a third. If the player challenged is bluffing and has no word, or if he has a word but is misspelling it, then HE becomes "a third of a ghost."

This game can be very enjoyable, and students will find it an excellent way to practice spelling and in other ways to familiarize themselves with English words.

If you would like to investigate the subject of language games further, you might want to consult a collection called *Games for Second Language Learning*, by Gertrude Nye Dorry. This is a small 58-page paperback published in 1966 by McGraw-Hill Book Company, 330 West 42nd Street, New York, New York 10036. It costs a little over one dollar. There are other collections of language games, but I have found that these are mainly for native speakers and thus are not suitable for our purposes. In any case, you can have a good start with the games suggested in this article. Eventually, you may even invent a language game of your own! . . .

PICTURES FOR PRACTICE

CAROL J. KREIDLER

Modern language pedagogy has developed the audio-lingual approach in which the emphasis is on developing the students' abilities to understand, speak, read, and write the language. The audio-lingual approach to language teaching is characterized by several statements which are undoubtedly well-known to you. The statement which is most important for own discussion here today is "Language is a set of habits." O'Connor and Twaddell make the following statement regarding initial stages of school-learning of a foreign language.

> The work of the descriptive analysts has revealed the complexity of language habits, and we are nowadays aware of the enormous amount of practice needed to make these recognitions and variations and selections truly automatic and habitual and usable. When a FL habit differs structurally from a conflicting NL habit, hundreds of repetitions (simple repetitions, and repetitions within variation and selection practice) are needed to form and confirm the desired new habit. Indeed, the strategy of planning a FL class is precisely the organizing of classroom time to assure the necessary repetitions of the essential patterns, without attention-killing boredom.[1]

If this, then, is our task, any aid which helps us to accomplish it is most welcome.

There are a variety of aids available to the classroom teacher which will both add variety to the class and relieve the teacher of the necessity of talking all the time. Among these aids are the tape recorder, record player, movies, charts, pictures, film strips, puppets, songs, games, flannel boards, chalkboards, and so on. As the title of this paper implies, we will limit ourselves to a discussion of the use of still pictures—those that are commercially available or easily made by the teacher.

The most effective practice for the automatic control of language is

---

[1] "Intensive Training for an Oral Approach in Language Teaching," *The Modern Language Journal* (St. Louis: National Federation of Modern Language Teaching Association), XLIV, No. 2, Part 2 (February, 1960), 5.

varied, fast-moving, and related to a situation or environment. The problem of creating interest while drilling rapidly in real situations is a considerable one. Since pictures are a recognized convention for an actual situation, they can provide a visual cue which will call to the student's mind the situation to which he should respond.

Maxine Buell suggests three important contributions pictures make to language teaching. First, pictures are practical

> . . . in helping connect new and unfamiliar terms with the ideas or concepts symbolized by these terms. Pictures help make concrete what might otherwise remain verbal abstraction for the student . . . Pictures help us avoid verbalism in our teaching; they give reality to what we are explaining. Second, pictures help the teacher suggest contexts which are outside the classroom setting. Some contexts are very difficult to recreate in words alone, and, if the teacher does manage to recreate them, it is only with the loss of valuable time. The third advantage follows closely. Pictures help the teacher change contexts rapidly and easily.[2]

Pictures, then, can be of help to the teacher in the various segments of the class time devoted to language teaching. Most of us would agree that class time is divided into two parts: presentation and practice. The introduction or presentation of a new point takes comparatively little class time, although it may take a great deal of teacher time to plan. The use of pictures in presenting a new structure, a pronunciation point, a vocabulary contrast or context, a situation for a reading selection or composition can make the following exercise much more meaningful and often unambiguous.

The practice segment of the class time is not only the larger segment, but also much harder work for both teacher and student. Practice may be divided into two types: drill and testing, both of which are important at various stages of learning the language. *Drill* is the rapid, quick-moving practice of a teacher-determined point or contrast—practice which will lead to the automatic handling of that point. Substitution drills and transformation or conversion drills are examples of the *drill-*type of practice. *Testing* is the practice of previously drilled points—a cumulative practice. In testing practice, the student is asked to call on all that he has been taught to react to the situation. Telling a story or writing a composition or some uses of dialogues are examples of testing practice. Pictures may be used either as the cue which provides the stimulus for rapid drill or as the context for testing practice.

In the presentation segment of the lesson and in the testing aspect of

[2] Maxine Guin Buell, "Picture Exercises for Oral Drill of Structure Patterns," *Language Learning*, III, 1 and 2 (January–June, 1950), 14.

practice, the use of pictures has been widespread for some time. Posters and wall-charts, in addition to providing classroom decoration, can set the context for introducing a dialogue, and they can stimulate oral and written composition. Movies and filmstrips add a variety of developed situations which can stimulate composition. A series of drawings on the chalkboard can stimulate story-telling. Most of us have made use of these aids in our teaching. It is in the area of pictures for drill practice that much less has been developed for teaching English to speakers of other languages. It is this type of practice—drill—that I would like to emphasize.

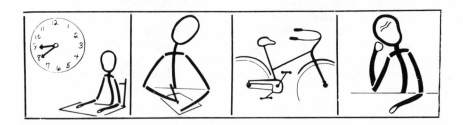

Let us see now how pictures might be used in class time to relieve "attention-killing boredom." Since the teaching of language involves teaching the students to handle the basic grammatical structures, to use the proper vocabulary items in those structures, and to pronounce those vocabulary items well, I would like to discuss these parts of language teaching and how pictures can be used as an aid for teaching them. The emphasis will be on drill-type practice, but I will mention the use of pictures in presentation and the testing-type practice.

THE TEACHING OF PRONUNCIATION

Focus on pronunciation begins when a pronunciation point is determined by the teacher. This point will probably be presented and practiced in contrast with another sound. The teacher will want to practice the contrast in minimal pairs, other single words, and then in larger utterances. Let us assume we wish to practice /i/ contrasted with /iy/. Pictures might be used in the following ways in this part of the lesson:[3]

For presentation the teacher holds up a picture of a *ship* and a *sheep* saying, *It's a ship, It's a sheep,* or *It's a pick, It's a peak.* This has the advantage of assuring the student that there is a difference which he must master.

In the teaching of pronunciation the teacher spends a great deal of

[3] All items used as examples in presentation or drills are picturable.

time in having the student recognize the sound and in guiding the student's imitation of a model. At this point pictures do not play a large part in class activity. When the class progresses to the testing phase, the production of the sounds without the teacher as a constant model, pictures can be of help.

Assuming the identification structure is already mastered, the teacher might select a number of items with the contrasting /i/ and /iy/. With the teacher flashing the picture, the students respond, *It's a sheep, It's a ship, It's a peak, It's a key, It's a bridge, It's a pick, It's a fish, It's a tree, It's a pig, It's a three.*

If the contrast is taught at a later stage, the structure might be a more advanced one:

> You must have seen a pig   before.
> sheep
> key
> bridge
> pick
> peak
> fish
> tree
> ship

After a number of verbs have been introduced, /iy/ and /i/ may be tested with pictures of action. Notice how these pictures are handled. The cue is written on the back of the card. Moving the pictures from the back of the pile to the front allows the teacher to know which picture the class is looking at without craning his neck. For example:

> He is fixing the radio.
> playing pingpong.
> reading the newspaper.
> sleeping.
> feeding the dog.
> stealing the monkey.
> crossing the street.
> drinking milk.
> swimming.
> singing a song.

We all agree that review is an extremely important part of our work. Pictures can be used to provide a quick review of sound contrast; those pictures used originally to present the contrasts can be used in a quick-moving exercise using the identification structure for review of the sounds at any time after they have been taught.

THE TEACHING OF VOCABULARY

Lessons in vocabulary no longer take the form of definition-centered explanations. The audio-lingual approach takes into account three aspects in the presentation of vocabulary: the item, the structure, and the context. Each item is presented in a structure, and if possible, the structure is presented in a context.

Let us assume that the area we wish to present and practice is food. The context is "having a meal"—in this case, breakfast. The structure we will be practicing is: *I like coffee; I would like a cup of coffee*—count nouns or countables versus mass nouns or uncountables. Much of the learning that takes place here is the learning of the names of the items. We have: orange juice, cereal, fruit, coffee, milk, eggs, toast, etc. Drill exercises might consist of flashing the pictures with the structure set. For example:

I like oranges.	*Then:* I would like a glass of orange juice.
milk.	glass of milk.
coffee.	cup of coffee.
fruit.	dish of fruit.
cereal.	bowl of cereal.
toast.	slice or piece of toast.
cheese.	slice or piece of cheese.

then mixing the items forcing a choice between:

I'd like some oranges. *and* I'd like a glass of orange juice.

Testing might consist of having students *tell* what they have had for breakfast, holding up the picture at the same time.

Items such as adjectives are often more easily presented and drilled with their opposites:

A is	large.	B is	small.
	long.		short.
	fast.		slow.
	wide.		narrow.
	tall.		short.
	old.		young.
	new.		old.
	cheap.		expensive.
	wet.		dry.

and later:

A is happier	than B.
B is sadder	than A.
A is heavier	than B.
B is lighter	than A.
A is fatter	than B.
B is thinner	than A.
A is thicker	than B.
B is thinner	than A.

THE TEACHING OF GRAMMAR

There are two types of commercially available pictures which can be used for drilling: context-oriented pictures and structure-oriented pictures. Context-oriented pictures[4] are those with a context set by the picture, such as a home scene, beach scene, or sports scenes. Each picture includes several objects, or actions, or relationships which may be used to practice several types of structures. Structure-oriented pictures consist of actions, objects, or relationships also. In one set of commercially-available aids the pictures are placed in chart form[5] in groups of nine to twelve items chosen for the types of structures they will drill. In the other set of aids,[6] the pictures are on individual cards, color-keyed by grammatical category, but flexible enough to allow the teacher to construct his own drills. Although these pictures may be used for vocabulary or pronunciation drill, usually the items pictured are of such high frequency that the most effective use is for drilling points of grammar. Any of these pictures could be drawn by the teacher or taken from magazines.

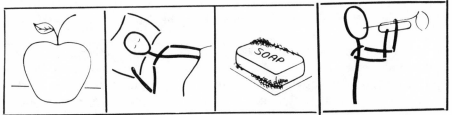

[4] *The ABC American English Charts* with *Teacher's Manual* (New York: American Book Co., 1960).
[5] Robert Lado and Charles C. Fries, et al., *English Pattern Practice Charts* (Ann Arbor, Michigan: University of Michigan Press, 1958).
[6] Carol J. Kreidler and M. Beatrice Sutherland, *Flash-Pictures: A Set of 252 Cards Used as an Aid to Teachers of English as a Foreign Language* (Ann Arbor, Michigan: 1963) (Distributed by Follett's Michigan Bookstore).

The pictures of adjectives with their opposites might also be used to present negatives. Let us take a picture indicating a strong man and a weak man. Presentation might be set up as follows: The teacher indicates the strong man and says, "He's strong." The teacher indicates the weak man and says, "He's weak. He isn't strong." The teacher indicates the strong man and says, "He's strong. He isn't weak."

There are a great many kinds of exercises which lend themselves to drill-type practice with pictures. These exercises include substitution and transformation or conversion, with all their variations. I would like to emphasize that the order of the structures is not necessarily the order in which I would teach them. A much more complicated structure may precede a much simpler one.

One of the most frequently used types of exercise is the substitution drill. In this the teacher sets the pattern by giving approximately three substitutions in the pattern, encouraging the students to join in when they feel confident of the pattern. The exercise would work like this:

> He's a doctor.
> dentist.
> musician.
> farmer.
> waiter.
> policeman.
> mechanic.
> clerk.

The number of new responses the teacher tries to elicit in such a drill without reviewing the items depends on the ability of the class, their familiarity with the vocabulary item, and the length of the response desired.

This substitution exercise works in the same way whether a chart or individual pictures are used. Any chart, however, is limited to the number of contexts illustrated. If there are twelve illustrations on one chart, one need not use all twelve in a drill, but it is impossible to use more than twelve contexts. Individual pictures, if there is a large enough collection, allow for more, varied contexts in which to practice a pattern.

A good set of pictures can be used to practice quite a number of structures from the simple pattern which was just demonstrated to the more complex ones. For example:

> He's waiting for the bus now.
> driving the car
> cutting the cake
> setting the table

at a later stage:

> Did he pick up the magazine yesterday?
> ride the bike
> shop

still later:

> I would like to watch TV, but I don't have time.
> wash my clothes,
> hold the baby,

and even later:

> Have you eaten lunch yet? Yes, I just ate lunch.
> bought a coat   bought a coat.
> written a letter   wrote a letter.
> thrown away the paper   threw it away.

It is even possible to get a fast-moving drill going by using the pictures of a boy and girl. These can be drawn on the chalkboard more easily. Standing between the two faces (*he* ♂ and *she* ♀) and using gestures, the teacher can practice all of the pronouns. The gestures should always be from the point of view of the student. Thus, when the teacher points to himself, the students should respond *you*. When the teacher points to an individual student, the student responds *I*.

> I'm working.
> He's
> She's
> They're
> We're
> You're

Another type of exercise in which pictures or drawings are useful is the transformation or conversion drill.

> He's a doctor;   he's not a dentist.
> dentist;   musician.
> musician;   farmer.
> farmer;   waiter.
> waiter;   mechanic.

Three symbols on the chalkboard can also help in the conversion drill. These are: + affirmative, − negative, and ? question. Then the picture may be held close to the appropriate symbols, forming a combination of substitution and conversion drills. Also verbal cues may be supplied: *walk, drive, fly, eat, practice English, sing, dance, laugh.*

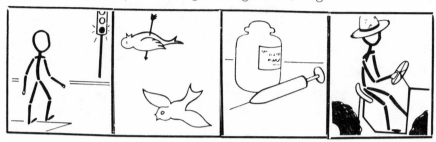

The context-oriented pictures that I mentioned can be used for practicing verbs in answer to such questions as *What is he doing? What does he do? What did he do? What has he done?* Such pictures also often indicate relationships, so prepositions are easily practiced with them. One definite advantage of this type of picture is the cultural advantage it provides. It is much easier to show a picture of a supermarket than to try to explain one.

Testing practice with pictures often takes the form of story-telling or writing compositions. Pictures can be used to stimulate the imagination of the student. A series of familiar pictures from which the student constructs a story can also be a help. Such pictures can give the student cues to which some structures may be attached. In other words, he has a "home base" from which to work.

For example, we might have the students tell about John and Mary's date. Pictures can be lined up in the chalk tray, and various structures can be used in writing about the pictures. Depending on the level of the student, more complicated patterns might be elicited.

This is John. He's a student. That is Mary. She's a nurse. John is handsome. Mary is beautiful. (Of course, the students might write: John is a handsome student and Mary is a beautiful nurse.) John called up Mary. He asked, "Would you go to the movies with me tonight?" Mary said, "Yes, thank you." In the evening they went downtown by bus. They went to a movie. After the movie they danced. They went home by taxi.

It is also a common practice to use a context-oriented picture for composition. In addition to some of the commercially available picture books for compositions, it is possible to use certain comic strips which do not use captions. Donald Duck, Henry, and Ferd'nand are examples of some of the cartoons which might be used.

Pictures are fun to make and one receives a great deal of satisfaction from using his own creations. The often heard statement, "I can't draw," has little importance. If the essence of the object is caught, this is most important. As long as one is willing to laugh at himself, he need not worry about his drawing ability.

There are, however, several criteria for pictures which one must keep in mind when selecting or drawing those which are to be used for drill. First of all, they must be relatively free from ambiguity. The picture should call to the student's mind one quickly recognizable situation. The meaning of each of the pictures must be established the first time that it is used, and the correct response must be obtained each time the picture is flashed, *if* quick-moving, smooth drill is to result.

Second, pictures for drill must be easy to see and to handle. If the pictures being used are in chart form they must be placed so that all of the students can see them. A pointer will allow the teacher to indicate a part of the chart without obscuring the view of the students. If the pictures are individual ones, they should be drawn or mounted on a card which can be seen by the whole class and still manipulated easily.

The third characteristic of a good picture for drill is that it is relatively free from cultural misinterpretation. This characteristic is probably more important for pictures which are used in teaching in other countries. There are stories of the misinterpretation of pictures because of the colors used or the shapes of buildings. What passes for a church in the Western countries would not be the typical kind of building for religious services in the Far East or in Moslem countries. In most of the classrooms in this country, the student is a resident of the cultural community and familiar with most of the concepts we would be picturing. If he is not familiar with them, he must learn them.

Drill such as the kind I have tried to illustrate is most useful at the earlier stages of learning a new language. It is in the early stages where correct habits must be formed. Other habits can then build on the solid foundation of these correct habits. However, for quite a while in the learning of the language remedial drill will be necessary. In testing practice a teacher may discover several students having trouble with a particular structure. This then is the point at which drill is necessary again. Pictures can help make this drill more meaningful and add variety to the class hour.

THE LANGUAGE LABORATORY:
Uses and Misuses

KENNETH CROFT

A LITTLE BIT OF HISTORY

As most of you are aware, the concept of the language laboratory which we have today is not very old. Most of our experience with labs has been gained within the last fifteen years or so—since World War II. Our experience with audio devices, however, dates back a little farther. Before and during World War II, some of you may have had occasion to use facilities at your own school for listening to language records or for practicing language lessons with dictaphones or soundscribers.

The notion of the language laboratory certainly didn't loom large in those days probably because the playback and recording equipment was rather primitive compared with what we have nowadays. The low fidelity of the recordings severely limited their usefulness in foreign language study. My opinion at the time, as I recall, was that recording and listening devices available were useful for teaching intonation, but that was about all.

With the coming of high fidelity sound reproduction, the language laboratory began to take shape. During the last ten years or so there has been a virtual boom in the manufacture of lab equipment—tape recorders, headsets, microphones, recording tape, and soundproofing. There have been other markets for the same kinds of equipment, and because of the intense competition among manufacturers, we now have unusually fine and reasonably priced lab equipment.

The language laboratory as we know it today did not develop overnight. The term "laboratory" at the present time gives us a mental picture of several rows of separate compartments or booths, each enclosed on three sides to about eye level; the students can sit down at one of these booths, put on headphones, and practice a language lesson in semiprivacy. Also, the language laboratory is usually equipped with a console which can serve as a source for one or more programs; and the console ordinarily serves as a monitoring station for the teacher. This is the general picture, the result of many compromises, much experimentation, and ten to twelve years of experience.

Some of you may have seen earlier models of language laboratories, say, around 1950, which were much more elaborate than this. There were labs, for example, set up with fully enclosed booths—similar to telephone booths, but roomier—and each was equipped with two tape recorders: one for listening and the other for recording. Headsets were not necessary in this arrangement because the prevoiced material coming from the speaker of one machine was recorded along with the student's responses on the other machine.

The biggest boost to the popularity of the language laboratory seems to have come after the development of the binaural or stereo type of recorder. This kind of machine made lab operations much simpler and reduced the requirements for equipment and space. The binaural recorder gives the student prerecorded cues or stimuli to respond to and also records the student's responses to these cues or stimuli. Only one tape is needed for this purpose. The machine uses two tracks—the upper half of the tape for the cues, which can not be erased, and the lower half of the tape for the student's responses, which can be erased. We show the two tracks in the diagram below.

The shaded areas indicate voiced material.

CUES:
RESPONSES:

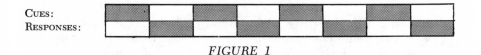

FIGURE 1

When the student gets to the end of his lesson, he can then listen to his own performance which has been recorded on the lower track, and the teacher can listen to it, too. The tape is reusable; the student's old responses are automatically erased each time he records new ones.

LITERATURE ON THE LANGUAGE LABORATORY

There's a sizable body of literature on language laboratories—entire books, chapters in books, and hundreds of articles on the subject. Almost every issue of the *Modern Language Journal* has an article on some aspect of the language laboratory. I made no attempt to review all the literature before this conference. I reviewed some of it and made up a list of recent items which will guide you to fairly detailed treatments of laboratory planning, types of equipment, and using equipment to best advantage. This is the bibliography at the end of the paper. Virtually all the literature has to do with the teaching of foreign languages to American students, but the experience, the advice, and the conclusions, to a large extent, are equally applicable to the teaching of English to speakers of other languages.

Chapter 17 of Lado's book (item 7 on the bibliography) provides a good summary of general laboratory practices. Hutchinson's survey (item

6) deals with current practices in high school labs; his book also contains a glossary of laboratory terms and an excellent bibliography up to
1961. The Hayes pamphlet (item 3) is especially useful for planning and
selecting equipment for the laboratory according to the requirements and
standards of different schools. Stack's book (item 9) describes and illustrates a large variety of drills and exercises and tests for use in the lab,
and it also provides a good deal of information about procedures in
operating a lab; this book, I should mention, is undergoing an extensive
revision, and a second edition will appear, I think, sometime this year.
I will refer to some of these publications again and mention others later.
One very important matter which needs still more attention than that
given in the literature is the making of master tapes. This is something,
of course, that requires a good deal of practice. I suppose the best
guidance is found in the leaflets supplied by the manufacturers of tape
recorders; but the voicing and recording of good master tapes is no
simple chore, and lab directors and supervisors should have thorough
training in this aspect of lab operations.

TYPES OF LABORATORIES

Lado defines the language laboratory as a special room for students to
practice with sound equipment—a place where students get audiolingual
practice outside of class. The amount and types of equipment are not
specified. The equipment may range from nothing more than one simple
playback machine and some chairs to the complete package type of
laboratory offered by some manufacturers with an elaborate console, an
overhead projector, synchronized tape and filmstrip apparatus, every
booth equipped with a binaural machine, etc.

Binaural machines, of course, make the lab more versatile. These
machines make possible about every kind of lab activity that's been
devised. Stack describes two modes of operation in the laboratory—the
broadcast mode and the library mode; these in part depend on the
equipment available.

The *broadcast* mode refers to activities in which all the students of a
class are doing the same thing at the same time—that is, responding to
the same cues which come from a tape played at the console. The individual booths may have nothing more than headphones and a selector
switch; the students select the program desired, listen to the cues, and
speak into the air. With a microphone, together with headphones, in
each booth and appropriate wiring to the console, a monitoring system
can be set up, so the teacher can hear the students' performance and give
guidance on individual problems or difficulties. If the headphones are
audioactive, the students can hear their own responses.

The *library* mode refers to the activities of a student working alone at
his own speed. Of course, a laboratory equipped for the library mode can

do everything the broadcast type can do. Besides headphones, microphone, and a selector switch, each booth has a binaural tape recorder, and the student works with his own prerecorded tape. The student's responses are recorded on the student track of the tape he uses.

For reasons of economy, many laboratories are set up as combinations of the two types. Some booths have tape recorders, but most booths have only headsets and mikes. There is no reason why these combinations shouldn't work out very well. Our experience at the American Language Institute bears this out, I believe. It took us four years to get a fully equipped lab. The first year—in 1961—our lab was entirely of the broadcast type, with a console and thirty-six student positions arranged in six rows. The second year we installed tape recorders in twelve booths, the third year twelve more, and this past year, the final installation was completed. After the first year we were able to use the combination approach—some students operating according to the broadcast mode and others according to the library mode.

EFFECTIVENESS OF THE LAB

The literature concerned with the effectiveness of the language laboratory seems to give more attention to how labs are being used and less attention to the type of equipment used. Hutchinson's pamphlet (item 5 on the bibliography) makes five points, which are fairly representative in evaluation studies concerning language labs. It is worthwhile, I think, to note these here:

> First, the teacher must be interested in getting the most out of the equipment and materials; and he must have some skill in the effective use of these aids in helping students develop skills of listening and speaking with comprehension.
>
> Second, the teaching materials must be designed not only to develop the listening and speaking skills efficiently but also to integrate class and laboratory work.
>
> Third, the testing and grading program must give due weight to achievement in listening and speaking.
>
> Fourth, the practice sessions must be frequent enough and long enough to enable students to develop the skills of listening and speaking.
>
> Fifth, the equipment must be good enough and flexible enough to permit efficient operation on a regular basis.

You notice the order in which he lists the five elements which make for effectiveness: (1) the teacher, (2) the teaching materials, (3) the testing and grading program, (4) the student practice sessions, and (5) the equipment. Equipment is noted last.

Hutchinson also summarizes a number of completed research studies concerning the language lab and mentions specific points indicated by the research. For example, in working with groups of French students—experimental groups and control groups—it was found that students who had only one lab practice period a week made no more gains than those in the control group. But students who had daily practice made dramatic gains. It was also shown that positive results could be achieved with two lab periods per week. Another study suggests that audioactive headphones are probably superior to unactivated headphones in the teaching of pronunciation. This same study indicated that the instructor's reinforcement of the student's self-correction and practice is extremely important.

Hutchinson also reports on an experiment to determine whether students of German would have more skill in reading and writing after two years if they were taught by the audiolingual method (including lab practice) instead of the grammar-and-reading method. At the end of the two-year period, the traditional students were about the same as the audiolingual students in reading, but the traditional students were superior in writing; the traditional students were also superior in translating from German to English, but in translating from English to German the groups were about equal. In speaking, as you might expect, the audiolingual students were far superior.

Preliminary reports of long-range studies of language laboratories already indicate that labs help students appreciably in learning foreign languages more efficiently.

INTERNALIZING STRUCTURAL PATTERNS

I was asked to spend part of the time here today talking about the kinds of drills which are best or at least suitable for the language laboratory. This can perhaps be accomplished most effectively by describing and illustrating some of the drills we have prepared for use in our own lab and mentioning others which I have observed in use at other labs.

As I mentioned earlier, Stack's book notes a large variety of drills. Lado's book describes and illustrates several kinds, too. And a large part of the volume edited by Gravit and Valdman is devoted to exercises and drills for the language laboratory.

In connection with the last item mentioned, *Structural Drill and the Language Laboratory* (item 2 on the bibliography), we should note that most drills designed for the language laboratory are "structural" drills. The terms "structural drill" and "pattern practice" seem to be pretty much synonymous. Such drills are developed to help the student internalize certain structures or patterns on all three levels: phonological, morphological, and syntactical. "Internalize," by the way, is just another way of saying "learn to manipulate automatically." If we internalize a pattern, we learn to manipulate the pattern automatically.

We should also note that most drills designed for the language laboratory so far were prepared for first- and second-level language students. At our own Institute this corresponds roughly to elementary and intermediate students. Experimental material for higher level students has been prepared at several institutions, but I'm not sure that any of it is generally available as yet.

A large segment of the drill material at our Institute is set up according to Stack's anticipation mode in four phases:

	1	2	3	4
CUE:	Stimulus		Corrected Response	
RESPONSE:		Attempted Response		Repetition

FIGURE 2

1. Cue is prerecorded.
2. PAUSE. The student responds. He anticipates the correct answer.
3. The correct response is also prerecorded.
4. PAUSE. The student repeats the correct response.

Let's see how this works with a concrete example, say, the substitution of a pronoun for a noun object:

	1	2	3	4
CUE:	I see the house.		I see it.		Bob hears . . .
RESPONSE:		I it see.		I see it.	

FIGURE 3

Laboratory practice, to my way of thinking, is merely supplementary to classwork. The goals of the classroom experience, then, also apply to the laboratory experience, at least in regard to listening and speaking. From this point of view, four main types of drills appear to be most appropriate: those involving imitation, substitution, expansion, and transformation.

IMITATION AND SUBSTITUTION DRILLS

Imitation drills are the easiest to devise and probably the most basic. The instructions to the students are simply "Repeat after me" or "Repeat after us." One popular type is drill on minimal pairs—words in pairs or in groups of three or four, which differ by one phoneme. For example, for practicing the *l-r* distinction in word-initial position, a drill might consist of such pairs as *lead-read, light-right, long-wrong, etc.* Another widely used kind of imitation drill is the dialogue for memorization. The utterances are broken up into small segments, and pauses are inserted after each segment to allow for student repetition. It goes without saying that the sentences and phrases should be short, particularly at the start; long utterances for repetition spread the student's attention over too wide a variety of details. There is a tendency on the part of many teachers to slow down the tempo in recording dialogue drill material. A little of this can be done without affecting the naturalness of speech; some people ordinarily talk slower than others. But a good deal of slowing will result in distortion, which should be avoided. Also, exaggeration of certain sound features should be avoided, such as overloudness of stressed syllables or extra high pitch where only normal high pitch is required.

Substitution drills afford practice on grammatical patterns, intonation patterns, and vocabulary. These are ordinarily prepared with frames, with one, or sometimes two, slots to be filled by the student. The drillmaker may select pattern sentences from previously memorized material, or he may devise new pattern sentences for the purpose. Let's take a pattern sentence like

Why did he bring the *watch?*

In place of *watch* we might substitute *key, pen, brush, car, note.* The objective would not ordinarily be the learning of these vocabulary items. The substitution of vocabulary in a frame focuses the student's attention on one slot—away from some pattern or pronunciation habit the teacher hopes to make automatic for the student. In this case it might be the word order for one type of interrogative question: question word, auxiliary, subject, verb, etc.; or, it might be the loss of "h" in "he" following an auxiliary in rapid speech. After setting up the frame with proper intonation, rhythm, etc., the drill is carried out by cues consisting of one word at a time which the student puts into the substitution slot.

EXPANSION AND TRANSFORMATION DRILLS

Expansion drills involve the addition of utterances or parts of utterances to the cues given. A widely used expansion drill provides practice on tag questions. For example, let's take a sentence like

John works hard.

The student, following his instruction, might be expected to say

John works hard, doesn't he?

After the placement of "doesn't he" becomes familiar, the subject of the sentence can be changed to *Mary* for a while to elicit "doesn't she" in the response and then, perhaps, to a plural noun to elicit "don't they," etc. After that, the subjects can be mixed, so that an element of choice is introduced—that is, the choice of "doesn't he," "doesn't she," or "don't they" depending on the subject of the cue sentence. Many of the teaching objectives which apply to substitution drills also apply to expansion drills.

Transformation drills are plentiful in the average foreign language textbook, including textbooks for English as a second language. Like substitution drills, they are useful for internalizing structural patterns. The term "transformation" has caused a little confusion, because it is also used in connection with certain kinds of grammatical analysis and presentation. But exercises involving transformation within sentences have been around a long time, familiar to language teachers in such instructions as "change the statements to questions" or "change the sentences to the passive."

Probably the easiest transformations to manipulate are those which call for no additions or deletions. This kind can be illustrated by the simple change of statements with the verb *be* to questions:

> The students are here.
> Are the students here?

A change of intonation, of course, goes with the change of word order.

But in addition to shifting, transformation drills often involve other kinds of alterations, such as replacing one item with another, bringing in new items, or dropping parts of the sentence. Simply converting a sentence to the passive requires several simultaneous operations:

> John completes the lesson.
> The lesson is completed by John.

The *-s* ending is replaced by *-d;* the words *is* and *by* are added and located according to a pattern; the front of the sentence goes to the end, and the end goes to the front.

The last example shows a combination of drill types: substitution, expansion, and transformation. *Combination* drills seem to be more common than the "pure" types, since most drills require more than just one operation.

SUMMARY

In summary, let me go back to the title of this presentation, "The Language Laboratory—Uses and Misuses." I have talked a good deal about *uses,* and by implication, mostly, have given some indications of *misuses.* I have shown, I think, that the language laboratory plays, or can play, an important role in the foreign language teaching program, including English as a second language.

The most significant point I have tried to make, and I will restate it here, is this: the main value of the language laboratory lies not so much in the kind of equipment you have, but in the way you make use of what you have.

BIBLIOGRAPHY

1. BRISLEY, LEONARD, CARL DELLACCIO, FRANCIS J. FUNKE, DONALD J. HAMLIN, and M. PHILLIP LEAMON. *Good Teaching Practices: A Survey of High-School Foreign-Language Classes.* New York: Modern Language Association of America, 1961.

2. GRAVIT, FRANCIS W., and ALBERT VALDMAN (eds.). *Structural Drill and the Language Laboratory. Report of the Third Laboratory Conference Held at Indiana University, March 29–31, 1962.* (Indiana University Research Center in Anthropology, Folklore, and Linguistics, Publication 27.) Bloomington: Indiana University, 1963.

3. HAYES, ALFRED S. *Language Laboratory Facilities: Technical Guide for the Selection, Purchase, Use, and Maintenance.* (Office of Education Bulletin 1963, No. 37 OE-21024.) Washington: U.S. Government Printing Office, 1963.

4. HOCKING, ELTON. *Language Laboratory and Language Learning.* (Monograph No. 2.) Washington, D.C.: National Education Association Department of Visual Instruction, 1964.

5. HUTCHINSON, JOSEPH C. *The Language Laboratory . . . How Effective Is It?* (U.S. Department of Health, Education, and Welfare, Office of Education, OE-27021.) Washington: U.S. Government Printing Office, 1964.

6. ————. *Modern Foreign Languages in High School: The Language Laboratory.* (Office of Education Bulletin 1961, No. 23, OE-27013.) Washington: U.S. Government Printing Office, 1961.

7. LADO, ROBERT. *Language Teaching: A Scientific Approach.* New York: McGraw-Hill Book Company, 1964.

8. MODERN LANGUAGE ASSOCIATION OF AMERICA. *A Dozen Do's and Don't's for Planning and Operating a Language Lab or an Electronic Classroom in a High School.* New York: MLA Materials Center, no date.

9. STACK, EDWARD M. *The Language Laboratory and Modern Language Teaching.* New York: Oxford University Press, 1960.

SECTION NINE

OTHER SELECTED TOPICS

This section, although seemingly miscellaneous, does have a common theme. The authors deal with certain aspects of "meaning" and its communication in second-language instruction, but the general subject of meaning does not receive systematic treatment here. In addition, the papers seem to focus on the advanced-level student. Prator proposes that language training can be made more meaningful and functional through an increased use of communicative activities in language classes; by means of a few simple adjustments he shows that a number of classroom exercises and drills may become less manipulative and more communicative. (Transition from the level of manipulation to the level of communication was considered at length in Section One.) Bowen discusses the enormous variety of form and expression in English: variation in dialect and variation in register especially; he points to a particular need in regard to ESL instruction: "to provide the base from which future flexibility and linguistic versatility can be developed." Croft notes that language categories—grammatical and lexical—play a significant role in what we call the native speakers' world view and the patterned habits and responses that accompany such a view; these categories, which are analyzable by the methods of linguists and linguistic anthropologists, cause a great deal of interference in second-language learning.

At this point in time, the advanced-level student is a major concern to us. We believe that we do a better job with our students at the beginning and intermediate levels than we do at the advanced level. In the audiolingual method we start out with mim-mem and patt-prac and work with these manipulative activities for a long time; gradually we introduce more and more communicative activities. Theoretically, at least, we should eventually reach the point where genuine communication replaces manipulation completely. What bothers many of us is that oftentimes our terminal product does not meet our expectations. I believe that we still lack a clear understanding of many problems facing the advanced-level student and the teacher of advanced-level students. As mentioned in my paper on language and

categories, "We don't know (and perhaps will never know) everything
that underlies language behavior." However, we continually add
to our knowledge through insights, experience, and (at least partial)
successes. One day we may even have a unified body of theory for
teaching students at the advanced level.

MEANING IN COMMUNICATION

Prator notes the de-emphasis on meaning carried over from
linguistic analysis to second-language teaching. He suggests that
"Perhaps most serious of all as a cause of the difficulties we are now
experiencing in advanced instruction, we seem to have largely
lost sight of the role of communication in language teaching. If
meaning is not considered to be important, then neither is communication.
Yet, even on the theoretical level, it should be easy to convince
ourselves that communication is an essential component of language,
that language bereft of its communicative function is not language at
all but mere parroting."

The long-range goal we have set for our students is communication
within a relevant range of experience; ideally this would equal the
students' competence in their native language. Bowen (in Section One)
puts it this way: the desired terminal behavior is "a useful control
of his second language in situations that demand real and authentic
communication." Prator, Rivers, and others express a similar point of
view. In regard to intermediate-level classroom activities, Bowen
suggests the teacher ask two questions concerning each activity: "(1)
Does the response to this stimulus represent a skill the student will need
when he is on his own? and (2) Does this activity stretch the
student's capacity by requiring that he express a thought of his own,
one that the teacher cannot fully predict? Then, of course, the teacher
must know if he is offering enough of these activities that require
independent student action, enough so that the student can operate
effectively when eventually he is left to his own resources."

The papers by Rivers (Section Two), Norris (Section Four),
Slager and Kaplan (Section Five), Twaddell (Section Six), and the
ones in this section point up specific problems of students at or
approaching the advanced level and they make realistic suggestions—
some of them tentative—for the solution of these problems. For the
most part these are problems of meaningful communication.

The overall process in second-language learning, Prator notes, "may
be regarded as a prolonged and very gradual shift from manipulation
to communication which is accomplished through progressive
decontrol." If we work more assiduously at decontrol throughout
the early and middle stages of instruction, it certainly seems reasonable

to expect that our advanced students will be able to arrive faster
at their ultimate goal: true communication, without external control.

THE IMPORTANCE OF REGISTER

In this section Bowen notes that every speech act is characterized
by the sender, the receiver, the message, and the situation. Following
Halliday, McIntosh, and Strevens, he defines *dialect* in terms of
the language user and *register* in terms of its use, involving receiver,
message, and situation. He gives more attention to register than to
dialect. "Since dialect depends on the user or speaker," he points out,
"it is reasonable to assume that flexibility in this area should be a
concern only on the level of recognition. Few people need to speak
more than one dialect. So we select a dialect, probably the one
most natural to the teacher, and present it consistently. But variation
in register depends . . . on the use the language is put to, and one
speaker may participate in communication of wide variety. He must
be able to adapt himself easily and quickly, or suffer the consequences
of restricted communication."

Register systems are considered on three scales: *key, mode,* and
pitch. Following Joos and Gleason, Bowen describes key, a kind
of formality scale, as consisting of five levels: "*consultative* is the level
we most normally operate on; *deliberative* is more formal, and
casual less formal. *Oratorical* and *intimate* are extremes of formality and
informality." The term "mode" applies to the written language, with
a set of "literary" keys: *hyperformal, formal, semiformal, informal,*
and *personal.* He mentions that traditionally the consultative key has
been emphasized in second-language instruction, but that the student
"should also have experience in and should be able to control with
at least a limited degree of proficiency the two adjacent levels, the
casual and deliberative keys, but he will have little need for the
extremes, the oratorical and intimate keys." The formal level has been
given similar emphasis, with insufficient attention to semiformal
and informal writing. The other set of dimensions, pitch, concerns "an
adjustment made by the speaker on the basis of specific information
he has about the receiver of the message . . . *status, technicality,
polish,* and *norm.*" These are factors in the particular situation: whom you
are speaking to, the amount of information on a subject the speaker
expects the hearer(s) to have, the appropriate dignity, and the
appropriate norm of expression for the listener and the occasion.

Bowen begins and ends his paper with samples of English from
different registers. He concludes with a brief discussion of pedagogy:
"We seem to recognize that, with appropriate assistance from
linguistic analysis and contrastive studies between languages, we

have been able to develop effective texts and methods to teach on the beginning levels, but then what's to be done afterward? My answer is broadened understanding, comprehension, and at least the beginning of a productive mastery of the register systems of the second language. I'm convinced we have fallen far short of this in many respects. It is my conviction that ranges of variation . . . should be defined, extensively illustrated, and taught as a major content of advanced language courses." He also mentions the device of "translating" from one register to another in order to give the student "specific information on how register differences are signaled, experience in hearing and reading identified samples, and practice in performing within the restrictions of a particular combination of key, mode, and pitch patterns."

LANGUAGE CATEGORIES

Croft deals with interference in second-language learning from language categories—"the structuring of the way people habitually think about and understand phenomena they deal with in their everyday lives." Both grammatical and lexical categories are considered. His approach is contrastive analysis, similar to the approach we use in comparing and contrasting patterns of phonology, morphology, and syntax of the native language on the one hand and the target language on the other. For illustrative purposes he discusses categories of measurement, number categories, pronoun systems, money, color classes, zoological classes, foodstuffs, gender classes, and others.

Traditionally, he points out, linguists have mapped out and described grammatical categories as a regular part of their analytical work. "In recent years," he continues, "linguistic anthropologists have been busy mapping out categories of (other) cultural phenomena utilizing theories, research methods, and analytical devices which are similar to those of the linguist." The second part of Croft's paper outlines the methodology of linguistic anthropologists in discovering and describing language categories that lack the formal characteristics of grammatical categories; this amounts to analysis of semantic components. "The devices include the paradigm, the taxonomy, and distributional analysis for identification and mapping semantic categories of a language—categories that reflect a system of knowledge built up around a people's view of what the world is like."

A modified version of the Sapir-Whorf Hypothesis underlies Croft's treatment. He emphasizes that "semantic (or lexical) categories are discoverable and describable by means of componential analysis. And when they are known, they can be learned by language students, just as grammatical categories are learned. . . . Learning lexical categories may be a step higher in sophistication, but these categories should receive systematic treatment [in language training] and be brought under the student's control on his route to nativelike fluency in a foreign language."

SELECTED READINGS

BROOKS, NELSON. *Language and Language Learning: Theory and Practice.* 2d ed. Chapter 6: "Language and Culture." New York: Harcourt Brace Jovanovich, 1964.

————. "Teaching Culture in the Foreign Language Classroom." *Foreign Language Annals* 1(1968):204–17.

CARROLL, JOHN B. "Linguistic Relativity, Contrastive Linguistics, and Language Learning." *IRAL* 1(1963):1–20.

FRIES, CHARLES C. *Teaching and Learning English as a Foreign Language.* Ann Arbor: Chapter 5: "Contextual Orientation." The University of Michigan Press, 1945.

JOOS, MARTIN. *The Five Clocks.* New York: Harcourt Brace Jovanovich, 1967.

LADO, ROBERT. "How to Test Cross-Cultural Understanding." In *Studies in Languages and Linguistics in Honor of Charles C. Fries.* Edited by Albert H. Marckwardt. Ann Arbor: The English Language Institute, The University of Michigan, 1964.

————. *Language Teaching: A Scientific Approach.* Chapter 15: "Cultural Content and Literature." New York: McGraw-Hill Book Company, 1964.

————. *Linguistics across Cultures: Applied Linguistics for Language Teachers.* Chapter 6: "How to Compare Two Cultures." Ann Arbor: The University of Michigan Press, 1957.

MARCKWARDT, ALBERT H. "A Note to the Language Teaching Profession." *The Linguistic Reporter* 13(Spring 1971):7–9.

MOULTON, WILLIAM G. *A Linguistic Guide to Language Learning.* 2d ed. Chapter 7: "Meaning." New York: The Modern Language Association, 1970.

NOSTRAND, HOWARD LEE. "Describing and Teaching the Sociocultural Context of a Foreign Language and Literature." In *Trends in Language Teaching.* Edited by Albert Valdman. New York: McGraw-Hill Book Company, 1966.

RIVERS, WILGA M. *The Psychologist and the Foreign-Language Teacher.* Chapter 13: "Meaning and Allusions," Chicago: The University of Chicago Press, 1964.

————. *Teaching Foreign-Language Skills.* Chapter 11: "Cultural Understanding." Chicago: The University of Chicago Press, 1968.

TROIKE, RUDOLPH C. "TESOL and Joos's Five Clocks." *TESOL Quarterly* 5(1971):39–45.

DEVELOPMENT
OF A
MANIPULATION-COMMUNICATION SCALE

CLIFFORD H. PRATOR

To judge by the topics of papers read at scholarly meetings, teachers have been increasingly worried for a decade or more about the effectiveness of the instruction in English as a second language which goes on in the United States at the intermediate and advanced levels. We are comparatively satisfied with our elementary classes and have produced a respectable number of successful texts for beginners or near-beginners. But at more advanced levels we are bedeviled by uncertainties as to our aims, lack of conviction in our choice of classroom activities, and a persistent shortage of good teaching materials.

The purpose of the present paper is to investigate briefly the causes of this situation and to suggest a theoretical guideline which may be of help in remedying our deficiencies.

LANGUAGE AS COMMUNICATION

In the opening sentence of his *Gallic War,* Julius Caesar notes the fact that "all Gaul is divided into three parts." The most notable fact about most language departments is somewhat similar. All, or almost all, are divided into two quite distinct, often antagonistic parts: language and literature. The language courses, which are usually assigned to the youngest and most defenseless members of the staff, tend today to be devoted to drill work of a rather mechanical sort and are likely to have little intellectual content. On the other hand, the courses in literature, typically reserved for senior personnel, are either taught largely in the mother tongue of the student or, if conducted in the second language, make no deliberate systematic attempt to help the student improve his practical command of that language. In the two sets of courses, aims, methods, and subject matter are utterly dissimilar. If another paraphrase is permissible, language is language, and literature is literature, and never the twain shall meet.

Yet, it is just such a meeting that is called for in the intermediate or advanced class in English as a second language. The unfortunate dichotomy prevailing in our language departments means that we have little precedent, few models for the kind of course in which a gradual and orderly transition is made from activities in which the major emphasis is on habit formation and the development of basic linguistic skills to activities designed primarily to encourage the free communication of thought. It is apparent, then, that some of the difficulty we experience in pushing on beyond the beginning level stems directly from the prevalent concept of departmental organization.

An even more important source of our difficulty may lie in our current excessive dependence on the structural linguists as the fountainhead of our attitudes toward language teaching. There is no gainsaying the fact that we teachers of English as a second language owe the linguists a tremendous debt of gratitude. One can no more deny the idea that language teaching must be grounded on linguistics—that is to say, on the body of knowledge we possess about the nature of language and of specific languages—than one can deny virtue, home, and mother. But it should be equally obvious that our discipline should rest on other foundations as well, particularly on that branch of psychology which deals with the nature of the learner and of the language-learning process.

Furthermore, American linguists have been notably uninterested in certain aspects of language with which the teacher must concern himself, especially in advanced classes. Since Bloomfield, the focus of attention in linguistic research has been the spoken language and little attention has been paid to writing above the level of graphemics. Grammatical analysis has been developed almost exclusively within the limits of the individual sentence, and there has been little study of the relationships which exist between sentences in larger units such as the paragraph. Yet, the advanced student of English as a second language must be taught composition.

THE IMPORTANCE OF MEANING

In their effort to develop more rigorous methods of linguistic analysis, the Bloomfieldians have tended to downgrade the importance of meaning as an element of language. However healthy this de-emphasis of meaning may have been in analytical work, it should never have been extended to the practical activities of the language classroom. In following the linguists too trustingly on this point, we language teachers have very often fallen into grievous error: extended drills on nonsense syllables, failure to make sure that our students understood the sentences they were so assiduously repeating, the use of language which bore no relationship to the realities of the environmental situation, exercises made up of totally disconnected sentences.

Perhaps most serious of all as a cause of the difficulties we are now experiencing in advanced instruction, we seem to have largely lost sight of the role of communication in language teaching. If meaning is not considered to be important, then neither is communication. Yet, even on the theoretical level, it should be easy to convince ourselves that communication is an essential component of language, that language bereft of its communicative function is not language at all but mere parroting.

The teacher who underestimates the importance of communication is likely to attach correspondingly greater weight to another element of language which has a clear methodological significance—its systematic nature. One of the greatest services the linguists have rendered us is to insist on the fact that a language is basically a system of structural signals by means of which a speaker indicates the relationship between content words. It follows that a primary aim of instruction must be to practice these arrangements of signals, these structural patterns, until they can be handled automatically as a matter of habit. Hence, our fully justified fondness for pattern practice.

We must realize, however, that pattern practice and communication are to a considerable degree antithetical. If our students are to form correct speech habits through pattern practice, they must not be allowed to practice errors. Therefore, strict controls must be exercised, and the proper words and structures are supplied in the form of an external model which the student is required to imitate. On the other hand, the beginning and essence of communication is the presence of a thought that the speaker wishes to share with a hearer, followed by that mysterious process whereby he produces from within himself the words and patterns with which to express that thought. True communication implies the absence of external controls.

FROM MANIPULATION TO COMMUNICATION

For the purposes of this paper, then, we may define communicative classroom activities as those in which the student himself is allowed to find the words and structures he uses. The other type of activity, in which the words and structures are supplied to him directly by the teacher, tape, or book, may be called—for want of a better word—a manipulative activity. In this sense, an example of pure manipulation would be a drill in which the students were asked merely to repeat sentences after the teacher. An example of pure communication would be a free conversation among the members of a class.

As was pointed out at last year's NAFSA Conference, however, when we begin to analyze activities from this point of view, we soon discover that most of them do not fall entirely within either category but are mixtures of communication and manipulation in various proportions. Thus, a teacher can frame a question in such a way as to control the form of the student's answer to a considerable degree but still to leave him some freedom in the choice of words: "Before you came to school this morning, what had you already done at home?" That one seems to involve a rather larger element of communication than of manipulation.

What all this has to do with the problems of advanced English instruction begins to become apparent when we reflect that the principal methodological change which should characterize the progression from the lower to the upper levels of language teaching is precisely the increased freedom of expression which students are allowed in the higher classes. In the beginning stages the teacher exerts such rigorous control as to reduce the possibility of error to a minimum; at least, this is what happens in classes taught by the methods that are most widely approved today. At some later stage the time must inevitably come when these controls disappear, when oral pattern practice is replaced by the discussion of ideas, and dictation is superseded by free composition. The whole process may be regarded as a prolonged and very gradual shift from manipulation to communication which is accomplished through progressive decontrol. We determine the speed of the transition by allowing the student the possibility of making certain errors only when we are reasonably sure that he will no longer be likely to make them.

It is fortunate that the movement from manipulation to communication does not have to be made abruptly, and it is probable that the shift should never be total, even in the most advanced classes. Therein lies the importance of analyzing all the great range of possible language-teaching techniques from the point of view of their manipulation-communication content, and of arranging them in our minds along a sort of scale extending from the most manipulative to the most communicative types.

In the development of such a scale, it may be helpful to divide classroom activities into at least four major groups: completely manipulative, predominantly manipulative, predominantly communicative, and completely communicative. For ease of reference, we can label these as groups one, two, three, and four. Obviously, the dimensions of this paper will not permit an attempt at a complete classification of this sort, but a number of specific examples may be useful.

GROUP ONE AND GROUP TWO ACTIVITIES

One of the currently most popular activities in language classes is the single-slot substitution drill: the teacher gives a model sentence, such as "My father is a doctor," and indicates that the students are to construct similar sentences by substituting for *doctor* a series of nouns of profession—*salesman, farmer, fisherman,* etc.—which are also supplied orally by the teacher. In this form the exercise is certainly completely manipulative and hence belongs in our group one. But by any of a number of slight changes it can be turned into a group-two activity and thus—even in a very elementary class—bring us slightly closer to our ultimate goal of using language for purposes of communication. For instance, the students could be allowed individually to substitute the name of their father's real profession. Such a change would, incidentally, avoid the element of silliness inherent in having the son of a professor chorusing that his father is a janitor. Another change which would permit a very short step toward communication would be to cue the exercise visually, by means of a series of pictures, instead of cuing it orally. In this situation, though the structure is determined by the teacher, the student is permitted to supply at least a single word in each sentence. (It is to be hoped that this argument may have some weight with those too numerous instructors who are deeply fearful of losing dignity if they use visual aids with adult students.)

As has already been pointed out, the most typical group one activity is probably the repetition of sentences by the students in immediate imitation of the teacher. Yet, an element of communication can be introduced into even this type of exercise by allowing a significant period of time to elapse between the hearing of the model and the attempt at imitation. In a beginning class, this might take the form of returning to a repetition drill after having moved on to some other type of exercise; except that, the second time round, the students would be asked to reproduce such sentences as they could remember without benefit of model. Clearly, in this delayed repetition the possibility of error and the need for the student to draw upon his own inner linguistic resources would be greater than in the original version of the activity. In an advanced class the same principle could be applied by asking students to retell an anecdote quite some time after it has been told them by the teacher.

This would seem to be a good place to consider memorization, and especially the memorization of material in dialogue form. The recitation of freshly memorized dialogue, whether it be recited with full comprehension by both participants or not, whether it be in perfectly authentic conversational form or not, cannot be said to involve any considerable element of communication as that term is defined in this paper. It is almost pure manipulation since the opportunity for the speakers to supply all or part of the language is practically nil. On the other hand, if students are encouraged to paraphrase all or portions of a dialogue, then they are certainly moving into the area of communication. One wonders why our textbooks so seldom contain versions of dialogues in which some portions of sentences are left blank, to be filled in by student improvisation.

GROUP THREE AND FOUR ACTIVITIES

In advanced classes, though it may occasionally be advisable to use a group one exercise, the greater emphasis should probably be on activities which fall into groups two and three. Since reading figures prominently in most advanced classes, it is interesting to apply our scale to various activities usually connected with reading. Following our definitions, we would be forced to classify silent reading, in which no overt linguistic activity of any sort is demanded of the student, as belonging to group one—completely manipulative, hence, not often recommendable for use in class at the advanced level. Reading aloud in direct imitation of a teacher would also, of course, fall into group one. But reading aloud without an immediate oral model to follow would require the student to supply the appropriate sounds and sound sequences, and would be classified as a group-two activity, and should therefore probably have a place in advanced instruction.

Questioning of various types ordinarily follows reading. In measuring different types against our manipulation-communication scale, good use can be made of Gurrey's well-known classification of questions as step-one, step-two, and step-three. He labels as step-one a question the answer to which can be found in the exact words of the text. Since the student has only to locate and read the appropriate words, questioning of this sort would appear to be a predominantly manipulative activity, suitable as a starting point in advanced classes provided that the teacher then moves on to questioning of a predominantly communicative type such as step-two and step-three questions. In Gurrey's thinking, a step-two question is one the student can answer by remembering information supplied by the text but not by using the exact words of the text. A step-three question relates to the student's own experience, and its content is merely suggested by the text. Obviously, this latter type approaches very close to pure communication; the only remaining control lies in the form of the question itself.

Students in advanced classes are usually asked to write compositions. If these are assigned without advance preparation of any kind, the writing of them is a group-four activity, completely communicative. It is surely preferable to lead up to composition through a series of related group-two or -three activities. Consulting our scale, we might decide to begin the series with a dictation dealing with the content of the eventual essay to be written, then to move on to another dictation on the same subject but one in which sentences were left incomplete to be filled in by the student, before finally assigning the related composition. Or we might prefer to base the composition on a text which has been read, and to prepare for it through a graded series of questions of a progressively more communicative sort.

Perhaps enough has been said to permit us to judge whether or not the kind of manipulation-communication scale here described can serve us effectively as a theoretical guideline in our organization of classes and textbooks. It seems to be a way of reconfirming, through a new logical approach, quite a few of our established ideas and convictions. On other points, however, it brings us to certain conclusions which we may find upsetting, and therefore challenging.

CONCLUSIONS

From the point of view developed in this paper, a typical class would be seen as made up of several cycles of activities, with each cycle related to the teaching of a corresponding small unit of subject matter. Within each cycle the activities would be so arranged as to constitute a gradual progression from manipulation to communication. The same progression would characterize the whole movement from elementary to advanced English courses, though at the point where manipulative activities disappeared altogether it might be well to stop thinking of the work as teaching English as a second language.

One result of the application of the scale might be a blurring of the sharp line which now separates language courses from literature courses. We might be encouraged to push through more often to communication in very elementary language courses. We might realize the naiveté we now frequently display in trusting that our beginners will somehow find adequate occasion outside the class for using communicatively the structures that we have taught them but that have never been so used in class. We might be helped to realize that we simply cannot be sure that our students have mastered a given structure until we have heard them produce it in a communication situation free of all controls. We might even come to consent to the supreme heresy of including in early literature courses a solid element of manipulation so that they could make a more direct contribution to the development of language skills.

A MULTIPLE-REGISTER APPROACH
TO TEACHING ENGLISH

J. DONALD BOWEN

Madame Chairman, Mr. Vice President, Honored Guests, and Esteemed and Distinguished Colleagues in the noble calling of the Teaching Profession:

I deem it an honor and a privilege to have been invited to come before you on this occasion, an invitation which I have accepted with the profoundest pleasure and gratitude. It is my purpose, as I stand here tonight, to share a few of the experiences I have had in my career of imparting knowledge to the rising generation, to those who will carry on when we have passed our time upon this sphere. I hope and trust that these experiences will not be devoid of interest for those of you who are toiling in the same vineyard, and that together we may reap a bounteous harvest.

Ladies and gentlemen:

I am indeed happy to have been invited by your Vice President, Mr. Horacio Foladori, to address you tonight on the subject "A Multiple-Register Approach to Teaching English." I hope that I will be able to share a few thoughts that you will find both interesting and pertinent to your assignments as teachers of English.

Good evening, friends:

Mr. Foladori has asked me to speak to you tonight on the general subject of teaching English. I hope I'll be able to say a few things that will be of some interest to you, and maybe that will help you be better teachers.

Hi, everybody,

Horacio asked me to come over here and talk to you all about how to teach English. He said I could talk about any of the angles of teaching English I wanted to, but not to get too all-fired technical or nobody'd understand a word I said.

With these introductions I'd like to begin a discussion of some of the problems of language teaching that can be related to the enormous variety of form and expression that has been developed in any language used for a multitude of purposes by a great number of speakers, or more properly, what we can call a world language.

I'm certain that no teacher of English is unaware of the existence of variation in language. We have a long tradition, not only of recognizing variation, but of judging it on a moral scale of right and wrong. Certain forms are proper and admissible in the classroom and are therefore encouraged. Other forms are quite improper and must be firmly opposed. In between there are some forms that we may accept with hesitation or reluctance. They may not be the best, but we tolerate them.

I do not intend to recommend that the reader should necessarily change his mind about value judgments in language usage. Virtually all teachers are convinced that some kinds of English are satisfactory and adequate, other kinds are questionable, and some are altogether undesirable, and classes will continue to be offered on the basis of these judgments.

All I really wish to do is to briefly analyze some of the types and ranges of variation, and perhaps to suggest that we should examine our teaching practices on the basis of a consideration of which varieties of language will be most useful and most helpful to our students.

Every act of using language is characterized by four elements:

Sender
Receiver
Message
Situation

The particular variety of language that occurs depends greatly on the sender and the situation, considerably on the receiver, and to some extent on the message. It's not quite accurate to try to assume a clear separation of these elements. Sometimes the sender is closely identified with the message, or the message and the receiver may be very much a part of the situation, etc.

For the sake of convenience in analysis, I'd like to borrow the classification proposed by Halliday, McIntosh, and Strevens in their book, *The Linguistic Sciences and Language Teaching* (1964), where they define variety according to the user of a language as a function of *dialect* and variety according to the use of a language as a function of *register*. Thus, dialect depends on the sender and register on the other elements: the receiver, the message, and the situation.

VARIATION IN DIALECT

Dialect differences can be measured in at least six dimensions. The most familiar is territorial, or geographic dialect. We are quite familiar with at least the broad implications of dialect geography. In teaching English as a world language it is not uncommon to enormously simplify the problem and pretend there are only two pertinent varieties between which a choice must be made: British and American English. Indeed there are these varieties, though we should probably say two families of English: the British kinds and the American kinds, nor should we forget other important areas where other kinds of English are spoken natively. All of these can be analyzed in great detail and mapped for the areas they cover. If we desire to limit the area of reference, we can designate a general area (say Northern America), a more specific region (North Central American), a particular state (Illinois), or part of a state (Northern Illinois), or a city (Chicago), or even a part of a city (the South Side). Dialect Atlas studies have shown that geographical features are both important and complex, that there is rarely a clear line between dialects. Rather there are various shadings of differences, onto which we impose boundaries for our own convenience. And as just pointed out, boundaries can be used or ignored, as it suits our purposes.

A second dimension is social. Our speech patterns vary according to the class we belong to. This is even more difficult to define and chart, and again there are numerous overlaps and shadings. And it should be pointed out that within each geographical and social dialect there is an enormous amount of variation in the patterns, part of which will be explained later in this paper.

Another dimension of dialect difference is in the age of speakers. Young people talk differently from older ones, and in the course of a lifetime, a person passes from group to group, adopting new forms and discarding older ones in accordance with the needs of his group. We do not expect a small child to say things like: "The prevocalic or postvocalic aspiration /h/ is opposed to the even, unaspirated onset or decay of the vowel." Nor do we expect the dean of the diplomatic corps to say: "What's the matter said the doctor, what's the matter said the nurse, what's the matter said the lady with the alligator purse."

Still another dimension is the sex of the speaker. This can very nicely be illustrated in Spanish, where a man cannot say "Estoy contenta" because he is the wrong sex. There are other differences, many of which are much more subtle. In English a man doesn't usually say "Oh dear me" or "Goodness gracious." Some of the things he *does* say may be considered inappropriate in print, but you will understand that there are indeed differences.

Another dimension is the life role of the speaker. This dimension does not affect most of us very directly, but it does exist as a possible source of linguistic variation. A ruling monarch, for example, may express his wishes with the pronoun *we*, as a sign of his position. We are told that in Thai there are whole sets of forms used only when speaking to the king. Their very use indicates that the message is directed to the sovereign.

Finally there is the dialect dimension of generation. Each generation represents a stage in the development of the language as it changes over a period of time. This sort of change appears most convincingly in the written language, and when we attempt orally to resurrect past forms, as in:

> With hym ther was his sone, a yong squier,
> A lovyere and a lusty bacheler.

It seems to be a characteristic reaction of every generation that its members feel that the next one is going to the dogs and is taking the language with it. During their teens, when young people are seeking their personal identification and are striving for their independence as individuals, there is characteristically a considerable amount of innovation especially for use among members of the in-group. This tendency excites and alarms the older generation, who by now have forgotten their own teen-age innovations, as has everybody else. As Gleason has pointed out in his interesting book *Linguistics and English Grammar* (1965), there is no need to worry, for what is permanent and essentially durable in their speech was no doubt fixed long before adolescence. Slang is only useful because it's a form of private language. As soon as others "get hep," it ceases to serve this function and is soon dropped. There are a few exceptions where slang terms are adopted in the normal speech of the wider community, but these are relatively rare.

VARIATION IN REGISTER

There are much more interesting variations in language in the dimensions of register, characterized by the situation, the receiver, and to a lesser extent the message. Differences in the register systems can be classified on three scales: *key, mode,* and *pitch,* each of which can be described separately, though there are correlations that suggest a certain amount of overlap.

KEY

One system can be referred to as the *key* of linguistic expression. Key is well described in Joos' brief but interesting monograph *The Five Clocks* (1962) and in Gleason's chapter entitled "Language Variation." Key is a concept that represents a kind of formality scale. Gleason lists and defines five levels: *consultative* is the level we most normally operate on; *deliberative* is more formal, and *casual* less formal. *Oratorical* and *intimate* are the extremes of formality and informality. Each of these levels is further described by Gleason as follows:

Oratorical—Elaborate, intricate, ornate, completely composed with balanced periods and parallel constructions. It is used almost exclusively by specialists such as lawyers, preachers, politicians, etc., and is always recognized as appropriate to a very formal situation.

Deliberative—Used in speaking to medium-sized or large groups, no informal (i.e. verbal) feedback. It is planned in advance and deliberately maintains distance between speakers and hearers. As differentiated from consultative key, it is characterized by sentences that are more sharply defined, by fewer run-on sentences, by more extensive vocabulary, with lots of synonyms or near synonyms used to avoid lexical repetition, thus showing a concern for style of expression by the speaker. It is often very difficult for a native speaker to learn to perform on this level, though he will understand what he hears and will usually appreciate the skills shown by others.

Consultative—Conversation between two persons (usually), both active participants, exchanging roles as speaker, and supplying appropriate feedback symbols while listening. Not planned far in advance, but monitored continually. It is characterized by loose grammatical constructions, frequent restarts, fairly short phrases, and simple connectors.

Casual—Complete rapport between speaker and hearer, with the frequent use of slang as an indication of in-group relationship (private or semiprivate language).

It is characterized by the omission of unstressed words at the beginnings of sentences, as in "Gotta match? Wanta come with us? Darn it—broke my finger nail," and the like.

Intimate—Completely private, personal within families. The intimate key is the language one makes love in.

Of these it should be obvious that the most useful to a student of a second language is the middle level, the consultative key, which is the central point in the system. He should also have experience in and should be able to control with at least a limited degree of proficiency the two adjacent levels, the casual and deliberative keys, but he will have little need for the extremes, the oratorical and intimate keys.

In spite of the need the student has for the three middle levels, traditional teaching has concentrated almost exclusively on the deliberative key. Thus a second-language student is taught to say and recognize "What do you have?" only to find that in the world of real communication he is likely to hear "What've you got?" or even "Whaddaya got?"

This emphasis on the deliberative key in second-language teaching reflects the experience of teaching native speakers. Through formal training an effort is made to elaborate and improve the native-speaking student's facility in his own language. This student has mastered consultative and casual (and intimate) in informal situations before coming to school and in out-of-school activities. He needs only the deliberative key (and perhaps, if he chooses to major in one of the speech arts, the oratorical).

Not teaching or not adequately teaching consultative and casual speech keys in a second-language classroom has been a typical area of major neglect. If the school doesn't teach these keys, the chances are the student will be denied them, because other opportunities to learn them are rarely provided in any systematic way. Yet in many cases consultative and even casual speech will eventually be more useful to him than deliberative.

MODE

Another register function is *mode*, by which is meant oral language vs. written. Most teachers are well aware of the considerable difference between oral and written English, especially since the popularity of the audio-lingual approach has emphasized the importance of the spoken language. We should recognize, however, that the distinction oral-written is not a simple one. The written language is a separate system with its own set of keys. These written or literary keys may tend, as a system, to show more regularity and perhaps more formality than oral language on the same level, but the important point is that the same relationship exists among the five levels.

Literary keys can be characterized as follows, from most to least formal: *hyperformal, formal, semiformal, informal, personal*. Each level can be defined as follows:

Hyperformal: The written equivalent of the oration. A composition written for its heightened effect. Poetry which follows a strict formal pattern, such as a sonnet.

Formal: The writing found in professional journals, carefully edited and elaborated.

Semiformal: Business letters, statements or letters of recommendation, reports, project write-ups.

Informal: Correspondence to family members or close friends. Characterized by use of numerous written contractions, standard abbreviations, simplified spellings, sentence fragments.

Personal: Notes one writes to himself. An example can be seen in the following items from a housewife's shopping list:

```
ban       (bananas)
sug       (sugar)
b  p      (baking powder)
gr  pep   (green pepper)
let       (lettuce)
```

As the following chart shows, key and mode can be listed as two dimensions:

	MODE	
	ORAL	WRITTEN
K	Oratorical	Hyperformal
	Deliberative	Formal
e	Consultative	Semiformal
	Casual	Informal
y	Intimate	Personal

The written mode may also display dialect differences, though these are usually fewer in number and less conspicuous than in the spoken mode. There are, for example, a few differences in British and U.S. spelling conventions that identify the provenience of the writer, such as color-colour, defense-defence, analyze-analyse, tire-tyre, theater-theatre, and a few others.

Again we can say that traditional language classes have emphasized the formal level, and often the hyperformal level, and have not always given sufficient recognition to semiformal and informal writing.

PITCH

Another series of dimensions of register can be labeled *pitch*, which can be described as an adjustment made by the speaker on the basis of specific information he has about the receiver of a message. There are at least four of these, analyzable under the rubrics *status, technicality, polish,* and *norm.*

The *status* of the person addressed, in relation to the speaker, can make an enormous difference in the forms used. This is to say that a student doesn't talk to the dean of the college in the same way he talks to a table waiter. We regularly employ forms or pronunciations that imply deference when we owe respect to the person we address, so that our relative positions are clearly indicated.

Possibly the distinctions implied could be described in terms of the keys of the spoken language. There are differences, however, that cannot be easily accounted for strictly in terms of formality levels, such as the language used in speaking to one's own children compared to the language used with one's spouse. In both cases the key is intimate, but there are features such as intonation patterns and vocabulary selection, that clearly mark a difference best considered as "status," contrasting a horizontal with a vertical social relationship.

Another dimension is *technicality*, which concerns the amount of information about the subject which the speaker expects the hearer to have. At a professional conference the speaker will be able to take certain things for granted, because he is talking to specialists in his own field. In addressing English teachers, for example, it is possible to talk of sentence fragments, subordinating conjunction, participial constructions, prepositions, split infinitives, and the speaker will be confident that he will be correctly understood. But the same speaker addressing parents of students in an elementary school class must exercise much more caution in discussing his professional field. He cannot assume his audience will know the specific meanings of words he uses every day in his professional life.

Another dimension is *polish*, which measures the dignity we estimate to be appropriate for our listener and for the occasion. This ranges from profanity and obscenity at one extreme to euphemism at the other.

Finally there is the dimension of *norm*. In playing our part before this or that particular listener or listeners we conform to what we consider to be the appropriate norm of expression. I, on one occasion, utterly shocked the wife of one of my new colleagues, when as a young instructor I used the word *ain't* during conversation at a reception. I'm not completely certain that this serious mistake is not the reason I am no longer teaching at the august institution where this occurred. My listener considered this a grievous infraction of proper linguistic behavior and made no attempt to conceal her shock.

THE NEED FOR FLEXIBILITY AND VERSATILITY

This discussion of variation in language usage on the basis of dialect and register has undoubtedly been far from adequate in terms of the broad spectrum of differences that can be observed in human communication. It is not easy to adequately describe in very simple terms the ranges that can be realized within each classification and to indicate the extensive amount of overlap that makes almost any classification somewhat arbitrary. What is important for the purpose of this paper is to establish an appreciation for the range of variation that exists in any language, particularly in English. Faced with an enormous and complex amount of variety, the teacher, knowing that all of it cannot be taught, must decide what to present and in what sequence to explain and drill each of the varieties that are to be included in the curriculum.

I have suggested that in much of our traditional teaching we have tended to concentrate on the relatively formal level of the deliberative key. In doing so we have followed the example of first language teaching, where formal patterns are added as a peculiar contribution of our educational system to the informal mastery of the language that has been achieved in the process of growing up. But second-language teaching is different in precisely this area: the need to present in a systematically structured way a much greater variety of registers. Otherwise the student is left with no means of developing the flexibility of action and response that are desirable in a bilingual.

We may very well limit our teaching to avoid unnecessary exposure to variation. I have suggested that the extremes of the oratorical and intimate keys are of little use to a student who will not likely operate on either level. If we knew just what varieties our students needed, especially if their needs were for only one or only a few varieties, we could improve our efficiency by teaching that variety or those varieties. But we don't know. Especially we don't know if we are teaching young students who do not yet themselves know how they will use their second language.

We have many students. The future needs of some may be simple, of others complex. But we are not in a position to identify those needs now. Therefore, we have to recognize the necessity of keeping our training fairly general. We need to provide the base from which future flexibility and linguistic versatility can be developed. Then when our students become travellers, scholarship grantees, newspapermen, diplomats, radio announcers, technical specialists at international conventions, etc., they can more readily develop the specific skills they will need.

This may sound logical in the abstract. But how does one do this? I have two things to say—the first a suggestion, the second a caution. The suggestion is to look to the experience of a native speaker, who masters a considerable range of variation in his own language, rarely or never the entire range, but a considerable range. How does he do it? We're not really sure how it happens, but we do know he's exposed to it, and without this exposure there is little likelihood he would develop his own range.

So we should expose our students to variety. How should we start? Here's where the difference between dialect and register comes in handy. Since dialect depends on the user or speaker, it is reasonable to assume that flexibility in this area should be a concern only on the level of recognition. Few people need to speak more than one dialect. So we select a dialect, probably the one most natural to the teacher, and present it consistently.

But variation in register is a different matter. Here variety depends on the situation, the hearer, and the message, that is to say, on the use the language is put to, and one speaker may participate in communication experiences of wide variety. He must be able to adapt himself easily and quickly, or suffer the consequences of restricted communication. At this point he must be trained to shift keys, to adapt modes, and to make adjustments in pitch to different hearers, to different situations, and to differences in message content. This must be a part of his productive training. The schools, and more specifically the language classrooms, must accept responsibility for providing specifics for the useful varieties and ranges of register, and must do so on the productive level. An ability to receive and interpret is not enough.

Perhaps it is worth pointing out that it is not really the situation that determines the form of a message, but rather the conventions as to the kind of language considered appropriate to the situation. This is not a terribly important distinction, but it may serve to point up the fact that communication is between human beings. Everything else in the communication situation is incidental to the process of transferring an idea from the mind of one person to the mind of another.

MASTERY OF THE REGISTER SYSTEM

The caution is illustrated in a quotation from Halliday, McIntosh, and Strevens (p. 88): "The choice of items from the wrong register, and the mixing of different registers, are among the most frequent mistakes made by a non-native speaker of a language." Why is this so? Well, there are at least two reasons: one, the register system is very complex. It is not easy to master. A native speaker counts on the experiences of his whole lifetime to develop a feeling for what is appropriate in any particular situation. And sometimes even then he is not fully successful in matching message and occasion.

The second reason is one we can perhaps do something about. Nobody has ever taught register systematically. Little wonder a second-language student has difficulty. He has been left to shift for himself in a learning situation which seldom provides the cultural contexts of reality at the time he needs them to define variations of expression. So we are faced with advanced students who studiously avoid all English contractions because their teacher thought that contractions were substandard and therefore protected the students from them. The result is a student who sounds like a book and who can't understand a word of spoken English from anyone but his teacher. This student is in the position of the

American newspaperman who, in preparation for a tour of duty as a foreign correspondent in France, studied elementary French, only to find out later that nobody in France speaks elementary French.

The very nature of language teaching means that the teacher must develop efficiency of presentation in the classroom. When we consider that, conservatively estimated, a native speaker spends 11,680 hours learning his language by the age of eight, but that four years of high school language study gives the student less than 700 contact hours shared with twenty-five or thirty classmates, we can see that the so-called mother method cannot be used to teach a second language. We must be more efficient, which means our classes must be structured. We cannot wait for chance to define or fill out patterns of usage. We must describe and present them systematically and contrastively.

In discussing language pedagogy the question of appropriate materials for courses on the intermediate level often arises. And what we should be doing in our advanced classes is a subject of discussion at almost every meeting or conference of the language-teaching profession. We seem to recognize that, with appropriate assistance from linguistic analysis and contrastive studies between languages, we have been able to develop effective texts and methods to teach on the beginning levels, but then what's to be done afterward. My answer is a broadened understanding, comprehension, and at least the beginning of a productive mastery of the register systems of the second language. I'm convinced we have fallen far short of this in many respects.

It is my conviction that ranges of variation in the dimensions of usage discussed earlier in this paper should be defined, extensively illustrated, and taught as the major content of advanced language courses. At the present time advanced courses are typically restricted to literature. Literature is important and appropriate in the language classroom, and certainly has a place in a liberal arts curriculum. But it is only one mode and, unless carefully selected, may fail to illustrate an adequately broad range of keys and pitches. Furthermore literature derives much of its value as an artistic elaboration of language, which automatically removes it from the arena of common communication in any register. Let's keep literature in the advanced curriculum; its values cannot be denied. But let's add generous samples of other varieties of the language.

Frequently we can begin from a literary composition and "translate" to other registers. By doing this we can see different keys, modes, and pitches in contrast with each other, which will emphasize the specific points of difference. This is precisely what the student needs: specific information on how register differences are signalled, experience in hearing and reading identified samples, and practice in performing within the restrictions of a particular combination of key, mode, and pitch patterns.

EXAMPLES FROM A VARIETY OF REGISTERS

I would like to end this presentation by listing some samples of American English from a variety of registers, which can readily be analyzed in terms of their register functions, with an identification of the probable circumstances surrounding the production of each sample.

No. 1.   Ask not what your country can do for you, rather ask what you can do for your country.

No. 2.   I don't know what you'll get out of it. Maybe you oughta do it for nothin'.

No. 3.   Don't ask me what there is in it for you. Why don't you do something for someone else once in a while.

No. 4.   Members are advised that this is one of the club's regular service projects. There will be no compensation for participation.

No. 5.   Seek not thine own profit, but strive to serve thy fellow man.

No. 6.   Look here, you're supposed to do this for me without getting paid. What do you think I give you an allowance for?

No. 7.   Look, Gus. I know this is a business, but we have to help out on community projects. Chalk it up to advertising—it's good will.

No. 8.   And so my fellow citizens, I earnestly solicit your cooperation and request that you join me early Saturday morning on this much needed and worthwhile venture for beautifying our proud community.

No. 9.   I don't know why we have to do it. The teacher says so.

No. 10.   What's the cut?—Search me. Maybe nuthin'.

No. 11.   O.K. you guys, get your lazy so-and-so's out of those bunks. Fall out and police the area, and don't miss nothin' or you'll do it over.

No. 12.   Johnny, I wonder if you and Alice would help Mommy pick up all these toys. Daddy'll be home soon and we want the house all nice and clean for him.

No. 13.   Don't throw it. Stow it.

No. 14.   No Littering. $500 Fine.

No. 15.   Section II, Title One, Part A. Any person apprehended in the act of discarding or abandoning rubbish, garbage, junk, or allowing the same to escape from a moving vehicle, on property in the public domain or of otherwise littering any public right-of-way will upon conviction, be liable for a fine not to exceed five hundred dollars ($500) or thirty (30) days in jail, or both, at the discretion of the presiding judge.

No. 16.   The public is hereby advised that ordinances will herewith be strictly enforced.

No. 17.   Don't be a litterbug. Every litter bit hurts.

Admittedly it is a big order to develop a sensitivity to register differences in a second-language student and a bigger order to teach him to produce these differences consistently in appropriate contexts. Probably we won't succeed with all of our students, but in making an attempt we can offer two services: 1) better prepare students for a broad range of participation through the medium of their second language, helping them develop the base of flexibility from which a variety of presently unpredictable future needs can be served, and 2) partially solve the nagging problem of what to do at the advanced levels of language training.

LANGUAGE AND CATEGORIES
Some Notes for Foreign Language Teachers[1]

KENNETH CROFT

Some of you have probably had the experience of trying to make your way around in a foreign country where the metric system was used for weights and measures, and temperature was measured in centigrade units. In addition, you probably had to deal with a different monetary system; perhaps the units were not entirely unfamiliar in relation to each other, but they were different in terms of the buying power of American dollars and cents. Assuming you had a good command of the language of the country—even a very good command of it—you still might have encountered some interference in using it at times because the measuring units differed in value from those you were accustomed to using.

CATEGORIES OF MEASUREMENT

On three occasions I was a resident in Mexico City: the first time for about eleven months, the second time for about eight months, and the third time for about thirteen months. Each time I went to Mexico I had to go through a period of adjustment to the metric system in regard to distances, liquid measures, weights, the Celsius temperature scale, etc. I learned a few approximate equivalents to American measuring units once and did not have to relearn them later. For example, I found out that a kilogram was equal to approximately 2.2 pounds, so when I wanted to buy something like a pound of meat, I asked for half a kilo. I learned that a liter was a little more than a quart, and gasoline was sold by the liter; so instead of asking for ten gallons of gas, I asked for 40 liters. (This gave me about ten and a half gallons.)

Distances and temperature equivalents were not quite as simple, and they did require a certain amount of relearning. A meter, I discovered, was a little longer than a yard (one meter = 39.37 inches); this helped me with calculations of short distances. But a kilometer (1000 meters)

---

[1] Notes, for the most part, used in talking with groups of teachers of English to speakers of other languages during the summer of 1969 at the University of Southern California, the University of Illinois, and the California Polytechnic College at San Luis Obispo.

is equal to .621 miles—somewhat more than half a mile. Nevertheless, I often found myself thinking of a kilometer as approximately half a mile in making quick, rough calculations of distance to certain places and also in judging the speed limit—a certain number of kilometers per hour. People who were able to make mental calculations by using fractions, I noticed, came up with more accurate equivalents; one kilometer equals approximately ⅝ of a mile.

As any former student of chemistry or physics knows, the Fahrenheit temperature scale is convertible to the Celsius (Centigrade) scale and vice versa by a formula. However, relatively few people go around making this kind of conversion quickly without using pencil and paper. A couple of reference points are good to remember, namely that 0° C equals 32° F— the point at which water freezes—and 100° C equals 212° F—the point at which water boils. Once in a while the temperature in Mexico City goes down to zero—0° C, that is, not 0° F. It gave me a start when I heard, for the first time, that the temperature might drop to zero during the night. When you want to convert Fahrenheit to Centigrade, you subtract 32 and then multiply by ⅚. 70° F, my favorite temperature during the day, is about 21° C.

I became fairly expert in money conversion, perhaps because of necessity. My income was in dollars, and these had to be converted into Mexican pesos. Then everything was paid for in pesos. I noticed that inflation was taking place, faster than I've ever noticed it in the States, and I had to be careful that I didn't spend money at a faster rate than I received it. In terms of American money, the peso was worth about 17 cents at first; then it dropped to a little more than 12½ cents; later it dropped further to about 8 cents. What happened may be described in two ways: we say the peso was devalued on two occasions, but from another point of view—expressed by some Mexicans—the Americans raised the price of the dollar.

INTERFERENCE FROM LANGUAGE CATEGORIES

A great deal his been written and said about interference in language learning—interference from one's native language while learning a foreign language. We read and hear mostly about interference in phonology (sound structure), interference in morphology (word structure), and interference in syntax (sentence structure). The kind of interference noted above might be called interference in vocabulary, but I think it is more precise to call it interference from language categories—the structuring of the way that people habitually think about and understand phenomena they deal with in their everyday lives.

In regard to units of measure, you might say that I lived in a world of approximations; for me there were no exact equivalents—that is, not any

I could arrive at simply. Certainly the Mexican's analysis and understanding of distance, weight, temperature, and monetary values were quite different from mine. His thoughts concerning "how long" or "how far" were in terms of centimeters, meters, kilometers, and the like, whereas my thoughts were in terms of inches, feet, yards and miles. Similarly, his notion of weight was in terms of grams, kilograms, and metric tons; my notion of weight, on the other hand, was in terms of ounces, pounds, and "short" tons—categories somewhat differently graded. At a stand near the entrance to a movie one time I noticed that the price of candy was given as so much per 100 grams; I didn't know then, but I know now, that 100 grams equals 3½ ounces.

Learning the vocabulary of the metric system presents no great problem; actually, it is rather simple. The fundamental units are the meter and the gram. Designations of multiples and subdivisions of any unit can be arrived at by combining with the name of the unit the prefix *deka-*, *hecto-*, and *kilo-*, meaning, respectively, 10, 100, and 1000 and *deci-*, *centi-*, and *milli-*, meaning, respectively one-tenth, one-hundredth, and one-thousandth. It may be pointed out perhaps that the measuring units of the metric system are not native categories of any natural language. Nevertheless, they are very *real* categories in most European languages, and these categories provide a set of "grooves" for thinking about distance, weight, etc.—quite different from our set of "grooves."

The examples noted above demonstrate the kind of interference that may result when phenomena are categorized and viewed differently by the speakers of different languages. Whether formal linguistic categories or semantic categories, they still influence the thinking of the people who speak the language. According to Edward Sapir, ". . . the 'real world' is to a large extent unconsciously built up on the language habits of the group . . ."[2]

THE SAPIR-WHORF HYPOTHESIS

There are many statements in the writings of Edward Sapir[3] and Benjamin Lee Whorf[4] to the effect that our thoughts, our ideas, and our views of the universe are shaped considerably by our language—including, of course, the formal and semantic categories of our language. Some of these statements have been cited hundreds of times in linguistic and anthropological literature and have, in a sense, become classic statements; the notions contained in them have been designated as the "Sapir-Whorf

[2] "The Status of Linguistics as a Science." In *Selected Writings of Edward Sapir in Language, Culture, and Personality,* ed. by David G. Mandelbaum. Berkeley and Los Angeles: University of California Press, 1949, p. 162.
[3] *Ibid.,* pp. 1–166, *passim.*
[4] *Language, Thought, and Reality: Selected Writings of Benjamin Lee Whorf,* ed. by John B. Carroll. Cambridge, Mass.: The M.I.T. Press, 1956. *Passim.*

Hypothesis" (of linguistic relativity). Whorf states that "We cut nature up, organize it into concepts, and ascribe significances as we do, largely because we are parties to an agreement to organize it in this way—an agreement that holds throughout our speech community and is codified in the patterns of our language."[5]

Both Sapir and Whorf say there is relatively little if any awareness of the intricate workings of the language on the part of the speaker while he is speaking his native language. Whorf states ". . . that the phenomena of a language are to its speakers largely of a background character and outside the critical consciousness and control of the speaker. . . ."[6]

The Sapir-Whorf Hypothesis has been restated, explicated, and elaborated in various ways by social scientists, sometimes with evidence that tends to support it and sometimes with evidence that tends to refute it. After many years of research, however, there still appears to be insufficient evidence to prove anything conclusively about the S-W Hypothesis; it remains pretty much controversial. In 1953 Harry Hoijer stated the central idea of the S-W Hypothesis in this way: "Each language has its own peculiar and favorite devices, lexical and grammatical, which are employed in reporting, analyzing, and categorizing experience."[7]

Whorf's notion was that language directed the perceptions of its speakers besides providing habitual modes of analyzing experience into significant categories. But Hoijer was more conservative; he stated that "Languages . . . do not so much determine the perceptual and other faculties vis-à-vis experience as they influence and direct these faculties into prescribed channels."[8] This more conservative position seems to be favored by linguists and anthropologists today. I think John B. Carroll's restatement of the S-W Hypothesis, in the light of recent relativity theories, is not untypical: "Insofar as languages differ in the ways they encode experience, language users tend to sort out and distinguish experience differently according to the categories provided by their respective languages. These cognitions will tend to have certain effects on behavior."[9]

NUMBER CATEGORIES

Those of you who teach English to orientals will be familiar with this situation: There is a huge class of English nouns which we often refer to

[5] *Ibid.,* p. 213.
[6] *Ibid.,* p. 211.
[7] "The Sapir-Whorf Hypothesis." In *Language in Culture: Conference on the Interrelations of Language and Other Aspects of Culture,* ed. by Harry Hoijer. Chicago: The University of Chicago Press, 1954. p. 95.
[8] *Ibid.,* p. 94.
[9] "Linguistic Relativity, Contrastive Linguistics, and Language Learning." *International Review of Applied Linguistics* 1.1–20 (1963), p. 12.

as "count nouns" or "countable nouns." These for the most part have different forms for the SINGULAR (one) and PLURAL (more than one). The choice of the singular or plural affects the syntax; for example, we use *this, that,* and *is* with the singular and *these, those,* and *are* with the plural. But even after studying English for eight or ten years, many of my oriental students are still unable to make this singular-plural distinction consistently—that is, in the way that native speakers make it. Their tendency is to ignore the fact that English has separate categories denoting *one* and *more than one* and use only the former.

The speaker of Chinese, Japanese, or Korean is not forced by the conventions of his language to specify one or more than one when he talks about certain objects in the world and, consequently, is not compelled to think of them in such terms. In other words, singular and plural are not grammatical categories in Chinese, Japanese, and Korean, as they are in English and many other languages. Oriental languages have ways of expressing the difference between one and more than one, but if this difference is not particularly important in what the speaker is saying, he does not habitually express it. The English speaker, on the other hand, is forced by the conventions of his language to express this difference, whether it is important or not. I imagine the average native speaker of English would be hard put to find examples in which he considered the singular-plural distinction unnecessary, whereas the oriental, I imagine, would not be able to come up with a plentiful number of cases in his language in which he considered the distinction to be necessary. Here we see two separate ways of categorizing and reporting information about objects: indifference in regard to number on the one hand, and a compulsory distinction between one and more than one on the other.

PRONOUN SYSTEMS

In doing their analytical work, linguists map out the grammatical categories they find in a language. A linguist, for example, might show his analysis of the subject forms of English personal pronouns as in Figure 1. He would then point out that a gender distinction (masculine, feminine, and neuter) is found only in the third person singular, "you" is nonspecific as to number (singular or plural), and "we" means "I and one or more others."

Traditionally we show these pronouns as six points on a chart (see Figure 2), perhaps because the pronouns of other European languages generally pattern out this way.

If we now examine pronominal reference in Samoan similarly, we come out with a fairly different chart. (Compare Figure 3 with Figure 2.) Instead of the English two-way number system (singular and plural), we have a three-way number system: singular (one), dual (two), and plural

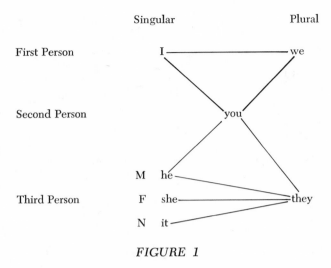

FIGURE 1

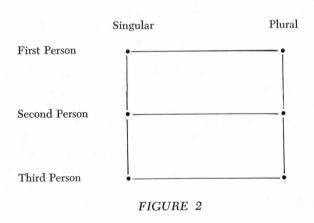

FIGURE 2

(more than two). The notion of singular in all persons compares well in both languages, except that the English gender distinction in the third-person singular is not found in Samoan. On the other hand, we find much more elaboration in Samoan when we compare the notion of "more than one" in the two languages. The Samoan dual appears to carry with it a good deal of the time something like the English idea of "couple."

People with only a European-language orientation generally find the dual requires at least a minor adjustment of habit: the notions of "you-more-than-one" and "they," for example, have to be redistributed as "you-couple," "you-more-than-two," and "they-couple," "they-more-than-two." More than just a minor adjustment is necessary for the notion of "we," for we find the inclusive and exclusive in both the first-person dual and

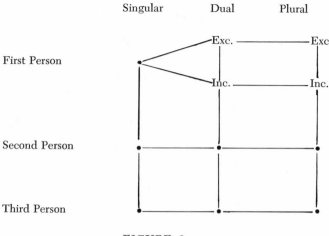

FIGURE 3

first-person plural. There's a four-way system in Samoan, all translated into English as *we:* "you(singular)-and-I" (inclusive), "I-and-one-other-but-not-you" (exclusive) and "you(singular)-and-I-and-one-or-more-others" (inclusive), "I-and-others-but-not-including-you" (exclusive).

Use of person-number contrasts for indicating pronominal reference, as shown in the English and Samoan examples above, may be less efficient sometimes than other kinds of contrast. Harold Conklin's componential analysis of Hanunoo pronouns is a good example of this, and I think he comes closer to a conceptual code in his kind of treatment.[10] Note first the traditional charting of Hanunoo pronouns in Figure 4. Conklin saw there were eight terms here in an assymetrical arrangement and suggested there might be an underlying scheme of components other than the usual ones for person and number. The ones he extracted from his data were: inclu-

	Singular	Dual	Plural
First Person	kuh	tah	mih (exclusive)
			tam (inclusive)
Second Person	muh	—	yuh
Third Person	yah	—	dah

FIGURE 4

[10] "Lexicographical Treatment of Folk Taxonomies." In *Problems in Lexicography,* ed. by Fred W. Householder and Sol Saporta. Bloomington, Ind.: Indiana University Research Center in Anthropology, Folklore, and Linguistics, 1962. pp. 134–35.

dah	$\overline{M}$	$\overline{S}$	$\overline{H}$
yuh	$\overline{M}$	$\overline{S}$	H
mih	$\overline{M}$	S	$\overline{H}$
tam	$\overline{M}$	S	H
yah	M	$\overline{S}$	$\overline{H}$
muh	M	$\overline{S}$	H
kuh	M	S	$\overline{H}$
tah	M	S	H

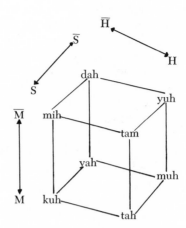

FIGURE 5

sion of the speaker (S) or exclusion of the speaker ($\overline{S}$), inclusion of the hearer (H) or exclusion of the hearer ($\overline{H}$), and minimal membership (M) or nonminimal membership ($\overline{M}$).[11] He then constructed a box with a pronoun at each corner, the location representing an intersection of these three dimensions of contrast. (See Figure 5.) All the pronouns on the front of the box include the speaker, and those on the back exclude the speaker; the pronouns on the right include the hearer, and those on the left exclude the hearer; the pronouns at the bottom show minimal membership, and those at the top nonminimal membership.

PARADIGMS

The kind of chart just described is sometimes called a *paradigm*, defined by Lounsbury as "any set of linguistic forms wherein: (a) the meaning of every form has a feature in common with the meanings of all the other forms of the set, and (b) the meaning of every form differs from that of every other form of the set by one or more additional features."[12]

[11] "Minimal membership" seems to be roughly equivalent to "finite number," and "nonminimal membership" to "indefinite number."
[12] "The Structural Analysis of Kinship Semantics." In *Proceedings of the Ninth International Congress of Linguistics*. The Hague: Mouton and Co., 1964.

The charts representing English and Samoan pronouns may be called paradigms, too, since they meet the criteria noted in (a) and (b). Conklin's paradigm of Hanunoo pronouns is reminiscent of the Prague School charts indicating distinctive phonological features. For example, the phonological components of Turkish vowels (eight altogether) might be shown by a box with a vowel at each corner, indicating three dimensions of contrast: high versus low, front versus nonfront, and rounded versus unrounded. We would not ordinarily call this a paradigm, however, because phonological features, rather than features of meaning, would be represented.

The paradigm is a componential analysis device which shows systematically the intersection of semantic features. Grammarians have used this device for a long time in the representation of grammatical meanings of linguistic forms—the representation of grammatical categories. More recently linguistic anthropologists have made use of the paradigm to sort out semantic components of other terminological systems, in an attempt to classify (categorize) cultural phenomena as viewed by native speakers of a given language. A notable example of this is the terminology of kinship systems,[13] but other *domains* (sets of semantically related terms), or at least parts of domains, seem to lend themselves to paradigmatic analysis, too. For instance, in the following arrangement of terms dealing with livestock we can clearly see the intersection of semantic components:[14]

sheep	ram	ewe	lamb
hogs	boar	sow	pig
horses	stallion	mare	colt
cattle	bull	cow	calf
chickens	rooster	hen	chick

TAXONOMIES

Another componential analysis device used by linguistic anthropologists for similar purposes (actually more widely used than the paradigm) is the *taxonomy*. Instead of showing intersections of semantic components, the taxonomy is a hierarchical arrangement of terms showing inclusion and contrast. In a simple taxonomy of, say, American money we could list coins—penny, nickel, dime, quarter, etc.—and bills—$1, $5, $10, $20, etc. We note these on a branching diagram in Figure 6. At the first level we

[13] A number of kinship studies on this model have been reprinted in *Cognitive Anthropology*, ed. by Stephen A. Tyler. New York: Holt, Rinehart and Winston, Inc., 1969.

[14] Cf. *Ibid.*, pp. 8–10. See also "Anthropological Aspects of Language: Animal Categories and Verbal Abuse," by Edmund Leach. In *New Directions in the Study of Language*, ed. by Eric Lenneberg. Cambridge, Mass.: The M.I.T. Press, 1964. p. 48.

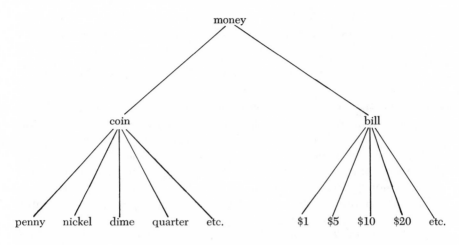

FIGURE 6

have the domain label "money." At the second level, "coin" and "bill" contrast but are included in the first-level term "money." At the third level, "penny, nickel, dime, quarter, etc." contrast but are included in the term "coin"; similarly, $1, $5, $10, $20, etc." contrast but are included in the term "bill." In a taxonomic arrangement, items at a lower level are kinds of items in higher levels.

The structure of domains may differ slightly to considerably from language to language. (Even the domains themselves may show a good deal of overlap from language to language.) Color categories provide a good illustration of how people throughout the world divide the color spectrum variously,[15] and they provide further examples of taxonomic arrangement. For English we might list eleven "basic" color terms: white, black, red, green, yellow, blue, brown, pink, purple, orange, and gray. At the next lower level we might, in turn, list the kinds of "red, green, brown, etc." As kinds of red we could list "maroon, scarlet, crimson, cock's comb, turkey red," and the like. Such terms as the latter are in my passive vocabulary, but I seldom use them in daily activities.

Conklin's list of Hanunoo color classes, on the other hand, is quite different:[16]

(ma)lagti?—white, light tints of other colors and mixtures.

[15] An excellent detailed treatment of color categories can be found in *Basic Color Terms: Their Universality and Evolution*, by Brent Berlin and Paul Kay. Berkeley and Los Angeles: University of California Press, 1969.
[16] "Hanunoo Color Categories." *Southwestern Journal of Anthropology* 11:339–44 (1955).

(*ma*)*bīru*—black, violet, indigo, blue, dark green, dark gray, and deep
shades of other colors.

(*ma*)*rara?*—maroon, red, orange, yellow, mixtures in which these qualities
seem to predominate.

(*ma*)*latuy*—light green, mixtures of green, yellow, and light brown.

Ordinarily, the meanings of color categories are expressed in terms of
hue, saturation, and brightness. Conklin notes, however, that certain other
components, namely dryness or desiccation and wetness or freshness (suc-
culence), are relevant semantic features in Hanunoo color terms.[17] He
also points out that a lower-level terminology can be applied when
greater color specification is required.[18]

Like the paradigm, the taxonomy attempts to show how the native
speakers of a given language slice up reality into named categories. There
is good evidence, I believe, that conceptual patterns and systems in lexicography can be discovered and mapped out by means of these devices.
The methodology of linguistic anthropologists in this regard, described in
several places, is rigorous and exacting.[19] Before leaving the matter of
taxonomies, I want to mention that only a few extensive ones have ever
been worked out in depth, and fewer still have ever been published.

Figure 7 gives a partial taxonomy of the Navaho animal kingdom.[20] We
can make a few inferences from this chart and check them with a more
complete set of data. "Land dwellers" at level one possibly contrasts with
a term for "water creatures," and it may be that the two are included in
some higher-level term. In an English-language classification we might
discriminate the two similarly—"land creatures" and "water creatures"—
but we would also have an "intermediate" class of "amphibious creatures."
At level two, we might guess that "walkers, fowl, crawlers, and insects"
overlap our English categories "animals (including 'human animals'),
birds, reptiles, and insects" pretty well. But at level three we would not

---

[17] *Ibid.*, pp. 342–43.

[18] *Ibid.*, p. 343. A question is sometimes raised about color perception when a given
language contains fewer color terms than we have. Actually, color categories of different languages reflect a different division of the spectrum; these categories may be
less finely graded than ours or perhaps more finely graded in some cases. The fact that
the same term in a particular language applies to what we call "blue" and "green"
doesn't mean that the speaker of the language can't see the difference between these
two "colors." If the need arises to make a distinction between the two, he has a way
of doing it. But habitually he labels what we call "blue" and "green" in the same
way.

[19] See Tyler's (*op. cit.*) Introduction, Parts I and II, particularly "Notes on Queries in
Ethnography" by Charles O. Frake and "Eliciting Folk Taxonomy in Ojibwa" by
Mary B. Black. Note also the bibliographical references accompanying these two
papers.

[20] "Navaho Systems of Classification: Some Implications for Ethnoscience," by Norma
Perchonock and Oswald Werner. *Ethnology* 8:229–42 (1969).

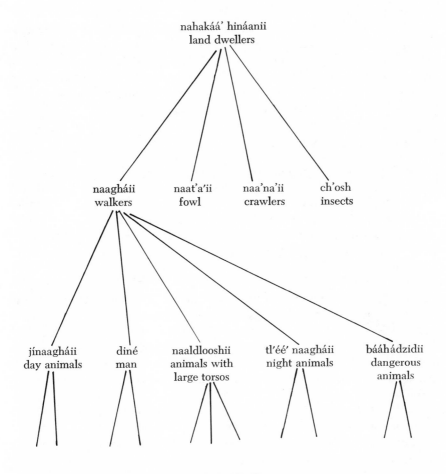

FIGURE 7

consider "man" as one among several classes of animals; except in some kind of scientific zoological classification, this would seem un-English. Also the classes "day animals, animals with large torsos, night animals, and dangerous animals" are unfamiliar. In English, I imagine we would classify animals as tame or wild at this level, then tame animals as pets or livestock at the next lower level, and then animal names at the following level—something like that. In regard to wild animals, we might distinguish game animals from non-game animals at the next lower level, and give animal names at the following level. This classification in English is all impressionistic and, I suppose, "folk."[21]

Partial taxonomies appear here and there is anthropological and lin-

[21] Cf. Leach, *op. cit.*, p. 41.

guistic literature, and many of them seem to be concerned with demonstration of method rather than providing taxonomic information. Now that a number of ethnographers have incorporated taxonomic mapping into their field procedures, we can expect to see an abundance of taxonomic studies in the future. Some ethnographers are even using computers to aid them in sorting and arranging their field data.

DISTRIBUTIONAL ANALYSIS

Paradigms and taxonomies are neat and orderly. But efforts in componential analysis at times produce only lists of terms and (sometimes) subclasses of these terms. Charting them seems to reveal nothing of particular significance. Nevertheless, the domains and categories under investigation are presumably no less important than others, so they must be treated in some fashion. Listing may be the most efficient means of presentation.

Nouns in many languages fall into classes we call *gender*. In English we use the labels "masculine, feminine, and neuter" and determine the gender of nouns by the pronouns used to substitute for them. These labels lack precision, but they are meaningful in most cases—less arbitrary than the gender labels for Spanish and French. In addition to formal grammatical distinctions in the English gender system, there are also semantic distinctions. And these distinctions influence our thinking about objects in the universe.

Gender classes in the Algonquian languages are labeled "animate" and "inanimate." These labels lack complete precision, too, in terms of Western science, but the two classes tend to force Algonquian speakers to make a mental separation between living and nonliving things. Navaho has an elaborate gender system—something like twelve gender classes—which appear to be based in part on shapes of objects.

Landar and Berlin have made studies of the eating vocabulary of Navaho and Tzeltal respectively.[22] Both languages contain seven verbs which we translate into English as "eat." One is a general verb for eating used, for example, in questions. The others divide all foodstuffs into six classes. Navaho categories, given by Landar, are (1) "eating in general," (2) "hard or chewy object," (3) "long, stringy object," (4) "meat," (5) "one round object," (6) "mushy matter," and (7) "separable objects." Tzeltal categories given by Berlin, are similar: (1) "eating in general," (2) "chewy object with pulp expectorated," (3) "meat," (4) "mushy or gelatin-like objects," (5) "individuated, hardish objects," (6) "breadstuffs," and (7) "foods which dissolve in the mouth with little mastication."

[22] "Seven Navaho Verbs for Eating," by Herbert Landar. *International Journal of American Linguistics* 30:94–96 (1964). "Categories of Eating in Tzeltal and Navaho," by Brent Berlin. *International Journal of American Linguistics* 33:1–6 (1967).

Berlin notes that "chili pepper" and "mushroom" are included in the category labeled "meat," and Tzeltal speakers readily offer folk theories to account for this. The documentation of his field experience in gathering and classifying food terms clearly shows that these categories have cultural significance to speakers of the language. But the food categories of both Navaho and Tzeltal are grammatical categories (as are the gender classes noted above); a particular food item governs the choice of verb. Landar and Berlin give descriptive labels in English to these categories based on something the class-members have in common. There may or may not be corresponding labels in Navaho and Tzeltal—probably not.

A taxonomic arrangement, as mentioned earlier, is an arrangement of semantic categories based on inclusion: items at a lower level are kinds of items at higher levels. Other semantic categories may be based on use or function or some other means of classification. Metzger and Williams have made a study of Tzeltal firewood using distributional analysis of linguistic contexts.[23] Their field methodology, involving the formulation of frames and eliciting of responses, led to the establishment of categories along various lines of cultural organization. Additional studies using this or similar techniques have been made of weddings, curers, diseases, deities, law, and perhaps other domains.[24]

CONCLUSION

As a high-school student of Spanish many years ago, I remember that my teacher and others told me I should learn to "think in the language." They assured me that when I reached that goal I would no longer speak Spanish hesitantly or haltingly; my responses would be automatic and "natural." My notion of "thinking in the language," I know, was pretty vague at that time. I probably considered my task as learning to put words together as the native speaker did, and this could be accomplished by learning a lot of words and the rules for putting them together. I wonder if the people who advised "learning to think in a foreign language" really understood the implications of that expression; I doubt it. My notion of that expression certainly changed later on when I became

[23] "Some Procedures and Results in the Study of Native Categories: Tzeltal 'Firewood'." *American Anthropologist* 68:389–407 (1966).
[24] "A Formal Ethnographic Analysis of Tenejapa Ladino Weddings," by Duane Metzger and Gerald Williams. *American Anthropologist* 65:1076–1101 (1963). "Tenejapa Medicine I: the Curer," by Duane Metzger and Gerald Williams. *Southwestern Journal of Anthropology* 19:216–34 (1963). "The Diagnosis of Disease among the Subanun of Mindanao," by Charles O. Frake. *American Anthropologist* 63:113–32 (1961). "Ethnographic Description and the Study of Law," by Mary Black and Duane Metzger. *American Anthropologist* 66 (Part 2, Special Publication):141–65 (1965). "A Structural Description of Subanun 'Religious Behavior'," by Charles O. Frake. In *Explorations in Cultural Anthropology*, ed. by W. H. Goodenough. New York: McGraw Hill, Inc., 1964.

an English teacher in Mexico and started gaining some familiarity with native languages spoken in that country.

As of now, I'm not sure that "learning to think in a foreign language" means anything. If it does mean something, it's certainly something much more ambitious then I previously realized. A language student would not only internalize the native speakers' patterned habits in regard to phonology, morphology, and syntax, he would also internalize the native speakers' collective view of the universe and the behavior patterns appropriate to and consistent with this view—both linguistic and nonlinguistic. It is inconceivable to me that linguistic and nonlinguistic behavior can be separated; even if we make such a separation (artificially), we still have to learn about the latter through language.

We don't know (and perhaps will never know) everything that underlies language behavior. Language categories—grammatical and lexical—certainly play a significant role in what we call the native speakers' world view and the patterned habits and responses that accompany such a view. This paper has dealt in part with interference from language categories in language learning. Traditionally, linguists have mapped out and described grammatical categories. In recent years, linguistic anthropologists have been busy mapping out categories of (other) cultural phenomena utilizing theories, research methods, and analytical devices which are similar to those of the linguist.

The other part of this paper has dealt with the methodology of linguistic anthropologists in discovering and describing language categories which lack the formal characteristics of grammatical categories; this amounts to analysis of semantic components. The devices include the paradigm, the taxonomy, and distributional analysis for identifying and mapping semantic categories of a language—categories which reflect a system of knowledge built up around a people's view of what the world is like. As an approach to ethnography, these procedures, descriptions, etc. are called *ethnoscience, ethnographic semantics,* or simply *componential analysis.*

My emphasis is on the fact that semantic (or lexical) categories are discoverable and describable by means of componential analysis. And when these categories are known, they can be learned by language students, just as grammatical categories are learned—perhaps with ease, perhaps with difficulty. I think it largely depends on how readily the student comes to accept the idea of diversity in the classification of cultural phenomena. We all know from experience that learning to accept the notion that one's own grammatical categories are not universal is no simple matter. Learning lexical categories may be a step higher in sophistication, but these categories should receive systematic treatment and be brought under the student's control on his route toward native-like fluency in a foreign language.